Magic in the Web

Magic in the Web

ACTION & LANGUAGE IN OTHELLO

ROBERT B. HEILMAN

GREENWOOD PRESS, PUBLISHERS
WESTPORT, CONNECTICUT

Library of Congress Cataloging in Publication Data

Heilman, Robert Bechtold, 1906–
    Magic in the web.

    Reprint of the ed. published by University of Kentucky Press, Lexington.
    Includes bibliographical references and index.
    1. Shakespeare, William, 1564–1616. Othello.
I. Title.
[PR2829.H4 1977]   822.3'3   77-21918
ISBN 0-8371-9784-8

COPYRIGHT © 1956 BY THE UNIVERSITY OF KENTUCKY PRESS

All rights reserved.

Originally published in 1956 by The University of Kentucky Press, Lexington

Reprinted with the permission of The University Press of Kentucky

Reprinted in 1977 by Greenwood Press
A division of Congressional Information Service, Inc.
88 Post Road West, Westport, Connecticut 06881

Library of Congress catalog card number 77-21918
ISBN 0-8371-9784-8

Printed in the United States of America

10 9 8 7 6 5 4 3 2

Contents

	PAGE
1 APPROACH	1
1. ASSUMPTIONS	2
2. INTERCONNECTIONS	17
2 IAGO: BEYOND THE GRIEVANCES	25
3 THE IAGO WORLD: STYLES IN DECEPTION	45
1. HONEST IAGO	46
2. SEEMING AND SEEING: OCULAR PROOF	50
3. LIGHT AND DARKNESS	64
4. IAGO AS ECONOMIST	73
5. DR. IAGO AND HIS POTIONS	86
4 THE IAGO WORLD: STYLES IN REVELATION	99
1. REDUCTION AND CONQUEST	100
2. THE HUNTER, THE INHUMAN DOG, AND THE SLAVE	104
3. THE GREATEST DISCORDS	113
4. CHAOS: THE WAR AT HOME	121
5 OTHELLO: ACTION AND LANGUAGE	137
6 THEMATIC FORM: VERSIONS OF LOVE	169
1. STYLES OF ACTION	170
2. DOCTRINE AND SYMBOL	193
7 THEMATIC FORM: WIT AND WITCHCRAFT	219
APPENDIX A. THE ENCHAFED FLOOD	231
APPENDIX B. THE BODY	234
NOTES	237
INDEX	289

To Eric Voegelin

Approach

This is one man's reading of *Othello*. I hope it will appear to illuminate some of the parts, and to speculate persuasively about the sum of the parts. If *Othello* is not the most complex of the tragedies, the problem of its over-all form is still a large one, and he who would account for the creative relationship of a large number of parts must be content if he seems generally to be moving in the right direction. There have been many analyses of parts and some studies of the whole. Here we endeavor to trace out the parts rather fully,[1] to observe their modes of combining, and thus to arrive at a theory of the whole. At best the theory is a cousin of the drama; such wit as the critic may have must follow the witchcraft of the dramatist (to take Iago's words out of context) from afar. But the cousin may help identify the drama, the wit tell how the witchcraft has gone. At the same time the critic, whatever he imparts, must at various points duplicate and parallel his predecessors[2] while assaying to be himself; so he runs the double risk of not encompassing the novelty which will absolve him of the suspicion of merely repeating what oft was thought, and of falling into innovations which in some quarters will seem dubious because such things were never thought. He can but hope to convince without simply establishing the accepted, and to achieve a justifying newness without falling into novelty for novelty's sake.

CHAPTER *1*

MAGIC IN THE WEB

1. ASSUMPTIONS

The parts which make up the whole are numerous and diverse. Othello is a part. Iago is a part. Iago's deception of Roderigo is a part. Iago's remarks on reputation, Desdemona's incredulity at the sexual misbehavior of wives, Emilia's revulsion against Iago, Cassio's drunken babbling are parts. All recognitions and reversals, all thoughts and feelings of characters are parts. The nighttime in which most of the major actions occur is a part. Iago's use of *honesty* is a part. All the uses of *honesty* are a part. All the metaphors of medicine and disease, the images from army life, the language of light and dark are parts.

The point is to keep the idea of the part flexible and inclusive, as a step toward adequate freedom in the description of structure. A view of the parts begotten of a preoccupation with gross anatomy will yield a coarse and constricted account of structure. On the other hand, compiling an unlimited serial list of parts would be futile. The main thing is to be aware of a part in all its relational possibilities.[3] Othello's farewell to arms (3.3.348ff.) is relevant to the specific situation of the moment, to Othello's personality generally, to Shakespeare's conception of the modes of response to disaster possible to human beings. Emilia's picking up of the handkerchief helps advance the action by contributing to Iago's deception of Othello, but it is also relevant to her character and to Shakespeare's conception of the modes of wifely devotion and marital relationship (not to mention its relations by contrast with actions of Desdemona and Bianca and of Emilia herself later). The theories of sex which Iago advances to Roderigo are relevant to his purpose of controlling Roderigo, to his modes of thought generally, and to Shakespeare's awareness of the whole realm of philosophies of love.

For working criticism, the broad categories of the parts whose relatedness is to be observed are two: plot and poetry. We might again find our metaphor in Iago's words and speak of the wit and witchcraft of the dramatist: the conscious designing and articulating; and the mysterious endowing of many parts—especially the poetic language—with dramatic value and meaning far in excess of the minimal logical requirements of the occasion: the magic in the web. This is less a theory of composition than an effort to suggest different aspects of the play that are only theoretically separable. Let us put it another way. If love is what *Othello* is "about," *Othello* is not only a play about love but a poem about love.[4] It has parts which interact in the mode of "pure" drama—people having such and such an effect on each other, irrespective of whether they communicate in verse, prose, or pantomime; it also has parts which interact in the manner of a poem. Again, this is a theoretical separation: the characters have such and such an effect by means of the words they speak; and conversely, an analysis of the words they speak involves the student regularly in a consideration of the "action" and interaction of the speakers. Yet when the dramatist has his characters speak in poetic language, he vastly complicates their communication with each other and with us. Figure, rhythm, poetic order do not merely make "more vivid" or "heighten" a literal prose statement that is otherwise unchanged; they constitute a fundamentally different statement by the introduction of the nuance, overtone, feeling, association, implication, and extension characteristic of them; in other words, by subtly carrying us beyond the finiteness, one-dimensionalism, and contextual restrictions of the pure statement determined only by the strict logical requirements of the immediate situation. When Othello summons Desdemona and dismisses Emilia, "Leave procreants alone . . .; / Cough or cry hem if anybody come. / Your mystery, your mystery!" (4.2.28-30), he not only dismisses Emilia, accuses Desdemona of infidelity, and betrays his own insane bitterness, but he converts the marriage into a brothel arrangement in which all three are involved, and by so doing establishes imaginative lines of connection with the role of Bianca and particularly with the Iago philosophy of sexual conduct.

MAGIC IN THE WEB

If we take all the lines of one character out of context and consider them as a unit, we have always a useful body of information; but if, when we study Iago's lines, we find that he consistently describes himself in images of hunting and trapping, we learn not only his plans of action but something of his attitude to occasions, to his victims, and to himself; and beyond that there is fixed for us an image of evil—one of those by which the drama interprets the human situation. When Othello says he threw away a "pearl," we recall that Brabantio, in acceding to Desdemona's departure, called her "jewel"; when Desdemona says she would rather have lost her purse than the handkerchief, we recall that Iago, who has stolen the handkerchief, has spoken of stealing a purse; we spontaneously make these connections, and, even if we go no further, our reading has brought forth linkings that cannot be expunged; but we often do go further, and seek out the formal order that is exemplified in these images that leap out of their own contexts and carry our imaginations into other parts of the play.[5] When to these we add many other instances in which poetic language, functioning doubly or triply, takes us beyond specific moments of action into others and on into general areas of character, feeling, and thought, we find that we have an immensely complicated verbal structure with which we must come to terms—the "poem about love," as I have called it. We are trying to describe what Traversi called "a new kind of dramatic unity."[6]

A play written in poetic form is simply not the same kind of literary work as a play written in prose; if one could imagine *Othello* translated into prose, it would be a different thing. This is true whether one is speaking of action or structure or meaning. The words put into a character's mouth, whatever immediate purposes of communication with other dramatis personae they may serve, are also the author's means of communicating with or "working on" the reader. The style is the character, of course. But the choice of one image or another sets off one kind or another of association, interconnection, possibility of meaning; a chosen metaphor is not simply a

4

APPROACH

neutral alternative, an ingenious transposition of a hypothetical literal statement which was prior to it; it is a unique definition of character, action, or theme, and it enters into the structure of meaning, which would be different if the metaphor were not present.[7] When Iago calls his false statements to Othello "poison," he exhibits the intellectual clarity required for self-identification and the moral callousness necessary to accept the identification. But when he also calls what he has told Othello "medicine," he uses a much more vibrant and exciting metaphor, one by which the author "says" vastly more to the reader: aside from expressing Iago's sardonic delight in an action which seems to be one thing but is another, it brings into focus the vast irony of Iago's frequent resemblance to the physician in his dealings with others, and the general state of affairs so often set forth in images of disease and disability; thus it is part of a "poetic" construction that deals vividly with the theme of evil. Suppose Iago had spoken only of his "tales" or "lies."

If I have said more about the parts that interact in the manner of a poem than about those which interact in the manner of a drama, it is simply that the latter are more familiar in the critical tradition. As terms for the two categories of structure (other students may discern other structural principles as inherent in the *materia dramatica*) I have so far used "plot" and "poetry." But these are not quite satisfactory, partly because willy-nilly they suggest a polar separation of elements that function integrally and that can be split apart only for critical inspection, and partly because to some readers "poetry" apparently means only "lyric" and therefore analysis of the poetic language of a play appears to reduce drama to lyric. But it should be evident, from the examples already cited and from the chapters that follow, that the poetic language of *Othello* is "dramatic"—in that it "works" or "acts," in relation to a given scene or episode, in relation to a character generally,[8] and in relation to areas of feeling and suggestion, of idea and theme, and of meaning that the drama is concerned with.[9] I will therefore use the term "verbal drama" for poetic language, or, more generally, for all the effects traceable, initially or finally, to what characters "say" and how they say it; and the term "actional drama" for what characters "do." These terms, alas, do not solve all the problems. For one thing, neither applies properly to matters of setting, properties, and costume, which are not necessarily passive or static[10] (and whose active influence one might call "circumstantial drama"[11]). More important, "doing" and "saying" are not always properly distinguishable; saying is often a very important way of doing. Further, "verbal drama" sounds pretty flat; but I prefer to have a very inclusive term and to avoid the confusion entailed by the use of "poetic drama," since the latter will primarily mean any drama written in verse. Again, "actional drama" may savor of tautology; but that risk I am willing to run for the sake of having the word *drama* in both phrases and of thus indicating the functional analogy and the structural coalescence of word and act. Actional drama and verbal drama work in collusion; both are imaginative languages, each potentially ambiguous and polysemous; they are fused in a harmonious structure of meaning. The play about love and the poem about love, though they have different structural foci, are one; they are *Othello*. For understanding its composition this "one" may be thought of as an organization of dramatic structures which, if not discrete entities, may be theoretically discriminated as objects of contemplation. After this preliminary comes critical synthesis, a formidable task. One cannot aspire to solve finally the problem of the fusion of actional and verbal drama; one can derive a certain solution from the text and hope that it is convincing. The magic in the web of *Othello* does not yield easily to rational accounting.[12]

Our business with the poetry or the verbal drama is, then, with its constructive or formative role. It is a subject that has not been much treated, except, at a virtually sterilizing distance, by vast editorial explications of a glossarial and syntactical sort, until recent years. One may speculate that one reason for its neglect is that Aristotle does not treat the subject adequately; what he says in the *Poetics* about language is limited and pedestrian and does not provide an approach to intrinsic aspects of Greek drama that are now beginning to be understood.[13] But it is no longer necessary to defend the position that poetic language is integral and not merely a convention, a traditional embellishment, or, in Hereward T. Price's phrase, a "detachable ornament"[14] that is conducive to a quotable charm and beauty; that it is not simply another vehicle of expression, chosen as a matter of taste, for getting to the same place that prose would carry one to, but a formal element that helps determine what the play becomes. In his study of Shakespeare's use of imagery generally, Professor Clemen remarks that in the tragedies the images become "an inherent part of the dramatic structure," resembling "a second line of action . . . and providing a 'counterpoint' to the events on the stage," and that in some tragedies Shakespeare "continually thought in images which are charged with symbolic meaning to such a degree that we could not understand the tragedy's significance and import without a proper understanding of its image-patterns," and speaks of the imagery as expressing "symbolically correspondences and interrelations which underlie the real action and often contain the essential meaning of the play."[15]

"Correspondences and interrelations" brings us to a characteristic of Shakespeare's verbal drama which the preceding paragraphs have alluded to a number of times—its notable repetitiveness, of images and likewise of abstract words. After Emilia has three times incredulously asked, "My husband?" Othello demands, "What needs this iterance, woman?" (5.2. 150). We all must play Othello to Shakespeare's Emilia: "iterance" forces itself upon us as a critical problem. The dramatist cannot conspicuously repeat words and rely upon figures of the same class (e.g., clothes, military life) without catching our eye and raising a question about what goes on. We are hardly likely to attribute this recurrency to the artist's carelessness or failing resourcefulness or to stop at description—an inert lexicon of repetitions. When editors devotedly multiply cross references to dictional or rhetorical echoes and anticipations, they act, one assumes, more from a sense of relationship than from a delight in coincidence. Speaking of *Antony and Cleopatra,* Professor Clemen uses a phrase that is valid for other plays: "this symbolical meaning of certain sequences of imagery."[16] As Paul Goodman puts it, Shakespeare's "profusion of images is so handled through a long play that it forms a systematic structure and is part of the plot." He elaborates on "a method that is characteristically Shakespearean: this is to present a line of thought by an independent development of the system of imagery. Put formally: when several characters independently and throughout the play employ the same system of images, the diction becomes an independent part of the plot implying a thought, action, etc., whatever is the principle of the system. For it is not in character for different characters to use the same images."[17] I suspect that it may be "in character for different characters to use the same images," which can be a device for suggesting similarities or even contrasts among them; or if the images belong dominantly to one character in one part of the play, and to another in another part, the change may be an important mark of dramatic progression, as when the almost pre-emptive use of animal imagery passes in mid-play from Iago to Othello.[18] But beyond all its possible uses in characterization, recurrent diction has still other functions. Goodman's phrase "independent development" is the key. For though speeches are in one sense not separable from the characters, in another sense they do become disengaged from particular speakers and enter the general verbal fund of the play. (The more rich and profuse the language, the more this is likely to be true, just as the more rich and powerful the literary work, the more likely it is to become disengaged from its own times, however much these times may be needed for exegetic purposes, and to enter the general timeless fund of literary possessions.) Reiterative language is particularly prone to acquire a continuity of its own and to become "an independent part of the plot"[19] whose effect we can attempt to gauge. It may create "mood" or "atmosphere": the pervasiveness of images of injury, pain, and torture in *Othello* has a very strong impact that is not wholly determined by who uses the images. But most of all the "system of imagery" introduces thoughts, ideas, themes—elements of the meaning that is the author's final organization of all his materials.[20] If various characters explicitly or implicitly invoke "nature" in a series of irreconcilable actions, the repetition of "nature" directs our attention to the problem of nature, raises our expectation that we will find a dramatic effort to deal with it, and actually guides us to the artist's disposition of it.

We come to the problem of "meaning" not only from the verbal drama, with its burden of thought that belongs to the whole drama as well as to the individual speakers, but from the very nature of the actional drama itself. Killing, for example, may take place for principle, passion, profit, or perversity, or for a mixture of motives, or with self-deception, or may be accompanied by this or that poetic language with its profoundly modifying power; we do not actually apprehend the action until we know what it amounts to. We have immediate, tentative responses; they are subject to change as the real nature of the action—the meaning—becomes clearer to us. Again, what happens after the killing—despair, remorse, justice, emptiness, etc.—is not merely a way of bringing about satisfactory feelings; it is a dramatic wrestling with the problem of the morally possible, and it seems probable that in different dramas it may produce a considerable range of emotional responses, some too complex for prediction. The affective quality of literary experience may be calculated with security only when the works are stereotyped and the readers strongly "typed"; the more mature the literature, the less is the affective quality identical—for all the works in a genre, for all competent auditors (readers) of one work, or even for one auditor (reader) at all the stages of his acquaintance with the work. One may conjecture that the pleasure felt may be deepened and refined with the growing awareness of the total statement made by all the dramatic devices.

If the critic's concern is "the total statement made by all the dramatic devices," he is committed to the structural analysis of the unique work rather than to the computing of its generic characteristics. *Othello* is "a tragedy" as well as "tragedy." The critic will presumably wish to mediate between the generic and the individual, to see how the abstract pattern is transformed in the immediate literary organism. Of the genre one is aware, but rather to see how *this* tragedy looks and works (what kind of tragic hero is Othello? how does the consummate portraiture of villainy modify the tragic tone?) than to establish its fidelity to formula, structural or affective. Generic analysis is especially useful when there is formal or tonal ambiguity, as with Chekhov; or when there is a serious question as to the nature of the achievement, as with Williams and Miller; and it is of course the main business if one is reconsidering a traditional classification, as one might with Euripides. The present essay will regard *Othello* not primarily as an instance of a category or the equivalent of any other "regular" example of the genre but as a tragedy that can be examined with respect to its own structure and meaning. Likewise, as a "poem" about love, *Othello* uses kinds of images that appear in other "poems" by Shakespeare; our problem, however, is not to catalogue Shakespeare's arsenal of images[21] but to try to analyze the composition of the images in this particular play.

To speak of "all the dramatic devices" is also to imply that, if tragedy is an imitation of an action, the action may be fully defined or placed only by a complete functional assessment of all the means of imitation. Now the plurality of methods of imitation is matched by a plurality in that which is imitated. The "action" of which criticism speaks is likely to be taken for a single, objective, isolatable doing by men as if in the world. Certainly an action is imitated. But the imitation is also of the picture of that action that is held in the mind of an individual artist; again, it is an imitation of his "intention" to uncover one reality rather than another in the action. The imitation is recognizable by other men who as individuals are different from the artist, but to them it is also revelatory. Here we border on the problem of the paradoxical interfusion of the mimetic and the creative of which Eliseo Vivas has written penetratingly.[22] But let us go further. The imitation is also of ideas, notions, attitudes which the artist shares with his own times—e.g., the concepts of "nature" that figure eminently in *Lear*. Beyond that, the imitation is also of other ideas, perceptions, intuitions peculiar to the artist's own contemplation of experience (where he rejects, modifies, or transcends the contemporary)—all the "insights" in virtue of which the final work partly eludes the seal of its own age and becomes profoundly meaningful in other times and places. (We speak now of great writers.) This is the ultimately individual in the work; yet here we come upon another, if more familiar, paradox—that through the most individual comes the "universal." Where the vision is freest, the contemporary and parochial have the most tenuous hold. It is when he endows his "action" with that aura of truth, that impression of having in some way seized upon human constants which tinctures the pleasurable feeling of all subsequent auditors with a sense of urgent significance, that the artist is calling upon all the resources of actional and verbal drama. Thus *Oedipus Rex* becomes something more than an imitation of an action as an action is minimally describable: it imitates also (more conspicuously, let us say, than *Trachiniae* and many plays by Euripides) a perception of human experiencing (being and doing) valid in some way for distant centuries and cultures. Iago is a machiavel, true; but he is something more, still fundamentally significant when the machiavel is remembered only in footnotes; into the imitation of the maneuvers of the false friend has gone a unique intuition of human potentialities.

So when we follow up mimesis far enough, we come to archetype and symbol. The relations may be of different orders.

MAGIC IN THE WEB

A poem (used here as a general term for literary work) may be said to imitate a poet's intentions but to symbolize some impulse or "drive" or "need" of his; in this sense the poem is "symbolic action," and the analysis of the mode of symbolic action for the poet may clarify the kind of symbolic experience it affords others—a problem with which Kenneth Burke has often dealt. In another sense, the poem imitates the poet's perspectives and beliefs, and these become symbolized in the poem.[23] All the parts of the poem, then, are parts not only of an action but also of the symbolic structure of perspective and belief—of the poet's world view, his affirmations or denials, his lament or his "prophecy." In that sense it is axiomatic that the poem is symbolic, whether or not the poet consciously calls attention to the second dimension of meaning; the burden of proof rests on the literalist.[24] The symbolic may be present in a mixture so rich as to be all-demanding or so thin as to be not worth bothering about. Its possibilities are greatest when the poem is concerned with characters in action. Once the character overflows our limited and limiting sense of him as one man and no more—and thus reveals what Longinus called greatness of conception—we move into the symbolic dimension and use the word *archetype* to describe that compression of possibilities which is so inclusive that all other characters of the same order seem but partial representations of the original idea. Iago is this kind of character; he is infinitely more than the skillful manipulator of a stratagem; the more we know him, the more we ask the question "What else?" to which we are driven when there is a symbolic dimension. A different case is that of Athena and the Eumenides in Aeschylus' *Oresteia;* quite aside from the fact that they are superhuman beings we have the sense of "something more than," for they are, as Eric Voegelin puts it, "theomorphic symbolizations of the forces of the soul."[25] Finally, the symbolic quality is an almost inevitable consequence of the use of poetic language; or more precisely, it is a function of the imaginative quality of the poetic language. We cannot have the multidimensionalism of poetic language—not to mention the barrier-breaking tendency of the verbal drama generally—without constantly being pushed beyond the bare action into all the reaches of meaning possible to literary art. A symbol, in Norman Friedman's words, is "An image alive with an idea; a fact saturated in value."[26]

Literary art: all that I have said implies that *Othello* is a work of literature as well as a set of directions for a theatrical performance. We must remember the "conditions of the stage," to be sure; but if the surviving text were but a blueprint for mimes, the product of an elder stagecraft, our interest in it could be only antiquarian.[27] The fact is that our interest is much more than antiquarian. I wish not to disparage the theater but to argue that some writing for the theater, such as Shakespeare's, at once satisfies the requirements of the theater and goes way beyond them; such writing provides a stage action pleasurable to the immediate audience and at the same time dramatic literature suitable for prolonged contemplation, indeed yielding its secrets, if it yields them, only after long study and thought by the reader. The printed play is somewhat like the symphonic score which the music critic, imagining the performance, may study rigorously to see how it is "composed." All this is hardly a new and bright idea, but it seems necessary to say it to counter an argument that keeps popping up—the Fallacy of the First Night or the Fallacy of the Single Reading. The victim of this fallacy can hardly believe that what the auditor would not get from the performance, or the reader from such reading as he would accord to a relatively straightforward work of prose, is not there, but he often talks as if this were true—as if, because he wrote for the theater, Shakespeare were restricted by the capacities of the ordinary theatergoer (as conjectured by a twentieth-century scholar); as if it were not possible at once to please in the theater and to overflow the theater and call upon the full resources of the readers of poetry; as if it were not possible to follow a character through a given action in such a way as to make him open to a working or tentative understanding, and yet to endow him with a substance that can exact scrutiny and meditation long after the staged action is over; as if all the imaginative transmutation of properties and scenes, all the generalizing of characters and actions, all the poetry—all the symbolic language and its impact on all else that we apprehend through it alone—as if all this, because it might be missed or but dimly grasped on a single occasion, were not there. But a poetic drama is a Janus (as I said earlier, it is both play and poem): it looks both toward the theater and toward the study or library; or it begins in one and ends in the other.[28] But from whichever direction one approaches it, his task is not easy; he can but approximate and hope that he comes close enough to the text to reflect some of its light.

To acknowledge the claims of Shakespeare's theater upon the critic is to acknowledge that one is never entirely free of history. In attempting a critical analysis of *Othello* as poetic drama one must constantly rely on the work of historical scholars. That should be understood. There are points, indeed, at which a historical reading is richer than one possible to a nonhistorical reader; not to be familiar, for instance, with the material of Partridge's *Shakespeare's Bawdy* would be to miss various secondary meanings in *Othello*, meanings which extend on into major structural characteristics of the drama. Contrariwise, one must wish to be free of the kind of restrictive historicism which would seek to explain Falstaff and Iago entirely in terms of Renaissance military regulations and practices.[29] It is perhaps a noble endeavor to aspire to see the literary object "as it is," to rid our apprehension of it of every modifying attitude, or preconception, or habit or possession of mind that belongs to us as individuals or to our times. But one kind of pursuer of objectivity leaves us with a serious problem (aside from the epistemological problem) when he tacitly identifies "as it is" with "as it was"; the real Shakespeare becomes an Elizabethan (or Jacobean) reality, and this reality is accessible to us only if we acquire an Elizabethan point of view. This conclusion rather begs the question of whether a completely

APPROACH

historical attitude may be achieved, whether a sense of being Elizabethan in point of view does not contain something of the illusory.[30] But a more fundamental difficulty in the identification of "as it is" with "as it was" is that it appears not to do entire justice to the great literary work such as the Shakespeare tragedy. For it is the very nature of the work of a transcendent genius that its value has multiple aspects, so that it necessarily "is," we may say figuratively, a number of different things at once—the play that succeeds in a given theater and the literary work that transcends the limits of the stage; the literal fable or action and the symbolic statement of a sense of reality; a plot that evokes immediate responses and a bearer of meanings that may not appear immediately; an instance of a genre and yet an individual of utmost independence, eluding the bonds of generic regularity; a creature of its times, consonant with their thought and feeling, and yet a free agent, communicating with other ages even in their own different idioms and yet reserving something that they continually pursue; "conformable to different cultures at different times," as Blackmur puts it, because of "the unity of the reality under all cultures at all times."[31] It is odd that we habitually call a great work "timeless" and yet in one frame of mind seek its essence in one brief time, the hour of its birth. I say "in one frame of mind" because the quest of the "as it was" is a highly specialized exploit, and we are not always specialists; to aspire always to see only with the eyes of a particular past would be uncomfortably close to doing intellectual push-ups—a worthy preparatory exercise, but hardly a substitute for the full imaginative activity that comes later. Perhaps when we render exclusive devotion to the "as it was," it is that we despair of the whole and modestly settle for the part, or, as Goodman has it, are driven to the part by failure to choose an adequate way of looking at the whole;[32] perhaps it is that since history deals with the past, things of the past seem to belong only to history; perhaps in an excessive fear of anachronism we forget that we have some small share in a faculty attributed to divine beings—that of perceiving all times in simultaneity; perhaps with the sickness for document and proof (one form of Othello's own disease) that besets an unstable era, we seem to have in the "as it was" a kind of knowledge comfortingly susceptible of final demonstration. To see the "as it is" we must rely in part on the "as it was," yet knowing that Shakespeare was, in Robert M. Smith's phrase, "not merely a mouthpiece of contemporary fashion";[33] at the same time we must remember that we cannot help reading Shakespeare as creatures of our own era, cannot and indeed should not, Maud Bodkin insists, "cancel the psychological awareness that our own age has conferred on us";[34] and we may even boldly surmise that at times a modern perspective will yield a fresh insight into the intricate imaginative workings of the artist's mind; and finally we may hope that in our happiest moments we are limited in our view of art neither to an older age nor to our own but—whether we proceed by analogy or by our portion of that persistent sense of human constants that is never entirely dulled by the thought styles peculiar to an age—are getting hold of the realities by which the work transcends the artist's age and our own,[35] and in virtue of which the tragic heroes, as Sewell puts it,[36] belong to "a world beyond the world, a universe outside time." If this be an illusion, it may nevertheless be a dynamic and fruitful illusion.

All this is to say that besides the historical truth there is a nonhistorical, accommodated to the historical mold and yet overflowing it to find its own complex design; what we have to seek is the patterns of permanence in the characters and their relationships. Iago "is" evil, we say; but what terms has Shakespeare found that make evil and its mode of working meaningful to other times? In answering such questions we try as best we may to follow the magic in the web, with our wit to spy out the artist's wit and witchcraft. Eventually we may find that wit and witchcraft are not only instruments of art but objects of the artist's contemplation.

APPROACH

2. INTERCONNECTIONS

Before seeking directly for the "patterns of permanence," I want to look in a little more detail at one aspect of the magic in the web about which I have already spoken briefly—the complex interconnectedness of the parts which may be discovered whether one uses the perspective of verbal drama or that of actional drama or, as is often required, a fusion of these. Since in the following chapters our search will take us into various formal patterns of interrelationship, the present section is something of a preview, but besides alerting the reader to the kind of process that will be used more systematically later, it will also bring into relief facets of the drama upon which the subsequent analysis will depend. With regard to connections: unless the plot movement of the drama has broken down (as often in Shaw), one is of course always, and primarily, aware of any segment of action as a part of an actional sequence; but we must also note all the connections superadded to plot, that is, all those arrangements of the web which introduce into our awareness of an episode or passage, however concentrated upon it our attention may be, a modifying awareness of other parts of the play.[37]

MODES OF IRONY   Without ignoring irony as a characteristic value of a mature literary work—the maintenance of disparate perspectives—I wish to regard it here as also a mode of interconnection, as illuminating discrepancy. Awareness of discrepancy means awareness of at least the two elements required to create a discrepancy; in a nonironic work such nexus would be lacking, and the texture would be correspondingly thinner. The ironic connection may be between elements close or distant; it may be completed in actional or verbal terms; and it may have different temporal aspects. It may complete itself in the "present" in which it comes into view, either as a contradiction of terms within that situation or as an overturn of a universal expectancy. Or it may bind past and present, or present and future, by a reversal of "ordinary probability" or of specific expectancies created by the terms of the plot.

The standard dramatic irony is that of a character's taking an action which does not lead where he expects it to; e.g., Othello, trying to punish an apparent wrong, commits a real wrong, much greater than the supposed one, and leaves himself infinitely worse off than if he had foregone the punitive satisfaction.[38] A lesser irony, though it may be valuable connectively, is that of circumstance, in which the human will operates minimally or not at all: Cassio is the first person whose death is formally plotted, but he is the principal survivor. As he says to his nocturnal assailant, Roderigo, "That thrust had been mine enemy indeed / But that my coat is better than thou know'st" (5.1.24-25). Thus he is able to succeed the very commander who fired him.

There are a number of ironic relations in which the future reverses the certainty, promise, oath, or hope expressed in the present. Othello is sure that his love of Desdemona will not interfere with his execution of duties at the front: if it happens, he says, "That my disports corrupt and taint my business, / Let housewives make a skillet of my helm" (1.3.272-273). It is just this domestication of the warrior that takes place:[39] Othello is overcome by the "family problem" and formally gives up the career of war.[40] Desdemona assures Cassio that she "will have my lord and you again / As friendly as you were" (3.3.6-7). This comes true but not in the intended sense: they are reunited only after her death and for a short time before Othello's.[41] When Othello wagers, "My life upon her faith!" (1.3.295), both terms ironically come true: she is faithful, and he pays with his life.[42] Or a literal statement may be countered by facts not known or foreseen:[43] when Desdemona fears that Othello may "shake me off / To beggarly divorcement" (4.2.

157-158), he has already resolved on steps that would make divorce seem like a friendly act.[44]

Again, there are relations of irony in which a character "speaks better than he knows," expressing truths which would not be expected of him, or making statements that are true in a way he does not intend or is not conscious of. When Desdemona asserts her faithfulness as Cassio's attorney, she uses a metaphor of fidelity which is literally prophetic:[45] "For thy solicitor shall rather die / Than give thy cause away" (3.3.27-28). Characters stumble into words which would be guides to right understanding or action if the speakers were not in some way inhibited from seizing upon the validity of their perceptions,[46] as when Brabantio says to Iago and Roderigo, "Upon malicious bravery dost thou come / To start my quiet" (1.1.100-101). When Othello repeats Iago's "lie on her," he annotates, "We say lie on her when they belie her" (4.1.35-36), i.e., "tell a lie on her." Half-mad as he is, he is toying, like a virtuoso in language, with the ambiguity of meaning in the phrase: the very verbal play leads him to the doorstep of truth. What is more, Iago's own provocative embellishment of his lie—"lie with her, lie on her"—has led his victim to the point from which he might see truth.[47]

The villain, who is by definition outside the community of tragic awareness, defines the tragic hero.[48] Iago's phrase, "loving his own pride and purposes" (1.1.12), though it refers only to Othello's appointment of a lieutenant, actually describes Othello's tragic role generally.[49] Derogatory statements, indeed, are often vibrant with strange accuracies that the reader perceives, indeed cannot help perceiving, if he is aware of the interplay of contexts. Iago's account of Othello's style, "bombast circumstance, / Horribly stuff'd with epithets of war" (1.1.13-14), is partly justified by Othello's addiction to rhetorical bravura.[50] In a simpler kind of play, the villain would merely speak unjustly. When Brabantio calls Iago "profane wretch" (1.1.115) and Desdemona playfully calls him "a most

19

profane and liberal counsellor" (2.1.165), we are aware, in each case, of the unfelt truth,[51] and, additionally, of the kind of verbal echo frequently woven into the fabric of the play. When Othello says sneeringly of Desdemona, "And she's obedient; as you say, obedient, / Very obedient" (4.1.266-267), i.e., obedient to any man that asks, the word that he uses sarcastically is true literally, in the sense in which he thinks it is not.[52] Or a character may ignorantly speak an untruth and then compound the irony by the inadvertent use of specifically corrective terms, as when Othello, having described the living Desdemona's hand as "Hot, hot, and moist" (3.4.39), uses these words of Desdemona dead: "Cold, cold, my girl? / Even like thy chastity" (5.2.275-276). Note his repetition of the antonyms.

Irony as a linking agent appears also in the variations of dynamic ideas held by different characters—for instance, the idea that one injury justifies another.[53] But here I aim not at inconclusiveness, nor am I ready to approach the larger structural design, just as in describing certain ironic modes I am intent not upon their significance for tone and theme, nor yet upon an exhaustive catalogue and a refined analytical differentiation of them. The sampling and the rough classifications, in this section and the notes, should be enough to suggest the pervasiveness and multifariousness of irony as one source of the rich interwovenness of the dramatic web.

Modes of Separation

The design of the web depends also on the proper distinction of parts which would otherwise fall together into a mass in which the forming powers of the multiple linkages we are observing would be obscured, diminished, or rendered irrelevant. Design is a tension of separative and unifying powers: in this sense the negative (separative) is essential to the affirmative (unifying) and is a relational mode. We need to be aware of the separative modes which lie beyond

APPROACH

the distinguishability of the characters and the discernible segmentation of the action in time.

Moody Prior has pointed out how variations in rhythm help to establish a series of changes in Othello's state of mind.[54] Paul Goodman argues that in Act 1 prose is used to "neutralize" the "motion and sound . . . in the context" and that "the prose prevents the war from stealing attention from the wedding."[55] To this we may add that the passages dealing with state business have not only a flatter rhythm but very little of the imagistic life that surges through the rest of the play.[56]

Style is used separatively. Iago and Roderigo, who share a number of scenes, are distinguished stylistically. Iago speaks a highly seasoned language, flooded with images; relatively, Roderigo is flat and much closer to "pure prose." At the height of Iago's power over him, Othello falls into a prose rhythm: "Iago has reduced Othello to his own element."[57] Elsewhere the shift between verse and prose is used to distinguish phases of character. In soliloquy Iago "drops into the verse of the Machiavellian villain," but as "honest Iago" he most frequently uses "the technique of reduction and denigration," which is "Shakespeare's major development of the prose convention."[58]

The characters are distinguished by consistent variations in poetic style.[59] Other students of the play have made a considerable study of rhythmical variation;[60] I shall be more concerned with variations in vocabulary.

Types of verbal links

Finally, we may observe interconnections made through the the content of comparisons, by conspicuous repetitions, and by the construction of a passage so that it is a junction point of many lines of verbal activity that run through the play.

A figure of speech acquires special meaning or vitality because the object or circumstance used in comparison draws on another part of the play. In Iago's comparison, "fools as gross / As ignorance made drunk" (3.3.404-405), "ignorance made drunk" exactly describes Cassio under Iago's hands and thus draws life from a preceding action. When Emilia speaks of wives "foul as slander" (4.2.19), her comparison would lack body but for our image of Iago slandering. When Othello says of Desdemona, "She was false as water" (5.2.134), his very choice of simile betrays him in his wrongness: in his immediate experience "water" has not been "false" (in the storm at sea, the Turks were drowned, the Venetians survived). Somewhat differently, Shakespeare may so juxtapose images that we detect the coexistence of overt and underlying meanings. The reader whose awareness has been informed by modern psychological theory will sense the sexual *double entendre* in the early lines of Cassio's prayer for the safety of Othello,[61] who has not yet reached Cyprus: "Great Jove, Othello guard, / And swell his sail with thine own pow'rful breath, / That he may bless this bay with his tall ship," which are followed immediately by the explicit image, "Make love's quick pants in Desdemona's arms" (2.1.77-80).

Key words or phrases repeated in different parts of the play may sharpen a character or a situation.[62]

When Cassio says he doesn't remember what happened when he was drunk, Iago exclaims, "Is't possible?" (2.3.288). Again when Othello trumpets his farewell to tranquillity and war, Iago's response is, "Is't possible . . . ?" (3.3.358). The habitual astonishment of deadpan innocence resembles that of the practical joker: these recurrent traces of the comedian in Iago (more of this later) heighten the shock of his savagery.

Concerning Othello's apparent jealousy Desdemona insists, "I never gave him cause" (3.4.158). Near the end Cassio says to Othello, "I never gave you cause" (5.2.299). His two victims point out that Othello, so insistent on "cause" in the legal sense, acts without cause (one of his rough resemblances to Iago)

APPROACH

Desdemona denies

> that mine eyes, mine ears, or any sense
> Delighted them in any other form.   (4.2.154-155)

Compare Emilia's lines on husbands and wives:

> Their wives have sense like them. They see, and smell,
> And have their palates both for sweet and sour,
> As husbands have.   (4.3.97-99)

The repeated use of the senses in defining a situation helps sharpen the opposition between Desdemona's statement of the individual case[63] (with its implied theory of conduct) and Emilia's explicit general theory.

Iago insists, "I am not what I am" (1.1.65); Othello urges "Speak of me as I am" (5.2.342). The verbal resemblance emphasizes the fact that Othello has the right sentiment. Yet to the extent that Othello does not entirely face or know what he is, the words ironically remind us that Iago has the greater self-understanding.

Of all the ways of binding together the parts by verbal, figural, and imaginal echo and interplay, the subtlest and yet surest is the construction of an individual speech in such a way as to make it a web of the threads of language, literal and metaphorical, that may be traced throughout the play. The magic in the web springs from all the concepts, impulses, perspectives, and symbols which create the general dramatic life of the play but are here drawn upon for the secret vitalization of a particular context.[64] Lodovico's lines that close the play (5.2.361-371) are in one sense a kind of conventional finishing off, an assertion of right feeling and community direction to palliate all the shocks of Act 5. The rhythm is respectably "official," unstirred by the shifts of pace and emphasis appropriate to a new surge of action or feeling. The tenor is that of a balance between the weariness after battle and the continuing will to struggle that appears in the last of several exhortations to move against Iago. Yet the speech is not flat or pat. Indeed, it has an "esemplastic" quality: it brings together, quite compactly, various lines of force, verbal and actional, that have extended through the drama:

> O Spartan dog,
> [The animal imagery, here climaxed in an epithet of meanness universally familiar.]
> More fell than anguish, hunger, or the sea!
> [Othello's early adventures. The anguish of all the major characters. The imagery of food and eating. The storm and sea imagery. The truth of this comparison in this play: the sea has been benevolent to the Venetians.]
> Look on the tragic loading of this bed.
> [The bed of Othello and Desdemona has been present or mentioned in every act of the drama.]
> This is thy work. The object poisons sight;
> [The imagery of poisoning. The sight theme.]
> Let it be hid. Gratiano, keep the house,
> [Hiding of facts or truths has been constant.]
> And seize upon the fortunes of the Moor,
> For they succeed on you.
> [The wealth theme. The status of Othello.]
> To you, Lord Governor,
> Remains the censure of this hellish villain.
> [The diabolism theme. Another regular term for the meanness of Iago.]
> The time, the place, the torture—O, enforce it!
> [The last reflection of the injury-disability-torture theme.]
> Myself will straight aboard, and to the state
> This heavy act with heavy heart relate.
> [The last instance of the recurrent note of heaviness.]

Such interconnections are abundant in *Othello*. We will look at some of them more fully, and endeavor to examine them in ways that may contribute to our sense of the ordering of the whole.

BEYOND THE GRIEVANCES

Iago

In tracing the interconnections of the parts that should permit us eventually to see the design of the whole, I am starting with Iago because important elements of the verbal and actional drama represent a "flow," so to speak, from Iago into the rest of the community. We need, then, to see what kind of general estimate of him is demanded by the evidence. But before we can examine his full character and "meaning," we must obviously try to assess his "case."

Some of the points below have been made a number of times, but not all of them have been made, as far as I know, nor have all those that have been made been brought together in a single picture. They should document rather fully the "orthodox view," as Kenneth Muir calls the general critical position stemming from Coleridge.[1] Arguments on the other side are also made continually.[2]

Iago's first grievance is that in disregard of Iago's practical experience (1.1.28-30), seniority (37), and political support of "three great ones of the city" (8), Othello gave the lieutenancy to Cassio, whose only equipment for the position, according to Iago, is theoretical training (19-27). The one fact that we can perhaps accept here is that Iago had some hope of getting the lieutenancy. The question, then, is whether Iago's hope, if it actually did exist, was a reasonable one and

CHAPTER 2

whether the disparity between his talents and deserts and those of Cassio was such that Othello's choice was a real injustice to Iago. The following points bear on an answer to this question.

1. We have only Iago's word on this. Iago's lines in 1.1 are at once so perturbed and so calculating (i.e., so touched by the Iago theatricalism that we shall observe repeatedly[3])—in his self-love,[4] his picture of Othello's refusal, and his scorn for Cassio—that immediately he seems not entirely trustworthy and that we automatically begin to probe for the facts. His style is less that of a normally sensitive man honestly injured than of an envious schemer furious at a failure in "playing the angles."[5]

2. Iago himself never again mentions his loss of the lieutenancy after 1.1.38. Once he makes a single-line reference to getting the lieutenancy (1.3.399), and twice, single-line references to getting Cassio out of it (2.1.173, 284). Such lines indicate his enmity to Cassio and possibly some interest in his position; they in no way establish the legitimacy of his claim to it.

3. Nobody else ever mentions Iago's professional disappointment.[6] No one ever offers him condolences or encouragements. Cassio never shows any sign of discomfort when he is with Iago; he is never defensive or apologetic or inclined to deal with Iago in the two telltale extremes of manner—putting him in his place or treating him with kid gloves. Othello's manner with Iago, before their especial relationship develops, is casual, easy, professional, and unself-conscious (even in the condescension which has been attributed to him). Most important: Emilia, who is a shrewd woman and who, until disillusioned at the very end by his treachery, obviously has the usual wifely sympathies with Iago, never says a word intimating that he has not got all that he has coming to him. On the contrary she is glad to aid and encourage Cassio in recovering the lieutenancy after he has lost it (3.1.44-53).

4. It has been argued: "That Othello regarded Iago as fit

IAGO: BEYOND THE GRIEVANCES

for the lieutenancy is proved by his appointing him to that office when Cassio has shown his incompetency by drunken brawling."[7] But the time and style of the appointment, on the contrary, make us doubt the fitness of the appointee. Iago is a very late afterthought for the position. When Othello first fires Cassio, he says nothing at all about replacing him; in fact, Othello plans to reinstate Cassio (3.1.53). Iago is quite right when he tells Cassio that the "punishment" is "more in policy than in malice" (2.3.274-275). There is no evidence that Othello ever thinks of Iago for the job until the moment he appoints him, and that is at the end of the long deception scene in 3.3, when Iago has promised to kill Cassio (474) and Othello himself is planning to kill Desdemona. He is only paying off his "best friend." He is what we now call "emotionally insane," a state which if anything would suggest, not a sudden recognition of military capacities formerly unappreciated in Iago, but a self-gratification in disregard of the relevant facts and likelihoods.[8]

5. The argument that Cassio's getting drunk proves him "incompetent" depends entirely on the expectation that a commander's assistant shall be without flaw or weakness. What would seem more to the point would be the expectation that the lieutenant will know what his problem is and be in the main able to deal with it. Cassio knows his weakness, takes his risk only under extreme social pressure and in the apparent absence of a service rule which would allow him an automatic way out of the situation, and he is overcome by shame at his misconduct—a shame that is morally as well as pragmatically grounded (2.3.262ff.). The self-knowledge and the standard of value suggest a "personal" competence above average. Besides all this, Desdemona argues that Cassio's "trespass" is "not almost a fault / T' incur a private check," and she attributes this view to "our common reason" (3.3.64-67). Othello does not deny this.

When Iago, in the campaign to unseat Cassio, is calling Montano's attention to Cassio's drunkenness, he says, "He is a soldier fit to stand by Caesar / And give direction" (2.3.127-128). Iago may be as untrustworthy here as in his denigration of Cassio in 1.1, and his purpose may be subtly served by the infusion of some praise. But it seems reasonable to suppose that if Cassio were really incompetent or Iago genuinely considered him so, Iago would hardly lose this opportunity to make that point too.

The affirmative argument for Cassio's over-all (i.e., technical and personal) competence is the fact that when the Duke and Senators order Othello home, they give Cassio the full command in Cyprus (4.1.248, 272; 4.2.224ff.). They ratify Othello's judgment by promoting Cassio. If Othello had made a bad appointment, we may assume that it would be known by the ultimate authority, and that this would be the time to rectify it. Likewise, if Iago had a strong case, this would be the time for the "three great ones" who allegedly pushed Iago's case before to intervene again in his behalf. When Othello is taken into custody, Cassio is given full command immediately by Lodovico: "And Cassio rules in Cyprus" (5.2.332). This is done despite the fact that Cassio is wounded. And it is done in the presence of Montano, who had been concerned about Cassio's drinking and had indeed been wounded by Cassio in the first nocturnal brawl. Since there are no protests against Cassio by Montano, who had seen him at his worst (and who, as former governor of Cyprus, could presumably have spoken with some weight), since the Venetian authorities obviously accept him as capable, and since his original sponsor, Othello, is in disgrace, it may be concluded that his record was more impressive than Iago originally contended.[9]

6. To return to 1.1: of the 66½ lines which precede the beginning of Iago's and Roderigo's effort to set Brabantio on Othello, 59½ are spoken by Iago: those concerning his case against Othello are split almost evenly between the allegation of injustice and the boast that he will get even: "I follow him to serve my turn upon him" (42). When it is important to make a case, the amount of time spent on describing the inten-

IAGO: BEYOND THE GRIEVANCES

tion and the style of revenge is disproportionate, and the disproportion opens up the possibility that the feeling of enmity is the only real truth here, that it is not of recent birth, that the appointment of Cassio is less a cause than an occasion, and that the angry account of it is something like a ritual preparation.

7. If Iago hurries over the contention that he has been treated unjustly, never recurs to it again, and thus is unconvincing in this matter, what does he say that is convincing? Note the following passages:

>   Rod. Thou told'st me thou didst hold him in thy hate.
>   Iago. Despise me if I do not. (1.1.7-8)
>
>   [*Iago to Roderigo*] Though I do hate him as I do hell pains. (1.1.155)
>
>   [*Iago to Roderigo*] I have told thee often, and I retell thee again and again, I hate the Moor. (1.3.372-373)
>
>   [*Iago in soliloquy*]   I hate the Moor. (1.3.392)
>
>   [*Iago in soliloquy*]   howbeit that I endure him not. (2.1.297)

Here is something that Iago does not hurriedly allege and then forget, something that he comes back to repeatedly, and something that is consistent with all of his conduct. In such statements must be sought the key to his being. Iago not only reasserts his hatred[10] of Othello but is also at pains to deny his love:

>   Now, sir, be judge yourself,
>   Whether I in any just term am affin'd
>   To love the Moor. (1.1.38-40)
>
>   I must show out a flag and sign of love,
>   Which is indeed but sign. (1.1.157-158)

The antiphony of love and hate in Iago's own words points beyond his character to theme.

Of the preceding points, the first five lead us to the inference that Iago suffered no injustice when Cassio was made lieutenant. Objectively, Iago can be undergoing nothing more than the experience, which all of humanity knows, of that disappointment which is inevitable when the hope for a given preferment is felt by more than one person. Furthermore, the emphases of Iago's own lines (points 2, 6, 7) cast considerable doubt on the possibility that he himself has a profound sense of grievance or "cause." What is powerful and unmistakable in his lines is malice. On the fringe is the case-making, which I have called "ritual preparation."

MERE SUSPICION
Iago's second case against Othello is that Emilia and Othello may have committed adultery. This suspicion is set forth in two passages:

> I hate the Moor;
> And it is thought abroad that 'twixt my sheets
> 'Has done my office. I know not if't be true;
> Yet I, for mere suspicion in that kind,
> Will do as if for surety.   (1.3.392-396)

> But partly led to diet my revenge,
> For that I do suspect the lusty Moor
> Hath leap'd into my seat; the thought whereof
> Doth, like a poisonous mineral, gnaw my inwards;
> And nothing can or shall content my soul
> Till I am even'd with him, wife for wife.   (2.1.303-308)

The question here is less complicated than in the examination of Iago's complaint on the score of the lieutenancy, for on the matter of fact we are clear: Iago has not been wronged.[11] The only issue, then, is whether he really entertains the suspicion about which he talks in these ten lines. The following considerations are apposite:

1. Iago mentions this suspicion to no one else. He complains about the lieutenancy to Roderigo; there is no reason why Iago, whose sensibilities are not precisely delicate and who freely exhibits his character to Roderigo, should not also mention this suspicion, as a "gnawing" of his "inwards" would incline him to do.

2. In fact, Iago makes no other reference, direct or oblique,

IAGO: BEYOND THE GRIEVANCES

to this suspicion. Yet his soliloquies, the conventional instruments of self-disclosure, total 128 lines (1.3.389-410; 2.1.295-321; 2.3.342-368, 388-394; 3.3.321-333; 4.1.45-49, 94-104), not to mention various asides. Only 10 lines deal with the suspicion. As with the lieutenancy, Iago is less concerned to make a case than to make plans against the man he hates. His most astonishing failure to claim violated honor is after Emilia's disclosure, at 5.2.225ff., of what really happened to the handkerchief. Here an allegation of adultery might have been very helpful to Iago, who could at least play for the advantages of the *crime de passion*. But by now he has forgot that he was suspicious, or, more properly, that he had contended he was suspicious.

3. The charge against Othello is an afterthought, as the syntax in the first quotation makes clear: "I hate the Moor; / *And* it is thought abroad, etc." (italics mine). Rarely is a conjunction used so effectively: the hate is prior, and a motive is then discovered and happily pounced upon.¹² As in the steps of "revenge," Iago is improvising, else he would hardly admit the questionableness of the rumor before sweeping it into his arsenal of morality.

4. We need not work the criterion of intellectual consistency too hard, especially with Iago, but it is worth noting that "it is thought abroad" is cognate with "reputation," which Iago roundly debunks to Cassio. Granted, gossip about someone else and about oneself may seem fundamentally different. But observe Iago's "theory of reputation": "You have lost no reputation at all unless you repute yourself such a loser" (2.3.270-272). Analogously, what is "thought abroad" is meaningless unless one chooses to think it too. Compare Othello's real distress about his "honor": "A fixed figure for the time of scorn."

5. The second passage (2.1.303ff.) would actually be more impressive without the first, since the words chosen by Iago give some impression of vigor of feeling. The existence of the first, however, permits us to see how, with time, Iago has

31

been able to improve his version of a grievance that at first he picked up casually.[13] But he has not really convinced himself, or he would make more of this, especially in moments of triumph. Iago is too shrewd not to sense the desirability of some ritual suffering. The rite "purifies"—in Iago's case, frees him to devote all energies to the business at hand.

6. The suspicion is inconsistent with all we know of Iago. For one thing, it implies lack of information in the best informed character in the play—the hardboiled reporter who knows what is what and is fooled by nothing. The knowingness of manner which he assumes for his own purposes has a basis in fact: his real knowingness is assumed by the others, virtually all of whom at one time or another ask him for the facts or the truth of a matter. He is not the person to remain in the dark about the facts and to nurture an untested suspicion into an inner poison—unless he wishes to.[14]

Further, the alleged suspicion would be utterly inconsistent with Iago's shrewd (within limits) estimates of people. The man who so competently judges stimulus and response (his area of human understanding) that he is fooling all of the people nearly all of the time could not conceivably be fooled by adulterers no more scheming than the other characters in the play or suspect an adultery by people in whose character there is so little to evidence its probability. Besides, Iago repeatedly sneers at the simplicity and gullibility of Othello and plots to work on his "free and open nature." This is not a person whom he can seriously suspect of having carried on a liaison undetected.

7. If the suspicion of adultery were genuine and primary, the resultant hatred would fall on Emilia as much as on Othello. But except for the few lines in which he mentions the suspected misbehavior, Iago lets escape him no indication, direct or indirect, that he fears wrongdoing by Emilia.[15]

These points make it impossible to suppose that Iago took seriously the "suspicion" that Othello slept with Emilia. He can maintain it only on the theoretical ground, which is of

IAGO: BEYOND THE GRIEVANCES

course congenial to him, that adultery is universal. Besides, there is some ground for surmising that, even in a climate of cuckoldry jokes—a climate of which he may take advantage—Iago's personality frees him from excessive concern about Emilia's chastity.

What casts further doubt on the validity of these two grievances of Iago is that there are two of them and that both injuries have been done by the same man. Iago's case is too good; as a hunter of motives he has bagged more than the legal limit.[16] Yet some tendency to hyperbole of conception, some ironic attitude to his role as grievance-monger, makes him inflate his case with a third wrong. A little after he has spoken his "poisonous mineral" lines and promised to make Othello incurably jealous, he is improvising his procedure: "I'll have our Michael Cassio on the hip, / Abuse him to the Moor in the rank garb / (For I fear Cassio with my nightcap too)" (2.1.314-316). Again, there is no evidence whatsoever which would permit us to think the suspicion valid: the relations of Cassio and Emilia are marked by an easy and unconstrained friendliness which would be highly improbable if any of the tensions of a triangle were present. On the arrival at Cyprus, Cassio kisses Emilia openly and freely; Iago makes no comment except for an entertainer's joke[17] palpably without concealed depths. Further, Cassio could hardly deceive such a ferret as Iago, whose attitude to Cassio appears in the phrase "this honest fool" (2.3.359).

Into the statement of this third grievance, however, there enters a new and very curious element. The statement is familiar in one respect, namely, its having the tone of an afterthought. Just as earlier Iago said, "I hate the Moor," and then quickly added, "*And* it is thought abroad that 'twixt my sheets, etc.," so now he tells how he will "get" Cassio (as a part of the process of getting Othello) and then quickly adds, "For I fear Cassio, etc." But there is this difference: whereas the earlier afterthought about Othello was developed to the extent of two independent statements and thus acquired

33

a certain air of substantialness, the later afterthought about Cassio is hurried over in a single-line parenthesis (which some editors enclose in parentheses) in a sentence that then goes on for three and a half lines more about the method of working on Othello. Now the mechanics of revenge are a lesser subject than the emotions produced by a sexual wrong; yet here the mechanics take up eight lines of a sentence in which the emotion is expressed in a one-line parenthesis. The point to recall here is that this grammatical reversal, this ostentatious subordination of an element of intrinsic importance, is a standard comic device, especially in popular entertainment. Not only is the grievance unimportant to Iago, but also he knows that he is syntactically demoting it and thus in effect making a conscious joke of his profession of fear.[18] An actor would be called on to manage the line with the subtlest possible suggestion of the "double take."

Shakespeare adds a special note of the sinister to his evil by infusing the sardonic humor that might go with an entertainer rather than a destroyer. In fact, Iago repeatedly becomes the "comedian of evil," the zestful gamesman" with an actor's delight in his tricks;[19] in him the sadism underlying the laughter of the "harmless practical joke" expands to full size. His comic cover may range from a leaping gleeful enthusiasm to sidemouth contempt to the almost imperceptibly mobile deadpan—as here in the reference to Cassio, which has the controlled ambiguousness of the verbal maneuverings by which he later suborns distrust and murder. He is both kidding the justification game for those who can catch the half-hidden accent, and offering a case to those who incline to hear only the words.

THE PRINCIPLE OF JUSTIFICATION

If Iago really had the motives he alleges, the interpreter's task is easy: Iago executed an excessive vengeance.[20] But if we reject these motives, we have a number of problems to deal with, and the first of them is the *raison d'être* of the justifications,[21] which have been interpreted by some editors[22] as evidence of conscience. True, at times Iago exhibits an intellectual clarity that may be mistaken for a moral impulse. But not conscience—rather, an automatic movement of exculpation analogous to the twitching of tissues after death. He essays a kind of protective coloring. In so doing, he exemplifies the apparent impossibility of "pure" action against the community by one who has not withdrawn from it into open enmity but who, still in it, mechanically makes a token payment or formal obeisance to some of its standards of conduct.[23] Too, Iago has a positive cast of mind that impels him to move initially in the world of conventional demonstration. He does not take himself as a datum but must place himself in the existent order; so he finds what "law" he falls under—the still familiar one that one wrong justifies a greater. This quick, mechanical, even flippant, gesture at *rapprochement* hints just faintly of a flight from isolation: the shadowy miming of conscience in an essentially conscienceless person trying to get by among consciences. Isolation, however, is the condition of the destroyer, and in the final scene of the play Iago embraces his condition. But he has to "grow" to this.

When the quality of an evil character is at once so fully concealed from those about him (except from Roderigo, who is too suddenly immersed in his own hopeless passion to be perceptive) and so completely displayed for the audience as is Iago, the aesthetic danger is that he will be felt simply as a conventional villain, held off at a distance, and not assimilated in his full human meaning. It is in the light of this danger that Iago's grievance game may be more fully understood. The enumeration of wrongs, whatever else it does, is good strategy for bringing the villain home to the reader and auditor. How shall the dramatist deal maturely with human evil? If he writes classic tragedy, he can exhibit the "flaw" of the good man with whom, as we show by pity and fear, we are identified. But the "bad man" is likely to become simply an enemy to be put down, an enemy whose threat permits an assumption of the sufficiency of one's own virtue, shuts off self-inspection, and thus produces moral complacency—the psychological structure of melodrama. The problem, then, is to reduce the distance between villain and spectator, or to universalize the bad man,[24] or in still other words to cause him to be sensed as the incarnation and concentration of motives which, whether acted upon literally or symbolically, or "sublimated," or partly or totally suppressed, are found generally. Iago's justifications serve in part to make him, in Conrad's phrase, "one of us." As Muir has said, "Yet we are all, in some measure, Iagos, just as we are all Othellos."[25] Iago's looking for causes, his citing of wrongs, his disappointment—by these Shakespeare brings him partly within the circle of recognizable humanity and forbids us to write him off as unique. In his efforts to be or look "normal" we can see our own impulses at work. And if from within the circle of the apparently human the monstrous can emerge and mature, we are invited to entertain a view of humanity in which the monstrous is always a latent possibility, to see a full-size version of ordinary hypocrisy, love of trouble, malice, etc. If, finally, the justifications which establish an individual as a fellow mortal turn out to be spurious, we may have been led on to a view of that which is justified—vengefulness, destructiveness—as a constant reality rather than as alien, freakish, a foreign invasion of the moral realm. In Iago, Shakespeare made his fullest and most daring exploration of the potential evil of Everyman.

As a figure of evil, Iago is a datum,[26] spontaneous and omnipresent and native; he is an "insider," always susceptible of activation; he belongs in neither of two extreme categories— that of the mysterious visitation of disaster from without; and that of the completely explicable psychological phenomenon embodying a handy formula of cause and effect. In one direction, Iago has affiliations with the forces of evil in the morality play, and thus may be understood as a potentiality of the soul, striving to become the whole of it;[27] the "shadow-side of Othello," as Miss Bodkin puts it,[28] creeping over the whole (as with Roderigo, who is likewise receptive to the expanding dark

IAGO: BEYOND THE GRIEVANCES

side). Yet Iago is not an abstraction but a pronouncedly concrete individual—an individual, however, who carries certain impulses on to such a logical fullness that in contemplating him we are in the end driven to conceptualization (thus reversing the progress of the morality character from initial allegorical status into a fullness of personality in which we apprehend him directly as an individual). My main interpretation of Iago may gain some weight from the fact that there are some truly extraordinary parallels between him and a more recent literary character who has been much studied—namely, Claggart in *Billy Budd,* another drama hedged by the conditions of war and military life, and concerned with "an antipathy spontaneous and profound."[29] Melville might be portraying Iago when he draws on the concept of "natural depravity" and lists, among the characteristics of Claggart, respectability, the use of reason as "an ambidexter implement for effecting the irrational," "uncommon prudence," the use of "retaliation . . . in monstrous disproportion to the supposed offence," the fact that he "justified animosity into a sort of retributive righteousness," the "monomania in the man."[30] Iago also has the sense of personal antithesis which is implicitly present in Claggart: "If Cassio do remain, / He hath a daily beauty in his life / That makes me ugly" (5.1.18-20). The perception to which every villain with a mind is doomed is here used by Shakespeare to set forth in precise words that aspect of evil which he has already set forth in action, namely, its springing into full life at the implicit challenge of a counterexistence. Dormant evil is awakened by the juxtaposition of conspicuous good (Claggart by the arrival of Budd)—duplicity by integrity, mendacity by truthfulness, hate by love. Iago's hatred of Othello is activated when Othello, as successful lover, inclines to love all the world, and of Cassio when he is deep in a reciprocal friendly love with both Othello and Desdemona. Thus a commonplace psychological phenomenon, which in one direction shades off into the light comedy of taste ("I do not like thee, Dr. Fell"), is deepened by Shakespeare and presented ultimately in the light of its metaphysical implications. An observation of temperament is made the door to a view of spiritual reality.

THE MONSTER BEGOT UPON ITSELF

Othello has long been discussed as a "drama of jealousy," i.e., Iago's jealousy of Emilia, and, centrally, Othello's of Desdemona. I have argued that this account of Iago's role is untenable. I believe, also, that we get a very limited view of the play if we take its main substance to be Othello's jealousy. Though a number of lines bear on the subject of Othello's jealousy,[31] this is not the primary reality with him. What he suffers from may be called "secondary jealousy": it is induced, not spontaneous, and it takes root and gains strength not because of an addiction to sexual suspiciousness but because of other characteristics. Our problem, to which we shall return, is what lies beneath the surface of his jealousy, what is "primary" in him, what inner trouble makes him prone to acquiesce in the invention of a great imaginary evil for himself.

Not that there is not a jealousy theme.[32] If we go back for another look at Iago, we find passages in which he shows what must be called jealousy. He may have no case for the lieutenancy, but he is certainly jealous of Cassio as lieutenant. I think it is fair to say that he is jealous of Cassio's "book learning" (1.1.24-26)—of trained intelligence.[33] The witticisms and verses with which he entertains Emilia and Desdemona betray a jealousy of the human race insofar as it is capable of being sensible, orderly, and well behaved (2.1.110-161). He is jealous of Desdemona's "goodness," which he proposes to turn into a trap to catch the others (2.3.366-368). He is jealous of her devotion to Othello and of the friendly intimacy between her and Cassio (2.1.168-180, 223-270)—and in this feeling there are strange depths which we must explore more fully in Chapter VI.

Iago's jealousy is indeed pervasive.[34] Further, he instinctively adopts a quasi-Aristotelian program: the catharsis of jealousy

IAGO: BEYOND THE GRIEVANCES

by jealousy; that is, his jealousy works itself off, or is purged, by the creation of a soothing counterjealousy. Not that it is "purified" but that it finds an outlet. He arouses the paternal jealousy of Brabantio,[35] plays on that of Roderigo, creates that of Othello and fertilizes it by warning him against it.[36] His sponsoring of jealousy in others works so well because he can spot the infectible (not Desdemona, notably); he has an "inside"[37] knowledge of the disease: "Trifles light as air / Are to the jealous confirmations strong / As proofs of holy writ" (3.3.322-324).

What, then, is the nature of Iago's jealousy? In contrast with Othello's "secondary jealousy," it is "primary jealousy," and it is because this motif is present that *Othello* may indeed be considered a "drama of jealousy." "Primary jealousy" is not induced but spontaneous; it is not occasional but chronic; it is not the product of exceptional circumstances acting upon the character, but the character's essential mode of responding to circumstances. It is the basic determinant of moral direction. It has been called, correctly I think, envy.[38] Not that Iago is an allegorical figure of *invidia,* for he is a "round" character. He is a concentration of all the pure spite at the heart, yet with an endowment of supplementary traits that make him accepted by the community, as is symbolically necessary, and enough art in justification to be somewhat convincing to "us" (who cannot utterly disclaim kinship with him)—until in the extremities which he has brought about the malice stands out alone, the sum of his being.

Though the sexual jealousy which he momentarily parades has, I believe we shall see, one special, unsuspected area of truth, the fact is that Iago might be a happier man if Emilia were unfaithful: what is frustrating to Iagos is the lack of authentic grievances.[39] The pathology of the type is implied in what Desdemona and Emilia say about sexual jealousy. When Desdemona, somewhat misreading Othello, says that he is "made of no such baseness / As jealous creatures are" (3.4.27-28), she uses, in *baseness,* a word of great defining value:

39

Shakespeare, as we shall see, takes pains to attribute meanness and vulgarity to Iago. Emilia's theory of "jealous souls" tells us more about Iago: "They are not ever jealous for the cause, / But jealous for they are jealous. 'Tis a monster / Begot upon itself, born on itself" (3.4.159-162). This is exactly the definition of the man who lives in envy. Causes are irrelevant. Iago says almost the same thing when he pretends to warn Othello to look out for him: "As I confess it is my nature's plague / To spy into abuses, and oft my jealousy / Shapes faults that are not" (3.3.146-148). His tactic of deprecation actually gives away the truth about primary jealousy: that the impulse comes from within, not from without, and that it is a lust for the downfall of others (cf. Marlowe's Envy: "I cannot read, and therefore wish all books were burnt"). Finally, Iago's native resentfulness of human quality, which drives him to invent injustices against himself as occasions for attack, appears unequivocally in his statement, at which we have already glanced, of the profit in Cassio's death. Again the syntax is telling: "He hath a daily beauty in his life / That makes me ugly; *and besides,* the Moor / May unfold me to him" (5.1.19-21; my italics). This precisely duplicates the revelatory style of an earlier passage: "I hate the Moor; / *And* it is thought abroad, etc." (1.3.392-393). The real motive comes first—the *invidia;* then, with an *and* betraying the afterthought,[40] Iago adds the justification or the tactical consideration.

If this situation suggests the word *motiveless,* we should remember that *motiveless* is not the same as *unaccountable* or *incomprehensible* or *meaningless.* Indeed, to place Iago outside the circuit of commonplace cause and effect[41] is to make him not a lesser but an ampler character. As a figure of autonomous evil or "floating hatred" (a fact of experience not reducible to the common formulae of conduct), he does create difficulty for readers who require "positive" or specific situational causes for all actions. Even when we have found causes, however, we have acknowledged them to be inadequate; yet we have never considered the extent of Iago's hatred improb-

IAGO: BEYOND THE GRIEVANCES

able in itself; perhaps, then, even while motive-hunting, we have subconsciously tended to solve the problem by regarding Iago as human depravity in action. He is clearly a condensation of evil that is more than an isolatable, localized impulse to bad conduct. We cannot avoid thinking of him symbolically or metaphysically;[42] yet we can always see him as an individual, and besides, as a type—the type whose only excursion from moral indifference is a destructive hatred of achievements of spirit. Here we might find the metaphor "mass mind" useful.[43]

THE CHRISTIAN MYTH

Since the malice comes before the occasion that brings it into play, we might say that Iago is "original evil." It would then be not difficult to regard him as the devil incarnate and to turn the play into a parable echoing Genesis: Satan takes on his false colors, sets out to disturb the happy pair in their "fertile climate" (1.1.70), picks Othello some very bad fruit from the Tree of Knowledge (Desdemona unknowingly adds to his willingness to eat it), and thus causes him to ruin his garden himself. Or we might picture Satan as attacking a specifically Christian community and playing upon or bringing about failures in Christian practice that are disastrous to the community; Othello would then be the wavering Christian (who falls into self-righteousness, moral censoriousness, and wrath, and commits the sins of murder and suicide), and Desdemona the embodiment of Christian virtues (humility, obedience, fidelity, etc.) and perhaps even a sacrificial figure[44] ("the divine Desdemona," 2.1.73)—brought to an atoning death by a Judas ("base Judean")[45] who says, "I kiss'd thee ere I kill'd thee" (5.2.347, 358).

Reading *Othello* as a myth of Satan[46] would in one sense be very plausible, for the world of the play is emphatically Christian, as the language abundantly indicates.[47] To discover a profounder level of Christian thought and feeling, we could examine the action in terms of Christian doctrine (Iago's rejection of the love of fellow men, Othello's moral self-assurance,

Roderigo's lust, and so on), or consider the play "a study of sin in the private individual, worked out in terms of the theory of reason, will, and appetite,"[48] or chart the ironies to which the Christian influence contributes (the self-acknowledged hater seems to be the friend of all; Othello, quickest and most untiring in Christian allusion, fails in Christian virtues; Desdemona, most capable of growth in Christian spirit, is murdered). Although reading *Othello* as if it were explicitly a dramatization of a Christian world view can be very enlightening,[49] the Christian materials are so much in the foreground and are so numerous and distinct that they hardly offer a structural problem or provide a final way into the problems of verbal and actional drama.[50]

If we start by simply calling Iago a "devil," we risk using the myth of evil as a substitute for the analysis of the individual; his diabolical identity, if it is there, must be earned in the dramatic progression and discovered as a kind of substructure. What goes on in the play is less to be defined by than to define *devil*. In some characteristics Shakespeare's Iago anticipates Milton's Satan.[51] But we come to the generic or archetypal only after we have gone as far as we can with the unique person; not that we can come to it if it isn't there; but that, instead of initially dissolving the single human being in the mythic, we keep always a sharp sense of this single being and of the mythic, which we may think of as an auxiliary mode of conception forced upon us by the vast range of the individual. If we can hypothetically imagine Shakespeare starting (from Cinthio) with an idea of a literally "diabolical" character, his problem was to naturalize and actualize the mythical Satan, to incarnate the devil in such a way that the human dimension is primary and that the incarnation draws all it can from Everyman. This process of the realizing of Iago we try to follow in all the details of the actional and verbal drama. We do not exclude a mythic reading. But if we use it, our formulation should have a double predicate: "Iago is a human being and the devil too."[52]

IAGO: BEYOND THE GRIEVANCES

Or to put this another way by picking up a point made earlier in this chapter. In that old dispute, which began in the nineteenth century and continues in the present day, as to whether Iago is to be equated with "Evil" or is to be explained in terms of more or less commonplace "motives" (real grievances, class feelings, or even psychoanalytically discoverable troubles), one must sympathize with the anti-Evil position if to say that Iago "is" Evil means that he is a symbol and not a character. I happen to believe that we learn more about him if we say that he "is" Evil; but Evil must be more than a grand abstraction to evoke our horror, must be understood in terms of recurrent human manifestations that are made concrete in Iago. To rephrase: "Iago is Evil and is Iago—a somewhat ailing Everyman—too."[53] Several meanings are present simultaneously, not discordantly but integrally,[54] and they may be responded to "spontaneously and unconsciously" by the "multi-consciousness" of the audience.[55]

Multiple iago

To return for a moment to the Melville analogy, we may observe how Melville tidied up the plot (almost as if he were turning a novel into drama) by using a one-to-one line-up of spiritual antitypes (Claggart and Budd) and a referee, whereas Shakespeare placed Iago in a many-sided tension with a plurality of Billy Budds, all with their share of innocence and naivete. Shakespeare's intuition of the methods of evil is still at one point identical with Melville's: malevolence appears as benevolence: to Budd, Claggart seems well disposed, and Iago is equally regarded as reliable by Othello, Cassio, and Desdemona (and in a different way by Roderigo, who, naive but not innocent, is most inclined to suspicion). Iago's multiple histrionic feat permits an extraordinary probing of the issues compounded in his character. Primarily there is the study of the individual personality, which we have already glanced at fleetingly, and which offers many other complications, especially in his relations with Desdemona. But the individual is also generic, in the characteristic style of the poet who is at once portrait painter and typological analyst, so that one may observe the appearance of both a class of responses and a category of humanity which is an identifiable molding of Everyman. And the individual, as we have seen in the preceding section, also takes on a mythic cast. Further, Iago's actions have philosophic implications, and he formally explicates a number of ideas in which a philosophic bias is apparent. The maintenance of all these perspectives is the comprehensive technique for defining dramatically the evil embodied in Iago.[56] In both the actional and the verbal drama what he is and means is given a presentation which, though in some aspects it is forthright, is in others indirect, withdrawn, impalpably present, by the subtle texture of lighting and sound and figure deeply influencing the imagination. The magic in the web produces a character so full and flexible that it can accommodate itself to the psychological habits of different generations: Iago may be understood as Invidia or as the Machiavel or as the Jealous Man or as the False Friend; he can be sensed at his narrowest as the villain of melodrama or at his widest as Satan[57]—a projection of "the forces within and without us that threaten our supreme values."[58] Yet he is so far from any stereotype that there is always something of the enigmatic about him.[59] What we can understand is the malice toward a world understood, desired, lived in up to a point, and yet in spirit not to be possessed on his own terms. What we must seek, then, is the demonic strategies against the spiritual order, and the kinds of weakness that entice the strategies. Iago's evil is successful when he can take advantage of some readiness in his victim.[60] Iago is not an unconquerable giant of evil ruining innocents, nor is he a petty trickster giving only a little mechanical aid to corrupt giants as they destroy themselves; he and Othello are both large figures; the question is not "whose play it is"[61] but the kinds of evil force and susceptibility to evil, the kinds of temptation and openness to temptation—in other words, the human constants—embodied in Iago and Othello and in their interplay.

The Iago World

STYLES IN DECEPTION

To look at the "flow" from Iago into the community—the many-channeled influence revealed in the verbal and actional drama—is to study a relationship in which we may observe both certain powers and methods on one side and certain susceptibilities on the other, both what Iago is and what kinds of psychic and moral breaches he picks out in the community. In the present chapter we deal mainly with Iago's techniques of infiltration, that aspect of his maneuvering which reveals him to us through his modes of concealment from others: his multiple perfecting of what Fielding was long after to call "hypocrisy"—the simulation of virtues which are polar opposites of one's vices. We shall look, in the next chapter, at the manifold styles, literal or symbolic, in which Iago lets us know him "directly"—his vices acted out, named defiantly, or incarnated in his linguistic and intellectual manners.

The Iago world: active evil, and the human context of rejection or of acceptance unwitting, secretly willing, or imposed by ends in view. It may not be possible to identify a "key" readiness in a victim, especially a victim like Othello, who is vulnerable in more ways than one. But his most visible failure is an obtuseness to facts, an astigmatism by which he sees innocence as guilt, and guilt as innocence. These principal misseeings, as we shall find, are expressed in and given resonance

CHAPTER 3

by a manifold, unending metamorphosis of opposites (dark as light, poison as medicine, fantasy as evidence, and the like). To this systematic confounding of truth there is a choral ring of *honest* and *honesty*, flowing from the dissonant chord "honest Iago."

1. HONEST IAGO

The most conspicuous irony is Othello's thinking Iago is "honest" and Desdemona is not "honest." The use of this one word with two meanings quietly emphasizes the tie between the two reversals of truth by which Othello destroys himself. Having bound himself to evil, he converts it into honor; and having married Desdemona, he makes a dishonest woman of her. To effect this singular transaction, he reasons a priori when he should not, that is, in judging Iago's honesty, and fails to reason a priori when he should, that is, in assessing Desdemona's love.[1] We shall see more of how he reasons, and is taught to reason.

Iago himself uses the word *honest* just as frequently as Othello, and more than half the times he uses it he is, in one tone or another, applying it to himself. The word is used of Desdemona only a third as many times as it is used of Iago, of Cassio still less frequently, and of everybody else hardly at all. Iago has succeeded, then, in attaching the issue of honesty to himself, quite in the manner of a modern politician identifying himself, to the exclusion of others, with a movement or attitude or virtue. He has the air of an old hand at the game; we see it, not being learned before our eyes, but practiced easily; improvised in detail, perhaps, but enough an old part of himself to approach perfection on the occasion which "triggers" the release of his habitual resentfulness into one large gamble. Empson argues that the word *honest* was in transition, marking the emergence of "a sort of jovial cult of independence"; that the word ministered to a certain personal and philosophical (and perhaps social) defensiveness (against patronizing, un-

THE IAGO WORLD: STYLES IN DECEPTION

dervaluing, etc.) and could be used by Iago in senses that he could, and we should, feel to be literally and perhaps creditably applicable; and that these facts greatly complicate the revelation of self and the kind of chicane found in the honesty passages.[2] If this theory is sound, it is still true that even when speaking literally or "truly," Iago is also "working a line" and getting others to work it too; one may have a certain status as a matter of fact and yet use the status as an instrument. Human beings do it regularly; as Empson says, Shakespeare did not invent "a unique psychology" for Iago, nor, we may add, for his victims. Once the drama has begun, "honesty" comes into play very quickly: the personality breaks into the open. "Whip me such honest knaves!" cries Iago in the first scene (1.1.49), in his scorn for faithful servants repudiating the "old" honesty and taking on the "new," as well as setting up the contrast in Emilia's prayer, near the end, that heaven "put in every honest hand a whip" to torment slanderers (4.2.142). It is Emilia's own hand that soon carries the most stinging whip, but in the meantime the "honest knaves" have had a rough time of it.

As is proper in one whose slickness has passed off his instrument of policy as the disinterested real thing, Iago expresses explicit contempt for the simplicity and honesty of those on whom his "honesty" operates—Othello, Cassio, and, in a way, even Desdemona (1.3.406; 2.3.359, 345-347), and he enjoys contemplating his own role: "But I'll set down the pegs that make this music, / As honest as I am" (2.1.202-203). Repeatedly we detect the conscious histrionism in Iago, the egotistic relish of his artistry in seduction, and, in this, an infallible clue to the private reality of the man who conducts a public business in terms of a claimed and paraded virtue: the theatricalization of merit betrays the racket and, as a full-time hypnosis of a community, is the mark of a competent diabolist. So Iago to Cassio: "As I am an honest man, I thought you had receiv'd some bodily wound" (2.3.266-267). He "protests" that, in urging Cassio to secure Desdemona's help in recovering Othello's favor, he "advises" Cassio "in the sincerity of love and honest kindness" (333-334). He wins doubly, securing Cassio's aid in his plot and, additionally, Cassio's strengthened sense of his character: "Good night, honest Iago" (341). Cassio leaves; Iago, alone, turns right to the audience and justifies: "This advice is free . . . and honest" (343). He enters zestfully into his own casuistry, in the spirit of "Let's see, can I take in the audience too?" Here again Shakespeare adds a dash of the comic to the ruthless man; the sinister is enlarged when the moral destroyer is a zestful athlete of deception; in the antics of malice, a lover of footlights.

The patent ironies of the honesty motif spread out in various directions.[3] To call another man honest is almost a prelude to receiving injury at his hands. Desdemona insists on Cassio's "honest face" (3.3.50); he inadvertently assists in her destruction. Desdemona calls Iago "an honest fellow" (3.3.5), and Cassio strengthens his earlier estimate of Iago: "I never knew / A Florentine more kind and honest" (3.1.42-43); within a hundred lines Iago begins destroying them both—by leading Othello to question their honesty. "Is he not honest?" "Honest, my lord?" "Honest? Ay, honest" (3.3.103). In establishing publicly the bond between honesty and himself, Iago has profited not only by arrogating a certain moral status to himself but also by becoming an "expert" in the field. The expert now moves ahead by repeatedly calling attention to his "thoughts"[4] (97-162) but at the same time by showing some diffidence about their validity ("honesty" in action). Thus these three lines—

I dare be sworn I think that he is honest	(125);
Why then, I think Cassio's an honest man	(129);
I do not think but Desdemona's honest	(225)—

appear to be somewhat unwilling disclosure of real thoughts, appear to say what Othello wants to hear, yet convert their ostensible affirmations into negations by the implied fallibility of the speaker. The virtue of modest self-doubt (a version of honesty) has served to implant evil doubts of others: "I think

THE IAGO WORLD: STYLES IN DECEPTION

my wife be honest, and think she is not" (384). Othello is now far enough along so that his expert can discard the "I think" which conveys the meaning "I do not think" and risk a verb of possibility: "She may be honest yet" (433). The campaign of "honesty" against honesty succeeds: Othello is unable to believe two strong assertions of Emilia that Desdemona is "honest" (4.2.12, 17), he bitterly commands Desdemona to "damn" herself by an oath, namely, "Swear thou art honest" (38), and Desdemona at last has to express as a hope that which she had utterly taken for granted, "I hope my noble lord esteems me honest" (65).

It is more than an ironic effect when *honesty* regularly marks bamboozlement and when dishonesty can effect its purposes by talking honesty, or, to apply Empson, when "honesty" of one kind can talk honesty of another kind.[5] The irony discloses tragic confusion and, further beyond, that human fallibility of the innocent or the axe-grinders that helps malice succeed; it illuminates a human paradigm—the demagogue's succeeding by getting his public to accept him unconditionally in his own terms (so that other human beings can then not be accepted in terms appropriate to them). The play dramatizes generically the danger that exists, when, in a framework of action (as opposed to discussion), there is regular verbalizing about a virtue—that claiming of virtue (the first recourse of a scoundrel) and that conceding of the claim that obscure from all the real direction of the action. This claiming and this conceding can take place only in an air where corruption, actual or latent, and naivete inadvertently collaborate in yielding to imposture. We are given a clue to this in the very first words spoken to Othello by Iago, who, reporting with a pretense of indignation the abuse of Othello by Brabantio, comments, "I lack iniquity / Sometimes to do me service" (1.2.3-4). The assertion of an insufficiency of utilitarian vice is almost a classical revelation of dishonesty. (Compare Iago's following reference to "the little godliness I have," line 9: here the modest

49

claim to only a minimum of virtue is the technique for implying the presence of a sufficiency.) Othello has presumably been hearing this sort of thing for some time, and we may suppose that with more of an eye to moral reality he would at least have doubts about Iago. But he is representative in his obtuseness.[6]

Iago never mentions his honesty to Roderigo, and Roderigo never calls him honest. There is neither occasion nor room for such maneuvers; early in the game Iago has urged, "Let us be conjunctive in our revenge against him" (1.3.374-375). The contrast of the "honesty scenes" with the Roderigo scenes is dramatically useful: in the latter, Iago's unvarnished crudity underscores the genius with which he puts on and uses his veneer when dealing with all the others. Too, the Roderigo scenes give a kind of relief: evil is out in the open. Yet here the candor itself is a part of the faking, for Iago is still dishonestly making Roderigo believe in his eventual success in dishonesty. The assumption of dishonesty as a norm[7] permits an ever-extending come-on game in which the naive aspirant to evil and the lover of good may be conjoined as consenting victims of a Iago both Tartuffish and gangsterish. It is a powerful dramatization of evil: the power and the willingness to kill, and the ingenuity that can at once maneuver a group toward violence and evoke the choral refrain of "honest" which inhibits doubt and enlarges the sense of security at the very point of attack.

Now for some other specific forms in which Shakespeare presents the operating of honest Iago.

2. SEEMING AND SEEING: OCULAR PROOF

Honest Iago works principally by upsetting the probabilities upon which men rely in coping with experience. He is a master of disguise. He seems the finest friend to those whom he

THE IAGO WORLD: STYLES IN DECEPTION

destroys. He stage-manages two nocturnal brawls (2.3; 5.1) without the participants' suspecting that they are not acting spontaneously; he puts on a play within a play (4.1) which convinces Othello that Desdemona has been unfaithful. Iago's hand is regularly quicker than Othello's eye; he waves a magic wand, and Othello sees what he is told to see. Iago is not ranting idly when he speaks of using "heavenly shows" (2.3.358). *Shows* is, revealingly, a favorite word of his.[8]

Iago's manipulation of appearances[9] raises the problem of appearance and reality. It is almost as if Shakespeare took off consciously from the tradition of the disguise to elaborate a myth of the human being's normal incapacity to deal with the issue of surface and substance. It is a myth at which he works in a series of plays, but he gives it, in *Lear* and *Othello*, a special formulation: the tragic protagonist struggles with appearance and reality when another agent is deliberately confusing them.[10]

Iago succeeds in puddling the clear spirit of Othello (3.4.143) not only because he is a wily tactician but because his tactics flow from his convictions: reality is either relative or meaninglessly undifferentiated, and appearance is fluid and controllable. Whenever Iago is creating confusion, he at heart believes that the confounded elements are not properly distinguishable anyway; so he feels no inhibiting discrepancy between inner and outer, between idea and action, and all his energies are freed to utilize the flux. His jocular description of women as "pictures out of doors, / Bells in your parlours, wildcats in your kitchen, / Saints in your injuries, etc." 2.1.110-112) clearly implies an essential shiftingness of character, a fluidity of appearance which allows no sense of a stable reality. When he entertains Desdemona and Emilia with the couplets in which he undermines all distinctions between fair and foul, witty and foolish (2.1.130ff.), he does appear to identify a reality of character; but all he really offers is a biological common denominator worthless in a world of real individuals. Some kind of belief pours vitality into his persuading Roderigo that, despite appearances, Desdemona loves Cassio and that Cassio is most adept at "putting on the mere form of civil and humane seeming for the better compassing of his salt and most hidden loose affection" and has "an eye can stamp and counterfeit advantages" (2.1.242-249). The doctrine he holds and preaches is that the world is a treacherous mass of quicksands and boobytraps.[11] His genius is to make it just that for others, to make it habitable only for those constitutionally able to live in ceaseless suspicion.

Iago, the man who "looks dead with grieving" (2.3.177) to fool Othello, persuades Othello, who "thinks men honest that but seem to be so" (1.3.405-406), not only to act in a certain way but also to change his principles of action. More than once Iago aims at this ultimate subversion: not merely to suborn a ruinous mistake, but to have the mistake grounded in principle. In the long deception scene Iago first raises the problem of appearance:

> *Iago.* Men should be what they seem;
> Or those that be not, would they might seem none!
> *Oth.* Certain, men should be what they seem. (3.3.126-128)

Iago is doing more than plumping down a truism. For one thing, he is characteristically gambling, skirting the dangerous edge of discovery,[12] and this just after Othello himself has pointed out to him those aspects of appearance—the hesitancies of the unwilling witness—which Othello says would be suspect in anyone else (3.3.121-123). But more than that, he is planting a general idea in Othello's head—the doctrine that "all men are not what they seem"; and Othello officially embarks on a philosophic voyage for which he is ill equipped, the exploration of the different realms of *being* and *seeming*. Now if Othello were an entirely accurate follower of Iago, he would have to extend his doubts to Iago. Since he does not, except for a verbal flurry or two, doubt Iago, his implied principle

THE IAGO WORLD: STYLES IN DECEPTION

is the more limited one that "not all men are what they seem." So he needs to distinguish among men, including Iago (which is not too much to expect of the experienced commander of men). But Othello also fails at this point; we can see him getting morally involved by the insufficiency of his intellectual efforts. Oddly, he even takes a logical leap by which he outstrips the guide whom otherwise he follows with passionate docility. Iago's attack on appearances implicitly boils down to this: "Appearances of good are not trustworthy, those of evil are" (a selective skepticism familiar to us in the twentieth century, who are inclined, despite our ritual optimism, to regard an appearance of good as a trap for the unwary). This principle, if he apprehended it with any alertness, would still force Othello to keep a sharp eye on Iago. Instead, he acts in a way that carries him beyond Iago's doctrine to this: "Appearances of evil are trustworthy, those of good are not unless accompanied by displays of hostility to the supposedly evil." These formulations serve only the purpose of letting us see into what logically preposterous conduct[13] Iago has led Othello —preposterous but, we may conjecture, representative: the followers of the pretentiously virtuous in public life must be presumed to think like this.

Iago insinuates that Desdemona looks one thing but is another.[14] She "did deceive her father"; she actually loved you "when she seem'd to shake and fear your looks"; to think that one "so young, could give out such a seeming / To seel her father's eyes" (3.3.201-210)! Othello now infers the reality of evil from appearances that indicate, however incredibly, that it is a possibility; and he begins looking, of all things, for appearances that will prove it. Yet he cannot altogether quell his intuitive sense of the harmony of appearance and reality in Desdemona. Though he might also infer her inability to separate them[15] from his own "hardness to dissemble," as he calls it (3.4.34), he makes himself act as Iago has tutored him. In fact, he applies his schooling in two ways that help promote

53

disaster. He himself "dissembles"; to detect falseness, he puts on as much of a false appearance as he can; in thus shifting, without ethical concern, from being to seeming he augments confusion instead of finding light. On the other hand, he continues actively to war against the reassuring appearances of good which he has learned to find deceptive. When he strikes Desdemona in public and she cries, he sneers, "O well-painted passion!" (4.1.268). But, very skillfully, Shakespeare has Othello's accusations again run afoul of his direct response to her as she appears to him. In the mock-brothel scene she seems "lovely fair"; thou, he says to her, "smell'st so sweet"; and he asks, "Was this fair paper . . . / Made to write 'whore' upon?" (4.2.68-72). Repeatedly he senses a beauty which is more than apt line and color. But instead of giving rein to his almost instinctive feeling of the consonance of things,[16] he sticks to his prejudgment and can only marvel at the discrepancy of the seen and the real, "So sweet was ne'er so fatal" (5.2.20). So he kills her. Then in self-defense he takes his last stand on the doctrine of discrepancy to which Iago has enticed him; just after admitting that he has killed her, he begins to argue: "I know this act shows horrible and grim" (5.2.203). Here, almost at the end, not only Iago's thought, but his characteristic word *shows*.[17] Iago's deepest victory is that confusion of mind which lets Othello try to believe and explain that a murder looks much worse than it is.

But Othello comes to see what—or at least a part of what— he has done. Shakespeare manages this recognition with a typically full exploitation of theme: he has Othello formally state his acknowledgment in terms of appearance. In the only passage in which he addresses the dead Desdemona directly, his first words are: "Now, how dost thou look now?" (5.2.272) —as if consciously repeating the close examinations in which he had hunted for signs of guilt. Now he knows how she looks and what her look means: "This look of thine will hurl my soul from heaven" (274). His "journey's end," after the ex-

THE IAGO WORLD: STYLES IN DECEPTION

ploratory voyage into the realms of appearance and reality, is the costly discovery, once available without travel, that his original assumption of their identity is, for everything of importance in his life, valid.

THE HEART AND THE SLEEVE

The identity of appearance and reality in Desdemona is nicely put in Cassio's praise of her as one that "in th' essential vesture of creation / Does tire the ingener" (2.1.64-65). She is created with an "essential vesture," i.e., clothed with virtues: the outer and inner, the seen and the unseen,[18] are the same. Compare Desdemona's "essential vesture" with Iago's adherence to those who are "trimm'd in forms and visages of duty" and throw "but shows of service on their lords" and who, "when they have lin'd their coats, / Do themselves homage" (1.1.50-54). Here we have a conscious split between "essence" and "vesture," and, with fascinating appropriateness, between three layers of dress—trimming (good form), coat (admissible self-interest), and lining (the racket).

Such clothing imagery, reinforcing the abstract terms in which honest Iago usually argues *(deceive, shows, seeming),* is an admirable phase of the verbal drama that reveals the many-layered manipulator of appearances and that greatly strengthens our sense of his duplicity. Iago goes on:

> Heaven is my judge, not I for love and duty,
> But seeming so, for my peculiar end;
> For when my outward action doth demonstrate
> The native act and figure of my heart
> In compliment extern, 'tis not long after
> But I will wear my heart upon my sleeve
> For daws to peck at. I am not what I am.   (59-65)

"I am not what I am"—a highly charged summation of all Iago's poetry of deceit—is a self-characterization not of a man slipping tentatively into deception, but of a man deeply committed to a belief in the irrationality of all appearance and hence pe-

55

culiarly gifted for evil-doing by the manipulation of "seeming."[19] How right is *sleeve* for the external and the visible: it is dress, of course, but also a part of the dress especially available for display and gesture, the hallmarks of the Iago style; and further, it is on the periphery, away from the vital—in a word, almost a counterpoint to *heart*. Yet a man can move his sleeve over his heart, in token of humility, reverence, fidelity; Iago is a master of simulating the creditable emotion, that is, really, concealing the heart with the sleeve. He will not "wear" the heart—as if he were rejecting a mode of dress practiced only by the unheeding. He indeed is not heedless, for, on the three times in fourteen lines that he uses the word *heart* (51, 62, 64), this universal symbol of the spontaneous and outgoing (cordial, heartfelt) is for him the innermost invisible core of self-regard. But his very figure for its inviolability has betrayed another meaning of which he is unaware—that he is harboring something dead, a heart that would be only carrion for crows ("for daws to peck at").

The man of unexposed heart speaks naturally of "clothing" himself or others to suit his purposes;[20] creates a situation which can be solved only by a prolonged "unfolding";[21] and not only "puts on" but "takes off," as when he plans to "strip"[22] Cassio of his lieutenancy (2.1.173). In telling Othello about Cassio's fight, he ventures into a more inward and curious form of undressing someone else. The quarrelers, he says, had been friendly, "in terms like bride and groom / Devesting them for bed" (2.3.180-181), a figure which lends an air of devotion, love, and candid revelation at the very time Iago is working out his hate of others and revealing only what suits him. We are aware of "devesting" at two levels—that which Iago himself pretends to be doing while he is covering up the real facts that he knows; and that which appears in the content of the comparison. The striking rhetorical use of the bridal night to define friendship, with its unmistakable allusion to Othello's own immediate experience, is explicable only on the ground that Iago is strongly attracted by the image of disrobing. This same image he drags in, and carries much further, a little later when he is working on Othello: "Or to be naked with her friend in bed / An hour, or more, not meaning any harm?" (4.1.3-4). Iago is "undressing" Desdemona. But at the same time he is "devesting" himself for us, since he is giving us some clues to subterranean motives which, as we shall see in Chapter VI, are a powerful influence on his actions. And his words also serve to link[23] this scene to a later one—by the contrast between his visual undressing of Desdemona and, in an entirely different key, her actual undressing. Against Iago's oblique sexuality is her devoted love, and against his opaqueness and intensity, her simplicity and, depressed and anxious though she is, her relative unconstraint; hence the "theme" of "devesting" has been seen in two sharply different lights, the fancied disrobing having the note of the concealed obsession, and the actual the sobriety of deep feeling scarcely modified by the astringent joking of Emilia.[24] For the sobriety is that not only of great love but also of the ironic nexus of love and death which figures largely in the last two acts (see Chapter VI). In a brilliant but casual stroke this ambiguity of the situation is fully caught up by the clothing imagery. Desdemona, who has asked that her "wedding sheets" be laid on the bed (4.2.105), now commands Emilia, "If I do die before thee, prithee shroud me / In one of those same sheets" (4.3.24-25). Her final dress will symbolize the love which as a reality survives death but which in life could not break through the appearance of evil with which it had been invested. If dress is appearance, then in her death appearance and reality are one. Desdemona's despairing prescription for her shroud anticipates her final success in being seen as she is—after her death.

All through the bedroom scene, up to her death, Othello cannot see her truth, a failure the more marked for the analogy between the revealingness of her "nightly wearing" and her transparency of manner. His distance from her is subtly suggested by the fact that he himself stays dressed, as if he were neither a lover nor a sharer of the bedroom but an impersonal official. There is an analogy, too, between his remaining clothed and his maintaining a disguise of himself, pressing back the impulse to love and exonerate, and in the struggle taking on a strangeness of demeanor that to Desdemona is as terrifying as his words. She is undisguised; it is his own disguise that keeps him from seeing her. For him, the Iago principle defeats the Desdemona principle. But he is soon to be stripped—like other victims of Iago—of all delusions and defenses, even finally of his sword, and he describes himself in terms that apply more widely than he suspects; "naked as I am" (5.2.258)—a fitting outcome for the man who could not see beyond the Iago sleeve and could not see the "essential vesture of creation" in Desdemona.[25]

THE SEEN AND THE UNSEEN

Manipulating appearances is really a way of inducing blindness. Yet when Othello is being conspicuously deceived by the seeming, he is under the illusion that he is seeing particularly well, for Iago has tutored his vision. Iago, who instinctively turns to visual evidence,[26] shows an aptitude for getting others to "see things his way"—to observe the apparent facts and to act accordingly:[27]

> [*to Brabantio*] Look to your house, your daughter, and
> your bags! (1.1.80)
> [*to Roderigo*] Didst thou not see her paddle with the palm of his hand? Didst not mark that? (2.1.259-260)
> [*to Montano*] You see this fellow that is gone before.
> He is a soldier fit to stand by Caesar
> And give direction; and do but see his vice. (2.3.126-128)

Thus we are prepared for his introduction of an extensive vocabulary of seeing[28] in the big deception scene, 3.3. In the achievement of the ideal relation, in which Iago's "See" elicits

THE IAGO WORLD: STYLES IN DECEPTION

a responsive "I see" from Othello, Iago winds through several preliminary moves: he spurs Othello to ask him what he has seen;[29] in his best gamesman's style he gives ironic warnings against what he sees;[30] he ventures a direct command, "Look to your wife; observe her well with Cassio; / Wear your eye thus, not jealous nor secure," and adds, "Look to't" (197-200); and finally he subverts Othello's confidence in the Desdemona that he has seen,[31] and hence in his own past seeing.

At Venice, Othello was very sure that emotions would not interfere with his powers of seeing;[32] love would not "seel with wanton dullness / My speculative and offic'd instruments" (1.3.270-271). It was just a few lines after this that Brabantio warned him bitterly: "Look to her, Moor, if thou hast eyes to see. / She has deceiv'd her father, and may thee" (1.3.293-294). Iago, who heard both these speeches, now deliberately picks them up for use against Othello; yet he reintroduces the earlier words obliquely, counting upon a subliminal association in Othello, just as Shakespeare, by his poetic method, characteristically stirs the reader to sense the relation between distant passages. Without mentioning Brabantio directly, Iago uses almost his exact words[33] about Desdemona—"did deceive her father"—and then goes right on to attach to the problem of "seeming" the problem of "seeing": "She that, so young, could give out such a seeming / To seel her father's eyes up close as oak" (3.3.206-210). Iago's sliest trick is his repetition of the image from falconry, as a sort of delayed antiphon; Othello said, in effect, "Desdemona won't seel my eyes," and Iago implicitly retorts, "But she did seel her father's eyes."[34] After Othello's boast, Brabantio questioned his seeing and suggested the imminence of deception; now Iago reminds him of the deception, so that the configuration of *deceive-seel-eyes* is repeated from Act 1. The linking of the passages shows Othello becoming blind by thinking he is now seeing an earlier blindness for the first time. And the traditional tragic irony of the blind hero confident of his sight is developed by the rich vocabulary of seeing[35] as Othello, under Iago's guidance, goes questing for visual evidence to support his new intuition of truth.

Visual evidence: Othello is being led into a theory of truth— a new thematic climax to the drama of seeing. Before the *deceive-seel* crux he was beginning to feel his way toward it;[36] now, in a threat to Iago, comes an overt statement of it: "Villain, be sure thou prove my love a whore! / Be sure of it; give me ocular proof"; "Make me to see't; or at the least so prove, etc." (359-360, 364). Othello not only sees badly; he thinks badly about seeing. Just as he unconsciously formulates an untenable theory of appearances, so he also comes up with an inadequate theory of evidence. The key passage is "give me ocular proof," and it is restated in "Make me to see't; or at the least so prove, etc." Although he formally classifies *proving* as an alternative to *seeing*, his working theory is, "Seeing is proving," and on that basis he proceeds against Desdemona. Now the pragmatic difficulty of "seeing is believing" is that it puts you at the mercy of anyone whose hand is quicker than your eye. But its more serious difficulty is metaphysical, and it is hardly surprising that Othello, one of the most unphilosophical of Shakespeare's heroes, should choose to apply a doctrine of limited validity exactly where it can have least relevance. His implicit basis of action is that love or the failure or betrayal of love can be "proved" in the same way that a single action can be logically proved to have taken place. He drops into "the pitfall of reasoning about love and of admitting testimony against it," for "With love, reason and justice have ultimately nothing to do."[37] He wants a quality of life, ultimately a fact of spirit, to be established by a laboratory demonstration before his eyes. He anticipates Lear, who requires that his daughters give a measurement of their love on the spot.

Whatever his intellectual shortcomings,[38] Othello has some affinity with other Shakespeare heroes, for Shakespearian tragic method repeatedly entangles the hero in a mode of thought

THE IAGO WORLD: STYLES IN DECEPTION

incompatible with the situation or actions to which he applies it. Specifically, he tries to test, count, measure, prove, or calculate when he is dealing, not with objects or quantities or even recurrent processes, but with intangibles, with qualities or with spirit. He substitutes a rational check-up for imaginative apprehension; he takes on the style of the security police when he needs an intuitive perception of symbols; when the myth of love calls for his most flexible awareness of personality and for faith, he adopts a technique of rigorous verification. The recurrent treatment of this intellectual error in Shakespeare suggests that it is one of the archetypal sources of disaster for the tragic hero. If we shift our focus to the villains, we see that they are marked by an overdose of applied rationalism,[39] and their essential mode of betrayal is to stir up the same excess in their victims.

In structure, Shakespeare characteristically introduces alternatives. So now the language of the play indicates limits and alternatives to Othello's system of "ocular proof," and it does this at both pragmatic and metaphysical levels. When Othello strikes Desdemona in public, Lodovico tells him, "My lord, this would not be believ'd in Venice, / Though I should swear I saw't" (4.1.258-254). The Venetians would err in the single case, we know; yet in opposing "belief"—their experiential knowledge of the reality of the two characters—to the visual evidence of a single act, they would in the long run be on safer ground. Desdemona herself exemplifies the wise doubting of immediate evidence when it conflicts with experienced truth; after the scene in which Othello violently demands the handkerchief, her first words are "I ne'er saw this before" (3.4.100). In effect she questions the reliability of what she has seen, just as Othello might do in his whole "proving" of her. The point is not whether she judges right or wrong at the moment, but whether the principle that she intuitively follows is a saving one, a better one than Othello's.[40] (If she were acting on Othello's theory of evidence, she might be expected to say,

"Now that I see what he's really like, I'll take my own steps.")
But withholding judgment is not the only way open here; it is also possible to practice a different kind of seeing. To doubt the seen is to imply the unseen: may one not "see" it? It is exciting to find that Desdemona has already taken precisely that step, when, in making what is virtually a reply to Brabantio's exclamation, "To fall in love with what she fear'd to look on!" (1.3.98), she has told what she really "saw" in Othello: "I saw Othello's visage in his mind" (1.3.253). Here is a doctrine of sight more profound and veracious than Othello's system of ocular proof, for it rests firmly on the imaginative perception of quality that may deny or transcend the visual evidence.[41] It is only one step from the presentation of transcendent vision as a dramatic fact to a metaphysical notion that might also have saved Othello—that is, the reality of the unseen. This notion happens to be put into words by Iago even as he ranges himself against it: "Her honour is an essence that's not seen" (4.1.16). To positivist Iago, honor is, like reputation, unreal. But the rest of the drama validates the truth which Iago is implicitly denying, the reality of essences physically unseen.

Othello accepts the saving truth only after he has fatally pursued ocular proof through Act 3, listening to Iago and interrogating Desdemona;[42] through Act 4, in which, in a sort of laboratory test, Othello, like an invisible experimenter peering through a screen, watches a demonstration that appears to prove everything (Cassio talking to Iago about his love troubles),[43] and in which he cross-examines both Emilia and Desdemona;[44] and in Act 5, in which at the very execution he berates Desdemona with his ocular proof[45] and then, as the others gaze in horror,[46] states his case: "I saw it in his hand" (5.2.215). It is after "it"—the handkerchief—turns out to prove, with Oedipean irony, the opposite of what he supposed,[47] that he symbolically revokes his optical code. Once he ordered Desdemona, "Out of my sight!" (4.1.258), rejecting the visual

THE IAGO WORLD: STYLES IN DECEPTION

evidence that, if he could but see it aright, would clear up the case.[48] Now he knows that, with his faulty seeing,[49] he cannot stand, or does not deserve, the rejected image of truth: "Whip me, ye devils, / From the possession of this heavenly sight!" (5.2.277-278).

"Heavenly sight": before the murder, Othello assured himself, "Forth of my heart those charms, thine eyes, are blotted" (5.1.35). These were the eyes that "saw Othello's visage in his mind," the eyes of Desdemona,[50] who, when Emilia exclaimed, "I would you had never seen him!" formally rejected the "Out of my sight" solution, finding "grace and favour" in "even his stubbornness, his checks, his frowns" (4.3.18-21). So when Emilia describes Othello's crime—"hast kill'd the sweetest innocent / That e'er did lift up eye" (5.2.199-200)— her phrase really defines Desdemona as a spiritually perceptive woman.

The language forces upon us the fact that in the choice between Desdemona and Iago, Othello had a choice between two kinds of seeing. Wide-eyed, he fell for the cicerone who kept pointing at signs of apparent evil, becoming virtually an archetype of the informer who calls attention to certain occurrences and circumstances and by skillful emphasis encourages an insecure community to make interpretations that are bound to be followed by a panicky reflexive destructiveness. What he is bringing into focus seems always to be evidence. He has a favorite family of words: *see—look—behold—mark*. As late as the next to last scene, in which his victim is Bianca, Iago is calling attention to appearances, urging others to "perceive," "behold," "look," "see" (5.1.104ff.), and inviting the sense of wrongdoing.

This is one of Shakespeare's ways of dramatizing evil. In the hands of this guide, Othello has theorized about appearance and reality with ruinous incompetence; he has tried to pierce apparent disguises and to "unfold" the truth—with the result that in the end he finds himself "naked"; he has adopted a theory of visual evidence which has caused him to fail to see actuality, to "see" instead phantasmal evidence, to misread what he does see, and to be unable to recover sound vision until it is too late. If experience turns on the problem of appearance, the evil force, operating from the basic position that appearance and reality are fluid and therefore have only the form that is given them at any moment, falsifies and confounds appearance. If this problem is further set forth by the imagery of clothes, evil is shown disguising itself persuasively, trying to strip its enemies, purporting to bare the truth; what is more, Iago, in the pseudo disclosure of Desdemona's supposed adultery, does a verbal "undressing" of her that discloses to us his private striptease. But above all, he is helping others to see—pointing, pointing, pointing. Shakespeare's full development of Iago in this last role indicates his fascination with the man who has an extended index finger, the demonstrator, the one who focuses the sight of other observers and even appears to withhold judgment. In this figure he finds wide potentialities for the delineation of evil.

Iago purports to be making visible what has been unseen or even concealed, to be effecting an enlightenment. In a world founded on ocular proof, the evil person simulates the light-bearer. Shakespeare, as we see in the next section, makes dramatic capital of this way of confronting the world.

3. LIGHT AND DARKNESS

At the most obvious level of perception *Othello* makes use of a startling contrast—that between the "fair" Desdemona, as she is repeatedly called, and her black lover, Othello of the "sooty bosom" (1.2.66, 70). Now this opposition of fair and black, of light and dark, does not lie passively in the text, or remain an idle accident of stage make-up, but is always, though not obtrusively, pressed upon us, for it has more than one form in the play.[51] At the very start Iago, whose imagining of sex

THE IAGO WORLD: STYLES IN DECEPTION

is always vivid, shouts to Brabantio, "an old black ram / Is tupping your white ewe" (1.1.88-89); and he adds a suggestion, the first of many such, of the darkness of hell: "the devil will make a grandsire of you" (91); Roderigo mildly echoes the contrast when he says that Brabantio's "fair daughter" is in the "clasps of a lascivious Moor" (1.1.123, 127). The Moor himself is aware of his wife's fairness. He can call her "fair" (1.3.125; 2.1.184) as matter-of-factly as others do (4.2.118, 230), but he has much more than a matter-of-fact awareness: in killing her, he wants not to "scar that whiter skin of hers than snow" (5.2.4). By now, the black-white opposition has extended beyond the literal and pictorial into the symbolic: the fair Desdemona is innocent, and the language of the play has had the effect of making Othello doubly black.

In this scenic symbolism honest Iago, who corrupts appearances and the seeing process (section 2, preceding), has a role that is appropriate and characterizing. He describes his budding plot in terms that establish identifications to be used throughout the play: hell as black, heaven as white—

> Divinity of hell!
> When devils will the blackest sins put on,
> They do suggest at first with heavenly shows,
> As I do now. (2.3.356-359)

The Iago evil is redefined for us: his method is planned confusion, the metamorphosis of opposites, the use of "shows" that keep things from being seen in their "true colors." With fair Desdemona as subject, he will proceed thus: "So will I turn her virtue into pitch" (2.3.366)—from her goodness (fairness) produce black evil. In a passage poetically akin to this, Othello indicates the large possibilities of such an action: "and when I love thee not, / Chaos is come again" (3.3.91-92)—chaos, the primordial darkness. Immediately Iago maneuvers his way into "blackest sins"—his magician's transformation of all things into the dark-hellish-foul. Almost in passing he suggests to Othello that "foul things" often enter "palaces,"

"uncleanly apprehensions" even a "pure" breast (3.3.137-139).
Shakespeare measures the success of Iago's tricks by having
Othello use a matching metaphor: "Her name, that was as
fresh / As Dian's visage, is now begrim'd and black / As mine
own face" (3.3.386-388). Iago has made the good "begrim'd
and black," as he proposed; now he can directly call Desdemona "foul" (4.1.213, 215). Othello, on the other hand, still
wrestles with the contradiction between his old vision and his
new, requiring a paradoxical phrase such as "fair devil" (3.3.
478; cf. 4.1.255; 4.2.67-68, 71-72); after her death he can only
consign Desdemona to hell, simply not understanding the
counterinsistences of Emilia (5.2.130, 135), and charge her
with a foulness that he says Iago hated (148-149, 200).

To Othello, Desdemona seems to have changed objectively.
Closely tied in with the poetic recording of this change—a recording which takes advantage of the literal dramatic facts
(black and white)—is a like imaging of another change, which
is made possible by the dramatic use of Othello's own blackness. Of his dark skin we are reminded in various ways in
Act 1 (1.1.88; 1.2.66, 70; 1.3.65, 117), most significantly when
Brabantio exclaims, "To fall in love with what she fear'd to
look on!" (1.3.98). It is to this that Desdemona is really replying when she says, "I saw Othello's visage in his mind"
(253). His darkness is, in effect, denied; the reality is an inner
brightness. After this the Duke's summing up, which looks
at first like a pair of tag lines, is really a poetic continuation
of a theme: "If virtue no delighted beauty lack, / Your son-in-law is far more fair than black" (1.3.290-291). In punning,
the Duke introduces the paradox of black as fair, the happy
counterpart of the grim paradox of fair as black in which
Othello will later express his horror. "Virtue" is identified
with "fair," just as the two coincide in Desdemona; Othello's
blackness is declared skin-deep. And the first darkness that
Iago creates is thus dissipated.

From now, the fair Othello believes "colored" stories and
becomes, we may say, unfair. When he is called out by the

THE IAGO WORLD: STYLES IN DECEPTION

"foul rout" in Cyprus and begins to get angry, he speaks of the "passion" that has "collied" his "best judgment" (2.3.205-210)—that is, made it black like coal. These are good words for what happens to him in the next act when Iago really goes to work on him.[52] It is at this time that he twice thinks of his own color, saying "Haply, for I am black" (3.3.263) and describing Desdemona's name: "begrim'd and black / As mine own face." The awareness of color suggests, if ever so lightly, a new blackness of his own—at least of mood. A minute later he invokes the dark powers: "Arise, black vengeance, from the hollow hell!" (3.3.447). After he has had his black vengeance, he disputes with Emilia in images that mark his advance in darkness. When he exclaims that Desdemona is "like a liar gone to burning hell," Emilia retorts, "O, the more angel she, / And you the blacker devil!" (5.2.129-131)—an antithesis that is kept rebounding through the scene.[53] "Black Othello" has lost the "virtue" which made him "fair" and has earned a new blackness.

What we have been looking at is "verbal drama," an action of language that has served not to decorate the event but to express it dynamically by extending a difference of color into a symbolic contrast of good and evil. But we find more than a contrast: we find also a rendering of evil in action. In blackening Desdemona for Othello and in driving Othello to "black vengeance," Iago has twice turned virtue into pitch: he confuses light and dark, makes one into the other—a principle of corruption to which humanity is always susceptible. Just as when he is confronting Othello with the problem of appearance and reality and making it insoluble, so now he succeeds because his operative machinery springs from a credo: not only is he a cool manipulator, but he has faith in the indiscriminate, undifferentiable human universe which he strives to make all-effective. He can persuade Othello to take light for dark because he believes they are either infinitely convertible or much the same. His verses for Desdemona, worried on the Cyprus shore, are more than idle entertainment; they are a comic version of his least-common-denominator principle.[54] In these rhymes he characterizes women as witty and foolish, and as foul or fair or black; but these differences are meaningless, for women are identical in sexuality. A "black" woman will "find a white that shall her blackness fit" (2.1.134); a "fair" woman is never foolish, for "even her folly help'd her to an heir" (138); and in sum, "There's none so foul, and foolish thereunto, / But does foul pranks which fair and wise ones do" (142-143). Even jokes are utilized to present the Iago faith that will become a ruinous Othello heresy.

It is natural for the master of "heavenly shows" boldly to claim the light, indeed the light of heaven. When he wants to swear fidelity to Othello in getting revenge on Desdemona, Iago kneels and calls out, "Witness, you ever-burning lights above" (3.3.463). This scene is ironically duplicated when Desdemona, actually talking to Iago, is swearing her fidelity to Othello. She also kneels: "by this light of heaven, / I know not how I lost him. Here I kneel" (4.2.150-151). The darkbringer's sardonic invocation of light is contrasted with the earnest invocation of the light-seeker who suffers from the Iago darkness, in which she has been accused of adultery. When Emilia asks her if she would betray her husband, Desdemona again characteristically invokes the light: "No, by this heavenly light!" (4.3.65). Emilia's quick response gives us a fourth use of "heavenly light" and another contrast: "Nor I neither by this heavenly light. / I might do't as well i' th' dark" (66-67). A foil for—and even a relief from—Desdemona's girlish seriousness, Emilia takes us back to the worldly jokes of Iago, but with variations: he betrays a philosophy, she plays a game; he pretends to light, she boldly claims the dark.

THAT THE NIGHT COME

Othello is predominantly a night play. Even in daytime scenes we are hardly conscious that it is day. References to daylight are so few and casual as hardly to be

THE IAGO WORLD: STYLES IN DECEPTION

noticeable (1.3.381; 3.1.34) ; indeed, one gay reference to dawn —"By th' mass, 'tis morning!" (2.3.384)—is ironic in effect, for the words are spoken by Iago after a successful night of troublemaking in Cyprus. Iago picks the nighttime for all of his main operations; indeed, at least half the action of the play takes place during the hours of darkness[55] that give most scope to Iago and that are a powerful symbol of the darkness of life represented: Iago's planned evil and the groping ignorance and misunderstanding of the others. Not only is the night there in the stage directions or on the actual stage,. but the spoken words repeatedly remind us of the night. The word *night* itself, nearly always in a passage that focuses our attention on some nocturnal setting, is used a score of times.[56]

In *Othello* night is not just an accident or an idle setting, nor is it a property of melodrama, a cliché of fearfulness for a cliché-hungry public. Night is not passive but active; it brings not merely physical darkness but spiritual darkness, for it marks the triumph of the enemy of light (of the fair, the innocent). Shakespeare undermines the cliché response by investing night with still other potentialities. Consider Desdemona's command: "Lay on my bed my wedding sheets, remember" (4.2.105). Though these lines are a part of the context of growing moral shadows, there is in Desdemona's words something at war with the tone of foreboding: as long as the bed can be thought of as the marital bed, we cannot exclude the possibility that the nocturnal rites might be those of fulfillment rather than sacrifice. From Act 1, indeed, there has been another potentiality in night. When he is called forth in the first midnight alarum, Othello can cry in the high spirits of the bridegroom, "The goodness of the night upon you, friends!" (1.2.35). The evil that comes at night, then, does not come expectedly, or in place of nothing; it is a reversal, a driving out of something else. Twice Othello's bridal night is interrupted. The fact that what happens at night is always an interruption compels us to think of the night also

69

as the night of married love. Thus the dark is sinister not because it is a conventional accompaniment, a metonym, for evil, but because the evil that happens at night drives out a good. In this ironic juxtaposition of love and hate—of light and dark—*Othello* comes closest to moving us as deeply as the other major tragedies. It is as though Shakespeare had kept his human actors balanced upon a delicate borderline of life— a borderline between two realities that are as opposed as night and day and yet may yield to or replace each other in a flash.[57]

If the long night of the play might have been fair as well as dark, then Iago's role is the clearer. He makes it explicit in the dark-light couplet that ends Act 1: "I have't! It is engend'red! Hell and night / Must bring this monstrous birth to the world's light" (1.3.409-410). This couplet does everything: Hell and night, virtually interchangeable throughout the play, are here overtly allied;[58] the rhyming of *night* and *light* sets off the antithetic forces in their symbolic investitures; and the paradoxical inversions of order which provide the structure of Iago's program for evil are contained in the double-barreled metaphor—the metaphor of bringing death to life, and darkness to light.[59]

Yet there is another complication: while Iago is working to turn light into darkness, there is a kind of counterforce that tries to bring light into the darkness. If the night itself is symbolic, there is a comparable symbolic value in the lights that must be used at night. Lights are introduced very deliberately—much too frequently and conspicuously for us not to become conscious of them—whether they lead the way to understanding or ironically emphasize a failure of understanding. In Act 1, the one time when Iago's dark night is conquered, the conquest takes place amidst a continual flow of lights. As soon as Brabantio, the immediate and incidental victim of Iago's obfuscation, decides there may be something to the reports shouted at him, he calls repeatedly for lights (1.1.141-145). He and his servants come down "with torches," and he

THE IAGO WORLD: STYLES IN DECEPTION

calls again, "Get moe tapers!" (161, 167). In effect he seeks the light of knowledge, and he finds it; pleased or not, he does not act in ignorance, and thus he defeats the darkness which is Iago's climate. Four consecutive parties appear on the stage with "lights" or "torches" (1.2.1, 28-29, 55; 1.3.1); they all have weapons, too (cf. 1.2.55), but the fact is that matters are settled in the spirit of lights rather than weapons. The truth is told and understood, and everyone acts in terms of it.

The night scenes in Act 5 are so written, as is Shakespeare's wont, that they can be read more meaningfully by reference to Act 1. Again in Act 5 it is night, and Iago is now making his big push. Roderigo has been wounded by Cassio, and Cassio by Iago. Cassio calls, "O, help, ho! light! a surgeon!" (5.1.30), and after a delay and other calls for help, somebody comes—comes, as Gratiano says, "with light and weapons" (47). The newcomer is, of all people, Iago, "with a light"! What a fine stroke this is: the very source of darkness as the dispeller of darkness. But like one group of entering characters in the Venice scene (1.2.55), Iago carries a light *and weapons:* his equipment defines his pretense and his actuality. In Act 1, light conquered the weapons; here, weapons conquer the light. As lightbearer (Lucifer in modern dress) Iago is all on the side of chaos: he pretends ignorance, he pretends helpfulness, he intentionally misidentifies. Willfully postponing the use of "light," he uses his weapon to dispatch the wounded Roderigo, and with mock indignation utters the words that exactly define his own role: "Kill men i' th' dark?" (5.1.63). *Then* he calls loudly for "light" (73, 88) and, in explaining that Cassio was "set on in the dark" (112), reverts to that magnified distress over indecency that brings him close to the often irresistible role of comedian. In this scene his whole "style" is epitomized: turning virtue into pitch; matching the darkness of ignorance and of evil action with the darkness of night; and for all this, adopting the style of the light-bringer.

Not to follow through this much of the dark-light pattern

would be to miss all of the elaborate preparation for the final scene in Desdemona's bedroom. When Othello comes in to kill her, he enters—the last such entrance in the play—"with a light" (5.2.1). Here we have a final version, different from all the others, of the man who carries light, or seeks it, in the darkness. In Act 1 those who call for light, or bring light to bear on the situation, find the times propitious, and they succeed. In 5.1 the ostensible seeker and bringer of light, Iago, really wants to prolong and deepen darkness, and he succeeds. Now, in 5.2, the man who has sought light, Othello, is reaching the climax of his failure; he is under the illusion that he has the light, and therefore he cannot see what he is really doing. He addresses the "chaste stars," which might be a conventional invoking of cosmic justice but for the fact that "heavenly light" has repeatedly been invoked before—with a histrionic simulation of fidelity by Iago, with a jest by Emilia, and twice with utmost earnestness by Desdemona. Othello is like Desdemona in his earnestness, but his seizure of "her" symbol underlines the delusion which puts him at a great remove from her spirit. Then Othello, in his blackness towering over Desdemona of the skin "whiter . . . than snow," begins to talk about light, in those affecting lines that draw something from the earlier persistent exploitation of the dark-light theme:

> Put out the light, and then put out the light.
> If I quench thee, thou flaming minister,
> I can again thy former light restore,
> Should I repent me; but once put out thy light,
> Thou cunning'st pattern of excelling nature,
> I know not where is that Promethean heat
> That can thy light relume. (5.2.7-13)

In one aspect the strikingly juxtaposed images—of the literal extinction of a light and of the metaphorical extinction of a life—are simply images of thought and feeling, and their burden is the very slight Hamletic element in Othello. In another aspect they are the climax of the symbolic clash of light and

THE IAGO WORLD: STYLES IN DECEPTION

dark which has gone on from the beginning. To put out the light is not only to end a life; it is also to blot out a portion of the good and true, and to give a victory to the forces of darkness. The irony is that, in terms of the story, the dark need not win; the black may become fair, and light can prevail against darkness. But these transformations are not inevitable either; man is fallible and may destroy the fair; he may mistake the Iago darkness for light and—put out the true light. The kind of imagery permits us to see that Othello is at last carrying out the Iago will, the lust for darkness.

Yet there is another dim possibility in the image of "Promethean heat" to which Othello is led in his thoughts of irrevocability. Here there is a little more than a simple reference to the story of Prometheus. The Promethean suggests the titanic, immense struggle, agony: these are the terms in which the light may be "relumed"—not the light of an individual life but, in the symbolism of the play, the light of truth which sustains the quality of life. In this sense tragedy is a reluming. In *Othello* it is accomplished by the agony with which the hero recognizes what he has done and, as far as he is able, what he is. Othello tries to become "fair" again.

4. IAGO AS ECONOMIST

When Iago addresses to Othello his homily on values—"Good name . . . / Is the . . . jewel of their souls. / Who steals my purse steals trash" (3.3.155-157)—he chooses words so compact and memorizable that they have come into a kind of separate fame, and, like any other purple passage, seem a special added attraction, displayed for admiration during a brief pause in the forward movement. But they are more than that, for they tell us something important about Iago; they are not only deceptive in themselves but they lead us into another of his styles of deception and of his "strategies against the spiritual order," and so into the readiness of another victim besides Othello.

There are two stylistic lifelines between Iago's speech and the drama as a whole. For one thing, his use of *jewel, enriches, makes poor,* and *purse* to set forth the value of "good name" exemplifies the frequent presentation of nonmaterial value in "economic" terms such as *gold, sell, buy, profit, dear,* etc.[60] Such terms constitute a precise, unsentimental vocabulary for keeping before us the problem of values, especially with reference to the gain and loss that are always possible, and at times they connect separate passages revealingly.[61] The second link between Iago's lines and the rest of the drama is a verbal stratagem whose remarkableness is almost rubbed out by familiarity—the use of images of theft: *steals, filches, robs.* Iago might say abstractly, "Good name *is* more valuable than material wealth"; or he might use a direct economic metaphor, with "purse *is* trash" as a parallel to "good name *is* jewel"; or he might amplify the economic metaphor by contrasting the *loss* of one with the loss of the other. But Shakespeare elects none of these methods; he chooses instead an image of *theft.* On the face of it this ought to seem shocking, even obtrusive. It does not seem so, however, and at least one of the reasons is that the motif of theft is used regularly in the action and the language of the drama.

Images of economics and images of theft go well together: where values are denoted by *jewel, riches, prize,* etc., thievery is the right symbol for deprivation.[62] As we trace the value terms and the imagery of theft—"a subtle way of influencing and leading the audience through the play without their knowing it"[63]—we find that these are often closely related to a certain kind of action, action in the field of what we may call "financial affairs" or practical economics. This complex of verbal and actional drama tells us something about various characters, but a great deal about Iago, who not only has a marked penchant for terms from business[64] but also operates literally, if not openly, on the financial front.

THE IAGO WORLD: STYLES IN DECEPTION

Though to call Iago the Economic Man would overemphasize one aspect of him, the term does suggest the kind of self-revelation which Iago makes in that inner drama of exchange and values in which the good-name-is-jewel speech is a key point.[65] That self-revelation begins in the opening scene of the play, the first 80 lines of which are spoken by Iago and Roderigo. For a minor character whom we tend to forget, Roderigo has a rather substantial role; the fact is that he is more important than he may seem.[66] Shakespeare gives him dramatic usefulness by making him a lesser, semitragic analogue of Othello,[67] a victim with a somewhat different readiness; by providing us, through Iago's deception of him, with another view of Iago as deceiver and hence strengthening our sense of his technical competence as manipulator;[68] and by endowing Roderigo with an apparent innocuousness that lets Iago be entirely off guard before him, so that from their dialogue we learn much about Iago. The quality of their relationship, as Coleridge noted, is expressed in the first speech of the play, when Roderigo rebukes Iago, "who hast had my purse / As if the strings were thine" (1.1.2-3). This monetary definition of friendship, besides telling us something about Roderigo, is a tip-off to a real interest of Iago's. But even at that we are a little surprised to see with what bluntness Iago later insists on a supply of money when he encourages Roderigo not to despair of having Desdemona just because she is married. Ten times—with "put money in thy purse" or "make money" or "provide money"—he directly tells Roderigo to produce the cash (1.3.345-379). Crude as this is, Roderigo falls into line immediately, as if charmed: "I am chang'd. I'll go sell all my land" (388). But what actually is Iago's project? Up to this moment the audience has seen Iago as a man with an apparent grievance and with a heart for revenge—a situation which is not without associations of nobility. What, then, is he up to now? To sponging or petty bilking?[69] As if quite aware of the problem, Shakespeare has Iago rush to answer the question in soliloquy:

> Thus do I ever make my fool my purse;
> For I mine own gain'd knowledge should profane
> If I would time expend with such a snipe
> But for my sport and profit. (389-392)

So we have it: Iago is literally pursuing "purse" and "profit." He feels a momentary need to defend himself to himself: "sport" has a gentlemanly ring. But the quest of gain from "such a snipe" betrays, beyond the shrewdness in calculation, a streak of vulgarity—a streak that comes out in a number of ways.[70] The money code defines what one critic calls the world of "society"—the "kingdom of means, not ends."[71]

Iago knows how to influence people, indeed, but how good is his judgment of their quality? Is Roderigo merely a "snipe," or, as Iago calls him later, "this poor trash of Venice" (2.1. 312)? The answer is Roderigo's coming up with the acute perception that Desdemona is "full of most blessed condition" (2.1.254-255). Since this feeling for human quality is precisely what is absent in "poor trash"—"poor white trash," as we have come to say—we have an excellent glimpse into Iago's economics of character,[72] a clue to that faulty evaluation of the moral quality of human beings that will destroy him.[73] Roderigo progresses from a recognition of Desdemona to a recognition of himself: not only can he face facts—"My money is almost spent"—but he can almost gain something immaterial from his loss: "I shall have so much experience for my pains; and so, with no money at all, and a little more wit, return again to Venice" (2.3.371-375). Albeit for a very small way, Roderigo approaches the Shakespeare tragic character who at the very moment of loss ironically comes into a better kind of possession. Then Iago interposes with another sample of his moral economics: "How poor are they that have not patience!" (376), cleverly converting Roderigo's material poverty into a poverty of morale; and this challenge, plus a few words of cheer for the quest of sex which Roderigo even yet cannot relinquish, again reduces the latter to a tool. But once more, failure opens

THE IAGO WORLD: STYLES IN DECEPTION

Roderigo's eyes, and he begins to sense Iago's game: "I have wasted myself out of means. The jewels you have had from me to deliver to Desdemona would half have corrupted a votarist. You have told me she hath receiv'd them. . . . I tell you 'tis not very well. I will make myself known to Desdemona. If she will return me my jewels, I will give over my suit and repent my unlawful solicitation" (4.2.187-202). Roderigo is the one character whose course we see regularly in monetary terms. His rates of exchange clash with the insights of which he is capable: though he has come to understand Desdemona, himself, and to an extent Iago, he cannot by free repentance seal his recognitions but expects a price for his repentance. He is not a stereotyped gull, but as moral economist he lives in a fluctuating market that makes plausible Iago's finally persuading him to attempt murder and thus expose himself to murder.

Now Iago. Not until the final act do we learn the truth of what Roderigo has irresolutely suspected. Iago thus resolves on Roderigo's death:

> Live Roderigo,
> He calls me to a restitution large
> Of gold and jewels that I bobb'd from him
> As gifts to Desdemona. (5.1.14-17)

This is said so much in the flat style of a man coolly canvassing alternatives that we almost slide over a key point in the system of value terms. Here we learn that Iago has been not the needy friend, the costly agent, the inveterate touch artist, but the materialist as thief—and not the relatively forthright housebreaker but the double deceiver of one who takes him for a friend; not the picaro but the vicious man whom Dante punished in the eighth circle.

Iago's economic history shows him to be both vulgar and vicious—a notable definition of evil. He has not the shadow of a motive to rob Roderigo; contrariwise, he has at least monetary reasons for feeling gratitude to Roderigo. What we

77

can see at work is a kind of "pure malice" or "floating hatred." If this is true, the whole Roderigo plot has great dramatic utility, for it is directly related to the problem of "motiveless malignity." If Iago acts with "motiveless malignity" toward Roderigo, it is probable that he acts so toward Othello. His contempt for his purse-friend and follower Roderigo suggests that in speaking of Othello and Cassio he will characteristically undervalue the good and exaggerate any possible cause for animosity. Just as he underrates Roderigo, so his long opening complaint resembles the archetypal belittling of better men by one who has failed of an end. His "I know my price, I am worth no worse a place" (1.1.11) is the standard economics of self in the disappointed man. The cheating of Roderigo reveals, in Iago's opening diatribe against Othello, the influence of the "What's in it for me?" personality.

For Iago's spiritual defects, at once vulgar and demonic, Shakespeare has found a suitable dramatic formulation in the maneuvering of the thief, and the motif of thiefhood is woven tightly into the verbal and actional fabric. Indeed, in a play in which there is the elaborate and ordered use of light and dark at which we looked in the preceding section, Iago may easily be thought of as "the thief in the night." In his first attempted theft at night, Iago inaugurates a pattern which he will use several times: he tries to foist his own derangement on someone else. In arousing Brabantio in the opening scene, Iago does not call Othello "seducer" or "rapist," as we might expect, but shouts: "Awake! What, ho, Brabantio! Thieves! thieves! thieves! / Look to your house, your daughter, and your bags! / Thieves! thieves!" (1.1.79-81). In throwing in "your bags" he shows a characteristic inventiveness; but he also shows what kind of image comes readily to his mind. He dins the idea of robbery into Brabantio so convincingly (85, 86, 105) that Brabantio in turn screams at Othello, "Down with him, thief!" "O thou foul thief, where hast thou stow'd my daughter?" (1.2.57, 62) and charges more formally, to the Duke,

THE IAGO WORLD: STYLES IN DECEPTION

"She is abus'd, stol'n from me" (1.3.60). Othello admits that he has "ta'en away this old man's daughter" (78), but he escapes the plot that does not attack him within.[74]

As a part of the general intrigue against Othello, Iago also formulates a plot against Cassio—"To get his place" (1.3.399), that is, to steal it. He gets Cassio drunk, and Cassio is fired—the theft partly accomplished. The climax occurs when Othello and Iago enter the castle garden just as Cassio, having asked Desdemona for help in regaining the lieutenancy, leaves. To Othello's question, "Was not that Cassio . . .?" Iago replies: "Cassio, my lord? No, sure, I cannot think it, / That he would steal away so guilty-like, / Seeing you coming" (3.3.38-40). Iago here begins to steal Cassio's reputation—and by his characteristic method of conferring his own vice upon another: he makes Cassio, in his embarrassed departure, look like a thief! And Othello, whom he failed to destroy as thief, he will destroy as the detector of a thief.

Shortly after, as a part of the slowly evolving campaign to rob all three of precious possessions, Iago comes up with the best known words in the play—his deadpan essay on the relative values of purse and reputation:

> Good name in man and woman, dear my lord,
> Is the immediate jewel of their souls.
> Who steals my purse steals trash; 'tis something, nothing;
> 'Twas mine, 'tis his, and has been slave to thousands;
> But he that filches from me my good name
> Robs me of that which not enriches him
> And makes me poor indeed.   (3.3.155-161)

When we look at Iago's now almost proverbial phrases in the perspective of all the rest of the play, we see that they are something more than a happy accident of quotable words. For Iago is doing three things that are worth a little inspection: he is playing a rather risky game, he is offering a judgment of values, and he is uniquely applying his old image of theft to himself.

79

The risky game is clear: like Edmund in *Lear,* Iago is rather daringly telling his gull what he is doing, and this before the gull is under certain control. His complex personality contains more than a little of the gambler,[75] and, as we have seen, something of the actor. At the same time, by appearing reluctant to do what he is doing, he has the delicate satisfaction of directing a drama in which the gull in effect demands that he be imposed upon.[76] It's a better revenge than simple imposition, and it subtly executes a project phrased originally in blunter terms: "Make the Moor thank me, love me, and reward me / For making him egregiously an ass" (2.1.317-318).

In making his value judgment (by means of images from economics: jewel, trash), Iago takes us back to earlier actions of his: since we know by now that he is literally a purse lover, his words look like plain tactical hypocrisy. What is more, he has also expressed himself on the subject of good name. When Cassio, sobered up after his drunken fight, bemoans his loss of "reputation," Iago replies revealingly: "As I am an honest man, I thought you had receiv'd some bodily wound. There is more sense in that than in reputation. Reputation is an idle and most false imposition; oft got without merit and lost without deserving. You have lost no reputation at all unless you repute yourself such a loser" (2.3.266-272). Here we feel a profound echo of Iago's positivistic cast of mind: surely the reputation-is-an-imposition lines betray the fakery of the good-name-is-a-jewel speech.

What we think about Iago's attitude to his own lines depends in part upon whether we think the lines are "true." Roy Battenhouse argues that Iago can only lie and that his values are wrong, that he underrates material things and that his praise of good name pleases us only because it "flatters our 'higher' inclinations."[77] This is a healthy attack on the oversimplified acceptance of Iago's lines as pure "noble thoughts"; it enables us to sense in Iago's statement a hyperbolic form which suits his theatrical bent and which is artfully aimed at the strong "idealistic" or "ascetic" element in Othello. But it is one thing to say that Iago's formulation is excessive and unbalanced, and another thing to say that it is false; it is possible to bring purse value back into proper focus without going to the opposite extreme of demolishing good-name value. The latter may, like many truths, be accepted on the wrong grounds without being any the less true. ("Good name" will be suspect as a value only if we equate it with uninformed gossip rather than with the earned regard corresponding to, coextensive with, and inseparable from good character known in action. Cassio steers us to the profounder meaning in the play when he calls "reputation" the "immortal part of myself" and adds that "what remains is bestial.") Though it may be argued that as a Satanic character Iago is able only to lie, this approach runs the danger of oversimplifying him by reading him within allegorical restrictions instead of in his human complexity. What I am getting at is that Shakespeare achieves depth in the picture of villainy by making his evil man, not grossly impervious to the problem of value, but able to state an intellectual truth at the same time that all his moral impulses run counter to it. I suspect that even while he is falsely using a truth he may for the moment of formulation "feel" it to be "true"[78]—like Chaucer's Pardoner in his one moment of honest Christian exhortation to the Pilgrims. Only thus can he know wholly his own success in evil.

Iago's third, and most startling, exploit in this speech is his use of images of theft: *steal, filch, rob.* This is his own realm of action, and the irony is a fine one. For Iago, naming of what he is doing heightens the pleasure of the risky game; more important, it evidences that self-awareness which is the final intensification of the evil man's pleasure. He knows what he is doing and thus is able to savor it; he is not merely a raw emotion in action, aware only of the impulse to destroy, but one who, having a word for what he does, can enjoy contemplating his deed. Man cannot relish evil in ignorance; the successfully evil mind has some talent for definition.

Iago's definition sets forth the perfection of thiefhood: for the finest pleasure, he must steal a thing of highest value—not men's "trash," but the "jewel" of their "souls." Yet when Cassio called reputation his "immortal part," Iago sneered at reputation as an "imposition." Can he then really enjoy stealing "good name"? Indeed so. For Shakespeare has achieved a doubleness of character which partly explains the terrifyingness of Iago, making him on the one hand a habitual, principled debunker of the nonmaterial goods of mankind, but on the other hand an intelligent perceiver of the values by which men live. Hence the possibility that he may even "feel" the "truth" of his value judgment. Othello's and Cassio's words about reputation (2.3.195, 262ff.) he has heard, not with stupid incomprehension, but with an insight into their code which lets him know to inflict the most grievous damage upon those who live by it.[79] In active revenge he is not handicapped by his philosophical preferences.

Iago's distinction of two kinds of theft—vulgar theft or "trash"-stealing, and the more sinister nonprofit theft of character—is, as a piece of verbal drama, closely co-ordinated with the actional drama. Iago steals at both levels. In the Roderigo action he is the petty thief, the pursesnatcher; everywhere else he is the subtle thief: of the good name of Cassio and Desdemona, of the peace and happiness of Othello, even, indirectly, of Othello's good name. In defining Iago's evil Shakespeare has shown him in a wide range of spoliation—from petty larceny to character assassination; he is at once the common grabber and the diabolical thief of the spirit. This duality of the vulgar and the demonic, which extends through all of Iago's actions, is one of Shakespeare's great feats of characterization.[80]

As a figure on the exchange, Iago seems to be the winner taking all and making his victims "poor indeed." We need not labor the fact, however, that Iago uses only a short-term economics; he is a plunger in psychological pleasure, an emotional spendthrift who is indifferent to cost accounting. Iago has a good rational grasp of how to influence people, and the

THE IAGO WORLD: STYLES IN DECEPTION

vulgar streak of the profiteer; but in the failure of imagination he is reckless of his own coming impoverishment. But this is right; as we've said, he's a gambler; when resentful malice begins to run wild, it can no longer calculate the end; like the gambling spirit, it contains something of the suicidal.[81]

Thievery surrounds Iago like a personal atmosphere, and it spreads from him to permeate and infect the community: "My wayward husband hath a hundred times / Woo'd me to steal it" (3.3.292-293), says Emilia after she picks up the handkerchief, and words of stealing permeate the dialogue that follows (309-315). But beside Iago's plain, if concealed, robbery, Emilia's theft is half an accident, and when she sees what has happened, she tells the truth,[82] "He begg'd of me to steal't" (5.2.229). Ignorant of the theft of the handkerchief, Othello images Desdemona as a thief: "What sense had I of her stol'n hours of lust?" (3.3.338) and naively philosophizes: "He that is robb'd, not wanting what is stol'n, / Let him not know't, and he's not robb'd at all" (3.3.342-343). Here is a kind of passive tragic irony: in active tragic irony, the protagonist acts but does not know where his action tends; here he suffers, but does not know whence his suffering. Othello has indeed been robbed, but he knows neither who the robber is, nor that "knowing" and being robbed are identical.

Anyone familiar with Shakespeare's method would expect contrasts developed by the same verbal drama. Since Iago has talked so much about purses that he has made *purse* conspicuous, we stop short when we find Desdemona thus lamenting the loss of the handkerchief: "Believe me, I had rather have lost my purse / Full of crusadoes" (3.4.25-26). There is no reason to suppose that in her way Desdemona loves purses any less than Iago does. Yet her figure complicates the case by suggesting that purse love can coexist with clarity about basic values. We learn more of Desdemona's "economics" when she says to Emilia, "Not the world's mass of vanity could make me" (4.2.164) "do the act" which would "earn" the title of

83

"whore." Interesting how, in another reminiscence of the Christian myth, she continues to think of "the world" as a premium for adultery—the largest material temptation to a soul in trial, the realm of purses and of worldliness, with which love can come to terms only in comedy. Again she raises the question with Emilia, and again she avers, "Beshrew me if I would do such a wrong / For the whole world" (4.3.69, 80-81). Emilia deflates Desdemona's hyperbole, implicitly challenges her rhetoric, by a tour de force in the semantics of value terms: "the world" is, after all, "great price for a small vice"; for a lesser price, such as gowns, petticoats, no indeed; but to cuckold a husband into monarchy—a good bargain, surely; one would then rule "the world" and would have power to right the "wrong," as Desdemona calls it (69-85). As a jocular variation on a theme, this logical frolic is structurally analogous to Iago's verses on women (2.1.130ff.) which are an integral part of the fair-foul-light-dark theme. In fact, Emilia expounds playfully the purse economy to which Iago is strongly committed. But Shakespeare is using Emilia's gay exercise primarily as a counterweight to Desdemona's solemn incredulity; thus he shows his awareness of her inexperience and of her naive, enthusiastic, almost schoolgirlish style. Yet he does not question her values, nor do we; if we are made a little uncomfortable by her style, we are reassured by Emilia's worldly irony, which releases us from Desdemona's naive hyperbole without providing a tenable alternative to undercut her essential value judgment.[83] In fact, just after making fun of her style, Shakespeare goes on to support her moral economy by having Emilia shift from her agile game of wit to a serious but casuistical argument that "it is their husbands' faults / If wives do fall" (4.3.89-90). In morals (as in art), a shift from the problem of value to the problem of cause is a drop to a lesser level of discourse: Desdemona's new-young-wifely doctrine of chastity as unquestionable absolute looks very sound beside the moral buck-passing of Emilia's "The ills we do, their ills instruct us so"

THE IAGO WORLD: STYLES IN DECEPTION

(106). Here, perhaps from wifely bitterness,[84] Emilia falls into the manner of the mass mind principally imaged in Iago.[85] But she can think on the Iago level without being bound there forever. Like purses, worlds are a strand in the dramatic web, appearing again to complete a figure. Othello sets forth the value Desdemona had for him:

> Nay, had she been true,
> If heaven would make me such another world
> Of one entire and perfect chrysolite,
> I'ld not have sold her for it. (5.2.143-146)

In economics husband and wife are similar: Desdemona would not yield honor for the world; Othello would not give up his wife for a world of chrysolite. But they are not identical: Desdemona's charter of value is absolute, Othello's is conditional (the defect in his love), and whereas she is simply robbed, Othello acquiesces in being robbed. He has to learn that he is more than a victim, and it is just these images of value that illuminate the road he takes from a pathetic to a tragic role. At the first shock of supposed revelation he felt himself "robbed"—an innocent victim. But now in his world-of-chrysolite speech he is changed; his very verb shows a move from a passive to an active role. "I'ld not have *sold* her for it," he says. But he has still to advance from hypotheses ("would not have sold") to the recognition that he has acted, and acted voluntarily. Othello takes this step when he describes himself as "one whose hand / (Like the base Indian) threw a pearl away / Richer than all his tribe" (5.2.346-348). It has been Desdemona's fate to be wrongly valued. Brabantio spoke ironically in "giving" her to Othello and calling her "jewel" (1.3.193, 195). And now too late Othello recognizes her as a "pearl." But what is more important now is that he recognizes that he "threw" her away. This is his tragic climax: his acceptance, within his limits, of responsibility. This is the economics of the tragic hero.

MAGIC IN THE WEB

5. DR. IAGO AND HIS POTIONS

It comes naturally to our speech habits to call Othello, in the last three acts, a "sick" man. His violence of language and conduct comes from, and evidences, serious disorder; after he has publicly struck Desdemona, Lodovico asks, "Are his wits safe? Is he not light of brain?" (4.1.280). But aside from such lines as these the metaphor of illness is thoroughly embedded in the play. In one scene Othello has a literal illness; in two other scenes he suffers from a malaise on the borderline between the psychic and the physical, and between the assumed and the real.

In Act 4, goaded again by Iago, Othello falls into a partially incoherent prose in which he argues that his suspicions are verified by his "shadowing passion" (4.1.41)—i.e., this suffering that has a "blacking out" effect. Then he "Falls in a trance" (44). His physical "blacking out" is symbolically a darkening of vision; indeed, the "shadowing passion" carries many steps further a process that began when Othello, disturbed by the Cassio-Montano brawl, acknowledged that "passion" had "collied"—made black like coal—his "judgment" (2.3.206).

Two practitioners compete with first-aid remedies. Cassio suggests, "Rub him about the temples" (4.1.53), but Iago both overrules this treatment and gets rid of Cassio—a miniature of his success in larger operations. Iago figures quite literally as physician. He diagnoses: "My lord is fall'n into an epilepsy. / This is his second fit; he had one yesterday" (51-52). He counters Cassio's proposal with a prescription and a prognosis which show a knowledge of the case history:

<pre>
                    No, forbear.
    The lethargy must have his quiet course.
    If not, he foams at mouth, and by-and-by
    Break out to savage madness. Look, he stirs.
    Do you withdraw yourself a little while.
    He will recover straight.   (53-58)
</pre>

THE IAGO WORLD: STYLES IN DECEPTION

And when Othello "comes to" and thinks immediately of the cause of his suffering, Iago proffers a combination of encouragement and chiding which resembles the psychiatric part of the medical function: "Good sir, be a man," "Confine yourself but in a patient list" (66, 76ff.). We should never forget the carefully developed role of Iago as physician,[86] for it is the foundation for another telling definition of his evil—analogous to the portrait of Iago as the manipulator of appearances, the confounder of dark and light, and the robber of his friend.

For full light on Dr. Iago we need to look at other doctor-patient relationships. An earlier "illness" scene is tied very closely to the episode of the trance by some words spoken after Othello regains consciousness. Iago asks, "How is it, General? Have you not hurt your head?" (60) and Othello replies bitterly, "Dost thou mock me?" (61), for he scents a cuckoldry joke. Compare the earlier Othello-Desdemona exchange when Othello pretends to be ill:

> *Des.* Why do you speak so faintly?
> Are you not well?
> *Oth.* I have a pain upon my forehead, here.
> *Des.* Faith, that's with watching; 'twill away again.
> Let me but bind it hard, within this hour
> It will be well.
> *Oth.* Your napkin is too little.
> Let it alone. Come, I'll go in with you.
> *Des.* I am very sorry that you are not well. (3.3.282-289)

This brief episode is packed. While Othello jokes harshly, Desdemona implies a diagnosis ("not well"), postulates a cause ("with watching"), and prescribes a treatment: here it is she who is his physician. Now the "napkin" with which she proposes to make him "well" is not *any* handkerchief; it not only has a special associational value in their relationship, but has also a symbolic value (see Chapter VI). She doesn't have to hunt for it or plan an emotional coup; she has it with her and comes up with it spontaneously; her "love" is ready. But Othello doesn't even identify the handkerchief, much less the

87

proffered love; he is already far enough gone to reject the treatment he most needs. He pushes the handkerchief away; Desdemona is intent on him, not on things; and the handkerchief is dropped. The immediate theft by Emilia is not the completion of a "well-made" device, the picking up of an object that has been dropped that it may be picked up. Rather, the stage business is meaningful: an unrecognized good, a rejected good, can become an instrument of evil.

In the very next scene, in a striking reversal of roles, Othello, who has now been subject to the ministrations of Iago, briefly assumes the physician himself. "How do you, Desdemona?" he asks, and she replies "Well, my good lord" (3.4.35). He examines her hand, diagnoses, and prescribes: "Hot, hot, and moist. This hand of your requires / A sequester from liberty, fasting and prayer, / Much castigation, exercise devout" (3.4.39-41). Here Othello really slides over into the soul's leech—a role which he is again to adopt later. Then the leech who because he is sick suspects illness in a well person accentuates the irony by assuming an indisposition in order to trap the patient: "I have a salt and sorry rheum offends me. / Lend me thy handkerchief" (51-52), and for many lines he keeps demanding the handkerchief and explaining its value. As so often in Shakespeare, this scene gets some of its life from an earlier one which it partially replays. In 3.3 Desdemona offered the handkerchief, whereas now she does not know what has become of it; Othello refused the ministration of the handkerchief, whereas now he insistently calls for it. Whereas before, Othello symbolically rejected her love, he now calls loudly to her, not for the love, which he could have by recognizing it, but for proof of it, which she cannot give him. The doctor-patient is more profoundly ill than Desdemona realizes: "For let our finger ache, and it endues / Our other, healthful, members even to that sense / Of pain" (3.4.146-148). When he talks about himself, he often uses the metaphor of illness, as if compulsively. He is a victim, he thinks, of "the plague of great ones"[87] (3.3.273). The handkerchief story comes "o'er my memory," he says, "As doth the raven o'er the infected house" (4.1.20-21). Describing preferable alternate woes, Othello insists that he would have had "patience" if it had "pleas'd heaven" to rain "All kinds of sores and shames on my bare head" (4.2.47ff.). "Plague," "infected house," "sores and shames" tell us indirectly how ill Othello is.[88]

The doctor to whom Othello has newly entrusted himself, Iago, shows an eye ever alert to human distemper. He notes Cassio's "infirmity"[89] (2.3.132; cf. 43, 145); he calls Roderigo a "sick fool" (2.3.53); he defines Bianca's trouble, "the strumpet's plague" (4.1.97). In speaking of Desdemona's love he falls into the diagnostic and prognostic style of a specialist rehearsing classical symptoms: "Her eye must be fed; ... When the blood is made dull with the act of sport, there should be, again to inflame it and to give satiety a fresh appetite, loveliness in favour [etc.] ... her delicate tenderness will find itself abus'd, begin to heave the gorge, ... Very nature[90] will instruct her in it and compel her to some second choice" (2.1.227-237). Iago sounds a little like the scientist in advertisements.

Nor does Iago practice in one case only.[91] To Roderigo, who thinks "death" his only "physician" (1.3.311), Iago addresses a cheery question, "What wound did ever heal but by degrees?" (2.3.377)—and for a time snatches the case from the rival physician (to whom he will ultimately recommit the patient). He insists that he "would do much / To cure" Cassio of his "evil" (2.3.148-149)—his allergy to alcohol—and proposes a remedy for his loss of position: "This broken joint between you and her husband entreat her to splinter" (2.3.329). And after the final sword work, Iago promises Cassio, "I'll fetch the General's surgeon" (5.1.100). In each case Iago is clearly using his "patients": not healing them but making their condition worse. As a physician Iago is more than a generally bad man pretending to be good; he is the troublemaker and the destroyer masking himself as the healer and preserver, converting qualities into their opposites just as when he turns white into black and brings darkness by pretending to bring light. It is another dramatic way of translating the abstraction "evil" into concrete actuality.

Dr. Iago's basic potion, as we have seen it so far, has been words of hope. But for his most important case he has also another kind of medicine which we first hear about in the opening night scene. Brabantio is sure that Othello "hast practis'd on her with foul charms, / Abus'd her delicate youth with drugs or minerals / That weaken motion" (1.2.73-75). Since "practice" could mean "practice medicine" as well as "trick" or "scheme" (the more usual meaning), we have the first faint note of shady medical work, of the "false physician." There is also a serviceable ambiguity in "drugs or minerals," which, since they can be used for legitimate therapy or for bad ends, suggest the narrow borderline between good and evil practice. We get more of this when Brabantio charges before the Duke that Desdemona is "corrupted / By spells and medicines bought of mountebanks," since "nature" would be unable "so prepost'rously to err" (1.3.60-64). When Othello promises a defense "Of my whole course of love—what drugs, what charms" (91), Brabantio again accuses him of using "some mixtures pow'rful o'er the blood" or "some dram" (104-105). Then the Senator puts to Othello a question so phrased as to continue Brabantio's imagery and to wrest from it a still more basic version of ill-doing: "Did you by indirect and forced courses / Subdue and poison this young maid's affections?" (111-112). Everyone is soon satisfied that Othello used no drugs, minerals, medicines, mixtures, dram, or poison; yet into the play there has subtly entered a concept to be used later—that of the special means to an end which may, in variant circumstances, be construed as medicine or poison. Brabantio's second speech has given us, also, a fleeting image of the human figure who belongs in the realm of ambiguous potions—the "mountebank."

THE IAGO WORLD: STYLES IN DECEPTION

Now back to Iago, who even before the hearing is administering potions in his own style. While giving Roderigo directions for proceeding against Othello (through Brabantio), Iago has defined his own role with wonderful explicitness:

> Make after him, poison his delight,
> Proclaim him in the streets. Incense her kinsmen,
> And though he in a fertile climate dwell,
> Plague him with flies.   (1.1.68-71)

Poison and *plague:* here, almost before the play is started, Iago announces his trademarks.[92] The words are more than the chance verbal instruments of rancor; they inaugurate a poetic structure that is sustained throughout the play. For we are to see Iago administering poison and spreading a plague, and actually using such terms for his work. In the first scene, just as when he called thief, he succeeds in having pinned on his victim the evil which he himself performs: Othello is accused both of thievery and of using illicit medicines.

The early identification of Iago as a poisoner sets the stage for another remarkable dramatic definition of evil: the poisoner as physician (a parallel of the manipulator of appearances, the false light-bringer, the thief as adviser). In one sense the poisoner as physician is a rounding and a deepening of a flat machiavel; Shakespeare characteristically seizes upon a convention and endows it with such vitality that though to the trained eye the convention is still apparent its transitoriness has given way to something timeless. The villain has been enlarged from a stage-worn robot of naughtiness into a doer of evil comprehensible beyond time and place. The montaging of the healer upon the poisoner not only effects a coalescence of moral opposites that defines chaos, but reminds us that in virtue of his knowledge every doctor contains the poisoner: a potion can mean life or death to the man who drinks it. Hence we have a universal paradigm of evil, not a period piece from the antique mart. Physicians are rarely poisoners; they are subject to more than usual moral imperatives regarding human life because they have more than usual power over life and death. If we remember this, we appreciate Iago: Shakespeare gives him unusual mastery, skills, intelligence, without a vestige of moral controls, but with all the trappings of a profession in which those are axiomatic. Iago is impeded by no sullen integrity. He is given "charm" and "bedside manner"; he entertains gaily (2.1.100-161); he offers sympathy to Desdemona: "Do not weep, do not weep. Alas the day!" (4.2.124). Most of all, he elicits the trust that creates the confidant and adviser: it is he of whom the lost Desdemona begs help in winning Othello back (4.2.148ff.). This Iago does not date; in one direction he reminds us of the archetypal "doc" of the criminal world; in another, of the exuberant faith in "personality" and of the confidence that the exercise of rational skills autonomously effects good.

As poisoner, Dr. Iago develops gradually. First he thinks merely to "abuse Othello's ear" (1.3.401); by the next act his role crystallizes, and he puts his plan thus: "I'll pour this pestilence into his ear" (2.3.362)—an image that must remind us of the literal poisoning as in *Hamlet,* and, by contrast, of the willingness with which Othello, awake, lends his ear. In his next soliloquy Iago becomes more forthright and expansive:[93]

> The Moor already changes with my poison.
> Dangerous conceits are in their natures poisons
> Which at the first are scarce found to distaste,
> But with a little act upon the blood
> Burn like the mines of sulphur.   (3.3.325-329)

Just as Iago knows he is a thief, he knows he is a poisoner; he does not conceal his deed from himself but gloats in it—again the self-knowledge essential to pleasure in evil. Equally essential is the contemplation of success:

> Look where he comes! Not poppy nor mandragora,
> Nor all the drowsy syrups of the world,
> Shall ever medicine thee to that sweet sleep
> Which thou ow'dst yesterday.   (330-333)

He nurses his patient toward an incurable condition. But Iago's dual role is set forth with most effective shock when, under his goading, Othello has a kind of fit—a scene which we can now see in perspective. Just after Othello falls, Iago exclaims, "Work on, / My medicine, work! Thus credulous fools are caught" (4.1.45-46). This is the climax of the poetic structure of the physician-poisoner: the two functions coalesce as Iago uses *medicine,* the commonest word in the vocabulary of healing, to denote his poisoning of Othello's mind; to describe the conversion of order into disorder, he uses a word connoting the reduction of disorder to order. Repeatedly *Othello* presents the diabolical principle as a reversal of the human norms which guarantee ordinary safety in existence.

Othello comes to, is lectured by Iago, and withdraws. What Iago once foresaw as a possibility, "practising upon" Othello's "peace and quiet / Even to madness" (2.1.319-320), he now embodies in a prognostic resolve: "Othello shall go mad" (4.1. 101). The patient responds rapidly to further treatment, and as if he were mysteriously driven to act as he has been acted against, he thus elects the mode of Desdemona's death: "Get me some poison, Iago, this night. . . . This night, Iago!" (4.1. 216-219). The poisoned man will deal out his own poison, getting it from the poisoner who has acted as physician to him and to his intended victim. Then a shock, as the pseudo physician rejects the literal method which provides the metaphor for his favorite instrument: "Do it not with poison. Strangle her in her bed, even the bed she hath contaminated" (220-221). Is he not here eliminating an agency which he would be most likely to seize upon with glee? I think not. He reserves "poison" as a private instrument, he deprives Othello of a mechanical assistance which might let him think his criminal responsibility shared, and he appeals to his desire for "justice." In falling for this proposal, Othello prepares for himself an ineffaceable concrete image of his destruction of their love, their marital unity. The greater the "justice" of punishment, the greater the horror of injustice when the facts are known. By rejecting literal poison, Iago prepares a more tormenting poison for his victim.[94] And, as we shall see, he manages also to indulge another passion besides his malice.

Iago has gloated over the fact that his poison will "Burn like the mines of sulphur" (3.3.329). Shakespeare does not throw away this image of burning,[95] but uses it repeatedly. Othello exclaims, "If there be cords, or knives, / Poison, or fire, or suffocating streams, / I'll not endure it" (3.3.388-390), without recognizing that he is already suffering from a fiery poison. When Desdemona speaks innocently of the "love I bear to Cassio," he cries "Fire and brimstone!" (4.1.244-245). And when near the end he calls for punishment, he specifies tortures which have the effect of "implementing" Iago's prophecy: "roast me in sulphur! / Wash me in steep-down gulfs of liquid fire!" (5.2.279-280). The frequent naming of poison increases the meaning of Lodovico's comment when Othello as he dies falls on the bed that contains the body of Desdemona: "The object poisons sight; / Let it be hid" (5.2.364-365). In one sense this is a command for the traditional covering of the dead, but the word *poisons* contributes a strange intensity: to the reader aware of the poetic structure, it is as if the poison that came from Iago had gone over into his victims and made them, not serene in death, not cleansed, but something grotesque and disfigured.

But the poisoner-doctor motif, fine as it is for presenting the suffering of victims, serves primarily to give vitality to the idea of evil as treachery. His inner drama of treachery by poison Shakespeare carries one brilliant step further, using three brief passages to do it. When Othello is sure Desdemona has been unfaithful, he summons "black vengeance" and "hate" and then soars on to this climax: "Swell, bosom, with thy fraught, / For 'tis of aspics' tongues!" (3.3.449-450). By the poison in his breast Othello means, of course, his bitterness; but we cannot fail to see it also as something put there—injected—by Iago. Thus Othello adds a new stroke, almost a

THE IAGO WORLD: STYLES IN DECEPTION

transforming one, to the portrait of Iago: after all that has been done with poison, we can but see Iago as the asp. The identity is vouched for by a single detail—"aspics' tongues": the asp injects venom with its tongue, Iago by the tongue which he uses in speech. Nor does Shakespeare drop the idea here. When Emilia learns what Othello's inner gnawing is and tries to assure him that Desdemona is honest, she adds, "If you think other, / Remove your thought; it doth abuse your bosom" (4.2.13-14)—the bosom that Othello implored to "swell" with its "fraught." The passages are interrelated still more closely by Emilia's next lines: "If any wretch have put this in your head, / Let heaven requite it with the serpent's curse!" (15-16). She does not know of whom she speaks, but for us Iago is again revealed as an essentially snakelike figure, this time with his destiny asserted—to crawl on his belly and eat dirt. Still a third time Iago is so identified, this time by Lodovico, whose voice becomes increasingly authoritative in the final scene: "Where is that viper?" (5.2.285).

In the most telling of his transformations Iago becomes the poisonous reptile: initially he is the aggrieved human being, who, whatever his own ills, can still seem to minister to the ills of others; then the physician but dimly conceals the poisoner; at last the poisoner unfolds, and there at the center is the asp. As the developing characterization brings the nonhuman or the antihuman into sharper relief, the highly articulate Iago talks less and less; in the final scene he almost gives up human communication. The stage directions of another day might have said that he "hisses" the abuse which makes up most of his talk in Act. 5. The reptile images finally used for Iago, with their irresistible associations of treachery and debasement, mark the evildoer's ultimate loss of humanity. For a while Iago has marked resemblances to humanity: he can make friends, he has charm, he wins confidence, and most of all he has a familiar difficulty—a grievance. He even thinks of the grievance in the very terms in which he seeks vengeance: the thought that Othello has been the lover of Emilia, he says, "Doth, like a poisonous mineral, gnaw my inwards" (2.1.306). It is of course, as Coleridge said, Othello's inwards that will be gnawed; not that Iago does not feel a gnawing, but he refuses to diagnose it correctly as the ailment of his type, the essential *invidia*. Instead he invents a protective sexual jealousy; it is his human desire to look "human"; it is one of the devices by which he becomes an ancestor, not of nineteenth-century stage villains but of a dangerous type of man in the twentieth century. It is the resemblance to humanity that gives the shock to the emergence of inhumanity—a development wonderfully charted by the asp-serpent-viper series.

Though the failure of humanity is traced by various other means, the snake images, with their rich imaginative ties, are especially effective. The Genesis association enters unmistakably in Emilia's phrase "the serpent's curse." So we have the ancient false friend, Satan himself—a mythic expansion which genericizes the individual but still leaves him intact, unabstracted. The words in which Othello's indignation bursts forth carry the identification further:

> I look down towards his feet—but that's a fable.
> If that thou be'st a devil, I cannot kill thee.
>
> Will you, I pray, demand that demi-devil
> Why he hath thus ensnar'd my soul and body?
> (5.2.286-287, 301-302)

"Demi-devil" sums up very well the course of the human being who, simulating the physician, has become poisoner, then viper —betrayer raised to the mythical power. As Iago's diabolism thus emerges distinct from the interwoven texture of action and language, we see how the myth of the devil enters into the play—not as a formula which squeezes out the individuality of Iago, nor as a pure idea of which the dramatic parts are an allegorical projection, but as an added dimension, a collateral presence that makes us sense the inclusiveness of the fable.

THE IAGO WORLD: STYLES IN DECEPTION

We can see still more of what Shakespeare is doing, particularly of the tightness of his structure, if we compare the final transmogrification of Iago with a scene in Dante's *Inferno*. The jump to the *Inferno* is not a hard one, what with the constant verbal opposition of the heavenly and the infernal, the cry of "devil" often directed at both Othello and Iago, such images as those of burning sulphur and those used by Othello in summoning an infernal punishment for himself. Shakespeare's metaphorical turning of man into snake is a moral parallel to the transformation spectacularly described by Dante in Canto XXV—the literal metamorphosis of men into snakes. There is of course the difference that Dante's sinners are not poisoners or betrayers, but thieves. Yet for that reason the Dante analogy is more valuable than if it presented an immediate point-by-point parallel, since by it we can see more of the imaginative unity of *Othello*. For Iago is not only a poisoner but a thief—a thief of purses and good names in whom thiefhood is exhaustively canvassed. To turn this man, by a series of images, into a snake, is to do independently what Dante did; the comparable act of imagination by Dante—not to mention the comparable mythopoeic act by which the author of Genesis made the thief of souls assume the snake form voluntarily—implies an archetype of representation which recurrently visits the human imagination needing a measure of debasement. But when, as an elaboration of the thief-into-snake fable, Iago is also imaged as a poisoner, the poetic structure is tightened and enriched: the thief and poisoner both become the snake, the one by a transcendent moral propriety, the other by a logical progression of character when venom has become the motive and the instrument of all vital action.

The aesthetic parallel between Shakespeare and Dante is an aspect of the parallel in moral awareness. Dante's transfiguration scene belongs to his history of torments for sins of fraud and malice—the worst category of evil-doing into which Iago fits exactly. And at the end of the scene occurs this key line:

97

"The soul that had become a brute, fled hissing."[96] Shakespeare's theme is precisely the decline of soul into brute—of the man who could take the form of the healer and even display some talent in the role, but who chose instead to mislead, to steal from, and to poison his fellows and who thus, in the end, came to be called "viper" and "demi-devil."

The Iago World

STYLES IN REVELATION

Shakespeare has indirectly characterized Iago by a series of figurative part-portraits which are analogically related, almost in the fashion of those diverse accounts of the elephant given by a number of blind men each of whom felt a different part of the beast—side, trunk, ear, and so on. But in *Othello* the "part-portraits" are not the products of different minds and none of them purports to be complete; instead of existing separately, they coexist, interwoven in a single complex interpretative artwork which simultaneously uses various perspectives and thus gives us, not simply a full front or a profile, but something like an all-dimensional view of Iago. In Chapter III we looked at different faces of "honest Iago"—i.e., the styles of deception possible to evil: the disturbing of appearances, the robbing of trustful associates, the confounding of light and dark, the spreading of disease in the guise of a cure. All these modes of portraiture, with their exploitation of the literal and the figurative, of actional and verbal drama, complement each other in creating an extraordinary image of evil. The climactic stroke is the emergence of the diabolical personality from the multiple folds of humane seeming.

If virtuosity in deception be the primary mode of the diabolical personality, nevertheless the personality may reveal itself to us forthrightly, that is, without disguise. Iago not only

CHAPTER 4

"pretends," he "is." He not only infiltrates but appears in the open and attacks directly. The unaltered self falls into characteristic styles of language and action that, some in major ways and some in minor, are functional in placing him and interpreting the "flow" from him to the community. And we see how the community identifies him.

1. REDUCTION AND CONQUEST

Iago, who finds the sum of truth in the least common denominator, repeatedly expresses his views in terms of bodily functions.[1] Though nearly all characters use metaphors of eating and drinking in a self-regarding way,[2] Iago uses them conspicuously to express his contempt, in which he anticipates the parvenu sensibility, for those who do not get on profitably in the world ("Wears out his time, . . . / For naught but provender"—1.1.47-48; cf. 4.1.95-96), and to demote others to his own spiritual rank:[3] "Her eye must be fed; . . . to give satiety a fresh appetite," "The wine she drinks is made of grapes" (2.1.227, 231, 256-257). He likes to have (or help) things taste bitter for other people,[4] and to turn the sweet into the revolting:[5] "Foh! one may smell in such a will most rank" (3.3.232). He has a marked fondness for images of birth, and these he, the enemy of love, uses more frequently than any other character: "There are many events in the womb of time, which will be delivered" (1.3.377-378). "I have't! It is engend'red! Hell and night / Must bring this monstrous birth to the world's light" (1.3.408-409). To Othello he complains tactically: "I'll love no friend, sith love breeds such offence" (3.3.380). For the most part "offence" is just what "love breeds" in this play. One of Shakespeare's acute ways of characterizing the Iago world is to have images of birth used almost exclusively in connection with wrongdoing.[6] In the play of love itself there is almost no note of the renewal of life; fertility belongs to evil.[7]

THE IAGO WORLD: STYLES IN REVELATION

Iago's use of images from the physical world is always, in one way or another, a symbolic effecting of malice, a means of controlling life when it threatens to become qualitatively superior, a revelation of an impulse to exercise moral power in the name of his own limitations. The wealth of nautical imagery that he uses, though in part an accident of profession, is also to some extent a symbol of mastery, a reduction of experience to the terms of his own area of competence: "boarded a land carack" (1.2.50) cuts Othello's marriage down to the least common denominator. He has some authority in the realm of sea and storm,* literal and figurative. He ministers to Brabantio's "floodgate and o'erbearing" grief (1.3.56), but he controls Roderigo's emotional storm: "No more of drowning, do you hear?" (1.3.387). He takes Desdemona safely through an actual storm and then whips up the tempests of feeling that destroy her. He talks repeatedly (2.3.59, 63, 133, 147) of troubling the "isle" (surrounded by the sea, the home of storms) and stirs up a new storm of drinking, fights, and blood. In all this, his sense of power comes through in the nautical metaphor that he ironically chooses: "If consequence do but approve my dream, / My boat sails freely, both with wind and stream" (2.3.64-65).

Iago's instinct for destructive power finds outlet in time as well as tide: he works to speed up or slow down the actions of others, so that the pace of time is a symbolic marking of the life that he has tampered with. Here there is an illuminating interplay between his influence and the "readiness in the victim," for what is involved is a sense of decorum in time,[8] a feeling for whether little time or much time is appropriate in a given context. One may act or call for action "now" or "in a little while" or "never" or "forever": the pendulum that ticks off the interval is related to moral balance. Iago, who tries to disturb every pendulum, blandly tutors Othello: "keep time in all" (4.1.93).

* For a fuller comment on the dramatic use of the storm, see Appendix A, "The Enchafed Flood."

101

Cassio's extraordinary urgency[9] in wanting his job back without delay comes both from Iago's pressure and from his own make-up.[10] Though Cassio is a good enough man to feel morally responsible for his misbehavior (he does not blame Iago for forcing drinks on him), he is in danger of seeming insincere precisely because his capacity for vigorous self-criticism coexists—rather representatively—with a faulty sense of appropriateness in time that underlies his passion to have the penalty suspended "now." But Desdemona's effort to hasten Cassio's reinstatement (3.3.22, 57, 60-63) is fundamentally generous, even though it is mixed with thoughtlessness and a little desire to exercise power. Of all the major characters, she attempts least to have the temporal order conform to personal ends.[11]

Othello is more unrestrained than Cassio in wanting to impose a subjective time upon the flux of experience: inscribed on his banner is "Away at once with love or jealousy!" (3.3.192). Othello's intention of eliminating any interval of doubt and anguish is simple failure of understanding; when this impulse makes him want to punish others immediately, his egotism has a moral as well as an intellectual quality. Desdemona wanted Cassio restored to favor in three days; Othello's final reply to this is his command to Iago, whose interest it is to keep things moving as fast as possible, "Within these three days let me hear thee say / That Cassio's not alive" (3.3.472-473). As for Desdemona, she is to die "tonight" (4.1.191, 216-219). To have revenge "now" is not only to try to reduce the irreducible time of suffering, but to fail to live with it for that time that might qualify the suffering by making guilt or innocence unmistakable. On the one hand Othello shrinks from the inevitable duration of evil—"A fixed figure for the time of scorn / To point his slow unmoving finger at!" (4.2.54-55); on the other, he wants to prolong the joy of revenge:[12] "I would have him nine years a-killing!" (4.1.188), a wish that puts him in the same boat as Iago, with his glee that no drugs "Shall ever medicine thee to . . . sleep" (3.3.332). In

THE IAGO WORLD: STYLES IN REVELATION

wanting to annihilate one event or eternize another,[13] he symbolically tries to dominate fact by feeling. He will have Cassio as an officer "never more" (2.3.249); he is "bound" to Iago "for ever," and he says farewell to a happy career "for ever" (3.3.213, 347-349). He denies time as a healer, extends to infinity the feeling of the hour; by such impropriety he brings about the irrevocable. His mind, he says, will "never" change; his "bloody thoughts" shall "ne'er look back, ne'er ebb to humble love" (3.3.453, 457-458). He introduces finality before things are final: this is a rashness that can harden the spirit.

Cassio and Othello, with their own uncriticized impulse to exert power by the molding of time, have a readiness which is quite open to Iago. When he exaggerates, it is not from a dangerous ignorance of reality, but from the will to injure (as when he says that Cassio is drunk every night—2.3.134) or to strengthen his control over a victim (as when he matches Othello's hyperbole, "I am bound to thee for ever," with an echo, "I am your own for ever"—3.3.479). He can advance one theory to Roderigo, "wit depends on dilatory time," and another to himself a few lines later, "Dull not device by coldness and delay" (2.3.379, 394). He can restrain the urgency of Roderigo (2.3.384) and of Cassio when he wants to go on watch (2.3.13-14) and when he wants help for his wound (5.1.87). On the other hand, when Roderigo sensibly decides that he will give up the pursuit of Desdemona, Iago stirs him to a new urgency (4.2.218, 249-250), and he ministers to Othello's urgency in wanting Cassio killed immediately (4.1.225). Nor should we miss his specification of time[14] to heighten his provocation of Othello: "Or to be naked with her friend in bed / An hour, or more" (4.1.4-5).

The last line that Iago speaks is, "From this time forth I never will speak word" (5.2.304). For once his adverb of time comes not from his "wit," for strategy's sake, but out of the depths. All the volubility by which he has been operating in the world has overlaid a spiritual isolation which, once he is

103

uncovered, is symbolically engraved in his final phrase, not only in the refusal to "speak word," but in the *never*. His is a hyperbole of ethos, Othello's of mood.

2. THE HUNTER, THE INHUMAN DOG, AND THE SLAVE

From the political maxim, "Divide and conquer," Iago has fashioned an unspoken rule of action: "Reduce and conquer." He would conquer by reducing, by cutting down the human being to something barely human or less than human; this is a way of putting into action the embracing enmity of the diabolical personality, its essential *invidia*. Reduction can be accomplished conceptually—by ways of thinking about human beings ("The wine she drinks is made of grapes") or by ways of thinking about oneself.

Iago actually thinks of himself as working like a hunter or trapper,[15] and not always a human one ("a hound on the trail"),[16] trickily capturing his victims by net or web. Watching Cassio chat courteously and gallantly with Desdemona, Iago becomes both spider and jailer: "With as little a web as this will I ensnare as great a fly as Cassio. Ay, smile upon her, do! I will gyve thee in thine own courtship" (2.1.169-172). He has to control the overzealous hunting of Roderigo: "this poor trash of Venice, whom I trash / For his quick hunting" (2.1.312-313). He ends one of his strongest soliloquies resolving that he will "out of her own goodness make the net / That shall enmesh them all" (2.3.366-368). As Iago completes his figure of the net, Roderigo enters and complains in terms that show his awareness of the nature of their activity, "I do follow here in the chase, not like a hound that hunts, but one that fills up the cry" (369-370). So it is appropriate for Iago, a little later, to gloat over his "medicine," by which "credulous fools are caught" (4.1.46). As often, two imagistic approaches are

THE IAGO WORLD: STYLES IN REVELATION

fused in moments of intensely clear definition; this happens again when, at his enlightenment, Othello asks, "Will you, I pray, demand that demi-devil / Why he hath thus ensnar'd my soul and body?" (5.2.301-302). Iago is both fiend and trapper, and Othello senses the nature of his double action.

Such lines are strong instruments for the poetic dramatization of evil, for *hunted* and *trapped* have become almost clichés for desperateness of plight. What they signify is the human being reduced to the animal. Now it is exactly in the Iago style to treat people as animals, whether by hunting them or by thinking of them in a certain way—for instance, in his view of love, his stimulus-and-response psychology, his belief in universal gullibility. In looking at Iago as hunter and trapper we come close to the core of his evil—the threat to the soul. It is the predictable target of the dealer in poison who, as we saw in Chapter III, sinks into the brute.

In his barnyard view of life, Iago instinctively dehumanizes the human being, especially by treating love as a mechanical animality.[17] In exclamation, in definition, in comparison, as all readers know, he draws easily upon the animal world.[18] Not only does he think of men as animals, he leads them to become animals in their action.[19] Cassio's self-judgment, "I have lost the immortal part of myself, and what remains is bestial" (2.3.263-264), employs words that are thematically important. If in his misery he seems to overstate his single misdemeanor,[20] nevertheless he does recognize what the opposed realities finally are, and so he states the counterpoint of *immortal* and *bestial* that runs implicitly all through the drama. What Iago really stands for is destruction of the spirit.[21] Just this counterpoint flashes into Othello's speech the first time he uses an animal image:

> Exchange me for a goat
> When I shall turn the business of my soul
> Matching thy inference.   (3.3.180-183)
> To such exsufflicate and blown surmises,

105

With Cassio it was *immortal:bestial;* here it is *soul:goat.*[22] Thus the language keeps hammering in what Iago is really up to, and how well he succeeds: Othello's soul does become "busy" with such "surmises," and his humanity is debased. One flaring index of his decline is the way animal images sweep into his speech after—and *only* after—the suspicions planted by Iago begin to eat into him:[23] animal images for others, for experience generally, for himself. When he shouts, "I'll tear her all to pieces!" (3.3.431), he yields a great victory to Iago by becoming the wild animal; but when at the end he smites the "circumcised dog" (5.2.355-356)—ostensibly a Turk, actually himself—he strives to salvage something of his surrendered humanity by killing the beast that he has become.

But with predictable pride Iago endeavors to exempt himself from the consequences of his gnawing compulsion to conquer man by viewing him as animal. He will not work dully "like his master's ass" and he will not expose a heart "for daws to peck at," for "we have reason to cool . . . our unbitted lusts" (1.3.334-336). Though he addresses this to Roderigo, he thinks it meaningful only for himself; but the deeper irony is that he himself does not abide by it, does not even try to, for his will and reason are slaves to passions of his own (the cultist of reason customarily identifies only the irrationalities of others). Indeed Iago's thought leaves him without an adequate counterpoise to all passional drives. He significantly denies one kind of passion: "Ere I would say I would drown myself for the love of a guinea hen, I would change my humanity with a baboon" (316-318). (Compare Othello's "Exchange me for a goat.") When we recall Dante's doctrine that the will is subject to the guidance of love, and that to will rightly one must love rightly, we can see that Dante's history of the mind, as Francis Fergusson calls it, provides a measure for Iago; his denial of sexual passion—even of a callow infatuation—in effect eliminates from the sphere of possibility a great and devoted love which would bend the will effectively against "the blood and baseness of our natures." "Guinea hen" cuts out love by degrading its object. "Change my humanity with a baboon": better to be an ape than to love violently. And if loving to a hysterical extreme mark a fever of the soul for which reason might be a lenitive, yet to have no capacity for strong love is to remain outside of love, or, in Iago's figure, to be anthropoid rather than human. To be able to love includes the risk of excess.

Repeatedly the Shakespearian villain is the meeting ground of rationality and animality (as in Goneril and Regan). One dramatic problem is the recognition of the animality by those from whom the rationality has concealed it, and in this process the thematic dualism of *immortal:bestial* and *soul:goat* is brought in again to remind us of the alternatives, first in Othello's demand for proof, "Or, by the worth of man's[24] eternal soul, / Thou hadst been better have been born a dog" (3.3.361-362), and then implicitly in the speculation about Desdemona's traducer, as yet unknown: Desdemona prays, "heaven pardon him!" and Emilia, "hell gnaw his bones!" (4.2.135-136). These tentative identifications become direct and final in the dying words of Roderigo, "O inhuman dog!" (5.1.62), and in the concluding lines of Lodovico, "O Spartan dog" (5.2.361). The hunter who animalizes man is finally spotted as "the dog that hunts"[25] (and, we recall, as diabolical "viper"). If such terms begin by expressing the feelings of those who use them, they end by denoting a moral reality:[26] when the issue is the slender margin between man's humanity and his animality, evil takes the form of the theory that the margin is negligible or nonexistent, and of actions that try to demolish what margin there is. The final stroke in the portraiture of the "inhuman dog" is that at the end he has no image for himself, whereas those whom he has enticed over the margin but who still have lifelines to their humanity can face (at least in part) the imaged truth: Cassio repents the "beast" in himself and Othello punishes the "dog."

In some of its forms, the evil condensed in Iago is easily recognizable outside its dramatic context. The view of evil as the animalization of the human or the destruction of spirit will easily suggest familiar aspects of criminal life, or, on a larger scale, certain political developments of modern times. Behind all this lies the subtler phenomenon, with ramifications in many aspects of life, of the tendency to interpret—without any recognition of what is going on—human conduct and action in terms of neural mechanism (e.g., propaganda, advertising, "promotion" of all kinds, much political debate and maneuvering). Still further toward the center of things we come upon the aphorism: "Twentieth-century man is the first man to think he has no soul." In Iago, Shakespeare exhibited a rather wide grasp of certain potentialities in mankind.

ESSAY ON MAN
      Iago can talk of the animal called man in a vocabulary which could admit a profound, unreductive view of humanity: *nature, soul,* and *man.* Yet his very use of these terms is tinctured by his reductive cast of mind.[27] While he is capable of using *nature* tactically in the conventional sense of a universal order which, he intimates to Othello, Desdemona has violated (3.3.229-233), he uses it more spontaneously to mean the uncontrollable quest for sexual variety (2.1.237-239), thus introducing the dramatic possibility which was to become one of the great strands in *Lear*—the clash of good and evil as the competition of different meanings for possession of the philosophic term *nature.*[28] When he says that servants who line their coats "have some soul" (1.1.54) and that a sexual revenge on Othello can alone "content my soul" (2.1.307), he reduces the soul to the despiritualized locus of self-interest and revenge.[29]

His oath, "by the faith of man, / I know my price" (1.1.10-11), might seem a random one[30] but for the fact that it occurs in a context in which he compares Cassio to a "spinster" (24), sneers at "Many a duteous and knee-crooking knave" (45), and decrees a treatment for the type, "Whip me such honest knaves!" (49). What begins to emerge is the popular picture of "mas-

THE IAGO WORLD: STYLES IN REVELATION

culinity"—confident, assertive, eyeing the main chance, playing the cards close to the vest. To this type some frailty may be admitted, of the boisterous sort into which Cassio fell; as Iago puts it, "But men are men; the best sometimes forget" and "men in rage strike those that wish them best" (2.3.241, 243). Though Iago can enjoy a deadpan defense of man as the possessor of standard virtues,[31] his main concept of "man" implies ethical qualities only when these are needed as an instrument of control. Hence his "Come, be a man!" to Roderigo (1.3.340) and his "Are you a man? Have you a soul or sense?" to Othello (3.3.374). A "man" must not only expect betrayal but must accept all a "friend" asserts, despite the claims of probability and self-preservation; i.e., Iago creates a climate in which it becomes impossible to define listening to scandal as unmanly, or wise hesitation and inquiry as manly.[32] When he goes on, "Would you would bear your fortune like a man!" (4.1.62), his words skirt a truth that Othello might heed to his profit. But Iago hardly means bearing one's allotment of suffering; rather he inculcates for "man" an intellectual acceptance of and a brute putting up with gross evil, as appears in the radical theory of vice that he voices immediately: "Good sir, be a man. / Think every bearded fellow that's but yok'd / May draw with you" (66-68). Manliness is now the cynical acceptance of universal cuckoldry. But Iago reverts to a definition more conducive to the profitable direction of Othello's emotions: being "o'erwhelmed with . . . grief" and "in spleen" do not belong to "a man" (77-78, 88-90). In inculcating this I-can-take-it endurance, Iago really assimilates manliness to his own spiritual hardness; as always, his mode of ruining men is to make them like himself.

Shakespeare more than once shows interest in the problem of manliness,[33] that is, in the seizure of the term for the rejection rather than the maturing of spirit (as by Lady Macbeth, Goneril and Regan)—a problem whose universality is attested to by the latter-day currency of the Iago definition, with its omission of principle, love, forbearance, discrimination, etc.

109

MAGIC IN THE WEB

To this man-of-the-street manhood Shakespeare does not directly counterpose a fully developed antithetical concept, but he does work competing meanings into the text. In lamenting his drunkenness, Cassio names three stages: "sensible man," "fool," "beast" (2.3.309-310). Othello defines a "man that's just" as one in whom shows of emotion are "from the heart" (3.3.122-123). Montano says of Othello: "the man commands / Like a full soldier" (2.1.35-36). After hearing Othello's story of heroic deeds, Desdemona "wish'd / That heaven had made her such a man" (1.3.163); concerning Cassio she assures Othello, "You'll never meet a more sufficient man" (3.4.91); and when Othello has begun to abuse her, she concludes sadly, with an implied rebuke to herself, "Nay, we must think men are not gods" (3.4.148). Through these passages run the ideas of man as understanding or sensitive, as having honest feelings, competence, bravery, authority, but as being, ultimately, a little lower than the angels. Emilia adds a codicil to the definition when she demands of Iago that he deny Othello's charge that he instigated the murder of Desdemona: "Disprove this villain, if thou be'st a man" (5.2.172). Iago, who called on Othello to be a man, is now summoned to the same role. Now, however, not to toughness in the world, but to an unfolding of truth in action, to a truth of speech made possible by truth of being. Emilia's words fortify an implied definition of manhood, which, if not all-inclusive, is at least morally sustaining. To that consensus several speakers contribute. Yet one evil man, by pressing a single view of manliness as a hard-skinned watchfulness and endurance, uses it successfully as one weapon in a campaign to ruin a human being.

Iago also pursues his conquest of humanity by a rich vocabulary of the base, the inhuman, and the subhuman: repeatedly we hear "knave," "thief," "barbarian," "foul," "villainous," "trash," "fool."[34] The massing of such words—their spread among characters, their disappearance and return—creates one of the rhythms of the play. In Acts 1 and 2 the Iago style of contempt and abuse contrasts with the more civil tone of inter-

THE IAGO WORLD: STYLES IN REVELATION

spersed scenes in which Iago either has a minor role or is not present and in which, though there are tensions, the participants have some formal respect for each other as men and women, so that vulgarization does not gain a foothold. In Act 3 Iago moves into a more muted style to deal with Othello, and Othello now breaks out into a storm of vilification.[35] Othello under control, Iago reverts to his coarser vocabulary of disesteem, spreading verbal degradation among Cassio, Othello, Roderigo, and Bianca even to the end.[36] When he is cornered at last by Emilia's truth, his address to her is pure Iago: "Villanous whore!" and "Filth, thou liest!" (5.2.229, 231).

In all of this, the vilifying of others by Iago and by those under his spur, there is the note of humanity fallen to its lowest potential, even of the criminality shadowed elsewhere in the speech style.[37] All this rebounds on Iago, as it has to in the moral recovery that concludes the tragic rhythm (as opposed, say, to the rhythm of the literature of simple shock and disaster). Granted that the tragic rhythm requires the self-recognition of all the characters who have erred (of Othello and Emilia, and of Cassio and even Roderigo in their ways), and that the mere discovery of the villain by others is the epiphany of mystery fiction. But Iago works through other men's capacity for self-deception, so that their uncovering of the deceiver must then also be a discovery of themselves. Eventually there falls on Iago a torrent of the terms which have been his chief instruments for thinking of mankind and debasing it: before he is known as the traducer, "wretch," "rogue," "knave," "scurvy fellow"; after he is known, "villain," again and again.[38] This is verbal abuse too, but it is purgative and denotative; it is Iago's denigration of mankind come full circle, the debaser debased, that is, known in his baseness.[39]

Of all the metaphors for baseness of spirit, perhaps the one that best sums up Iago is *slave*. Except for two early uses,[40] Shakespeare reserves the word for Iago. Three times Iago himself uses it, always with an air of superiority, always rhetorically—in a sneer at Othello (2.3.351-352), in abuse of the

111

injurer of Cassio, "O murd'rous slave!" (5.1.61), and in apparent refusal to divulge his "worst of thoughts" to Othello, "I am not bound to that all slaves are free to" (3.3.135). He asserts freedom of thought, as if proudly. But he uses his freedom like a slave. This is seen, in time. Before Emilia knows the slanderer of Desdemona, she calls him, in her first outburst, "cogging, cozening slave" (4.2.132). This image for Iago's soul comes naturally to others. The last line spoken by Montano is: "For 'tis a damned slave" (5.2.243). Othello accuses:[41] "O cursed, cursed slave!" (5.2.276). Lodovico makes the irony explicit: "O thou Othello that wert once so good, / Fall'n in the practice of a damned slave" (5.2.291-292), and he calls for torture "For this slave" (332). The agreement upon this name for Iago is almost the fulfillment of a prophecy by Brabantio, who in the first night's action spoke of what he thought to be Othello's seduction of Desdemona by magic: "For if such actions may have passage free, / Bondslaves and pagans shall our statesmen be" (1.2.98-99). It is really Iago who engages in "such actions" and who is a kind of "statesman."

"Monster" and "dog" and "viper" denote the Iago flight from humanity, "villain" and "slave" his embracing the depths. *Slave* is a capacious term: it suggests a class mentality, a minimal human range. We need, naturally, to distinguish *slave* as one involuntarily held in bonds from *slave* as an image for one nominally at liberty but having the sensibility of one bound and inwardly compliant. The initial problem with the actual slaveholder is that he does not, or is not willing to, regard slaves as human beings. The problem for the observer of a nonslave order is the many he sees who do not, or are not willing to, regard themselves as human beings[42] (hence the possibility of utopias with slave classes; no man could invent these if he did not see slavishness as a human fact). This unwillingness to accept the burden of being human means a minimizing of the morally and spiritually possible—love is no more than casual lusts; learning can be despised as "bookish"; seeing is believing; other living beings are animals to be trapped

THE IAGO WORLD: STYLES IN REVELATION

or gulls to be tricked (by the manipulator of appearances, the false physician, the obscurantist lightbearer); the unqualified value of the material makes thievery instinctive; communication takes the form of a whispering campaign, and it is matched by an inclination to noisy brawling. *Slave* incarnates most of the Iago views and habits, the evidence of what I have elsewhere called the "mass mind."

"Inward compliance" means, not utter tranquillity, but the absence of revolt against narrow bounds. The mass mind may be passive; or if it revolts, it revolts against wider bounds for other men. It tries to absolutize its own confinement. Poverty of spirit means either inertness or envy of spiritual possessions. In such a way are we to understand the "jealousy" of Iago, which is a way of responding, not to a violation of love, but, like that of Melville's Claggart, to a violation of self-love, when richer qualities of spirit come into being near one and must be seen and felt. Iago has to endure such qualities in several people, but his overt hate is focused principally on Othello. Othello can say, "I fetch my life and being / From men of royal siege" (1.2.21-22), and Gratiano inherits his "fortunes" (5.2.366). Perhaps Iago, who we know is a thief, unconsciously covets this well-being. But the situation is rather a symbolic one—the royally descended nobleman as the traditional inheritor of qualities the reverse of the slave's. Othello, Cassio says, was "great of heart" (5.2.361). Cassio is only partly right, but there is in Othello something of that quality that Iago cannot stand and that his envy must destroy. It is good material for a picture of wreckage: the nobleman yielding to the slave.

3. THE GREATEST DISCORDS

If Iago's ability to shift from a vocabulary of quiet friendliness to one of violent abuse were translated into sound, one would expect to discover him at times using a low-voiced, even whispering manner, at others—in fact, most of the time—shouting with full lung-power. We would expect the man who regards men as brutes or wants to reduce them to brutes to find roaring and howling congenial. We would expect the diabolical personality and the aggressive slave-mind to be loud disturbers of the peace. And indeed sound—volume of sound—is thoroughly exploited in the characterization of Iago.

Fittingly, the drama as a whole is crammed with sound effects. Quite aside from the raising or intensifying of voice demanded by the content of lines, there is a remarkable utilization of sound as an instrument of drama—of sound literally produced by speakers or embedded in metaphor, reported as event or made by instruments, of sound raucous or harmonious. The threatening noises of the storm—"spoke aloud," "blast," "howling winds," and so on (2.1.5-7, 68)—yield to the cries of victory and safe arrival: "News," the Turks "bang'd," "A sail" (20, 21, 51, 54), to the reassuring loudness of shots and trumpets (56, 93-94, 180). Happy Othello can now rejoice in the blasts: "May the winds blow till they have waken'd death!" (188). The clatter of rejoicing continues as the Herald reads Othello's proclamation of "sport and revels" until "the bell have told eleven" (2.2.3-12). And this carnival of Act 2 is followed by Cassio's serenade of the newly married couple in Act 3. The best of the Clown's jokes, which are all auditory, is a pun whose relevance extends beyond the context. "The General so likes your music," he tells the musicians, "that he desires you, of all loves, to make no more noise with it" (3.1.12-14). *Noise,* meaning both music and noise, comes opportunely to suggest a transition in tone that is now under way. If all the music in the play is not noise, all of it is allied with trouble.[43]

On the "night of revels" decreed by Othello, Iago sings two songs which arouse Cassio's enthusiasm (2.3.71-99). But here the songs, which ordinarily would indicate spontaneous joyousness, are fraught with calculation (the "good fellow" is "selling himself"); in the carefree safety after the destruction

THE IAGO WORLD: STYLES IN REVELATION

of the enemy, Cassio is losing control and setting up a new danger; the music of victory ends in discords. When these discords have advanced far enough, Desdemona is obsessively reminded of the song of Barbara, who was deserted by her lover (4.3.26-33), and she sings it: this music is the product and expression of the disorder in life. Barbara "died singing" the song, Desdemona says (30): the ultimate ironic resolution of disorder. The irony is echoed in Emilia's final lines after Iago has wounded her: "What did thy song bode, lady? / Hark, canst thou hear me? I will play the swan, / And die in music. 'Willow, willow, willow' " (5.2.246-248). Emilia brings herself into harmony with both her mistress and her fate: amid the discords of her last day, this much concord she can find.[44]

After seeing the tie between music and trouble, we are able to read more sharply some of the lines spoken when, the storm behind them, Othello and Desdemona happily kiss. Othello hopes that the kisses will "the greatest discords be / That e'er our hearts shall make!" (2.1.200-201). As soon as Othello makes this definition of well-being in musical terms, Iago picks up his image: "O, you are well tun'd now! / But I'll set down the pegs that make this music, / As honest as I am" (201-203). The same man who sets about bringing darkness where there is light will bring discord where there is harmony; the two metaphors collaborate very well in bringing evil out of shadowy allegory into the firm, clear lines of action in the world. Iago's words describe a universal pattern of malice that works not so much against the individual being as against an organism formed by individuals, so that the wreckage is that of a community: Iago conceives of himself as incapacitating an *instrument* which is the relationship between two people. And the instrument is love, which is what Iago most of all must knock to pieces.

After he has "set down the pegs," Desdemona must sadly admit to Cassio, "My advocation is not now in tune" (3.4.123). Yet Othello, in the very midst of his resolution to kill her, thinks literally of her musical talent: "an admirable musician! O, she will sing the savageness out of a bear!" (4.1.199-201). As in other symbolic acts, Othello throws away the means of salvation and sticks to his savageness. This very savageness has become his harmony, so that a failure in murder—Cassio alive when Desdemona is dead—is felt as a discord: "Not Cassio kill'd? Then murther's out of tune, / And sweet revenge grows harsh" (5.2.115-116).

Iago not only destroys music and creates discord; from the beginning he strives for a condition in which music cannot exist. His campaign against harmony is managed with extraordinary "sound effects"; the discord of the spirit is present as an auditory commotion, sometimes growing to a brutal violence of sound. Iago is so likely to be thought of as the sly and subtle corrupter, the purring villain, the crafty consultant in the study, that we may overlook his role as loudmouthed disturber of the peace. But we must hear also the accents of the raucous bully to appreciate the depth and variety of Shakespeare's portrait. For in Iago, as we have already seen, Shakespeare has included what Melville has excluded from the narrower and more schematic Claggart—the dimension of vulgarity—and he has thus strengthened the impression of the potency and resourcefulness of the evil agent, whose universality permits him to operate simultaneously on different levels, through a flair for *sotto voce* scheming and an appetite for clangor. From the conventions of villainy Shakespeare has constructed a brazenness of spirit capable at once of earnest and thoughtful insinuation and of noisy cutthroat rowdyism.

Iago naturally plays for public uproar, though this may not always be essential to his ends. Brabantio could be told privately and quietly of his daughter's elopement, but Iago prefers a clamorous outcry. "Call up her father, / Rouse him," he directs Roderigo, and then, referring to Othello, "Proclaim him in the streets" (1.1.67-69). Roderigo's reply begins nine lines of sheer noise:

THE IAGO WORLD: STYLES IN REVELATION

> *Rod.* Here is her father's house. I'll call aloud.
> *Iago.* Do, with like timorous accent and dire yell
> As when, by night and negligence, the fire
> Is spied in populous cities.
> *Rod.* What, ho, Brabantio! Signior Brabantio, ho!
> *Iago.* Awake! What, ho, Brabantio! Thieves! thieves!
>   thieves!
> Look to your house, your daughter, and your bags!
> Thieves! thieves!
> *Bra.* [*above*]. What is the reason of this terrible sum-
>   mons?   (74-82)

This hyperbole of sound, blaring and echoing vowels, and onomatopoeia carry through the scene—another powerful symbol of the Iago world. Iago adds, "Awake the snorting citizens with the bell" (90), and soon Brabantio himself, the typical agent of the Iago personality, has burst into noisy alarums and outcries that keep up until the truth sinks in.[45]

At the first opportunity, Iago stirs up a racket in Cyprus: he tells Roderigo that "speaking too loud" (2.1.274) is a way to upset Cassio,[46] and soon he has a fracas in motion—cries for help, actual fighting, Cassio shouting insults and threats (2.3. 148-154). Iago acts promptly to keep up the hubbub while seeming to calm things down:

> [*aside to Roderigo*] Away, I say! Go out and cry a mutiny!
>   *They fight*
>   *Exit Roderigo*
> Nay, good Lieutenant. God's will, gentlemen!
> Help, ho!—Lieutenant—sir—Montano—sir—
> Help, masters!—Here's a goodly watch indeed!
> Who's that which rings the bell? Diablo, ho!
> The town will rise. God's will, Lieutenant, hold!
> You will be sham'd for ever.   (157-163)

Then he can enjoy the noise a second time by reporting to Othello on "the crying fellow," "the clamour," "the clink and fall of swords, / And Cassio high in oath" (230-235).

Othello, whose "peace and quiet" is the target of Iago's fusillade (2.1.319), conspicuously resents the noise: his first

117

and last commands are "Silence that dreadful bell!" (2.3.175) and "silence those whom this vile brawl distracted" (256), this last, ironically, addressed to Iago. The value of this is that whereas Othello as official is on one side of the fence, Othello as a person will forget the official and soon become the noisemaker; he will plunge into a bawling speech like Iago's own. As the technique makes us go on repeating, Iago wins by finding the Iago potential in another and bringing it out into overt action. He has discovered a universal paradigm of subversion. Othello, who is by no means without sensitiveness, becomes as vulgar as Iago; Iago's success in setting down the pegs is reflected in the vociferousness of Othello's accusations of Desdemona.[47] And we need to see the relevance of Othello's goodbye to war:

> Farewell the neighing steed and the shrill trump,
> The spirit-stirring drum, th' ear-piercing fife,
> The royal banner, and all quality,
> Pride, pomp, and circumstance of glorious war!
> And O ye mortal engines whose rude throats
> Th' immortal Jove's dread clamours counterfeit,
> Farewell! (3.3.351-357)

Nearly all of Othello's images of war are auditory. It is clear that in one sense he likes the clatter of it; there is something of the man of noise in Othello. At the same time his very fondness for noise betrays another of the weak spots which make him vulnerable: he hears war only in its inspiriting sounds, not in the horror of battle noises which Shakespeare could also use dramatically.[48] Yet there is a paradox here, for the military clangor is public, produced by a group, and at least in part disciplined—in other words a symbol of order, of an organized activity that can awaken traditional virtues. There is a difference between the trump, fife, drum, and cannon, on the one hand, and, on the other, the outcries of midnight fights, the clash of private weapons, and the "dreadful bell."

Iago's provocations have worked so well that others make

THE IAGO WORLD: STYLES IN REVELATION

most of the outcry in Act 5, which is rarely free of the discordant sounds of fighting, injury, grief, and despair. Cassio, wounded, cries out repeatedly (5.1.27, 30, 37) and is echoed by Gratiano (38). Roderigo, also wounded, calls for help, and the tension by sound continues in the responses of Lodovico (40, 42, 46). Iago now enters, in abrupt stichomythic dialogue asks repeatedly about the noise (48, 49, 53), and with loud indignation finishes off Roderigo (62). Bianca's entry produces another outcry (74-77, 84). In the midst of this unbroken nerve-racking pandemonium stands Iago's ostentatious "How silent is this town!" (64). Iago reproves the town for being quiet, as if noisiness were the only acceptable evidence of alertness against crime; then in the remainder of the line—"Ho! murther! murther!"—he at once remedies the defect and again turns loose his symptomatic passion for immediate uproar, the sign of total discord.

There is contrasting quietness as the final scene opens with Desdemona asleep; then a crescendo of sound with Desdemona's desperate pleas and Othello's accusations; then a climax of silence when he smothers her. Immediately the silence of the murder is broken in on by two kinds of sound—a "noise" from Desdemona (5.2.85, 93) which is at first a stirring of life and then has the effect of coming from beyond the world (117, 122, 124-125); and an urgent series of calls from Emilia "within" that is a communication from the outside, everyday world. Emilia comes in and hears Desdemona's final words: the voice from beyond the world animates the voice in the world, and from now on the strident words are Emilia's. Her loud vehemence is forced from her, not by native disposition, for she has on the whole been mild-voiced, but by a sense of outrage: she raises the voice of justice in a world torn by the noise of planned dissension. So violence of sound is given a new meaning, as though the world were righting itself in the same terms that marked its upset. Othello tries to quiet her—"Peace, you were best" (161), but she calls out the truth:

119

"I care not for thy sword; I'll make thee known, / Though I lost twenty lives. Help! help! O, help! / The Moor hath kill'd my mistress! Murther! murther!" (165-167). This is exactly analogous to Iago's rousing the town for evil ends. But now Iago himself is among those roused, and her accusing voice is turned on him—the ironic end-product of his earlier command to "call a mutiny." The best irony in the whole supporting drama of sound occurs when Iago, whose bent is to call for noise, must reverse himself: "Zounds, hold your peace!" (219), but now fails where he once succeeded. Emilia comes back: "'Twill out, 'twill out! I peace? / No, I will speak as liberal as the North" (219-220). She tells the story, is fatally wounded by Iago, and dies in song—the symbolic ending of Iago's game of setting down the pegs that make the music. The ending of his game is a spiritual failure, for the music that Iago hated was the music of love; Emilia acted in love and sings in love—the kind of victory that can come at the center of the tragic catastrophe.[49]

Iago, on the edge of being questioned about his motives, speaks his final lines: "Demand me nothing. What you know, you know. / From this time forth I never will speak word" (303-304). So the man who opened the play with a torrent of words, who reveled in loudness, and who was always voluble, shuts himself up in absolute silence: the demonic closure is the logical end of the man who would not wear his heart on his sleeve. If Iago's oral violence, his predilection for noise, shows, as I suggest, a vulgar side of him, the style of the street brawler and troublemaker, his resolve never to speak again exhibits an ultimate underworld toughness.[50] (Only the man able to will silence could have so well pretended unwillingness to speak earlier.) In his multidimensional portrait, Shakespeare gives us not only the sly plotter and the coarse rioter, either of whom might be fundamentally soft and self-pitying, but also now a steely-cored being who registers an advanced stage of dehumanization, the ultimate fanaticism of pride.[51] Shake-

THE IAGO WORLD: STYLES IN REVELATION

speare continued to be aware of this moral possibility, for he gave a similar turn to Goneril, whose final words are, "Ask me not what I know" (*Lear*, 5.3.160). In dramatizing these flights from the general world of intercourse, Shakespeare imaginatively identifies a type of personality which is familiar enough in our own day—that of the criminal or gangster who steadfastly refuses to "talk." In Iago there is still another mark of the type: he has killed Emilia, the confederate who has "betrayed" him to the law. Indeed, he goes beyond the isolation from the community that we observe in the criminal, who has his own subcommunity or enclave (Shakespeare was to trace the workings of this, as well as its disintegration, in the Goneril-Regan-Edmund tie-up). However, our business is not to find new epithets for Iago but to discover whatever analogues are useful in unfolding the multiplicities of his character. It is less important to say that Iago has marks of a "criminal type" than to see that in making him freeze up in absolute self-reliance Shakespeare has identified a basis of evil which may or may not appear in all criminal conduct—the hardness of spirit which closes upon itself and excludes every possibility of grace.[52] This is the final summation of a Iago whom we have seen—and have yet to see—in many other aspects.

The irony of Iago's hardness is that it looks not unlike steadfastness, courage, strength, for speaking no word also means being tight-lipped. In fact, he is manifesting an impermeability to torture of which few could be sure. It is the deepest of the numerous resources[53] which Shakespeare has given to the character in whom he explores the reality of evil.

4. CHAOS: THE WAR AT HOME

Iago's climactic strategy, one that embraces all his ways of dehumanizing men and is hardly separable from his passionate evocation of sheer noise, is his attack on peace and justice, in a word, his quest for the chaos that Othello unwittingly foretells. Chaos is dramatically realized[54] by the darkness or half-light or false light in which major parts of the action occur; by the masquerading of the killer as the healer; by the regression of men into animals; by the fighting and killing; by the growth of discord that is a fact of both sense and spirit. We have seen Iago's hand everywhere in this. The attack on peace and justice is brought home to us especially by the constant language of injury, punishment, and torture—of activities that are close to the heart of the Iago world. Iago does violence to human beings by the figures he applies to them, by direct verbal assaults, and by physical injury.

The poetry of damage and destruction gains invisible support from images of the body, the physical substance where passion is made manifest. Hearts and eyes are everywhere in the lines. Hands are given in gesture and read in error, real or deliberate. Parts of the body are specified to enhance the note of sexuality. To express a diversity of feeling, characters name noses, stomachs, lips, bare feet, heads hung at one side. Bodily images—of tongues, noses—may appear in a series of passages, tending to form a sequence, vibrant with subtle but persistent interconnections. Even figurative usage may keep the flesh vividly before us.* The physiological concreteness of Renaissance poetry is everywhere evident. The constant naming of parts of the body creates a less than conscious but unbroken awareness of the physical being which suffers physical injury and symbolizes psychic injury. We are not told that "the injury was painful"; rather we see it being inflicted by or on a body that in many ways is kept present before us. The drama is full of actual fighting, wounding, and murder, and, along with these, of the language of animosity, damage, injury, and torture. After a severe storm and a serious threat of war, the principals are safe on an island, their world nominally at peace; yet there is a war within peace—a representative Shake-

* See Appendix B for the evidence on which this paragraph is based.

THE IAGO WORLD: STYLES IN REVELATION

spearian paradox that is one of the ways of dramatizing the active presence of evil.

The "war at home" proceeds first intermittently from the beginning, after a while steadily. Under Iago's secret prodding, weapons are drawn in the opening scene (1.1.182; 1.2.57); Iago's hopes for truncheon blows and a "mutiny" on Cyprus (2.1.280-282) are realized when Cassio comes in "driving in" Roderigo, threatening to "beat the knave into a twiggen bottle" and to "knock" Montano "o'er the mazzard," and wounding him, so that, as Othello and others enter "with weapons," Montano is just able to say, "I am hurt to the death" (2.3.149-164; cf. 3.1.48).

At the end Iago stage-manages another fight: he encourages Roderigo to "knock out" Cassio's brains (4.2.236) and commands him, "Wear thy good rapier bare, and put it home" (5.1.2). Roderigo resolves, "He dies!" while Iago coolly reflects, "Now whether he kill Cassio, / Or Cassio him, or each do kill the other, / Every way makes my game" (10-14). Violence appears in two modes: Iago's distant and mathematical "No, he must die" is followed by Roderigo's quick rush, "Villain, thou diest!" and a "thrust" (22-24). This "battle" is a heightening of the second, as the second was of the first (at Venice): here Iago is not only prompter but active swordsman. Cassio wounds Roderigo, Iago slashes Cassio in the leg, and then finishes off Roderigo. The air constantly echoes with the language of injury and death: "maim'd for ever," "Murther! murther!" "bleed to death," "My leg is cut in two," "thus have mangled you," "Alas, he faints," "this injury."[55] Iago is at the center of this chaos vividly and ceaselessly forced upon our consciousness.

Suddenly we shift to the quiet decency of Desdemona's bedroom, but even in negations the words of Othello, responding to Iago's onslaught on peace, link this moment with the murderous outbreaks before and after: "shed her blood," "scar that whiter skin," "must die," "put out thy light," "pluck'd the

123

rose," "will kill thee," "strikes where it doth love" (5.2.3-22). Death is pre-experienced in the words: *kill* and its cognates are used again and again, the chief supports of the dialogue.[56] Othello speaks of Cassio's death, smothers Desdemona; the sense of torment goes on in his "I would not have thee linger in thy pain" (87). The murders of Scenes 1 and 2 are brought together in one effect by the succeeding annunciations—of Roderigo's death by Emilia, of Desdemona's by herself; then there is another protracted discordant run of *murder* and *kill*.[57] Emilia takes over, fiercely accusing, facing Othello's threat of injury (162-163), frantically proclaiming the murder, "I care not for thy sword; I'll make thee known / Though I lost twenty lives. Help! help! O, help! / The Moor hath kill'd my mistress! Murther! murther!" (165-167), always using words of violence: "lay their murders on your neck," "here lies murthered," "have set the murther on," "kill myself," "kill'd the sweetest innocent" (169-199). Othello points to the body, holds up "these hands" that killed her (201-202); Brabantio's death is mentioned (205-206); Emilia's handkerchief story brings on the third episode of violence in Act 5 (the fifth in the play)—Iago's threat with words and sword, Othello's attack on Iago, Iago's fatal wounding of Emilia, all these with continuing terms of death (233-238).

The point is not only the series of blows and killings, but the almost incredibly drawn-out verbal repercussions of these that maintain an extraordinary atmosphere of violence.[58] With his flair for injury and violence,[59] Iago dominates the verbal as well as the actional drama of the first two acts: "Whip me such honest knaves!" "Plague him with flies," "I do hate him as I do hell pains," "Your heart is burst," "gall him with some check."[60] He will have Cassio "on the hip" (2.1.314)—the wrestler about to be thrown. In reporting on the Roderigo-Cassio-Montano fight, he has opportunity for a verbal savoring of the domestic wars: "Swords out, and tilting one at other's breast," "crying out for help," "determin'd sword," "clink and

THE IAGO WORLD: STYLES IN REVELATION

fall of swords," "blow and thrust," "men in rage strike those that wish them best" (2.3.183, 226-243). Iago even uses pseudo injury: "And would in glorious action I had lost / Those legs that brought me to a part of it!" (2.3.186-187)—a universal pattern of pretentious regret (the verbal mimesis of suffering) which for Iago gratifies both his histrionic inclination and his deep-lying attraction to injury.[61]

The "Iago principle" which Iago arouses to action in Othello appears in his changed ideas and in a new brutality of style; we see him mastering violence, then being upset by it, then plunging into it.[62] He stops the near fight with Brabantio's party by his finely controlled command, "Keep up your bright swords, for the dew will rust them" (1.2.59), in which, while he may scorn the unused (bright) swords, he also shows self-possession: only dew, not blood, will rust these swords. He is courteous: "Good signior, you shall more command with years / Than with your weapons" (60-61). The very words that name violence subdue it. Not so in Act 2, when he is over-vehement in rebuking the brawlers, threatens death to whoever "stirs next to carve for his own rage" (2.3.173), admits his own passion (206ff.), and angrily condemns the "private and domestic quarrel" carried on "in a town of war" (213-215). For us, the antithesis ironically undercuts his expectation: the "war" is no longer real, but the "quarrel" is becoming destructive and menacing.

As Othello forgets the commander in himself (another irony) and grants his "quarrel" priority over all other claims, he takes over the language of pain and injury that in Acts 1 and 2 was Iago's: "pain upon my forehead," "hast set me on the rack," "If thou dost . . . torture me," "If there be cords, or knives, / Poison, or fire, or suffocating streams, / I'll not endure it."[63] From embracing his own wound, "Swell, bosom, with thy fraught, / For 'tis of aspics' tongues!" he turns to images of punishing the culprits: "tear her all to pieces," "swift means of death," "be hang'd for his labour," "that nose of yours . . .

that dog I shall throw't to," "How shall I murther him," "nine years a-killing," "chop her into messes."[64]

In one minor aspect the language of violence accompanies the turn toward justice at the end: Emilia so uses it,[65] and Othello calls for punishment, "Whip me, ye devils," etc. (5.2. 277ff.). Iago would "Whip . . . honest knaves" (1.1.49), Emilia would "lash . . . rascals" (4.2.143), Othello would have himself whipped—a series that marks the developing focus of tragedy. Yet Othello is never far from swordplay (5.2.244, 252-266), for his impulse to blame and strike is strong; he wounds Iago before turning to the summary violence of suicide. Gratiano's comment, "All that's spoke is marr'd" (357), maintains the tone of the Iago world without rest or peace.

Besides, Iago remains alive and intransigent. In other major tragedies, active evil is out of the way by now, so that pacification, if only in the mode of weariness, can begin. Here, the air is still heavy with the unresolved; at least a susurrus of violence hangs about the diminished community; this finale challenges the conventional expectation by substituting, for a tentative ordering of the chosen segment of human life and action, a mimesis of the current[66] of life, a mimesis which it accomplishes by letting the figure of evil live on, not now inflicting injury but keeping its spirit alive.[67] Montano orders, "Let him not pass, / But kill him rather" (241-242); Othello tries to kill him—a failure of violence which ironically is also a failure to bring such peace as the context can afford. Iago squeezes out a little more victory by noting, with a modeled placidity that jeers obliquely at the general disquiet, "I bleed, sir, but not kill'd" (288). In the personal triumph we see the strength of evil in man; as a version of Everyman, Iago endures.[68] For his toughness the institutional therapy is rack and screw: "Torments," "cunning cruelty," "the torture—O, enforce it!" (305, 333, 369). Ahead lies the desperate grapple, by machine laid on flesh, with demonic hardness of spirit. Peace is only partial. There are remainders of passion not

THE IAGO WORLD: STYLES IN REVELATION

spent, as with those storms that seem to clear the air but leave unconsumed cloud banks from which some lingering tumult will spring. In the widespread use of language of injury and violence, Desdemona has almost no share: true, she pleads not to be killed, and notes the distortions in Othello, and briefly her own pain, but since she escapes both the self-pitying and the accusatory, she exists apart from the idea and the mood of damage and death-dealing which at some time overtake all the others.[69] The stylistic exception is a mark of her livingness, a measure of what is requisite for life. In the pervasiveness of the brutal style to which all the others are at one time or another subject, we sense the encroachment of death upon life. In this symbolization of chaos there may be some special meaning for an age fed upon a daily, indeed almost a continuous, contemplation of violence in speech and deed.

And at the end Iago, the concentration of Everyman's malice, lives. It is, rightly, not assured that torture will lead to the death of the original torturer. Whatever the outcome, the very dealing with him will have its price in human resources already strained. It is through our sense of the still unended psychic cost that Shakespeare gives a singular final emphasis to the unresting destructiveness begot by the primitive and the calculating in fell conjunction.

THE BLOODY BOOK OF LAW

Iago is a "man of blood": he likes the word *bloody;*[70] he enjoys the ambiguous oath to carry out any command of Othello's, "What bloody business ever" (3.3. 469); he conquers by shedding the blood of others and triumphs even in shedding his own;[71] but above all he finds in blood a symbol for the purely physical being which for him contains all reality: "the blood and baseness of our natures," "lust of the blood," "when the blood is made dull with the act of sport" (1.3.332, 339; 2.1.230). So he concocts a "poison"

MAGIC IN THE WEB

to "act upon the blood" of Othello (3.3.328), so successfully that Lodovico wonders whether the letters from Venice "did . . . work upon his blood" (4.1.286). Once again the verbal drama reveals Iago finding the Iago principle in Othello and turning it loose.[72] As early as the first night fight in Cyprus, Othello admits, "My blood begins my safer guides to rule" (2.3.205). It is the first sign that Othello can blow up, and an artistically conceived one: his own blood, the Iago in him, stirs him up, leads him on to bloody business. Othello is to become obsessed with blood:

O, blood, blood, blood! (3.3.451)

Even so my bloody thoughts, with violent pace,
Shall ne'er look back, ne'er ebb to humble love. (3.3.457-458)

I will be found most cunning in my patience;
But (dost thou hear?) most bloody. (4.1.91-92)

Thy bed, lust-stain'd, shall with lust's blood be spotted.
(5.1.36)

Though shortly he makes a technical revision of plans, deciding that he'll "not shed her blood" (5.2.3)—an instance of the quasi-humane aestheticism by which the violent man may garnish or ostensibly transform his violence—Desdemona recognizes that he suffers from "Some bloody passion" (5.2.44).

Lodovico's words of summation after Othello's shedding of his own blood—"O bloody period!" (5.2.357)—take us, in the manner of an accomplished finale, back to an earlier phase of the blood motif. For Othello has exacted of himself the death penalty that was first named by the Duke to reassure Brabantio —"the bloody book of law" (1.3.67). "Blood" and "justice" may, then, be reconciled: the reconciliation of the Iago world and the human community. In acting against Desdemona and then against himself, Othello has adopted in part the style of the judge; yet we are entirely unable to forget the obsessive bloodiness of his thoughts. Does he then reconcile blood and justice? Or which prevails in him—the Iago side (blood) or

THE IAGO WORLD: STYLES IN REVELATION

the sense of community (justice)? With the Duke, law or the idea of justice is prior: is it thus with Othello? So we are led naturally from the theme of violence to the theme of justice. And thus at last Iago yields the primacy in this discussion to Othello, and we pass from the nature of the evil man's evil to the nature of the good man's response to that evil.

Nearly everybody whose mind is entered, however fleetingly, by the thought of justice speaks confidently as if justice were on his side—Iago, Roderigo, Brabantio.[73] Othello insists near the end, "I did proceed upon just grounds"[74] (5.2.138). Desdemona is the exception: she alone is more concerned to be just than to assert her justice.[75] Yet in some sort all may be said to want justice as an ally. While they all talk justice, Shakespeare elaborately pictures justice in action, so that in one sense the play advances by a series of scenes analogous to trials or court actions.

Othello begins where some plays end, with a formal legal hearing that clears things up. From the time when Brabantio first calls for court action (1.2.85-87), a series of legal terms makes us anticipate a trial.[76] The Duke hears the case; Brabantio makes an accusation; the defendant pleads not guilty and promises a full statement; Brabantio charges witchcraft. The Duke rules: "To vouch this is no proof, / Without more certain and more overt test" (1.3.106-107)—a structurally important statement, for in comparable scenes later we are to hear a great deal about "proof." Finally Othello not only takes the stand in his own defense[77] but summons Desdemona as a defense witness: if she testifies adversely, he says with assurance, not only demote me "but let your sentence / Even fall upon my life" (119-120). Their evidence is conclusive; the court is convinced; Brabantio withdraws his charge.

The point is not only that Iago's initial violence and provocation have failed, but that the organized, public processes of justice have succeeded. Since the participants, and Othello in particular, have been temperate and sensible, we see a world,

129

MAGIC IN THE WEB

not of corrupt institutions calling for romantic revolt, but of affirmative order, one that might be expected to be solidly resistant to challenge or threat. So we have some measure for later actions that have the form of justice, and, in the stability which is the target for the enemy of peace and justice to shoot at, a clue to his extraordinary success.

Othello moves from the justiciary center of the state to an island outpost; and from reliance upon an adequate court to a position of authority upon which others rely for justice. The successful defendant against unjust charges becomes the judge who must determine the justice of charges. The "worthy governor," as Montano calls him (2.1.30), will soon face the renewed efforts of the original *agent provocateur,* who plans a "mutiny" (2.1.282; 2.3.157). As official in charge, Othello exhibits less poise than the Duke during the much greater nocturnal alarums of Act 1. (We are reminded of the earlier scene by Othello's repetition of "What's the matter . . . ?"—2.3.176, 193—the same words the Duke earlier addressed to Brabantio—1.3.58.) Though the total situation in Cyprus is less complex and tense, Othello is irritable from the start, sharp in command, reproof, and even threat (2.3.169ff.). He seems temporarily cooler as he seeks evidence of Montano (190ff.) but then again rises into warmth of feeling and an exclamatory and condemnatory manner (204ff.). He knows something of himself—"And passion . . . / Assays to lead the way" (206-207) —but does not replot his course to allow for emotional drift. If the hearing was bound to result in some disciplinary action against Cassio, nevertheless we observe that the court has been somewhat intemperate and that the "judge" has become the creature of a single witness,[78] a witness who is to testify again a little later. The contrast with the Duke's hearing in Venice sharpens for us the deterioration in the administering of justice. The public hearing in Cyprus is thus intermediate: it logically precedes the episodes in which as "judge" Othello is still more passionate and more unjust. Iago's attack on justice

THE IAGO WORLD: STYLES IN REVELATION

is the more devastating in its effect because we can see his plots making headway through actions that are like legal procedures.

The next "hearing" is built up to by the legal metaphor in which the preparatory actions are couched. Iago foresees the trouble that can be created as Desdemona "pleads" and "repeals" (2.3.361-363) Cassio's case, which she takes with enthusiasm:

> I'll intermingle everything he does
> With Cassio's suit. Therefore be merry, Cassio,
> For thy solicitor shall rather die
> Than give thy cause away.   (3.3.25-28)

Her continuing use of legal terms[79] more firmly establishes her role as attorney, and it is this very role that contributes to her being placed beside her client as a defendant before the same court.

Othello is clearly sitting in judgment on Desdemona. Emotional as we have seen him to be, he still aspires (and his aspiration has its own complexity) to the judicial, but his occasional gestures in this direction, by reminding us of more competent hearings, underscore the breakdown that is going on. Othello makes the philosophic error of wanting to "see" matters that cannot be seen or be resolved by what is seen; yet he also wants to qualify the private intuition by methods which will bestow a public reliability upon actions at once private and official. The deception scene has many resemblances to the legal hearing, with Othello playing now the judge, now the jury, to Iago's prosecuting attorney.[80] As soon as the suspicion planted by Iago[81] begins to take root, Othello resolves to "prove" (3.3.190-191; cf. 196, 260). Now at this point he has one of his moments of illumination: "If she be false, O, then heaven mocks itself! / I'll not believe't" (278-279). Here is his cue: to give up legalism entirely and to rely on belief, by which, though he lost something, he would at least save

131

his humanity; or, if he will continue to act as a court, to take some account of probability. Instead we see him acting in terms of a familiar human paradox: though he is incurably irrational, he wants the reassuring illusion of acting only in terms of rational formulations (as Lear does also). His emotions make him in effect rule the defendant guilty, and then he tries to validate his feelings and actions by a rational proof which makes them obligatory. As he keeps talking about "proof" (360, 364, 365, 386), Iago offers circumstantial evidence—"strong circumstances / Which lead directly to the door of truth" (406-407), but Othello demands "a living reason" (409), i.e., direct evidence. Iago replies, "I do not like the office" but promises to "go on" since "I am enter'd in this cause so far" (410-412). At this point he can carry on the "case" only by perjury, and he comes up first with the story of Cassio's dream (413ff.), then with the story of Cassio's wiping his beard with the handkerchief (433ff.). These so perturb the court that prosecutor Iago can now venture on the slickest trick of the proceeding, namely, treating these stories as merely corroboratory evidence of a case already proved:

> And this may help to thicken other proofs
> That do demonstrate thinly.   (430-431)
>
> If it be that, or any that was hers,
> It speaks against her, with the other proofs.   (440-441)

There are no "other proofs." But the court is now in a fury, calling for "black vengeance, from the hollow hell" and "tyrannous hate" and swearing that "bloody thoughts, with violent pace" shall follow through to "wide revenge" (442-459). The trial analogy, loose as it is, helps determine the scene: the climax of disorder is violence, and cries for revenge, from the bench—and these sacramentalized by ritualistic kneeling (by both Othello and Iago), Othello's "sacred vow" "by yond marble heaven" (460-461), and Iago's formal oath of duty, "Witness, you ever-burning lights above" (463). The medley of

THE IAGO WORLD: STYLES IN REVELATION

roles infuses the words Othello speaks; in his speech of consecration (453ff.) the "icy current" and the "bloody thoughts" are respectively the facade and the reality of his incompatible aspiration and passion. He cannot hold them together; the effort at "poetic" integration fails, and the judge breaks down into abuse: "Damn her, lewd minx!" (475)—this as he sentences Cassio to death (472-473) and "withdraws" from the bench to ponder a suitable sentence of death against the "fair devil" (476-478).

The romantic view of life is reversed: this private court dispenses a justice catastrophically different from that of the public, institutional hearing in Act 1. Iago measures the extent of his victory when he rejoices that the "guiltless" suffer (4.1.48), for the social symbol of radical destructiveness is the corruption of justice. Othello has now virtually lost sight of his wavering impulse to be official and plunges into the bitter and the bloody. After he is given the maddening "evidence" of Iago's manipulated interview with Cassio, he roars violently: "she shall not live," "Hang her!" (4.1.192, 198). The enormity of his decision against Desdemona is that right now there is present to his mind another kind of evidence which is of great legal importance—the evidence of character. Even while damning her to Iago he is able himself to be a character witness—to recall her sweetness, her skills, her "plenteous wit and invention," her gentleness of disposition (4.1.194-201). His own phrase, "I do but say what she is" (198), is the key to his destruction: just as earlier, when he said "I'll not believe't" (3.3.279) and believed, so now he can throw out a truth which he imaginatively possesses in favor of a "fact" which he lets himself think is "proved." After he makes so substantive an error, which is philosophic as well as legal, there is a fine incongruity in his momentary resumption of the bench to complete the unfinished business of the sentencing. Iago suggests strangling her in the bed "she hath contaminated" (221) and Othello accepts with delight: "The justice of it pleases" (222);

133

i.e., what is "just" or "appropriate" is legal justice. Now, having sentenced the defendant and publicly struck and disgraced her, he reverts to an earlier legal stage, investigation: at Emilia he fires six staccato questions and statements, accusing, demanding proof of what he has already accepted as proved (4.2.1-11). In this irregular order of sentence before examination we see the plaintiff-judge unconsciously masking his complex feelings (hate, self-pity, even some self-punishment) in an appearance of procedural thoroughness which is never present in fact. He orders Emilia to summon the next witness, Desdemona. He interrogates her, puts her on oath ("Come, swear it, damn thyself"; "Swear thou art honest"—4.2.35, 38), sneers at her request to know the charges[82] ("What committed? / Committed?" "What committed?" "What committed?"—70, 72, 73, 76, 80), pities himself, and accuses her. The defendant has been found guilty in advance and is being reviled by the plaintiff, but it is precisely the tincture of the judicial in the words and in the procedure that maximizes the horror of the situation: private violence made official. Further, Shakespeare has so managed the scene—has so discerned the characteristics of the type—that it might be modeled on quasi-judicial procedures of many centuries later: the hearing, often before one man, of a witness in effect prejudged to be guilty on the findings of an investigator and therefore subject to abuse by the "judge" acting representatively as the injured party.

The drama has still to move on to an ultimate vision of disorder—the chaos that is reached after successive phases of intensifying violence and deteriorating justice. The drama may be said to begin with a successful formal court action, to advance by implicitly contrasting this with less adequate court actions that gradually shrink into simulations of the judicial, and to complete the series by a contrast of the quasi-courtly with brute action that supersedes the judicial. Justice: the imitation of justice: the negation of justice. Private passion controlled by public form: private passion endeavoring to find

THE IAGO WORLD: STYLES IN REVELATION

public form: private passion triumphant over public form. In these triads the second term shows a corruption of the first and yet saves something that in the third is lost entirely: in the unveneered brutishness of Iago (the decayed man of reason) the disintegration of order is carried further than in Othello's self-delusive efforts to justify violence. The middle term is the ambiguous one, the one of greatest poetic possibility; if we are always to grasp its ambivalence, we must always keep in mind both the Duke's court and Iago's annihilation of the court. This middle term is the action of Othello as a man of authority, from the judgment of Cassio to the murder of Desdemona. The murder scene is complicated by the efforts to create a facade of justice, the violence of the action by the desire to transcend violence, the barbarousness of the agent by a singular aspiration to humanity. And in all this we must remember, and we cannot overemphasize, that Othello had one sure way of ultimately transcending violence—by finding in his love the scope of charity.

The last act means, then, a profound exploration of Othello's personality. But this exploration has been prepared for long in advance, and we cannot read it satisfactorily without looking at the whole portrait of Othello in action and, too, at the image of himself which he entertains and aspires to use as a moral compass.

What we have examined so far is the various ways in which evil is made manifest—its modes of operation and its impact. Though this way of looking at *Othello* has for some chapters put Iago into the limelight, we have also seen contrasts and resemblances between him and others. In Othello himself we have seen: his confusion in judging and theorizing about appearances; his faulty seeing and his falling for "Seeing is believing"; his illusion that he has the light and that he can diagnose Desdemona; his picking up a half-baked idea of manliness; his passion to manipulate time; his falling into animal imagery that dehumanizes others, into the whole vocabulary

135

of abuse, into a brutal noisiness, into violence of speech and deed—yielding to "blood," and yet trying to be judicial. These devices of verbal and actional drama give a multifold description of the hero's tragic course. We can now look at his personality and see if we can find inner reasons for that course.

ACTION AND LANGUAGE

Othello

The problem of character presented by Othello's collapse before Iago's machinations in 3.3 is handled in three main ways. According to one view, the problem is insoluble: Othello believes Iago only "by virtue of the convention of the calumniator credited."[1] Among the analysts of character, the older tradition is that Othello is the victim of Iago and remains pretty much the "noble Moor" throughout; he is guilty only of being too innocent or foolish or simple or trusting or of losing his usual self-control.[2] According to the other main approach through character, Othello is not the "noble Moor" at all but has serious defects of character which cause his downfall[3]—defects such as habitual flight from reality[4] and as pride.[5] Resultant protests against the deidealizing of Othello[6] may in part be due to the fact that, after the long dominance of the Bradley view of Othello, the discoverers of his flaws tend to take his virtues for granted—courage, desire to do and be right, normal inclination to be open, the impalpable elements summarized as "charm," relative freedom from pettiness and duplicity. But these virtues may coexist with serious defects. I began my study holding the orthodox view of Othello's "nobility" but found the impression gradually modified by repeated readings of the lines. There is something in Othello's own rhetoric, I suspect, which can simultaneously support conflict-

CHAPTER 5

ing impressions of his personality. The sweep, the color, the resonance, the spontaneity, the frequent exoticism of the images —all this magniloquence suggests largeness and freedom of spirit, and it is at first easy to forget that self-deception, limitedness of feeling, and egotism may also inhabit this verbal expansiveness. If there is this ambiguity in the style, then the style is a fitting instrument for a complexity of character that we may subconsciously resist because of the obvious elements that have nourished the long tradition of calling Othello "simple." There is no master term for Othello—"nobility" or "simplicity" or "passionateness under control" or "pride" or "romantic idealism." In following his role one needs a number of different terms, as different facets of his personality come to the fore, or as one is attempting to name a moral quality or a secret impulse. In trying to trace a kind of weakness that leads to the quest for what, though neither satisfied with the term nor able to hit on an equally compact alternative, I call "positional assurance," I also use such terms as "puritanism," "stoicism," "self-love," "self-deception," and so on. Whatever the cost in uniformity, some such plurality of terms cannot be avoided, I believe, without imposing schematic readings.[7]

The arguments that Othello's yielding to Iago in 3.3 is explicable in terms of his character[8] usually turn on such points as these: Iago's irresistible technique and his long reputation for honesty; Othello's fine but simple "extrovert" nature, suited for action but not for perception and reflection; his deeply passionate nature, at best held under precarious control; his submerged sexuality, likely under stress to break out in violence; his unfamiliarity with Venetian ways; a "racial" self-consciousness, inferiority, and perhaps savagery. It is possible that Othello's characteristic quest for assurance of position may reflect in part an ethnic anxiety; once or twice he speaks in terms that may imply an alien's special doubt.[9] Yet such passages are few and incidental; the ideas do not come up again and again as they would do if they were naggingly present in his mind. Though Iago takes some trouble to work on Othello as an outsider and to arouse the suspicions of the foreigner,[10] Othello's passions simply do not mature according to this mold. He thinks of himself as the victim of women generally ("these delicate creatures . . . / . . . their appetites"—3.3.269-270), as the victim of marriage in high life (273ff.), as the "horned man" (4.1.63), rather than, let us say, as the "despised Moor." (Cf. Shylock's awareness of being a Jew.) Shakespeare strives, not for a particularist vulnerability and rancor, but for the human essence, and Othello's scope is lost sight of if we can understand him only by racial psychology.[11] *Othello* is not a treatise on mixed marriages, but a drama about Everyman, with the modifications necessary to individualize him. Othello's Moorishness, if it is anything more than a neutral heritage from Cinthio, is less a psychological or moral factor than a symbol of characteristic human problems currently denoted by such overly familiar terms as "insecurity" and "rejection." Moorishness, in this sense, is one of the ills that flesh is heir to.

The breakdown of Othello from Act 3 on is a collapse of certain props of assurance—the assurance of being loved and the assurance of position—upon which his personality rests and which, as we see long before then, he needs after the manner of a habit. When he murders Desdemona he no longer has the assurance of being loved, but, under the pressure of an alert instinct, he has provided himself with a new "positional assurance." This experience appears to me to be representative rather than idiosyncratic. We now seek the elements of personality that form the experience.

Othello has maximum poise when he can consciously rest on the assurance of being loved and the assurance of position. His confidence in Desdemona's love in Acts 1 and 2 and part of 3 penetrates all the dialogue that is not restricted to state business. When Iago's first attack is made in Act 1, Othello is explicit about the strength of his position: his "services [to] . . . the signiory"; his descent "From men of royal siege"; his "demerits" (i.e., merits) which "May speak (unbonneted) to as proud a fortune / As this that I have reach'd" (1.2.18-24).

He can face the court secure in "My parts, my title, and my perfect soul" (31). He needs no "prompter" (84) to tell him to fight or not. In the double assurance of the warrior depended on by the state and loved by a beautiful aristocrat Othello can acknowledge easily one area in which, though with only partial accuracy,[12] he sees his position as inferior: he is not a polished speaker (1.3.81, 86); yet he is not without sensitiveness in this, for he reverts to it later as one of the possible causes of Desdemona's defection (3.3.264). But the general tone is of "complacency" and "naive self-esteem."[13]

The hours of greatest assurance permit some glimpse of regions where under increased stress we might expect cracks to appear and to intensify the need for assurance. Take "the story of my life" as he says he rolled it off for Brabantio and Desdemona: "disastrous chances," "moving accidents," "hairbreadth scapes," "sold to slavery," "redemption," "travel's history," "anters vast and deserts idle," "hills whose heads touch heaven," "Cannibals," "Anthropophagi, and men whose heads / Do grow beneath their shoulders" (1.3.134-145). Experience has been turned to adventure, glamor, romance; the narrator is not the lessoned alumnus of suffering whose courage has been tempered into valor for the subtler and more nagging challenges of peace; in this picturesque and romantic account we cannot miss the immaturity[14]—an immaturity the more arresting in view of Othello's repeated references to his being no longer young (1.3.264; 3.3.265-266). Further, Othello has a histrionic side (in this there is an interesting affinity between him and Iago): not only does he have "a habit of approving self-dramatization,"[15] but he notes the impact of his role on the audience, of which he is candidly aware, and, letting the actor direct the historian, plays in part for effect. After he "found good means" (1.3.151) to get Desdemona to ask him for a complete personal history, his tale of the "distressful stroke" drew both tears and sighs (156-159). This is not to say that he had no feeling for Desdemona, but he singularly reminds us of the actor falling in love with his audience: he

OTHELLO: ACTION AND LANGUAGE

played his "dangers," she loved him "for" them, "And I lov'd her that she did pity them" (168). It is not to charge emotional chicanery to note that when the lover can define his emotion as a product of the loved one's pity for him, there is some failure of response to, and potentially of acceptance of, the whole being of the loved one, and there is a hint of latent self-pity or of aptitude for it.

If it is correct to see in Othello's history of his romance signs of immaturity, histrionism, and incompleteness of love, we have early in the play some clues to the ripening of his disaster and, as well, to his almost instinctive quest for assurance of position. Further, the new husband, routed out of the bridal bed, is almost too prompt to declare his fealty to "the flinty and steel couch of war" (1.3.231). He glosses: "I do agnize / A natural and prompt alacrity / I find in hardness" (232-234). This is the dutiful soldier, true; also, however, Othello pleasurably observing himself as the dutiful soldier. But more important than that is the physical stoicism of the romantic personality that has found a military outlet—a stoicism that can develop into toughness and even ruthlessness (akin to the hardness of spirit of the good man gone self-righteous, a recurrent theme of George Eliot's). This conscious muscular dutifulness becomes rather conspicuous when Othello promises the Senators that Desdemona's presence at Cyprus will not interfere with their "business" and his own "business" (268, 272). Under the military circumstances we cannot quarrel with the doctrine of "business first." But his style is very emphatic, and it is hardly a compliment to Desdemona to equate the substance of their married love with "light-wing'd toys / Of feather'd Cupid" (269-270). Despite flamboyance, there is a military heaviness in all this. Whatever Othello's military virtues, they hardly equip him for a demanding intimate personal relationship.

To point out that Othello has a tough side, and is somewhat graceless in his military virtue, and deceives himself, in addition to having some staginess of style and to being, in his love and his assessment of his own past experiences, less mature

141

than his years would warrant, is to try to identify the kinds of flaw that will make understandable the destruction of this tragic hero. Through these early windows we may see aspects of the inner Othello that will break out later: a kind of puritan hardness (the note of asceticism and of moral self-confidence) which can beget condemnatory rigor, and enough immaturity and self-deceptiveness to undermine the possibility of a modifying self-criticism: all of this a version of Everyman's pride. Now he has the assurance of being loved (which is not the assurance of "being loved and loving"; what he lacks without knowing it, is the assurance of giving). He has positional assurance: a sense of status, of propriety of attitude. And finally he is bent on protecting a position: the commandership in chief will sustain no irruption from the joys of private life.

After the storm Othello, the pleased recipient of an assuring love from the Cyprians, "I have found great love amongst them" (2.1.207), declares public festivities, in rejoicing for the Turkish disaster and in "celebration of his nuptial" (2.2.7-8). This glorification of his public and private good fortune, which is in the tradition of "V-day" revelry but also betrays a secret impulse to add public support to his assurance of position, is an ironic choice, since it provides opportunity for Iago's next experiments as *agent provocateur*. Not that Othello can't guess how such festivities may come out, for he delivers an official little homily to Cassio: "Let's teach ourselves that honourable stop, / Not to outsport discretion" (2.3.2-3).

In his handling of the "mutiny" scene, Othello, as we saw in Chapter IV, does not live up to the standard of justice set in the "hearing" in Act 1. Othello's irritability raises a question, since it appears to include something other than the administrator's expected response to a disturbance of the peace and to a momentary difficulty in obtaining evidence. It is hardly annoyance at being again routed out of the bridal bed, a discomfort that he twice endures with equanimity: as he says, " 'Tis the soldiers' life / To have their balmy slumbers wak'd with strife" (2.3.257-258). It can hardly be complete

OTHELLO: ACTION AND LANGUAGE

astonishment at the breach of good behavior; surely Othello has seen enough binges by military personnel to be able to anticipate unamiable outbreaks. This time he has commanded "each man to what sport and revels his addiction leads him" and declared "full liberty of feasting . . . till . . . eleven" (2.2.5-11); it is now presumably not much more than ten, since about 150 lines have been spoken since Iago said " 'tis not yet ten o' th' clock" (2.3.13). Perhaps, noting that Othello is quick to threaten death to the next person that makes a move (165, 174), we should simply say that he is excitable, choleric, "quick on the trigger." But what is the nature of this excitableness? Mingled with the legitimate concern for order there is a lack of impersonality, as if Othello were not entirely a figure of law, but a being in some way threatened by these goings-on. He has the kind of self-awareness which results less in self-appraisal than in hypersensitiveness about encroachment. He charges Iago to testify "On thy *love*" (178); he orders Montano, "Give *me* answer to't" (196); he talks of "*my* blood," "*my* safer guides," "*my* best judgment" (205-206). He makes an extraordinary assertion of power which is less that of the office than of the person occupying the office: "If *I* once stir / Or do but lift *this arm,* the best of you / Shall sink in *my* rebuke" (207-209), and he adds that whoever started this "Shall lose *me*" (213). It is as if he had felt a challenge, not to law and order, but to himself, or as if he personally were eliciting too little respect; some stirring from within his personality makes him uneasy; so he immediately and instinctively takes refuge in an unassailable "position": "What! in a town of war, / Yet wild, the people's hearts brimful of fear, / To manage private and domestic quarrel?" (213-215).

The only trouble is that this position is hardly in accord with facts. Though by legal technicality the town may be in a "state of war," the argument lacks psychological or moral weight, for we have been told by the third Gentleman (quoting Cassio) that the Turks were ruined by the storm (2.1.20ff., 31ff.); Othello cannot possibly believe it, for he has stated publicly,

"Our wars are done; the Turks are drown'd" (2.1.204); the people cannot believe it, for the public proclamation has informed them of "the mere [utter] perdition of the Turkish fleet" (2.2.3). How can anyone believe "the people's hearts brimful of fear" when they have been having five hours of officially proclaimed "sport and revels"? They may be a little disturbed by the uproar, as Iago later suggests (2.3.231-232), but this is not what Othello has been talking about. He is perhaps just forgetting that he has declared the war over, but the context suggests rather that he is feeling and trying to meet an intangible need to bolster himself, and that in being legalistic he is capable, as elsewhere, of the required self-deceit. With a greater stability under pressure, Othello might have dealt with the situation less simply by contemplating the possible justice of some self-censure for the hasty proclamation of revelry, by pushing his witnesses with firmer reason and persistence, and by some suspending of judgment. If we are aware of this option we can appreciate the quickness of his dash to an impregnable rock (not that he does not "believe" in his "town of war" rhetoric) and then his excessive promptness in establishing, as a further positional support, his gubernatorial detachment and integrity: "Cassio, I love thee; / But never more be officer of mine" (248-249). This "never more" is far-reaching, final. We can imagine a more intrinsically assured Othello who might himself take part of the blame and discipline Cassio by suspension for a limited time.[16]

Would I were satisfied

Iago's subversion of Othello in 3.3 may well appear too brilliant and successful if we regard Othello only as "of a constant, loving, noble nature" (2.1.298). It will hardly appear so if we keep in mind all the qualifications of character that Shakespeare has patiently, and on the whole very unobtrusively, dramatized—the unripeness of his sense of his own past, the flair for the picturesque and the histrionic, the stoicism of the flesh unmatched by an endurance of spirit,

OTHELLO: ACTION AND LANGUAGE

the capacity for occasional self-deception, the hypersensitivity to challenge, the inexperience in giving, the inclination to be irritable under responsibility and hasty in the absence of superior authority, the need to rely on position. It is not on any personality that Iago plays but on this particular personality—on Everyman in terms of his liability to doubt and unsureness, or of the romantic strain on which some critics lay strong emphasis,[17] or of his deficiency in charitable love. As soon as Iago lets it appear that he has a significant "thought," Othello pursues that thought as if he were relying on it; that is, he does not rely on something else that would permit him to encounter the thought at least on even terms, but, in the manner of one with no "position" to direct him, seeks out the thought as if it were a support and the circumambient world were fluid.[18] True, he once takes a position of "good sense" in rejecting hypothetical sources of jealousy and in giving himself a strengthening reminder of Desdemona's openeyed choice of him (180-189). But even the good sense tends to be simply the administrative neatness of the executive mind, which will not flounder for an instant but will sink or swim immediately. "No! To be once in doubt / Is once to be resolv'd" (179-180). He charts an orderly sequence of moves: to "see," then "doubt," then "prove," and then, "Away at once with love or jealousy!" (190-192). How ill equipped for the complications and stresses of personal life is the holder of this position, with his assembly-line sensibility, his self-deception, and, we may guess, his histrionic image of the quick executive act (as in the disciplining of Cassio).

When he promises Iago, "Fear not my government [self-control]" (256), he is again deceiving himself. In searching around for intellectual "positions" that will provide a rationale of what he believes to be his situation, he shows the immaturity of his reflective powers, an absence of self-criticism, an infusion of self-pity: "Why did I marry?" (242); "I am abus'd, and my relief / Must be to loathe her" (267-268); "'tis the plague of great ones" (273); "'Tis destiny unshunnable, like death"

145

(275). Othello thinks thus feebly because an unusual breadth of experience has for him never gone beyond the excitement of the picturesque; with all his opportunity for observation he has learned virtually nothing about the human capacity for good and for evil, about human variations from abstract patterns, about the plurality of available responses to apparent disaster. Here is also something of his puritanism, that is, of a disposition readily to convict mankind generally of habitual severe misconduct. He tends, as Leavis and Elliott say, to think of Desdemona as a type rather than as an individual.[19] He has not the flexibility of mind that can entertain qualifications. In soliloquy he has fewer lines than Shakespeare's other tragic heroes: he is less intelligent than they, less introspective; he has less inner life to lay bare[20] (less even than Iago). Not only does he have a sense of audience, but he needs an audience. For him reality lies less in transactions with himself than in transactions with others.

Othello's version of ignorance-is-bliss (336-347) is again the product of a mind which the kaleidoscopic flashing of life has deflected from a steady contemplation of the disagreeable surprises that are of its nature.[21] The farewell to war (349-357) is a histrionic farewell to a theatrical war, an affair of parade and pageantry which might be dreamed by one who had never been there. Othello menaces Iago with his "wak'd wrath" (363, 364-373) somewhat as he had threatened the drunken brawlers; thus he falls into another extreme without having touched at the midpoint of controlled inquiry. His demand for "proof" (360ff.) means, as we noted in Chapter III, a grave impropriety of method. When he insists, "I *will*[22] [be satisfied]" (393), he is "crying for certainty at any price,"[23] and exhibiting further his "egotistical self-absorption."[24] Here we can recall again that by loving enough, which includes the willingness to be mistaken, he could save himself.

After he is "satisfied" he stops trying to think: from now on, he only craves violence. Here is another aspect of his military toughness, and here is the primitivism, perhaps of "the

OTHELLO: ACTION AND LANGUAGE

Moor," but rather, I think, of the human being never transformed, as much as human beings can be, by the ripening process. His history is that of a man somehow skimmed over by the impulses of spiritual adulthood.[25] He never gained strength through giving himself. Othello is one version of the man who has never grown up; beside Macbeth and Antony—and even Hamlet—he is a child. For a period Shakespeare is concerned with the tragic discrepancy between years and wisdom; in *Lear* he goes on to explore the theme to the limits of possibility.

THE HONESTY GAME

As the assurance of love has dwindled, Othello has sought frantically for a compensating assurance; he cannot rest in the wisdom that it is better to suffer than to cause suffering, or even in a sense of tragic destiny; but he must lean on persons or passions. The irony of his leaning on his seducer is doubled by his insisting on the seducer's "honesty"; but this insistence is also revelatory. We find that Othello always harps on Iago's honesty when Iago is, or appears to be, doing him a favor or service (likewise Cassio, when he thinks he is getting something for nothing from Iago; only Desdemona is capable of referring disinterestedly to Iago's honesty—3.3.5). Even when he is assigning Iago to escort Desdemona to Cyprus, and the outcome depends largely on the chances of war and weather, Othello is impelled to name Iago's virtue, "A man he is of honesty and trust" (1.3.285), and to address his ancient, "Honest Iago, / My Desdemona must I leave to thee" (295-296). Aside from Othello's possible condescension and his falling in with Iago's obviously well established honesty game, we see something else: an implied need of justification, as if, even when Othello is generally triumphant, he requires additional assurance of the rightness of his action. If this is true, then he has latent uncertainties which will be troublesome when he is under pressure. The next time he praises Iago—"Iago is most honest" (2.3.6)—is when he and

Cassio are arranging for the victory-night watch: is this the hypnotized repetition of a key word, brought on by the mere mention of the name *Iago,* or is this an oblique indication of Othello's inarticulate desire to assure himself, even this late, that a proclamation partly aimed at glorifying himself and his bride was not ill considered? He is more overtly relying on Iago when he addresses him after the brawl: "Honest Iago, that looks dead with grieving, / Speak" (2.3.177). Othello is excited, and the situation is not clarifying itself for him as quickly as he thinks it ought to; he has let himself be maneuvered—by Iago's skill in faking concern as a means of catching Othello's eye—into calling on Iago before Cassio. Hence the "honest" implicitly reassures him on his procedure and on the testimony that will be forthcoming. Since Othello is somewhat self-conscious and defensive in this scene, he possibly has an obscure awareness of hurrying, hearing only one witness, and making no real effort to get Cassio to tell his story. How, then, gain assurance that all is well? By telling Iago in the lines that close the scene, "Thy honesty and love doth mince this matter, / Making it light to Cassio" (247-248). He can thus assume Cassio guilty of serious enough misconduct to justify the heavy penalty by which Othello seems to gain moral control of the situation (the issue is not only the appropriateness of the sentence but the extrajudicial vibrations in the temper of the judge).

This consistent pattern in the use of *honest* in Acts 1 and 2 reveals that Othello, in constantly repeating *honest* in 3.3, is doing something more than judiciously establishing the competence of the witness. It is easy to forget that Othello really has no business to inquire into the "monster in his thought" or his "horrible conceit" (3.3.107, 115). He cannot entertain Iago's imputations against Cassio without also entertaining allegations against his new wife. Yet he has some impulse to listen; some lack of equilibrium, some unripeness makes it possible to breed in him an untenable suspicion. Since he is, as Kirschbaum has pointed out, the only one of four people to whom Iago accuses Desdemona of infidelity that believes it, it is difficult to deny that "there is something in Othello's character which leads him to believe Iago's calumny."[26] Is it that the man who dashes so easily from the bridal bed to the couch of war—duty, of course, but duty without a pang—cannot help imagining, deep below the level of articulate consciousness, the possibility of another flight from the same bed? Does a hidden awareness of failure or deception from within force itself to the surface as a suspiciousness of failure or deception from without? If he wants to condescend, then, to eavesdrop, he must justify his uncriticized impulse by conferring upon gossip the status of gospel; hence, to Iago, "I know thou'rt full of love and honesty" (118)—the same self-sustaining words he used to Iago when he abruptly fired Cassio. Having now certified his own rectitude in listening to scandal, he has at the same time sharpened Iago's sense of his honesty as instrument (at which we glanced early in Chapter III): "It were not for . . . / . . . my manhood, honesty, or wisdom, / To let you know my thoughts" (152-154). If Othello now fails to press ahead into the dark of those thoughts, he will be implicitly challenging Iago's reliability. But the challenge would require resistance to habit as well as delay, and Othello cannot abide the temporary uncertainty which is essential to wise conclusions: he must have assurance now. He is not up to finding it in faith in Desdemona (or Cassio); he must lean directly on someone who promises support here and now. So he finds the required honesty in Iago: "This honest creature doubtless / Sees and knows more, much more, than he unfolds" (242-243) and "This fellow's of exceeding honesty" (258).

But Shakespeare has shrewdly given Othello a moment of doubt that is probable before the final surrender of the dupe: he swings briefly away from the Iago assurance toward the old Desdemona assurance. His threat to Iago leads to Iago's most striking use of honesty as a stratagem: to rescue himself in a pinch. He addresses first himself: "O wretched fool, / That liv'st to make thine honesty a vice!" (375-376); then the world, "Take note, take note, O world, / To be direct and honest is not safe" (377-378)—a pair of rhetoric-book apostrophes[27] whose moral ostentation would betray the speaker to anyone more mature and controlled than Othello. Othello flinches and virtually pleads, "Nay, stay. Thou shouldst be honest" (381), which has not only the obvious meaning, "All the evidence suggests that you are honest" but also the buried meaning, "My assurance cannot be taken away from me." Iago picks it right up for his next thrust in the duel: "I should be wise; for honesty's a fool / And loses that it works for" (382-383)— in effect, "I'll take my honesty home and won't play any more." After this works, Iago adopts the style of one mollified but still a little hurt as he promises to proceed in the "cause" in which he has come "so far, / Prick'd to't by foolish honesty and love" (412). He moves into the technique of the "big lie"—the rich tale of Cassio's dream—in the next line after "honesty and love," a huge incongruity in which there again flashes into sight the deadly-playful hand of the comedian, delightedly entertaining us with his destructive practical joke.

The honesty subdrama, with its "crucify me" climax, is more than an ironic condiment for the dramatic dish. It presents the vital conflict as a game, with two players, one using a device[28] that traps the other (in Chapter IV we saw Iago presenting himself as a trapper), the other being trapped because it is in his nature to be—lacking the repose to compare two sets of appearances, to suspend judgment, to trust to what is beyond "proof," to the unseen as against the "seen"; relying, too, on an old habit; but in the habit itself evincing an earlier and deeper need, a pitiable weakness correlative with his fearful violence. He endeavors to compensate for or to complete something incomplete in himself, to shore up an insufficiency, to find a remedy for some shakiness of personality of the sort we now call "insecurity." Miss Bodkin defines this as an inadequacy or shirking of moral understanding: Iago seems "so honest, so wise" because his words express half-truths that Othello formally ignored but secretly understood.[29] In a sense Othello passes the buck.

On the prop of Iago's honesty, Othello leans from Act 1 to Act 5. When Iago wounds Cassio, Othello exclaims "O brave Iago, honest and just" (5.1.31); in telling Desdemona that Cassio has been killed, he says, "Honest Iago hath ta'en order for't" (5.2.72)—i.e., since Iago is honest, the execution was just, and my order unassailable. When Othello is attempting to justify his murder of Desdemona to Emilia, he falls back on Iago again: "An honest man he is" (5.2.148), and, to quell her incredulity, "My friend, thy husband; honest, honest Iago" (154). The double *honest* is ironic, but it is not there for irony's sake; it comes out of a deep need in Othello. The double *honest* is echoed in his wordplay when he fails to kill Iago and loses his sword: "But why should honour outlive honesty?" (245). This is packed. Why should Othello ("all in honour") survive Desdemona, now known to be honest? Or survive that honesty once symbolized in Iago and now deflated? Or survive in reputation the loss of his own essential "honesty"?[30] This is the only time that *honesty* may apply to him. To describe his failure as loss of honesty yokes his violence in the name of justice with the weakness of his self-sustaining attribution of a reliable virtue to Iago: in a moral crisis, to depend on violence and to depend on another are the two extremes of a failure of self. Yet before it is over, Othello is trying to save his "honour": his last-minute prop.

Between the deception scene and the murder scene Othello is a creature of what Iago calls "passion most unfitting such a man." In fact, he uses an emotional double standard, accepting his passion and Iago's, but rejecting Desdemona's.[31] He yields to another game of Iago's (besides the honesty game)—the patience game, and formally rejects patience as a possible guide in his crisis.[32] And above all he rejects pity or at least fails to

151

be moved by pity, through which he might pass to the charitable love that surmounts a sense of injury.[33] This one saving course he never seriously considers.

CAUSE, SACRIFICE, MURDER
The murder scene requires and fulfills all the careful characterization of Othello that has gone before, for this exactly determines the tone and movement of the scene. It is the high point of the themes of violence and justice. It is another in a series of legal actions; like that in Act 1, it is concerned with a charge of sexual misconduct. In Act 1 there were a defendant, a corroborating witness, a judge, and a plaintiff given to recklessness but not incapable of reason and patience. Here we have only the defendant and the plaintiff—a plaintiff given to self-deception and passion.

Othello has now been severe or explosive, always on the edge of violence, on every appearance since Iago took him over in 3.3. But when he enters the bedroom he has become singularly calm. In fact, in the "Put out the light" speech (5.2.7ff.) he strikes a contemplative note that is rarely his, for he has the least reflective capacity of all Shakespeare's tragic heroes. So even at the time of murder the lines produce a paradoxical relief, as if a madman has suddenly come to sanity or a tempestuous youth to maturity; indeed, Othello hesitates and for a second or two it is almost possible to believe that he will burst out of his obsession and drop his resolve. The lover may break out of the paradoxical compound of lover and murderer (on which there has been much comment) and even now change the planned action. Is this simply effective theater, an additional reversal for tension's sake only? No, it is pure Othello. He yields to his love only sensorily; as a guide to action it is what he means to surmount. For he is up to something else. Under the impact of the light imagery and the following rose imagery we at first may underemphasize the less resonant lines that really define Othello's role:

OTHELLO: ACTION AND LANGUAGE

> It is the cause, it is the cause, my soul.
> Let me not name it to you, you chaste stars!
> It is the cause.
> Yet she must die, else she'll betray more men.
> O balmy breath, that dost almost persuade
> Justice to break her sword! (1-3, 6, 16-17)

"The cause"—that is, his action is legal, continuing from his decision to strangle her because "The justice of it pleases" (4.1.222). It is preventive justice, carried out lest the criminal "betray more men." Then Othello, having already in "chaste stars" ("heavenly lights") implicitly introduced the note of cosmic light and justice, goes on to exalt his image of justice: "This sorrow's heavenly; / It strikes where it doth love" (21-22). In one sense it is infatuation to convert the earthly court into a divine one; in another sense this "god pose"[34] marks the intensity of Othello's need for assurance. But simply in his conversion of himself into a judge we see his continuing quest for what I have called "positional assurance." Some tragic heroes desire the good but cannot encompass it. Othello "desires" the bad, that is, the death of Desdemona; but he also desires a good, namely, the conviction of right action. Hence he makes himself a judge, committed to action according to principles beyond his own desires and interests.[35] The transmutation appears to work better than in any of the earlier scenes in which he spasmodically assumed the black gown: as cosmic dispenser of justice Othello neutralizes for a time his violence of mind, and he becomes the almost philosophic contemplator of life and death. Aided by his capacity for self-deception, which springs into action spontaneously at need, he conceals from himself, and almost makes us forget, that he is a murderer; thus he calls forth the supposition that justice, as one critic puts it, may be "indistinguishable from man's need to find redress for what he cannot bear to find in human nature."[36]

After Desdemona awakes, the dialogue repeatedly draws upon

153

court procedure. She pleads, "guiltiness I know not" (39) and is warned by Othello: "Take heed of perjury" (51). But the irony is that Othello undermines his own role:

> Therefore confess thee freely of thy sin;
> For to deny each article with oath
> Cannot remove nor choke the strong conception
> That I do groan withal. Thou art to die.   (53-56)

The court has made up its mind in advance and sentenced her. The judge loses his composure, cites the circumstantial evidence that Iago gave him, and abuses the prisoner: "By heaven, I saw my handkerchief in's hand! / O perjur'd woman!" (62-63). If Shakespeare had dramatized evil only by such travestying of justice, he would have been very effective. But he has gone further.

Othello is not content with the role of judge. Note these lines:

> Have you pray'd tonight, Desdemon?
> If you bethink yourself of any crime
> Unreconcil'd as yet to heaven and grace,
> Solicit for it straight.
>   *Des.*   Then heaven
> Have mercy on me!
>   *Oth.*   Amen, with all my heart!
> Think on thy sins.
> Therefore confess thee freely of thy sin.
>   *Des.* Then Lord have mercy on me!
>   *Oth.*   I say amen.
>   (25, 26-28, 33-34, 40, 53, 57)

Though some of these lines might be spoken by a Christian judge, they belong rather to the Christian priest,[37] especially the priest in the role of confessor. This, then, is Othello's climactic means of placing himself on a pinnacle of assurance and of blinding himself to the true nature of what he does there. Though he has already inclined to assume the role of priest,[38] only now has he invested it with a brief air of dignity,

154

OTHELLO: ACTION AND LANGUAGE

which Shakespeare uses skillfully to dramatize the horror of Othello's conduct: to the coolness, the prayerfulness, the almost gentle calmness of the priest is added the frankness of the killer: "I would not kill thy unprepared spirit. / No, heaven forfend! I would not kill thy soul" (31-32). Repeatedly Othello talks of "killing" her—his voice quiet and controlled—at the same time that he urges her to save her soul.[39] The shock is that of a murder by rite, of an exotic depravity in which the selfless spiritual concern and the wholly selfish violence are confounded. The priest as killer is a remarkable dramatic conception: an ultimate violence is expressed by doing violence to all our preconceptions. This strategy is used doubly: the priestly role is worked out alongside the judicial role, so that we also have the judge as killer. But then the judge, we recall, is also the plaintiff and the prosecutor: and now he becomes also the executioner—as well as the confessor bent on the spiritual salvation of the criminal. In this merging of incompatible roles is the apex of Othello's self-deception, and here at last we can see that Othello was so easily deceived, so easily taken in by appearances and the false physician and the honesty game, because he had such great talent, and even a need, for self-deception. As we look further, we see that even his actions as confessor are equivocal: for if Desdemona confesses what he is convinced she must confess, she will give him the final assurance of his rectitude as judge and executioner. The revenger assumes the priest to hide the revenge; but even then he is not content but must convert the priestly function into an instrument of self-justification.

We would expect that the decorous mastery of incompatible roles could not last long, but that they would fly apart in a centrifugal burst if there were any rush of feeling about the small center of Othello's tenuously held calm. The stresses first occur when Desdemona defines her "sins" as the "loves I bear to you" (40); Othello's grip of his multiple role becomes looser when he is angered by her telling the true handkerchief story instead of the one he believes to be true (49-50, 58-61);

155

at her denial that she gave Cassio a token he finally explodes, "O perjur'd woman! thou dost stone my heart" (63). The judicial mask fades as the angry man gives way to feelings that he blames on the defendant (cf. his earlier "my heart is turn'd to stone"—4.1.193). He continues: "And mak'st me call what I intend to do / A murther, which I thought a sacrifice" (64-65), The synthetic role blows up: judge and priest are gone: what is left is the executioner serving the law of his own passion; the erstwhile Christian priest relapses into a state even more primitive than that of pre-Christian sacrifices.[40] He roars about the evidence, admits his "great revenge" against Cassio, twice shouts "strumpet" at Desdemona (74, 77, 79), kills her. The tension of his unsuccessful effort to ennoble his conduct is released in the act of violence and pushes him to the necessary haste: he can now depend only on the integrity of passion, he must act when it is quick and full, lest a dilution leave him with no assurance at all.[41] But the passion poured into the act of killing, he must again strive in a faint, incongruous, anticlimactic way to achieve a self-respect beyond the satisfaction of honor: "Not dead? not yet quite dead? / I that am cruel am yet merciful; / I would not have thee linger in thy pain" (85-87). This minor procedural humanity after the major, essential inhumanity is Othello's last gesture of self-deception.

The plurality of motives in Othello and the complexity of the actions to which the motives lead are such that, in tracing them, we have neglected the function of the "trial" and "execution" scene in the larger structure. The scene itself is, as I argued earlier,[42] ambivalent, having a doubleness analogous to that of Othello himself. It would be wrong to regard him as wholly barbarous, a loathsome monster of self-deception, or simply as the "noble Moor," admirably bent on justice but regrettably deflected by errors not entirely within his control, for he comes somewhere between these extremes, drawing something from both. And the scene which depicts such a

OTHELLO: ACTION AND LANGUAGE

character cannot be entirely a picture of horror and depravity. It has other values, and to assay its ambiguity we need to look at its relation to other scenes.

STYLES IN KILLING

Shakespeare's sense of the depravity of which men are capable who mean well or wish to think well of themselves went about as far as it could go in the scene of Desdemona's death, which travesties the Duke's administration of justice in Act 1, and of which Johnson, echoed by other editors, said, "It is not to be endured."[43] But Shakespeare could imagine still more about the husband as murderer, and this theme he amplifies in Iago's murder of Emilia. Othello kills Desdemona because, in her defense of Cassio, she seems to prove that she is betraying him. Iago kills Emilia because in her defense of Desdemona she is betraying him. Each husband feels the world he has built collapsing, and he acts in a reckless fury of revenge. Each abuses his wife, calling her whore and liar. Such rough parallels establish the second murder as a replica of the first, the intensifying repetition familiar in dramatic practice. Though in a sense it is that, there are meaningful differences. The clash between Iago and Emilia is very short. Between Emilia's telling Iago that he has told "an odious damned lie" (180) and his giving her the deathblow there are only 55 lines, during which the only lines that Iago speaks, all addressed to her, are these:

> With Cassio, mistress. Go to, charm your tongue.
> What, are you mad? I charge you get you home.
> Zounds, hold your peace!
> Be wise, and get you home.
> 　　　[*Here Iago threatens Emilia with his sword.*]
> Villanous whore!
> Filth, thou liest!　　　　　　(183, 194, 219, 223, 229, 231)

MAGIC IN THE WEB

This brevity of treatment, though it is a way of securing the necessary subordination of the secondary husband-wife relationship, does not violate the material; rather it is inherent in the character of Iago. Iago is the killer type who, though he can take infinite pains stalking quarry that has to be trapped, nevertheless hastens, coolly (as with Roderigo) or hotly (as with Emilia), to murder the present victim whose death he needs. Where strategic considerations do not intervene, he is direct and unceremonious. All the "reason" that he has devoted to the service of passion now yields, as excessive rationality always appears to do, to passion, overt and murderous.[44] His verbal style differs substantially from Othello's. Othello, it is true, pours heavy streams of abuse upon Desdemona, but up to a point his abuse is stylistically modified. Compare Iago's "Filth, thou liest"—three words containing two lies—with Othello's

> Come, swear it, damn thyself.
>
>   be double-damn'd—
> Swear thou art honest.
>
> Take heed of perjury.
>
> O perjur'd woman!   (4.2.35, 37-38; 5.2.51, 63)

Iago knows that Emilia does not lie but bluntly calls her liar; Othello believes that Desdemona lies but, instead of calling her liar,[45] expresses the imagined falsehood as a violation of oath or a perjury, thus partially transforming crude vilification, of which even the subhuman are capable, into a legal judgment. Iago characteristically vents bald abuse; Othello falls into bald abuse when he is unable to sustain the solemn legitimate condemnation to which he aspires. So in their killing: Iago kills with a rush of malice, Othello in a fury of revenge—but only after a late failure to maintain the form of judicial procedure. Each hates and destroys, but with a difference in style that persists into their last moments on stage: Iago turns mute, Othello goes out in rhetoric—two appropriate extremes.

OTHELLO: ACTION AND LANGUAGE

If we may speak hypothetically of a "case for revenge," we may summarize the over-all difference thus: Othello not only has no case for revenge, but in reaching for elevation of style he deceives himself about his motives. How, then, do the two murder scenes interact, or how does their copresence impinge on the meaning? To take boldly a modern view, Iago might seem to have a large advantage over Othello: candor is in repute with us, ornament is not, and of two killers we might well consider less obnoxious the one who went most forthrightly about his task, with no nonsense, no blinders, a frank knife to the heart. And if he didn't have a case that would stand very much inspection, still we could see why he felt the way he did, for we know that for the understanding of "unsocial conduct" we must look to its genesis. Othello is deceiving himself, and implicitly us, with a show of the judicial and the priestly, and this is offensive. He is covering his murderous impulse with a cloak of good manners, whereas we are likely to feel that a beast with good manners is still not only a beast, but what is worse, a pretentious beast. But this emphasis would be misleading. When tragedy involves both the individual and the community, the private error and its extensions in public disaster (e.g., *Oedipus, Macbeth, Lear*) and conversely the common modes of salvation, the "good manners" of the individual may be understood as the forms of community action and, as such, one means of meeting the never-ceasing threat of disorder and of channeling dynamic impulses toward organic order. Good manners may be a fraud, conceal a fraud, or let a man deceive himself, but they also contribute to order by making relationships, coherence, and common actions possible. If Othello deceives himself with his effort at legal (not to mention ecclesiastical) good form, at least his choice of a self-deceptive action is an effort to adopt the norms of community action. In his tragic failure to find the best form of action—to hear the transcendental imperative against vengeance (and thus incidentally to have time to learn the truth that would enable him to execute justice in the manner of the

Duke in Act 1)—he at least tries to avoid the extreme formlessness of uninhibited private action. In life as in art, the form of an action may reveal the content, at least at the level of implication. Order is still imaginable if there is an impulse to formal propriety, even though chaos invades the situation in which formal propriety puts a good face on murder (the judge or priest as executioner). This has its horror, as Shakespeare intends, but the unqualified private killing, when the killer has no sense of need to provide it with a common or sanctioned form, is the symbol of total disorder. Not that the imposition of a ritual form can justify an act of violence, but that the impulse to ritualization is essential to the preserving of order. What is at stake is the human community, whatever inhumanities may be encompassed within its forms, as against the total attack on the community.[46] When the impulse to ritualization, or to communal form, exists, tragedy is possible; without it, what is left is demonic melodrama.

But the paradox which we see in the style of Othello's killing of Desdemona—the paradox of an implicit remnant of order or of an impulse to order in the chaos of violated justice—if it appears tenuous, should appear less so when we recall that the portrayal of Othello does not end with the killing of his wife.

THE END OF THE CASE

Othello holds court until the end of the play: the judge (the judge-prosecutor-priest-executioner) has to find his own crime (in the tragic pattern created by Sophocles). The court which had heard only one witness must in time, simply by being a court—and this is one virtue of Othello's ritualizing impulse to be judicial—hear other witnesses. The late criminal returns from death to charge, "O, falsely, falsely murder'd!" (117), turning against Othello one of his favorite words of accusation, and to plead again, "A guiltless death I die" (122). Othello's assurance is never dependable; the court is promptly thrown on the defensive, reviles the victim (128ff.) to questioning Emilia, asserts, on the

OTHELLO: ACTION AND LANGUAGE

penalty of being "damn'd," that it "did proceed upon just grounds" (138), takes up the "honest Iago" defense of the sole witness and of itself (148, 154), and then, authority fading before the indignation of Emilia, falls into a slump while Emilia calls for help, cross-examines Iago, and blasts his testimony (169ff.). Othello confesses the death of Desdemona and then patiently, concessively (203, 210), almost wearily resumes the defense of the court action (200ff., 210ff.). This part of Act 5 is arranged with especial skill, since the movement comes inevitably from the characters and leads to maximum dramatic effect. There is an alternating rhythm of passion in Othello and Emilia: the first violence of his defense is overborne by her shock and incredulity, and when these have almost exhausted her, he is ready to present an orderly and relatively unimpassioned summary of the evidence. And it is just this complete judicial review of the case which leads at last to the hero's self-recognition in error (discovery of his "mistake" if not complete discovery of himself[47]) that distinguishes tragedy from the brute disaster that impinges only on the beholders. For Othello's defense of the court must name the handkerchief, and this arouses Emilia to a new frenzy in which she tells the true story of the handkerchief (219ff.). This is the ironic climax of the court metaphor: in the end the handkerchief does have evidential value—but the reverse of what Othello had supposed. The circumstantial evidence which he had admitted and relied on and which once apparently revealed Desdemona to Othello, now partly reveals Othello to himself.

Othello's first impulse, after his new vision of truth, is to execute summary justice on Iago, whom he attacks twice, the first time acting as a self-appointed deputy for an apparently tardy or ineffectual divine justice: "Are there no stones in heaven . . . ?" (234). Here is something again of Othello's inclination to spectacle, to the large mouth-filling stage effect; and the impulse to blame the outer agency of evil and thus avert recognition of inner responsiveness to it. But he does come to the judging of himself, according to his abilities; thus

161

the spirit of justice persists; human order is served by an implicit extension of the very ritual of the court that earlier permitted Othello to gloss over the role of revenger. The instinct for ritualization, though it may be directed toward self-deception, is related to the instinct for justice which includes self-judgment. The principle of the court is brought into play, and the individual is subordinated to it, regaining community. Iago, on the other hand, in the end simply closes up, hardens up in silence and resistance, hugs himself to himself in a shut-off, private world that, though it may break under the cruder instruments of retributive justice, is impermeable to spirit (cf. Othello's "free and open nature"—1.3.405).

It is possible to view the bowing before justice sentimentally, as we know from the turn which drama aspiring to seriousness took in the eighteenth century. It is, indeed, one of the more difficult feats to achieve a submission to justice—an acknowledgement of one's own errors—which is not also a prostration of dignity; in this the dramatist wrestles with the paradox of the attainment of self in the eclipse of self, and he becomes committed to cardinal problems of spirit. The greatness of *Othello* is not generally of that dimension. Shakespeare approaches the personality rather in terms of a not wholly overt conflict between the sense of justice and a vague appetite for eluding or circumventing its implications: he gives us a series of self-judgments whose rigor is modified by men's partiality to other objectives. From the start Roderigo judges Desdemona accurately, and he comes to judge himself: "I will give over my suit and repent my unlawful solicitation" (4.2.201-202). But he does neither. Cassio makes an uncompromising judgment of intoxication generally and of his own drinking: "I will ask him for my place again: he shall tell me I am a drunkard! Had I as many mouths as Hydra, such an answer would stop them all" (2.3.306-308). In his protracted self-condemnation (260-317) Cassio is almost hysterically thorough; yet he rushes immediately into his unhappy suit for reinstate-

OTHELLO: ACTION AND LANGUAGE

ment. Othello appears before the court of his own conscience, is sentenced to death by himself, and executed by himself. He takes on the same multiplicity of roles that had led to gross injustice in his dealing with Desdemona; his incompetence in the earlier case he purges by his sentencing himself now; justice is served finally by the death of the judge.[48]

Perhaps we should say only that "overt justice" is served. For the foreground action of the court (judicial self-judgment) is modified by a background action of the feelings (personal self-judgment) that admits a charity which is excluded from the sentencing itself. The total self-judgment is colored by elements of personality that we have discerned in other parts of the play. In other words, we have again a provocatively ambiguous court scene, but one which tellingly reverses the terms of the trial of Desdemona: there the private emotion was primary but was qualified by the form of justice; here the act of justice is primary but is qualified by the habits of private feeling. Two elements are tightly interwoven, and we would lose sight of one or the other if we judged Othello to be only the upright executor of justice or, conversely, only the self-regarding loser sunk in self-pity and self-justification.

He speaks accusingly of his failure to kill Iago and keeps his own weapon (5.2.243, 270-271). But here, too, is something of his love for executive despatch: the man who disposed quickly and neatly of the cases of Cassio and Desdemona has been inefficient in dealing with Iago, and on top of that he is hemmed in by Gratiano. He is able to check the comfort of warrior's memories—"O vain boast!" (264) but falls into the sheer defensiveness of "Who can control his fate?" (265), as if he were not actively concerned in the disaster. But, in another attempt to face the moral issue, he turns to Desdemona's body: "at compt," he says, "This look of thine will hurl my soul from heaven, / And fiends will snatch at it" (273-275). Yet even here he in some way slights the present by leaping from past to future: he less defines the quality of his

163

act than anticipates its consequences. In fact, he is a little disposed to revel in the hellish aftermath: "Whip me, . . . / . . . / Blow me about in winds! roast me in sulphur! / Wash me in steep-down gulfs of liquid fire!" (277-280). Here is the tendency to violence, even to spectacle;[49] the summoning of such penalties has a histrionic side. Indeed, Othello, the tough man of war, the stoic in body, equates punishment with physical torment, which, as he portrayed himself in Act 1, is just what he can best endure. "Facing the consequences," when these mean anguish of the flesh, may be a lesser task than facing one's spiritual state. When Lodovico asks Othello, in effect, to explain himself, Othello replies: "An honourable murderer, if you will; / For naught did I in hate, but all in honour" (294-295). Othello does say "murderer," and it is possible that combining "honourable" with "murderer" may be a bitter irony at his own expense. But the second line, as well as Othello's general incapacity for the oblique, makes it very likely that he means, not "nothing but a murderer, trying to look honorable," but "though, alas, a murderer, still an honorable man." "Naught . . . in hate" again displays self-deception: Othello does not know how close hate is to love, and he has forgot the intensity of his passion to destroy. In "all in honour" there is his old quest of assurance of position. Honor is a surrogate for the justice that has gone utterly wrong: in lieu of the lost "cause" it implies a code that ennobles the private lust for punitive action. Yet by "honor" he means less the "active honor" that implies obligation of self to others than the "passive honor" that asserts the obligation of others to oneself and one's accompanying privilege of imposing penalties on those who fail.

Amid spasmodic attacks on Iago, Othello approaches humility at only one moment:[50] when he asks Cassio's pardon for plotting his death (300). His terms of abuse for Iago are more frequent and more severe than the terms of judgment for himself. On hearing the final details of the handkerchief story, Othello cries "O fool! fool! fool!" (323). His epithet reminds him only of the least of his errors.[51] He somehow conveys the impression that his big mistake was not so much murder and revenge as it was depriving himself of Desdemona; he less repudiates the violence than deplores the silly mistakes which wiped out a very nice girl. To understand the incompleteness of the self-judgment we have only to recall the stern self-appraisal of Roderigo: "O, villain that I am!" (5.1.29). The impression of a not wholly disciplined partiality persists even in his death speech, that ingenuous apologia in which Othello bids the onlookers, "Speak of me as I am" (342), and then, with no more self-awareness than before, labors to present an "I am" which will at the last minute give all the assurance possible to a man about to be executed and all the help possible to those willing to "extenuate" his history. Othello's death sentence does represent a self-judgment or at least an invocation of justice as a public act; but while it is a penalty, it is also an act of desperation, a flight from bereavement. The guilt is never specified, but the extenuating circumstances are. The judge and prosecutor becomes, in the end, his own defense attorney, accepting the ultimate legal penalty but throwing himself morally on the mercy of the court of public opinion.[52] He has "done the state some service, and they know't" (339); what the observers of these events must report is "unlucky deeds" (341), as though no will had been involved; he was "wrought, / Perplex'd in the extreme" (345-346)—words which do not report that there was no effort at the delay that might have untangled the maze of difficulties; he "threw a pearl away"—a note of pitiable loss rather than of misconduct; his eyes "Drop tears" (350) rapidly—the marks of a grief and tenderness that appeal for sympathy and that might err but not overtly do evil. "Set you down this" he goes on (351), as if he (who in Act 1 thought in terms of "cue" and "prompter"[53]) and they were collaborating on a work of dramatic art. As in Act 1, Othello is conscious of his role and of his audience,

MAGIC IN THE WEB

particularly now when he sharply focuses all eyes and ears on himself and his last words and theatrically punctuates his death statement with the deathblow.[54] His final stroke in the picture of himself is this:

> And say besides that in Aleppo once,
> Where a malignant and a turban'd Turk
> Beat a Venetian and traduc'd the state,
> I took by th' throat the circumcised dog
> And smote him—thus.   (352-356)

In a last effort at security (self-esteem and popularity) he invites the Venetians to remember him as a hero of both state and religion. Ironically, his analogy—in which, as earlier (2.3.170), he plays for the stock response of turkophobia—also has the effect of making him a malignant dog.[55] This may be a self-betrayal or, as I suggested earlier, a symbolic effort at recovery by self-definition. But the effect of the moral judgment of self is obscured by the showmanship. Othello's last court plays for at least a murmur of applause.[56]

Othello is the least heroic of Shakespeare's tragic heroes. The need for justification, for a constant reconstruction of himself in acceptable terms, falls short of the achieved selfhood which can plunge with pride into great errors and face up with humility to what has been done. All passion spent, Othello obscures his vision by trying to keep his virtues in focus. The Moor, the warrior, the survivor of exotic adventures, the romantic historian of self, is oddly affiliated with the middle-class hero, and in his kind of awareness we detect a prevision of later domestic drama.[57]

It is these aspects of Othello's personality that are lost sight of when his ending is pictured as a rather glorious affair. His very defensiveness and sentiment and sense of loss and of good intention not quite explicably gone awry win an affection which a stern facing of spiritual reality might not. In Othello, the hero is—a rare thing—very close to Everyman in his latent capacity for violence and in all his ordinary self-protective de-

OTHELLO: ACTION AND LANGUAGE

vices. This is the underlying, though unidentified, reason why it is easy to "feel with" him. It is easy to feel with him, also, because he ends things with a beguiling masterfulness; he commands attention, without a disaffectingly conspicuous ostentation: his very use of reckless power matches a secret impulse. With his uninhibitedness, he provides the observer with a release for the unredeemed, though normally controlled, egotism that can aspire secretly both to self-justification and to easy authority over the eyes and hearts of others. Mature men resist the gratifications of these impulses when they come separately; if they are offered together, the double beguilement requires a sharper-eyed resistance. But Othello offers not only these satisfactions that may slide in unperceived; he is, besides, carrying out at least a partial justice. If he is not facing himself in the full truth of his deeds, he is unmistakably sentencing himself to the ultimate penalty—as a pusillanimous person could not do. And finally, to increase his claim upon our feelings, there come into our memories, beyond that seductive union of spectacle and self-punishment before our eyes, impressions of other qualities of his—of the zealous soldier, the loyal servant of the state, the candid and uncalculating man who, unlike Iago, desired the good. This is the complex, and not easily resistible, recipe for the "noble Moor." And a portion of that nobility, of the largeness of the public figure, is there. So are the failures, the self-centeredness, the blindness, the spiritual immaturity that we have described. Though it is easy to call Othello "simple," the characterization is far from simple, and it exacts of us the same double awareness as the trait of his which we may call aspiration—an impulse which may lead to nobility or to flight from actuality, or to something of both at once.[58] In all his major actions there is a comparable ambiguity.

In trying to win approval, from others and himself, Othello includes in his summation a one-line definition of himself which has been remembered better than any other part of his apologia—as "one that lov'd not wisely, but too well" (344). Was his vice really an excess of a virtue? Or should he have said "not wisely, nor enough"? One can guess that the constant quest of assurance might mean less a free giving of self than a taking for self. However, we cannot consider Othello as lover without also looking at others who love—and thus at the theme of love and its relation to the form of the whole.

Thematic Form

VERSIONS OF LOVE

Shakespeare presents love in almost innumerable poetic and dramatic forms. In one interpretation that recurs in a number of major dramas, love is a force that binds human beings despite differences that seem prohibitive; it is a means of surmounting great barriers and obstacles, of counterimperatives, even of human limitations. It transcends the family feud of Montagues and Capulets; it rises above the imperial rivalries of Rome and Egypt; and in *Othello* it unites the Venetian and the Moor despite formidable disparities of age, nation, and color, these to be felt perhaps as "after all only the dramatic heightenings of a simple truism . . . that love, any love, is a miracle."[1] Always, of course, Shakespeare is no less aware of the miracle than of the imperfections of circumstance and character that interfere with it or corrupt it. The very harmony that transcends old oppositions, *Othello* implies, brings into play a new competing divisiveness: synthesis, thesis, antithesis. If we call the impulse to harmony, love, the name for the divisive force is hate: the love of Othello and Desemona (and the lesser affection of Othello and Cassio) is the occasion for the flowering of Iago's hate.[2] The love which surmounts age and nation and color intimates an absolute reconciliation of contraries; hence it must call forth the most intense hate, the passion to separate (if this were a political

CHAPTER 6

myth, we would see in the lovers the possibility of unity in the world and in Iago all the divisiveness). These forces, opposed in what Granville-Barker calls a "conflict of being,"[3] can be understood, in Othello's words, as love and chaos: order and disorder, the bringing together and the tearing apart, the will to create and the will to destroy. Yet Iago is a dramatic vessel, not an allegory, of hate; he has a complex psychological make-up that can be unfolded. If his hate is autonomous, it is still true that that autonomous realm has its own particular structure. Likewise the love of Desdemona and Othello, though it point to the absolute powers of love, is a living experience, not an allegory of love. The transcendent unifying power that works in them is modified by their personalities and hence subject to incompleteness, distortion, and the troubles that flow from foolishness, ignorance, and good intentions.[4]

1. STYLES OF ACTION

The spatial form of Act 1 gives a clue to Shakespeare's way of perceiving the love theme. The act not only begins but also ends with Iago's openly stating his hatred and translating it into schemes against Othello. Twice in the first 150 lines and again twice in the last 50 Iago says unqualifiedly that he "hates" Othello (1.1.7-8, 155; 1.3.373, 392). In the beginning he gets Roderigo to stir up Brabantio against Othello; at the end persuades Roderigo to join him in "revenge" against Othello (1.3.375). In the beginning he repeatedly announces his freedom from the duty and the practice of love for Othello (1.1. 39-40, 59-60, 157-158). At the end he acknowledges the credo of self-love; rejects the idea of dying for love; and finally persuades Roderigo that Desdemona will soon tire of Othello and look for a livelier stimulus (1.3.315ff., 348ff.). So Iago has both ends of Act 1; thus his actions symbolically hem in or surround those of Othello and Desdemona, whose love is first dramatized in the middle of the act. What is the love that

THEMATIC FORM: VERSIONS OF LOVE

he would destroy? Is it "a revelation of community in things entirely of the spirit," "a spiritual union of two noble souls"?[5]

Othello is sure of his love for Desdemona; without it, he tells us in his second speech in the play, he would not his "unhoused free condition / Put into circumscription and confine / For the sea's worth" (1.2.26-28). Thus he shows his awareness of countervalues, in the manner, not indeed of one who regrets, but of one who is recording a transaction. He knows what he has traded in; the bargain is *his*; and it is this sense of himself as negotiator that continues on into his later complaints couched partly in the style of one who has bought defective goods. This incomplete giving, this note of calculation, is one element in his relationship with Desdemona. Then there is the histrionic, as we saw in Chapter V: Othello has acted out a melodrama of adventure, with special performances for Desdemona: his audience yielded tears and sighs and fell in love with the hero, and the hero, naively pleased with himself rather than yielding to her, "lov'd her that she did pity" (1.3.150-168). The Duke, charmed by the performance even in summary, and eager to get to state affairs, yields applause: "I think this tale would win my daughter too" (171). But even his acceptance of the romantic pattern does not obscure the fact that Othello evinces less of devotion than of flattered acceptance of adoration,[6] and we wonder what likelihood there is that, after this glamorous and one-sided beginning, the relationship will achieve depth and durability. He is now so emphatically the man of affairs that his role as lover is almost incidental, as if he were still a careless receiver of benefits rather than a fully reciprocating husband. Even with the Turks threatening, he is rather prompt in declaring his fondness for the hard bed of the warrior, and he goes out of his way to insist that sexual desire is not the reason for taking Desdemona to Cyprus (1.3.231-234, 262ff.). If one did not look carefully enough, this might seem entirely the "noble Othello," a serene conqueror of the lower animal being. But the conqueror's volubility makes one pause. What cloudy irresolutions trouble his awareness of sex? Is he a little unsure of himself here, perhaps mindful of trans-Mediterranean attitudes, fearful of seeming "the lascivious Moor" (a plausible motive in one so generally in need of assurance)? Or is he, by inclination and long practice, the man of public affairs whose private emotional life must tag along as best it may, an appendage rather than an element to be integrated or even an integrating force? Or is there simply a lapse of taste, a partner of his rhetorical tendency, in his vehement relegation of Desdemona to a secondary role that can in no way impinge on "serious and great business"? All these elements have a part in his somewhat protracted statement of his own virtue. Though we know that Othello must seem reliable as leader of the expedition, his heavy emphasis on the establishment of reliability is a giveaway, at least of a deficiency in adult self-awareness. There is a consistency in the conquest of physical hardship which he has reported, his quickness to go to war, and his denial of the pleasures of love. As an army man he has apparently had the love of subordinates; perhaps he comes too late to the love founded in sex and requiring a modification of self. The virtues of the military man may be the vices of the lover,[7] or the "noble egotism" of the hero may be an obstacle to personal life, since "self-centeredness doesn't mean self-knowledge."[8]

Further, the disavowal of sensuality is another index of self-deceptiveness. Not, I believe, that there is in Othello a powerful sexuality which he is unconsciously endeavoring to deny or disregard. The general incompleteness of response to Desdemona is the counterpart of a certain physical tepidness; there is a lack of warmth at all levels (it takes jealousy, as ministered to by Iago's aphrodisiac images, to beget intensity of sexual feeling). The lack of urgency, in turn, is symbolically a counterpart of his general deficiency of assurance: together, under pressure, they are convertible into a defensive violence. In denying the "young affects" Othello speaks something close to literal truth; but by implication he denies the power of the whole realm of passion and the irrational. He will order life rationally, as a good general should; no nonsense. The very believer in the magic-webbed handkerchief isn't going to let magic get out of hand; no upsetting passion for him. He rejects "light-wing'd toys" as Iago does "the love of a guinea hen." This is the area of self-deception.[9] His failure to experience a possibly saving irrationality ricochets, we may add, and he is ruined by a destructive irrationality. As in other ways, his experience is representative.

Younger, inexperienced, fascinated by a teller of romantic adventure stories,[10] and now confronted by a sudden nocturnal challenge, Desdemona might well be scared, tremulous, uncertain. But she has the self-possession of one whose new commitment, however romantic in origin, has enough depth to make for strength and security. In telling Brabantio of her new duty to Othello she is alert and resourceful, yet respectful and poised rather than "glib and sophisticated."[11] Then she presses spiritedly for permission to go to Cyprus, an action that is richly characterizing: we see her initiative; her realistic understanding of how her presence at home would affect her father; her romantic love projected from a hearing about into a sharing of adventures, and yet qualified by the facing of military actuality and deepened in two complementary ways: in one, by her explanation, now first made, that in the warrior she had also discerned an essential character ("I saw Othello's visage in his mind"—1.3.253); and in another, by her awareness, candidly stated, of love as a physical fact. "Soul" and "body" are both present in an unusually complete understanding of love.[12] She "did love the Moor to live with him," and if he goes to war alone, "The rites for which I love him are bereft me" (249, 258). "Rites" may mean the whole experience of living together, even of sharing life at the front; but it is difficult to exclude from it the sexual meaning.[13]

In her spontaneous plea to go to Cyprus, Desdemona may not be wise. But at least she is not being self-protective, whereas Othello, though he seconds her request (in one line—261), spends so much time (fourteen lines—262-275) explaining that he has the right reasons and rises to such a hyperbolic conclusion that we cannot fail to sense his self-protectiveness, and even some pompousness in his portrait of himself as the undeflectable commander. The contrast is compressed into a single line when the Duke orders, "You must hence tonight" (278):

Des. Tonight, my lord?
Duke. This night.
Oth. With all my heart. (279)

To Desdemona this is still an interruption of the bridal night. Othello has no consciousness of it. If his dutifulness is admirable, still his *"all* my heart" is singularly unqualified.[14] No shadow would be cast on his honor if he had some division of feeling or could manage some note of "I could not love thee, dear, so much, etc." But he crisply commands, "Come, Desdemona. I have but an hour / Of love" and is off to "obey the time" (299-301). In Othello, Shakespeare succeeds in showing something about the love of the hero for the girl who first caught his eye by adoring his exploits, a love in which an overexplicit temperateness reveals some incompleteness of response and in which the man of affairs, not quite consciously nourishing a large image of himself that he has seen in the mirror of affairs, has withheld the self from a transforming devotion. Thus his personal style oddly combines a certain chillness with a florid, flamboyant rhetoric. In his unredeemed egotism lies the force that can ironically convert the temperateness into its opposite—the chilly and florid into the passionate—and endow it with power to ruin.[15] Yet this history is not done simply. For the love that is diluted by a commander's hard pride in duty and by his self-awareness is found in a man of "personality" and courage and straightforwardness—and withal of a subtle self-distrust that is perhaps the inalienable underside of egotism. Strength may coexist with a kind of weakness, and pride joined to such weakness begets instability.[16]

After the storm Desdemona, who has shown no fear for

THEMATIC FORM: VERSIONS OF LOVE

herself, asks anxiously about Othello (2.1.88). Her tension is never relaxed until Othello arrives; yet, with the discipline of one who would not have her own feelings dominate the occasion, she acts a social role by encouraging Iago in his jokes about women[17] (2.1.118ff.). Then the happy reunion (184-214), during which Othello's lines, though for the first time they show some delight in the possession of Desdemona, still are subtly egocentric (there is, for instance, no inquiry into her well-being). His poststorm joyfulness, as well as his unwitting "I fear," suggests to various critics the happiness about to be dashed down. What is more important, I think, is the noticeable repetition of the first-person pronouns by Othello; it is in this unconsciously exhibited egocentricity that the threat of trouble lies. But it is also in this flush of exhilaration that he calls Desdemona to bed—"That profit's yet to come 'tween me and you" (2.3.10). If we believe, as some critics do, that Othello has more sexuality than he acknowledges, then here, in the carelessness of safe and victorious reunion, it breaks out;[18] but if we believe that his submerged passionateness is less of sex than of a lack of wisdom and of spiritual discipline and that he is characterized by a certain thinness of response in the total realm of sex and love, then here, under the most favorable circumstances, he is carried beyond himself into a warmth that, were it consistent, might make him a more complete and stable lover because it would exact a more thorough quenching of self. In victory he is assured; natural feelings flower; he can give himself. For a moment he is at a middle ground between deficiency of feeling and perversion of feeling.

When Desdemona takes up the "cause" of Cassio, she acts from friendly love (rather than self-regard), and her lines are full of the love theme;[19] glad to show her love by obedience, she leaves at Othello's request (3.3.85ff.). Then Othello's key words, "and when I love thee not, / Chaos is come again" (91-92)—his moment of warmest response, as if he were becoming engaged beyond the cherishing of her admiration and pity; his inadvertent prediction of what will happen; and above all,

175

his statement of Shakespeare's doctrine of love. Love is order, and Iago instinctively works for radical disorder, for chaos—in the human world, loss of humanity, a breaking free of animality. But Shakespeare has been careful to show in *Othello* all the areas of susceptibility to the strains that can be imposed by an earnest dealer in chaos. Iago could not thus work on Desdemona, who, whatever her own simplicity and her mild savoring of wifely influence, is in her love complete and secure.

HATE AS LOVE

Iago (the thief, the poisoner, the suborner of fights, the worker in the dark) defines himself when he says "I hate." As an open hater Iago would set up a less difficult problem, but in the actual Iago, destructiveness appears in another key—as friendship, helpfulness, selflessness, devotion to good causes. Hate takes on the guise of love (Iago as protector of property, healer, peacemaker, light-bringer); hence its overwhelming temporary power. In Iago's conduct Shakespeare has found a paradigm of experience affirmed constantly in other observations of life (for the relevancy of the paradigm in the political orbit, note Johnson on patriotism). In *Othello* it is one of the most ironic variations on the complex theme of love.

Iago can please anybody he wants to, and he "woos" whomever it suits his purposes to seem to love; in the world, evil can charm generally. He uses the word *love* with astonishing frequency. If you drown yourself, he assures Roderigo, "I shall never love thee after" (1.3.307), casting even his "morale-building" in the style of that coquetry with which he characteristically helps soften up a victim. He works on Cassio[20] directly: "I think you think I love you," "I protest, in the sincerity of love and honest kindness" (2.3.316, 333-334). Othello, wanting something of Iago, charges him "On thy love" or "If thou dost love me" (2.3.178; 3.3.115). Othello needs love (his problem of assurance again), and Iago plays to this need; he uses "love" as a weapon, along with "honesty,"

THEMATIC FORM: VERSIONS OF LOVE

again with the deep ironic pleasure of simulating what he is destroying.

In 3.3 Iago's style is exactly that of a lover bent on ensnaring a victim and betraying his real attitude to the victim in the obviousness of his devices: "My lord, you know I love you," and Othello, needing to acknowledge this, acknowledges it twice (117-118). When Iago is ready to tell a real lie about Desdemona, he attributes it to his "love and duty" (194). Othello is shocked by what he hears, and Iago promptly covers up with lover's strategy: a careful apology for "too much loving you" and a reassertion that all he says "Comes from my love" (213, 217). What emerges is a pattern of rival loves: Iago, the lover as operator, works to wean Othello from a counterlove and tie him to his own. It comes out in Othello's threat, "Villain, be sure thou prove my love a whore!" (359). The other love is on the way down, but the despairing fury of Othello is great enough to make Iago play the seducer's strongest card—the threat to pull out. "I thank you for this profit; and from hence / I'll love no friend, sith love breeds such offence" (379-380). In effect: "If you don't play my way, I won't love you any more." If we miss the coquetry, we miss the irony of the hater aping the lover to destroy love. The dalliance works; Othello can't escape the immediate lure, and Iago can revert to the style of heavy-handed devotion; he tells a lie, "Prick'd to't by foolish honesty and love" (412). Othello is finally given exactly the right words to mark the success of Iago's courtship:[21] first a denial of the old love, "All my fond love thus do I blow to heaven" (445), and then a declaration of the new allegiance: "Yield up, O love, thy crown and hearted throne / To tyrannous hate!" (448-449). He has shifted from the Desdemona principle to the Iago principle; he has committed himself to *hate,* using the very word by which Iago's essence has been set forth. Out with the old love: "my bloody thoughts, . . . / Shall ne'er look back, ne'er ebb to humble love" (457-458); and in with the new: "I greet thy love, / . . . with acceptance bounteous" (469-470). *Accept-*

ance is right; in love, Othello always has the manner of one who simply accepts. Now, with hate as his love, Othello orders Cassio's death, and Iago replies with his subtlest bit of love-making: "My friend is dead; 'tis done at your request" (474). It is not merely murder at "request"; it is murder of "my friend,"[22] as if he were murdering one love for the sake of another. Now since just before this he has said, "I'll love no friend," which is an involuntary assertion of truth as well as a verbal maneuver, "My friend is dead" is characteristically ambiguous. But Othello promptly promotes him, in words that are true in more than one sense: "Now art thou my lieutenant" (478), and Iago, echoing Othello's earlier, "I am bound to thee for ever" (213), closes the long scene with his largest assertion of attachment: "I am your own for ever" (479). The ambiguity of these words fittingly closes the "seduction scene." How right that Iago should choose a phrase that might be either the romantic cliché of the young lover or the reassuring hyperbole of the "deceiver" to his sentimental victim, and that, on the other hand, tells what has happened to Othello: he has made the Iago belief and motive his own, and the effect will be with him forever.[23]

After thus managing the "seduction scene," Iago acts in the assured manner of one who has evoked an infatuation that he can use as he pleases. Aside from having to work to make Othello carry out his many-sided hatred, he can treat his "loved one" with indifference and even contempt. He need not protest or ever mention his love again (just as with Roderigo and Cassio once he has them walking the paths that he has made them think will lead them where they want to go). But Othello, enthralled in the work of hate, takes his seducer's love for granted. He is charmed by Iago's "noble sense of thy friend's wrong" (5.1.32), for he counts on unearned emotional income as only a self-centered man could. And just before Emilia will tell him the truth, he triumphantly identifies his informer to her: "My friend, thy husband; honest, honest Iago" (5.2.154). "Friend" and "honest" sum up his infatuation.

THEMATIC FORM: VERSIONS OF LOVE

The amatory style, without which Iago could hardly have managed his great deception of Othello, complicates theme and helps reveal two characters. And it makes possible a second meaning in Emilia's indictment of Iago—"villany hath made mocks with love!" (5.2.151).

Roderigo, Cassio, Bianca, Emilia

Roderigo gives us another version of the lover sick with loss, and of the love inspired by Desdemona. Othello falls into brutality, but Roderigo, even when he is trying to outrage Brabantio, says nothing stronger than "gross clasps of a lascivious Moor" (1.1.127). Roderigo has been disappointed in a hope, whereas Othello, so he thinks, has been injured in a right; this is the difference between the periphery of brutal language and the full center, between the impulse to suicide and the impulse to murder. There is also a contrast between the self-conscious initial temperateness of Othello, and a devouring passion so strong that Roderigo can live with it only by maintaining the delusion that he will be able to satisfy it. Othello fears, Roderigo hopes, that Desdemona is adulterous. Yet Roderigo is not a stereotype of stupid lust; rather there is something of the pathetic in him, for he knows that his program is doomed from the start. He never really modifies the judgment that she is "of blessed condition," but he fumbles on in senseless schemes possible only to one driven, despite moments of enlightenment, by the hope of sleeping with her.

Cassio has a dual role: he is the friendly lover of Othello and Desdemona, and the careless and condescending lover of the "huswife" Bianca. He is happy in the new marriage (2.1.77-82), flamboyant in praise of Desdemona at seaside (83ff.), still enthusiastic but modestly reserved in contrast with Iago's sensual relish that night (2.3.18-27). Whatever the poor judgment and bad taste of Cassio's method of getting the lieutenancy back, the fact is that he feels free to rely on Desdemona's helpfulness and she to yield it, to speak of "the love

179

I bear to Cassio" and of her pleasure when he is eventually assigned to the governorship (4.1.244, 249). Ineptitude, yes; but it is the sureness of her passionate love for Othello that permits her to show candidly that she "lov'd Cassio," as she puts it, "with such general warranty of heaven / As I might love" (5.2.59-61). This is just what the egotist in Othello makes him incapable of understanding. Cassio's relationship with Bianca lets us see him with his own "positional assurance" —indeed, a lesser Othello, indulgently accepting more than he is giving, maintaining an attitude of business first, asking a favor, dismissing her when it suits his purpose.[24] The Othello-Cassio analogy becomes still clearer when Bianca turns out to be more than a stereotyped prostitute, a legitimate object of laughter because "out of her own love and flattery" (4.1.133-134) she hopes Cassio will marry her. For she enters again when Cassio is injured—terribly distressed, showing her love, trying to help, taking a risk when she might stay safely at home (5.1.74ff.). Here is a "strumpet" in action, thematically relevant because Othello has just been attacking Desdemona as a "strumpet." He has forced her into a category where fidelity is supposed not to be found; in rejecting a loving individual he is falling into the self-regard of a society (or the cynicism of a Iago) that uses hard categories to deny individuals. Both "strumpets" do love,[25] and neither gets her due.

Iago hates Bianca because she breaks out of the hard category of streetwalker and "dotes on Cassio" (4.1.97). His hate takes the form of society's sex judgments, a means of denying the individual who is disturbingly more than an animal, and the hate shows behind the tactics when he tries to implicate her in the attack on Cassio: "This is the fruit of whoring" (5.1.116). When Emilia tosses in "sincerely" the conventional proprieties, "Fie, fie upon thee, strumpet!" (121), Bianca defends herself firmly: "I am no strumpet, but of life as honest / As you that thus abuse me" (122-123). In terms of the action of the play to this point, it is true. She is more "honest" than Iago; like Desdemona, she has had one love; and she too protests against

THEMATIC FORM: VERSIONS OF LOVE

false charges. In the play of love, the honest whore has an illuminating role. The naive and devoted wife may be as undervalued as she, and she as singleminded as the wife. The figure of hate must endeavor to destroy both.

In sneering at Bianca, Emilia falls in with Iago's apparent attitude. She tries to serve two loves, sometimes compatible. The heavy tension she is under in Act 5 first shows when she steals the handkerchief; she is willing to pick it up and to seek Iago's praise, but intends no more than having a copy made for him and returning the original to Desdemona. But Shakespeare works the irony of the apparently harmless trick that suddenly gets out of control: Iago grabs the handkerchief, and Emilia is left wringing her hands. But Iago orders her to keep it quiet (3.3.319), and she does just that, even though she is present throughout the scene in which Othello gives Desdemona the history of the handkerchief and angrily demands that she produce it (3.4.33-98). She is caught by an unwilling commitment, a fear of confession, a belief that the storm is only temporary, and a hope that things "will turn out all right"; so she lets Desdemona "take it." Here there is something of the tight-lipped gangland "moll" that goes along appropriately with numerous suggestions of the gangster in Iago himself. Yet Emilia is not at ease; she doesn't say much, and she works off her uneasiness by attacking men (103-106, 159-162). It is good realistic portraiture. Emilia keeps quiet even after she has been interrogated by a palpably upset Othello and has heard the beginning and ending of the brothel scene. Is not this provocation enough to get her off the fence and make the loyalty to Desdemona active? Perhaps. On the other hand, she still does not guess how much is at stake; at most Othello must seem to be having a temporary fit of suspicion and ill temper; she knows that Desdemona's position is unassailable; and we may reasonably assume that she fails to think of the loss of the handkerchief as an active source of Othello's outbursts, if we take into account two facts: (1) from 3.4.102 to 5.2.214 neither Othello nor Desdemona again mentions the

181

handkerchief in her presence; (2) Emilia may be willingly forgetting.[26] Hence, when she attacks the supposed slanderer of Desdemona, she is the more voluble and earnest. That the handkerchief episode has, in whatever way, slipped below the threshold of consciousness, is attested to by Emilia's shock when, after the murder, Othello argues that Desdemona gave the handkerchief to Cassio as a "pledge of love" (5.2.214). Emilia's "O God! O heavenly pow'rs!" (218) surely indicates a sudden, new realization of what she has done. She has already prepared for a break with Iago in her unqualified attack on the unknown traducer of Desdemona and begun the break, when she identifies the traducer as Iago, by announcing: " 'Tis proper I obey him, but not now. / Perchance, Iago, I will ne'er go home" (196-197). Now, the handkerchief story clear, she completes the break and is killed by Iago. Her dying thoughts are all of Desdemona: her choice of loyalties is total.[27]

There are no clichés on wifely obedience: Desdemona chooses an obedience, Emilia a disobedience, that leads to death. Each chooses quality of life when by calculation she might get an extension of life; by disobeying, Emilia purges herself of an earlier obedience. The treatment of Emilia is one identifying mark of the high tragedy in which even apparently common-grained members of a society may be thought capable of making right choices instead of scheming self-protectively.

Epithets of War

In this drama of love the three leading men are professional soldiers, and for a while the action is under the shadow of war. So there is a certain amount of war talk, but only briefly; war reaches into the drama principally through its impact on the feelings and imaginations, and hence on the speech, of the actors. Though Iago, as everyone knows, seasons his language with a certain amount of military and naval rattle,[28] this style significantly disappears after Act 3, when Iago has an actual war going on the home front. His war against love breaks out obliquely in such terms as "boarded a land

THEMATIC FORM: VERSIONS OF LOVE

carack," "sounds a parley to provocation," "alarum to love," "Our General's wife is now the General" (1.2.50; 2.3.23, 27, 319). Far from being simply the casual metaphors of a bluff military man, these phrases imply attitudes: the marriage, imaged only in physical terms, is a kind of piracy; Desdemona's attractions are only physical; a wife becomes a "boss." The ancient ironic kinship of love and war—the myth of Mars and Venus—produces only a campfollower's view of life. When another soldier, Cassio, uses a similar figure for Desdemona— "our great captain's captain" (2.1.74)—the effect is different; the speaker is "thrice-gentle,"[29] as Desdemona calls him (3.4.122), and deeply appreciates Desdemona's quality, so that Othello gains stature in being declared her "man." So we have, not a cliché, "the soldier's" view of Othello's love, but contrasting views held by two different soldiers. Too, Cassio's own version of the Mars-Venus myth—the Bianca affair—goes, as we have seen, beyond the stereotype of casual lust, but without being sentimentalized.[30]

For the third soldier, war is variously business, romance, and symbol. In the early part of the play Othello is the businessman warrior, ever ready to meet the demands of vocation.[31] He is highly profession-conscious: he thinks of himself specifically as soldier rather than generically as man, and he talks much of lacking "the soft phrase of peace" and of "tented field" and of "broil and battle" (1.3.81-91). Yet businesslike as he is, he cannot talk realistically of war as only a business, or a sordid business; he sees it romantically, talks of it romantically, and produces a romantic result—Desdemona's attachment to him. So the drama produces a third version of the myth of war and love.

For Desdemona, the romance of war and the romance of love are intertwined. She wished to be or possess[32] a soldier, she fell in love with a soldier, and she interprets the sharing of a soldier's life as a realization of love in all its aspects. Here romantic glamor and realistically complete awareness of love are remarkably merged. Othello's first words to Desdemona

183

at Cyprus—"O my fair warrior!" (2.1.184)—remind us simultaneously of the war itself, of Desdemona's coming to the front, and of the role of war in their thought and feeling.[33] Then Othello proclaims a celebration of both the victory and "his nuptial" (2.2.1ff.)—war and love. The fair warrior tries to acknowledge the rules of war: in pleading for Cassio, she refers to the common opinion that "the wars must make examples / Out of their best" (3.3.65-66). Then Othello changes his tone; romance begins to disappear, and Desdemona finds herself a target—"stood within the blank of his displeasure" (3.4.128). She fires back, in thought only, yet promptly rebukes herself: "unhandsome warrior as I am!" (151). This aspect of the poem of love, which began with the romance of war,[34] now ends; even as she says "unhandsome warrior," Desdemona is moving significantly into a legal metaphor ("Arraigning his unkindness") : the new reality into which she is thrust is the problem of justice. She forgets rather than rejects the myth of the adventurous soldier-lover as she tries maturely to accommodate herself to the new Othello.

The new Othello, though not romantic, is in some ways more military than ever—rejecting "humble love," embracing hate, planning executions, unknowingly exciting comparisons with the kind of soldier he once was,[35] and yet saying goodbye to the warrior's life. He starts conventionally enough with a farewell to "tranquil mind" and "content." Then comes the shock: "tranquil mind" and "content" are followed by a striking series of defining terms—images of war:

> Farewell the plumed troop, and the big wars
> That make ambition virtue! O, farewell!
> Farewell the neighing steed and the shrill trump,
> The spirit-stirring drum, th' ear-piercing fife,
> The royal banner, and all quality,
> Pride, pomp, and circumstance of glorious war!
> And O ye mortal engines whose rude throats
> Th' immortal Jove's dread clamours counterfeit,
> Farewell! Othello's occupation's gone!   (3.3.349-357)

THEMATIC FORM: VERSIONS OF LOVE

Othello applies Shakespeare's doctrine of love. In drama after drama, love brings human beings together despite large barriers, making unity of diversity; for Othello, love creates the unity of the individual's life. If love fails, all the rest of life becomes empty.[36] And if all the rest of life is the practice of war, the renunciation is an extraordinary revelation of a latent paradox: "the tranquil mind" and "content" were found in the making of war, whereas now, in the technical peace that follows victory, there is a noisy and evil violence—continually forced upon us by the verbal and actional drama. War, a business turned into romance by Othello's perception of it, has now become a symbol. War was Othello's peace, and in peace he finds war; having no peace as a man, he must give up the peace of war. Shakespeare is moving toward the remarkable paradoxes that are at the heart of *King Lear*. Othello is not so great a figure as Lear, of course, and peace-in-war does not have the symbolic inclusiveness or depth of reason-in-madness or blindness-in-sight. Yet at this point there is in Othello something of the universal, and by that I mean the human tendency, which we are likely to conceal from ourselves, to find the life of war easier than the life of peace, to prefer the melodramatic life which seems to resolve the problem of good and evil, to the tragic life in which that problem is always confounding expectations. Othello is unfitted for tragic life. And in that he is characteristically tragic, for it is the nature of the tragic hero to want to live melodramatically or romantically, and his destiny to have to learn to live tragically. Nevertheless "farewell love, farewell arms" is more mature than the refrain of the banal romantic hero escaping to war: "farewell love, welcome arms."

And yet, we can see here why Othello is slow in coming to tragic insight. The paradox of peace in war is not as substantial as it might be, for Othello does not perceive war fully enough. Though his decision itself is unromantic, he has seen only half of what he renounces; if the war that seems inevitable now ("war is hell") was not inevitable then, it was at least possible, and possible to Shakespeare. But Shakespeare gives Othello none of it—no awareness of wounds and mutilation, confusion of motive, dishonor, brutishness, death, of what one scholar calls "the sordid actuality of Renaissance military life."[37] To Othello it is visual and auditory glamor—a parade-ground war.[38] At his age, and with all his experience, he is still the shiny-eyed novice in war. Yet what can be said for him is that he now knows this is gone. At the same time we wonder what another kind of warrior might think about a less colorful war in the light of private disaster.

Though he says farewell to war, Othello cannot help returning to the warrior. He thinks he could stand military hardship better than his present woes—if heaven had "Given to captivity me and my utmost hopes" (4.2.51). At the end the erring hero tends to become the erring military man; he grieves at the loss of his sword, claims he has another, plans to "assault" Gratiano (5.2.243-258), and thus gains his ear. Now—and we should not miss the characteristic Shakesperian contrast with the similar scene in Act 1—the old soldier again holds forth on his military glory, seasoning the stale hour of defeat with the last dashes of the "egoistic poetry of war":[39]

> Behold, I have a weapon.
> A better never did itself sustain
> Upon a soldier's thigh. I have seen the day
> That with this little arm and this good sword
> I have made my way through more impediments
> Than twenty times your stop.   (259-264)

But Othello has progressed: he cannot find peace in memories. Not that he has arrived at tragic maturity; he is less inclined to understand fully than to scourge himself—and to flay indeed not so much the transgressing man as the defunct warrior:

> But O vain boast!
> Who can control his fate? 'Tis not so now.
> Be not afraid, though you do see me weapon'd.
> Here is my journey's end, here is my butt,

THEMATIC FORM: VERSIONS OF LOVE

   And very seamark of my utmost sail.
   Do you go back dismay'd? 'Tis a lost fear.
   Man but a rush against Othello's breast,
   And he retires.   (264-271)

It may be argued that Othello's self-judgment is none the less penetrating because it is couched in metaphors from his profession. Yet the choice of metaphor partly determines what is to be said; here Othello certainly acknowledges a failure, but it is less a failure of commission than a falling into weariness or apathy or uncombativeness. His not charging Gratiano is again not an adequate symbol of his spiritual error, so that by focusing his own attention upon his lack of zest with his sword, he chastises himself for a failure that keeps his mind off a graver failure as a lover and as a human being. Through the consistency of Othello as a soldier Shakespeare displays the habits of a mind that repeatedly has difficulty in identifying and coming to grips with the deep center of his problems. The man who is thoroughly a soldier may not always realize the full spiritual potentialities of the man; the military career can encourage the immature and the histrionic. Even now, gloomily resigning the gesture of attack, Othello foresees picturesque, even quasi-military, punishments: "hurl my soul from heaven," "gulfs of liquid fire" (274, 280). And he goes on to that military self-execution which in one aspect is his last parade-ground spectacle.

   To see love partly in terms of war—even as an adjunct of war—is to provide a fresh and revealing dramatic perspective. The "epithets of war" are more than verbal mannerisms or neutral tags from trade.

THE LOVER'S DEATH

                           When the lover in the play of love is an army man, certain traditional associations, fraught with paradox, are easily set in motion—the affinity of war and love, of death-dealing and life-bringing. The fabled amorousness of the army man is prosaically echoed in the statistic of the wartime birth rate. The erotogenic war of nations finds a sociobiological analogy in the war of the sexes, which, as Aristophanes has shown, is easily convertible into the love of the sexes. The violent quarrel may take an erotic turn; the love-hate ambivalence is commonplace knowledge. "Fair warrior" is not only "fair army wife" or "fair lady at the front" but also "fair participant in love's combat." The mysterious resolutions of contraries—war as source of love, war as love, love as war—appear constantly in metaphor; the dark kinship of "fight" and "love" has a subterranean life in language itself.[40]

Thus the simple idea pairs of *war: death* and *love: life* are crossed and intertwined. From war, death; but from war, also, love; and, finally, the pairing of love and death, an imaginative yoking of long history. This yoking operates variously: there are the psychopathological forms[41] which, by the emphasis of distortion, alert us to the "normal"; the larger area of romantic feeling, extending from the cliché of "dying for love" to the grandiose Wagnerian idea of death as the end or ideal consummation of love;[42] the rich possibility of speaking of the act of love in terms of death—a metaphor which can range in tone from the broad joke to the acute irony—and of thus giving the vocabulary of death a new symbolic dimension. The Elizabethans were masters of this kind of effect. We need only recall the mad Lear's pungent ambiguity when he seasons his wild phrases of desperation—his expression of royal impotence, we might say—with a bitter sex allusion: "I will die bravely, like a smug bridegroom" (4.6.202).

When Shakespeare wrote that line, *Othello* might well have echoed in his mind. For Othello is a smug bridegroom, and at the end he dies bravely; but at the same time the actional and verbal drama are so managed that we cannot forget the symbolic meaning of *die*. The general marries; then he kills his wife; then he dies—beside her, on the bed. Thus love eventuates in death—with an ambiguity of which the play makes the most.[43]

Much of the action of *Othello* takes place, in a sense, on a

THEMATIC FORM: VERSIONS OF LOVE

bridal night—extended over several actual nights by two major interruptions. Here the counterpoint of light and darkness, which we traced in Chapter III, is the general outline for the development of a special nocturne. On the one hand, the interruptions[44] prompted by the pseudo bringer of light, Iago, whose motives we must return to later; on the other, the motif "that the night come." At first this is Desdemona's;[45] only in Cyprus does Othello, who in Venice was emphatically ready for a purely military "bed of down," call Desdemona to bed (2.3.8-9). Then the second consecutive interruption of a bridal night; and again Othello tells Desdemona, "come away to bed" (252).

A pattern of interference,[46] of imperfect consummation, is set up, and at the same time the bridal bed is made a concrete reality. The new sharing of the bed so strikes the imagination of Desdemona and Othello that from it both of them derive expressive images: "His bed shall seem a school" (3.3.24), and "She might lie by an emperor's side and command him tasks" (4.1.195-196). The novel, sharp awareness of the marital bed surely increases Othello's susceptibility to Iago's fluent images of the illicitly shared bed (4.1.3, 34, 69). The climax of all this is Iago's excited command, "Strangle her in bed, even the bed she hath contaminated" and Othello's hearty agreement—a shock which is not a theatrical trick but a logical dramatic pulling together of the linked parts we are tracing. Now for the third time Iago helps break into an Othello-and-Desdemona night, but this third time it is Othello who will spoil, and forever, the union—at the very time of physical actualizing at which it has already been twice disturbed. The husband will reverse his role as bringer of love and life.

But first Othello must accuse Desdemona directly, and he does this in a scene which fits exactly into this sequence: he makes believe that he is visiting Desdemona in a brothel (4.2. 26ff.). In this travesty of the bridal night the pretended use of the bed symbolically completes its "contamination," and Othello is ready for purgative murder. Of the irony of the

189

bridegroom as death-bringer Shakespeare makes the most, using not only the bedroom, but the bed itself, and for several scenes focusing our attention on Desdemona's preparing for bed. In the inevitable suggestions of the sex relation there is a possible variation in tone from the farcical and lusty to the romantic and intense. We remember Iago's "Well, happiness to their sheets!" (2.3.29). What makes the compelling effect here is the substitution of ominousness for all the other modes of anticipation. We can see how much Shakespeare is putting into this if we keep in mind that he is uniquely using dramatic materials capable of degenerating into the stuff of striptease and bedroom farce. Othello's command to Desdemona is not that of a lover: "Get you to bed on th' instant. I will be return'd forthwith. Dispatch your attendant there. Look't be done" (4.3.7-9). When Desdemona repeats the order and Emilia queries in sharp surprise, "Dismiss me?" (14), the note of threat is deepened. Desdemona's apprehensiveness appears in her inability to forget the Willow Song, which is not only about unhappy love but which in its closing line ties in with the "going to bed" theme: "If I court moe women, you'll couch with moe men" (57)—a line which, significantly, Desdemona has invented.[47] Shakespeare keeps concretely before us the intimations of sex in this place and time. Desdemona undresses: "Give me my nightly wearing" and "Prithee unpin me" (16, 21, 34). Beside the irony that she is undressing not for the marital bed but for death is another which grows out of her earlier command to Emilia, "Lay on my bed my wedding sheets" (4.2.105)—a symbolic reassertion of the fidelity denied by Othello, and an effort to renew the honeymoon of a marriage now monstrously threatened. Now, more depressed, she has a sharp new thought: "If I do die before thee, prithee shroud me / In one of those same sheets" (4.3.24-25). In one sense she would symbolically extend the marriage beyond life. But the marriage has been scarcely more than a bridal night, and the bridal night is now almost equated with death. What has served love will serve death; to the death that ends life

THEMATIC FORM: VERSIONS OF LOVE

it is but a step from the metaphorical death whence life begins. Beyond the manifest irony there is invoked something of the love-death mystery.

Whereas Desdemona would continue her authentic love in death, Othello would bury her suspected lust in death: "Strumpet, . . . / . . . / Thy bed, lust-stain'd, shall with lust's blood be spotted" (5.1.34-36). This metonym of the bed permits an essential ambiguity: the extremes of profound love and casual lust may, since they have a common element, perversely resemble one another (or one may even seek the other out—a problem posed by a subject to which we come shortly, the relation of Iago to Desdemona). Othello's promise to bloody the lust-stained bed, since it is made when he hears what he thinks is the killing of Cassio, serves to keep the final bedroom scene in our minds during the one public scene that intervenes between Desdemona's dismissal of Emilia and Othello's entering of the bedroom. Desdemona is in her bed throughout the scene; the bed is visible to the end of the play. We have only to reflect how different this scene would be, in effect and meaning, if the murder took place in the hall of the castle, say, or in the library. It would still be a passional crime, and there would still be the irony of destroying a true love, but all the overtone and ambiguity would be gone—the compounding of the cruel error by an imagined justness of unjust punishment; the convertibility of sexual love into hate; the transmutation of the marital bed—"Lay on my bed my wedding sheets, remember"—into the deathbed: "thou art on thy deathbed" (5.2.51), a transmutation at once monstrous and yet somehow breaking through a logical separation to express an obscure kinship intuitively felt. When the murderer enters and soliloquizes over the form on the bed, he is almost the physical lover: he smells the "rose" and kisses Desdemona lingeringly—a sensory indulgence (like his caressing relish of her snow-white, alabaster-smooth skin) discordant with his established purpose and judicial "mask" and yet exactly in accord with the prevalent ambiguity of the bedroom scenes.[48] The dual possibility

191

before the murderer-lover is implicit in Desdemona's words when she awakes: "Will you come to bed, my lord?" (5.2.24). It is as if Othello had a choice of life or death (as when Desdemona offered him the curative handkerchief), or, by virtue of the Elizabethan metaphor, a choice of death in one meaning or death in another. Yet his carrying out of the literal death which he chooses for her, and as a consequence for himself also, is overlaid with singular reminders of the other choice. His "smothering" her in bed, the physical contact, the suggested struggle or paroxysm, the moment of the total stillness and privacy (a blank in existence, suddenly ended by Emilia's calling "within")—here is a subtle transfer of terms, a metaphor of circumstances, by which one act becomes, without becoming, another. As Empson puts it, "It is as a sort of parody of the wedding night . . . that the scene is given its horror."[49] To the others who have come in, Emilia blurts out what has happened: "My mistress here lies murthered in her bed" (185); it is only seconds later that Othello first cries out in anguish and "Falls on the bed"[50] and Emilia lashes him, "Nay, lay thee down and roar!" (198). For a moment he is again beside Desdemona on the bed. Then there is the final union with her there—when Othello, at the climax of his deathbed speech, stabs himself with the intent of falling over her body. The double meaning of his words is unmistakable: "I kiss'd thee ere I kill'd thee. No way but this— / Killing myself, to die upon a kiss" (358-359). Once he had said, as if in wager, "My life upon her faith!" (1.3.295); now he yields his life upon her faithful body. When he entered her bedroom for the last time, he said, "I will kill thee, / And love thee after" (5.2.18-19). With all the preparation—the interrupted bridal night, Desdemona's getting ready for bed, the long focusing of attention on the bed—and with the bodily proximity before our eyes now, Othello's *die* cannot help having, in addition to its literal sense, the metaphorical sense of completing the sex act.[51] Othello finally seals the union only by killing his wife and himself: murder as the sex act. His last words are astonish-

THEMATIC FORM: VERSIONS OF LOVE

ingly close to Romeo's last words, "Thus with a kiss I die,"[52] and he might well apply to himself, with richer meaning than they have for Antony, Antony's words when he falls on his sword, "A bridegroom in my death."[53] For more than a decade the love-death ambiguity—love as death, death as love—particularly as it was made poetically viable by common metaphorical usage now lost, haunted Shakespeare's imagination, and he used it in closing three major dramas of love[54] (two of them with generals as heroes). But in the other two he did not have the pun so thoroughly prepared for and implied in the dramatic materials, or so concretely acted out, as in *Othello*. This powerful closing irony completes the tracing of a love that for the soldier Othello began in romance, never became grounded deep enough in actuality (physical and spiritual) to resist even a planted mirage of evil, and matured—as far as it could—only in the tragic pattern: in the discovery, at the cost of death, of a truth which man could have had simply by being open to it.

2. DOCTRINE AND SYMBOL

If *Othello* may be called the play of love, nevertheless, as I have said, it is not an allegory of love. But in different parts it does enunciate several doctrines of love which help to clarify the symbolic import of the action.

IAGO AS PHILOSOPHER OF LOVE

Under Iago's tutelage Othello the lover acquires not only what looks like information but also certain principles of knowledge. Out of passion for a certainty which he might have had by exercising the faith or the charity that love implies he falls into a philosophy that does him little good.

Iago's moral core, we have seen, is hate. Yet he can ape love. We might ask: what would such a man think about love if he theorized about it? What must a man think of that which he does not have but which he can fake and thus use instrumentally? Must he not disparage and minimize it? Here the problem is partly one of distinguishing Iago's beliefs from his strategies. He can encourage Roderigo to count on, and Othello to believe in, Desdemona's infidelity, and Cassio to count on her lovingkindness for strong intercession with Othello; and while hating Othello and plotting against him and Desdemona, he is capable of describing him as "of a constant, loving, noble nature" and her as "fram'd as fruitful / As the free elements" (2.3.347-348). Or he is capable of telling Othello, "There's millions now alive / That nightly lie in those unproper beds / Which they dare swear peculiar" just twenty lines after he has said in soliloquy, "And many worthy and chaste dames even thus, / All guiltless, meet reproach" (4.1.68-70, 47-48). We remember that Iago regards the world of reality and appearance as fluid, unjelled, subject to manipulation; the only truth is the one that has instrumental value in a given context. At the same time Iago is intellectually capable of recognizing realities—of character and value—that do not shift with context, that exist despite his preferences; of entertaining simultaneously the concept of "millions in unproper beds" and of "many worthy and chaste dames." By recognition of exceptions to what he believes to be the rule, he knows the good that alone makes evil enjoyable; if sex is the arena, the only victory is that over chastity and devotion. Antipoetic though he is at the core, there is yet something of the ironic poet in him, utilizing contradictory perspectives and even caught in ambivalence of feeling; there is insight in the judgment that Iago is "a case of dual personality,"[55] and that "in spite of his respect for the tortuous, he can also admire the open and truthful."[56] But even if we take "worthy and chaste dames" as literally "true" for Iago,[57] his hope and his operating faith are otherwise; without a faith in general depravity he could hardly be so consistent in style and so effective in causing others to adopt, for practical purposes, a positivist view of sex. At the heart

THEMATIC FORM: VERSIONS OF LOVE

of his working principle is the reduction of love to sensuality in flux.[58]

The reductive view of sex which, as we have seen, is implied in Iago's military and animal images of love early in the play prepares for his various discourses to Roderigo. In the first of these, when he must keep Roderigo from drowning himself, he passes quickly from a traditional exhortation[59] on the utility of will and reason to a theory of human nature that will minimize the need for self-discipline by Roderigo. If it were not for reason, he says, "the blood and baseness of our natures would conduct us to most prepost'rous conclusions" (1.3.332-333). What "you call love" is "a sect or scion" of "unbitted lusts" (336-337), "merely a lust of the blood and a permission of the will" (339-340). He is reducing the passion to a least common denominator that must behave according to certain simple rules, which he hardly expects will and reason to change. Desdemona's and Othello's love won't last long; it began violently and will subside accordingly; the Moor is changeable, Desdemona is changeable, both will reach satiety (347-358). Iago is sure that he can overcome the "sanctimony" (sacrament) and "frail vow" between them (361-362).

Concerning Desdemona, Iago needs to believe this true; concerning women generally, he does believe it to be true. He could not pretend to have suspicions of Othello and Cassio if infidelity were not the law of life. Cassio, he says in soliloquy, is "fram'd to make women false" (1.3.404). He makes epigrams and joking verses on the sexuality of women. So when he resumes encouraging Roderigo to hope for intercourse with Desdemona, we know that what he tells Roderigo for his own purposes is entirely consistent with his fundamental way of looking at love—as a purely physical, passing excitement, leading to satiety and disgust, and requiring new stimuli. He anticipates Edmund's naturalism:[60] "Very nature will instruct her in it and compel her to some second choice" (2.1.238).

Iago has a familiar reductive habit of mind. He is outside

195

the myth of love. He is a kind of scientist of sex. He positivizes it: it consists only of observable physical phenomena. "In Iago's world everything is catalogued from observation."[61] The invisible and the intangible are not real. There is no "idea" of love; we have only the evidence of sensory behavior, which is an absolute. Iago's theory of love is exactly consistent with his theory of reputation—"there is more sense in that [a bodily wound] than in reputation" (2.3.267-268)—and of honor—"Her honour is an essence that's not seen" (4.1.16). Note that the long addresses to Roderigo are the first extended prose passages in the play; the earlier of these concludes Act 1, just as the calculating prose of Goneril and Regan ends the first scene in *Lear.* Iago takes away the poetry of love—all the complex interaction of passion and imagination, of self and devotion, of flesh and spirit. He robs men of whatever transcends the physical facts of love—the personality of the thief at work on the philosophic plane; the obscurantist pretending to be the lightbearer; the promoter of what Eric Voegelin calls "spiritual eunuchism."[62] He commits Roderigo, who wants to believe it, to a philosophy of love; he converts Othello to the same philosophy—and Othello does not want to believe. In the end, Iago is engaged in philosophical corruption. He is not merely making statements which are not true, but making statements which might be true if the individual to whom they refer conformed to the general human rule which Iago advances for behavior of this order.[63] His success springs in part from the strength of his belief, in part from his playing upon a human inclination to accept a simplified likeness of truth, even though it promise disaster, rather than to labor with an exacting complex verity. For many human beings it is apparently easier to live with the idea of even a horrifying evil in someone else than to reckon with the complications of good and evil in another and in oneself.

By his style Iago cleverly creates the impression that he is talking about human generalities: *"Men* should be what they seem" (3.3.127), "it is my nature's plague / To spy into *abuses"*

THEMATIC FORM: VERSIONS OF LOVE

(146-147), "Good name in *man and woman* . . . / . . . jewel of their souls" (155-156), "*That cuckold* lives in bliss" (167), "the *souls* of all my tribe defend / From jealousy!" (175-176). The plurals, the generic singulars, the abstraction *jealousy* all subtly imply universal experience. Then Iago does literally generalize for Venice: "In Venice *they* do let heaven see the *pranks / They* dare not show *their husbands; their* best conscience" (202-203). A principle of action is suggested by the repetition of action: "She did deceive her father," "She that, so young, could give out such a seeming" (206, 209). If Desdemona departed from "nature" in marrying a man of different "clime," still she belongs to a class—really the class representing the novelty principle of sexuality: "Foh! one may smell in *such* a will most rank" (232). Hence the law of change may apply: she may "fall to match you with her country forms, / And happily repent" (237-238).

The turning point is Othello's soliloquy, for he now shows that he has adopted a general theory of sex which makes it virtually impossible for him to regain his shaken belief in Desdemona's fidelity. First he gives Iago credit, not for being a sleuth, but for knowledge of principles of human conduct: he "knows all qualities, with a learned spirit, / Of human dealings" (259-260). Then he states the principles to which he now adheres:

> O curse of marriage,
> That we can call these delicate creatures ours,
> And not their appetites!
>   Yet 'tis the plague of great ones;
> Prerogativ'd are they less than the base.
> 'Tis destiny unshunnable, like death.
> Even then this forked plague is fated to us
> When we do quicken.   (268-270, 273-277)

Iago's positivism has taken in Othello as it did Roderigo—more thoroughly, indeed, than Roderigo, who knew all the time that Desdemona was an exception to the rule which he was working by in the hope that it might hold for her. The play

197

of love is widened and deepened when to the other versions of love—the romantic, the friendly, the desperate, and others yet to be seen—is added the philosophic mode of defining love by the "laws" of sensuality: Othello thinks the universal itch is at work.[64] It would be a lesser play if he simply thought Desdemona unfaithful, i.e., had only made an error of fact. The most skillful trapper of men traps his victims philosophically, and traps them, as Iago does Othello, into a whole labyrinth of related intellectual confusions: his muddled reasoning about appearance and reality; his wanting to "see," as if all truth were visible; his determination to "prove"—the other face of a loss of the faith in love which alone could save him.[65]

The big job done, Iago's role as theorist of sex now thins out.[66] Othello goes on to apply his new philosophy—not only trying to convict Desdemona, but generalizing the case: "A liberal hand! The hearts of old gave hands; / But our new heraldry is hands, not hearts" (3.4.46-47), holding forth knowingly on "They that mean virtuously" (4.1.7), and sneering at "woman's tears" (256). The real horror of the brothel scene is not only that he is falsely accusing Desdemona but that he is reducing the person Desdemona into an impersonal exemplar of instinctive animal behavior, pushing down the extraordinary individual into the general mass of gross mechanical beings (4.2.27ff.). Both of them become neutral participants in a business arrangement. The symbolic poem which he is acting out is a spiritual murder and suicide (the forewarning of the actual murder and suicide); unconsciously Othello understands the implications of the philosophy he has learned from Iago.

Something might be said for having the actual death occur here where spiritual death—the reduction of the myth of love to the rules of sexuality—is symbolically presented (the *lust:death* equation, which we must still explore, could finely counterbalance the *love:death* paradox). But we still need to see how Iago's thought lowers the tone of the community and sweeps it toward chaos—the mounting noise, violence, plotting, and abuse. We have already noted how, as he speeds toward vio-

THEMATIC FORM: VERSIONS OF LOVE

lence, Othello falls into violence of language and virtually usurps Iago's animal imagery for human beings. He discovers his capacity for a vulgar style sharply contrasted with his early romantic manner;[67] up come the depths that help account for his quest of assurance; he falls into an abusive vocabulary of sex. To Iago: "prove my love a whore!" "Damn her, lewd minx!" "A fine woman! a fair woman! a sweet woman!" To Desdemona: "Devil," "whore," "public commoner," "impudent strumpet," "cunning whore of Venice," "strumpet," "strumpet" and after her death: "she was a whore" and "Cassio did top her."[68] Such verbal manners are not required of a husband who thinks he has been betrayed. The meanness comes both from the uncertainties in Othello's personality and the kind of ideas he has absorbed; the Iago commonness is diffused along with his malice, and the shock waves from Othello's abusive explosions are recorded in Emilia's angry incredulity ("whore? ... whore?"—4.2.115-137) and Desdemona's plea: "Am I that name, Iago?" "I cannot say 'whore.' / It doth abhor me now I speak the word" (4.2.118, 161-162). This is not false delicacy, for it comes from the same Desdemona who asked to travel with Othello lest "The rites for which I love him are bereft me."

In his actual and theoretical war against the myth of love, Iago brutalizes the world as far as he can. But Shakespeare equally dramatizes the powers of resistance to his philosophy. Emilia shares some of his ideas, as her questions indicate:

> What is it that they do
> When they change us for others? Is it sport?
> I think it is. And doth affection breed it?
> I think it doth. Is't frailty that thus errs?
> It is so too. And have not we affections,
> Desires for sport, and frailty, as men have?   (4.3.99-104)

But Emilia holds her "realism" flexibly; she knows that sensuality is a fact and also that chastity is a fact, and she values it. She is much more in the "world" than Desdemona, but she is capable of the "unworldly" devotion that is fatal to Iago.

199

Since his philosophy does not allow for this turn of events, he is really ruined by the inadequacies of his own system.[69] Called "subtle whore" by Othello (4.2.21) and "villanous whore"[70] by Iago (5.2.229), Emilia gives her life for Desdemona's truth. While Othello, pushed by Iago, is doing his best to turn love into whoredom, Bianca, repeatedly called "harlot" and "strumpet" by Iago, is turning whoredom into love. And under vicious attacks Desdemona remains chaste and devoted; it is just after she has been called "that cunning whore of Venice" that she directs Emilia, "Lay on my bed my wedding sheets." Three women under the weight of heavy abuse—under a malicious chorus of "strumpet" and "whore"—hold, in their different ways, to their faithfulness. They redeem the myth of love, in which Iago must disbelieve.

"I DO LOVE HER TOO"

Iago is not only a hater, a strategist in love, and a philosopher of love, but he is also, in his way, a lover. We need to define "in his way." But to say even so much is to add to a character already many-sided a new side disturbing in its possible incongruity with the others. Yet this new side, if it is there, may serve to hold together the others in a formal constitution of the character, at both psychological and symbolic levels, more nearly complete than we have so far seen. The hypothetical new side may also help to explain the "form" of certain segments of action otherwise perhaps obscure.

When Iago remarks casually of Desdemona, "Now I do love her too" (2.1.300), his words somehow make little impact. At first glimpse they sound like a sour joke. He goes on,

> Not out of absolute lust (though peradventure
> I stand accountant for as great a sin)
> But partly led to diet my revenge,
> For that I do suspect the lusty Moor
> Hath leap'd into my seat.   (301-305)

THEMATIC FORM: VERSIONS OF LOVE

Now the "love" seems invented, an afterthought, a retaliation fanciful in its irrelevance to possible overt action. Though Iago says sweepingly, "And nothing can or shall content my soul / Till I am even'd with him, wife for wife" (307-308), he does nothing to content his soul in this way but settles, apparently easily, for his second option, which is, to "put the Moor / At least into a jealousy so strong / That judgment cannot cure" (309-311). Have we anything, then, but an idea of getting even flashing through Iago's mind, a conception toyed with but dropped by a perhaps forgetful author? It may be. But if we go back to our theory that Iago had no real suspicion of Othello and Emilia, this *ad hoc* lust is deprived of its alleged source; we are then freed of an implausible theory of causation and compelled to take the only way out—the supposition that Iago is in his strange way sexually attracted to Desdemona.[71] The hypothesis has several advantages. First, it makes meaningful a phrase of Iago's otherwise difficult to interpret: "stand accountant for as great a sin," i.e., the "absolute lust" which he formally denies. Further, if his lust comes first, it enables us to understand why Iago should hit upon a suspicion of Othello and Emilia as a usable grievance: this is an instance of the now commonplace psychological phenomenon of a person's justifying his own misdeed by attributing a comparable misdeed to his victim (or to humanity generally)—in the universal argot, "projecting" it.[72] Lust is not morally caused; it is a moral cause. The primacy of Iago's own feelings will also help account for his theory about Cassio and Desdemona: "That Cassio loves her, I do well believe it; / That she loves him, 'tis apt and of great credit" (295-296). He is given a free field by everybody's misbehavior—a misbehavior which he images, that is, creates, because of his own passions and in terms of a particular passion of his.

"Now I do love her too" is a forthright primary statement. Having slipped into it, Iago faces the necessity of forgetting this "drive," for he cannot maintain the comforting fiction that he is fighting back against injustice if among his motives there looms up conspicuously a sexual passion for the virtuous wife of the man who he alleges is the chief wrongdoer against him. The self-revelatory technique of the soliloquy is uniquely used: Iago reveals himself as he gradually slides away from the initial revelation, slips "associationally" from one point to another, and ends twenty lines later at a quite different place, his pursuers having followed him through an elaborate evasive action in which their eyes have been kept on him at just such places as he wishes himself to be seen. He does not deny what he has said: he distracts attention from it. The twenty lines are a syntactical unit (they are traditionally punctuated as two sentences); that is to say that, in effect, he does not even stop for breath as he leads us on an elusive chase through a variety of subjects. He "loves"; then he qualifies, "not . . . absolute lust," but "to diet my revenge"; so he must be "even'd with him, wife for wife"; or there is the alternative of "jealousy," which can be worked through Roderigo and Cassio; he moves immediately into ten lines of plot mechanics and ends with a triumphant vision of the mad but grateful Moor—a very long way from "I do love her too" (300-320). It is a remarkable picture of the mental operations of a man who has slipped into a revelation which he then covers up, not with a betraying abruptness, but with an immensely slick sleight of words. Perhaps Iago is not doing his tongue-is-quicker-than-the-eye with conscious purpose, but Shakespeare has so written the speech as to make it a perfect diagram of an evasive movement given at least subconscious direction.

If Iago is really covering up something here, elsewhere his actions and words should betray it. And do they not? After Othello and Desdemona have gone to bed in Cyprus, Iago holds forth, despite a lukewarm reception of this by Cassio, with a drooling relish of the possibilities suggested by this occasion: "He hath not yet made wanton the night with her, and she is sport for Jove"; "And I'll warrant her, full of game"; "What an eye she has! Methinks it sounds a parley to provo-

THEMATIC FORM: VERSIONS OF LOVE

cation"; "And when she speaks, is it not an alarum to love?" (2.3.16-27). This is something more than the conventional enthusiasm for a handsome new bride. In observing the friendly intimacy between Cassio and Desdemona, Iago lingers over the physical details of their courtesies with an intensity of feeling that does not belong to a man simply planning to trap them: "He takes her by the palm. Ay, well said, whisper! . . . Ay, smile upon her, do! . . . it had been better you had not kiss'd your three fingers so oft—which now again you are most apt to play the sir in. Very good! well kiss'd! an excellent curtsy! 'Tis so, indeed. Yet again your fingers to your lips? Would they were clyster pipes for your sake!" (2.1.169-179). This is more than hatred of a military rival, we can see from the context. Just before, Iago has been making his epigrams on women and his verses, most of this turning on sexuality. In sixty lines Emilia speaks only three short lines; all the rest of the dialogue is between Iago and Desdemona. Bawdy talk is a familiar form of sexual endeavor, and it is not too hard to sense the symbolic erotic play in Iago's wit. Then what happens? Desdemona jokingly sums him up as a "profane and liberal counsellor" (165) and turns to talk to Cassio: it is just at this point that Iago fiercely observes their brief physical contact and all Cassio's gestures, as if he were feeding his rage on the successes of a rival. Iago knows, of course, that only courtesy is involved: yet it is as if, at the great distance which separates both of them from any personal feeling that Desdemona may have, Cassio had got a little closer than he. And he thinks Cassio "fram'd to make women false" (1.3.404).

Just a little later, Iago, continuing to work on Roderigo, is driven again to the painful subject of Cassio and Desdemona. He now comes up with the idea that Desdemona is in love with Cassio (2.1.221) and, in elaborating this, delivers a thirty-line prose speech—of which he spends almost one half abusing Cassio! All this is really a fantastic way to persuade Roderigo to hope that he will have Desdemona; if Cassio is on the inside, so much the worse for Roderigo; and getting rid of Cassio promises nothing. Iago drifts into this fiction because he is obsessed by Cassio's bordering on an intimacy denied to himself. But even if the design itself were sound enough to take in a less gullible victim than Roderigo, the long tirade against Cassio (240-253) is superfluous. It is not needed to convince Roderigo, and in it we sense something more than military rivalry and general personal antagonism. Note especially these parts: "civil and humane seeming for the better compassing of his salt and most hidden loose affection?" "handsome, young, and hath all those requisites in him that folly and green minds look after" (243-245, 250-252). This is the tone of sex rivalry, hypersensitive to "trifles light as air."

Iago cannot leave it alone; he keeps pushing his case in the relentless style of one who, whatever else he is doing, can't stop nagging himself with his own torment.[73] Roderigo argues back: Desdemona is "full of most blessed condition." Iago sneers, "Blessed fig's end!" and goes on, with growing intensity: "Didst thou not see her paddle with the palm of his hand? Didst not mark that?" "Lechery, by this hand! an index and obscure prologue to the history of lust and foul thoughts. They met so near with their lips that their breaths embrac'd together. Villanous thoughts, Roderigo! When these mutualities so marshal the way, hard at hand comes the master and main exercise, th' incorporate conclusion" (256-269). Iago "knows" this is not true of Desdemona, but is he not, with part of his mind, trying to convince, less Roderigo than himself, that it might be true? If true, it would compliment his cynicism. But his feeling goes beyond philosophical combativeness. There is a minute observation of physicality, a tactile awareness, a sleuthlike perception, almost empathic, of bodily movements and responses, that betrays in their tense observer the envy of these "mutualities"—and even beyond that, a perverse vicarious indulgence in them.[74]

Beneath Iago's freely acknowledged hate there struggles a half-buried impulse that escapes into these disturbed, feverish descriptions that go far beyond what is needed to control Rod-

THEMATIC FORM: VERSIONS OF LOVE

erigo. Should it not burst fully into Iago's own consciousness? It does; immediately after it keeps pressing up toward the surface in the dialogue with Roderigo, Iago soliloquizes, "Now I do love her too." There is this one outbreak, but the easement is also a shock, and Iago from now on keeps the impulse suppressed. But it affects the action, as we shall see, and it is reflected more than once by the verbal action, obviously in Iago's lip-smacking raptures over Desdemona's charms after she and Othello have gone to bed, but with a fascinating obliqueness elsewhere. Iago's extraordinary simile for Cassio and Montano before the fight—"like bride and groom / Devesting them for bed" (2.3.180-181)—reveals the persistence in Iago's mind of the images called up by the retirement of Othello and Desdemona not long before. He torments Othello with a tableau—"Or to be naked with her friend in bed / An hour, or more, not meaning any harm?" (4.1.3-4)—that, ingenious as Iago is, is too farfetched to be coldly planned; it is a display filtering through from a secret gallery of obsessive pictures deep in Iago's erotic imagination. With the same words he is "undressing" Desdemona and driving Othello mad; ironically, the pictorial by-product of his own lust is an aphrodisiac that begets in Othello a rare (and ambiguous) intensity of passion. (If we can view Iago as the mass mind, then we have here an analogue of popular erotica, appropriately commingling the lust and malice that for a time are present in Othello's feeling and that are deep in Iago's heart.) Reporting what Cassio "said" he "did" permits a verbal savoring of unattainable experience:

Oth. What? what?
Iago. Lie—
Oth. With her?
Iago. With her, on her; what you will.
(4.1.33-34)

It is not narrative necessity but the vicarious excitement of verbal specification that explains the "on," just as it does "behold her topp'd" and "mortal eyes do see them bolster" (3.3.

205

396-399). On the one hand, Iago is using the dirty-postcard technique of excitation; on the other, he himself, in his way, is seeing. Sometimes Iago is like the voyeur; in such places he reminds us somewhat of Faulkner's Popeye. Voyeurism may spring from different kinds of hopelessness.[75]

Now if we turn back to Act 1, we find other things more meaningful. When is Iago first sufficiently aroused to make an overt move against Othello? On Othello's marriage night. He complains of ill treatment in the army, but singularly tries to cause trouble between husband and wife. In the lurid images of the Othello-Desdemona intercourse ("ram . . . ewe") which he shouts at Brabantio appear not only Iago's design for trouble and his rhetorical pleasure, but also his own emotional involvement. When does Iago create his second disturbance? On the night when Othello and Desdemona for a second time go to bed together—and Iago, as we have seen, is abnormally conscious of what may be going on in their bedroom. In his repeated insistence to Roderigo that Desdemona must soon tire of Othello and find another lover we detect, if not hope for favor, the best alternative—hope for disfavor for a rival.[76] His instinctive hatred of Othello is intensified by the sexuality in his awareness of Desdemona; hence his automatic turning to sex as the realm of revenge.

Since Desdemona came to Cyprus under the "conveyance" of Iago (1.3.286), we might regard Iago as an antiromantic version of Tristram. This would at least be a way of emphasizing that his sexual jealousy (as distinguished from the general jealousy of his being) springs not from violated "honor" but from unfulfilled passion. It colors his detestation of Cassio as much as his fury at Othello. Iago's inquiries about Cassio's intimacy with Othello and Desdemona during their courtship (3.3.94ff.) then reflect his feeling about Cassio as well as his move against Othello. The "beware, my lord, of jealousy" speech (165ff.) is doubly meaningful. And the attack on Desdemona (her "will most rank") which runs through the seduction scene expresses not only the hate of an antitype but the

THEMATIC FORM: VERSIONS OF LOVE

malice of sexual feeling destined from its birth to nonrequital. In the fiction of Cassio's dream Iago can satisfy almost every motive: he can madden Othello, vilify Cassio and Desdemona, and snatch vicariously at the unattainable—in his savoring of bodily delight.[77] His mingled motives are most powerfully and subtly concentrated in decisive action in the next dialogue with Othello: three times Iago images Desdemona in bed ("naked in bed," "lie . . . on her"), the third and climactic time in a command: "Strangle her in bed, even the bed she hath contaminated" (4.1.220-221). We are now ready to see the deepest element in this complex passage. Iago writes a symbolic poem with one set of private symbols; Othello interprets it with another set of private symbols; thus Othello has the illusion of executing justice, while Iago has the satisfaction of making him destroy the love and life which Iago envies, at the scene of sexual enactment. "Contaminated" means one thing to Othello; to Iago another—her very choice of Othello. He too is punishing Desdemona. But what we might not infer, without a survey of Iago's erotic imaginings, is the sexuality grotesquely present in his vision of her death. The sensual and the sadistic are intertwined.[78]

To desire sexually, and to desire to injure, come together fittingly in Iago. His "love" and his philosophy of love are consistent. In his skepticism and his destructiveness, the theorist of love and the figure of hate—the questioner of true union and the active divider—are at one. The man of hate is jealous of all the potential good in the world; in Iago the sex jealousy is a specific extension of a general bias of personality.

The man of hate conquers by winning others to his theory of love. His own passion is one that, when he can think of it at all, he can think of only as a form of revenge. He wants his "love" to be a tool of hate, and indeed it is shot through with hate. There is high convertibility of elements in the lust-hate compound: hate for the unpossessed, hate for the once-possessed. Lust can be a mode of hate; possess once, without commitment; deny an enduring validity; thus destroy, acting out theory. Iago must fight against the love of Othello and Desdemona: that is the open plot and the metaphysical conflict of the drama. And the dramatic realization of the kind of human forces embodied in Iago is subtly enhanced by having him lusting, if only half-consciously, for Desdemona. It is not, I believe, really profitable to debate whether this is "true lust" or a pornographic indulgence of impotence or disorder, for the dramatic situation is clear. What is unmistakably present is sexual excitement without possibility of reciprocation or fulfillment. This is the dramatic icon of envy and malice; Iago can possess Desdemona in neither spirit nor body, though he is intensely aware of both. We can see now the sneering intensity of feeling in "turn her virtue into pitch." With Roderigo, with Cassio, and with Othello, the hate-figure Iago imitates love by will and reason; with Desdemona, the hate-figure imitates love by instinct. If the travesty of an opposite virtue is the ultimate self-defining action of a vice, Iago has expressed himself in a totality of modes.

Roderigo, Othello, and Iago have one thing in common: the vision, with its plain suffering or ambiguous pain, of Desdemona having intercourse with another man. With the action in Cyprus, and with the love-figure coming in from the sea, there is a teasing hint of the Cyprian myth. But it is hardly more than a tenuous allegorical possibility, for in Desdemona the love theme is given a different direction.

MAGIC IN THE WEB   Although Iago succeeds in dividing husband and wife, he fails in a profounder sense: Desdemona never wavers in the fidelity of which Iago denies the existence. When she protests Othello's harshness or asserts her innocence to him, she has the vigor of incredulity, but she does not fly off into the loud vehemence of offended self-love, just as in defending herself to Iago and Emilia she does not rise above a hurt amazement and a mild earnestness of asseveration. At the height of her happiness, Desdemona assures Othello, "What-

THEMATIC FORM: VERSIONS OF LOVE

e'er you be, I am obedient" (3.3.89); when he strikes her and abuses her, she continues to seek his commands and to do as he says, even when he sneers openly at her obedience (4.1.266-267). Before she knows that anything is wrong, she is solicitous about his headache; when it first appears that something is wrong, she is solicitous about his tears; after his outright accusations, her only concern is to "win my lord again" (4.2.149). Instead of looking around for someone to blame, she tries to make a case for Othello's incredible conduct, and she rebukes herself for blaming him. Later, her only theory for what has happened is, "It is my wretched fortune" (4.2.128)—a phrase which recalls the literal meaning of her name: "wretched" or "unhappy." But she does not use wretchedness as a ground for subordinating devotion to self-pity and self-justification; kneeling in the presence of Iago and Emilia, she swears that she "ever will . . . / . . . love him dearly" even though he divorce her (4.2.157-158). She rejects Emilia's wish that she had never seen Othello and accepts "his stubbornness, his checks, his frowns" (4.3.20). And the song that "will not go from" her mind has this line: "Let nobody blame him; his scorn I approve" (4.3.52). Desdemona has matured from the impressionable girl who was romantically charmed by tales of adventure, wondered at the "strange," and sighed for the "pitiful," so that she can without hyperbole define her "sins" paradoxically as the "loves I bear to you" (5.2.40). This is the Desdemona the drama creates for us, not a Desdemona who suffers for the guilt of filial disobedience.[79]

She has an un-Venetian ignorance of the world. She is naive in her astonishment that "women do abuse their husbands / In such gross kind" (4.3.62-63). She flatters the world by seeing it in her own image (just as Iago, by the same method, traduces it). Perhaps the lack of "sophistication" is a necessary part of her strength of devotion; there is no knowingness to dilute her love. It makes her overintricate to attribute "self-deception" and "deliberate blindness" to her.[80] Granted that Iago's cynicism and her naivete give untenably extreme views of human conduct, that her disbelief in the worldly woman described by Emilia (4.3.86) "is as romantically false as Othello's idealism";[81] nevertheless she may act "truly" despite believing "falsely" about the world. Yet the "romantically false" belief comes from the newlywed enthusiasm of a girl who spontaneously generalizes her own incapacity for sexual wandering. It amounts to an intellectual charity that is, after all, a counterpart of the charity of will that she is shortly to achieve. So, confident in her own and of Othello's truth, she inopportunely picks an angry challenge by Othello as the time to resume her plea for Cassio. She simply does not know that the ideal of love may govern Othello's conduct as imperfectly as that of adulterous wives. Perhaps she is willful, perhaps proud, in her way;[82] yet what comes through most directly in the lines is a misestimating of the situation, puzzlement, something like panic, along with a desire not to be overborne, or deflected from her promise to Cassio, by a frightening violence. The very "human" medley of impulses adds up to bad judgment—an avenue to tragedy somewhat like, though less decisive than, Cordelia's refusal to compete with her sisters in the game of love and land. And at the ill-timed moment she resumes her do-good role (from 3.4.50) she has already mishandled the issue of the handkerchief. She knows that it is gone, and she is seriously disturbed (3.4.23ff.), but upset by Othello's threatening pressure, she twice tells him it is not lost (83, 85), says she can show it to him "but . . . not now" (86), and jumps to the Cassio theme. Presumably Desdemona, though she "knows" the handkerchief is missing, does not "believe" that it is finally lost but hopes that some miracle will uncover it; "it is not lost" is a metaphor for this irrational but understandable combination of belief and hope. The lie comes from these emotions and fear, not from habitual or momentary trickiness. Were she not too disturbed to admit the loss, she might conceivably bring him to a more careful look at the case. Here again she has responsibility in the tragedy.

Yet it may be virtually impossible for Desdemona, young

THEMATIC FORM: VERSIONS OF LOVE

and inexperienced, to be practically wise about the missing handkerchief after Othello has said ominously, "To lose't or give't away were such perdition / As nothing else could match" (67-68). For now she learns that the handkerchief is deeply symbolic; and here we look through another open window on the inner structure of the drama. The handkerchief, far from being only the trivial object that Rymer saw,[83] has a specific symbolic status and, beyond that, the dramatic role of leading us in to the crowning statement in the play of love.

The handkerchief is a talisman: kept by a wife, it guarantees her husband's love; if it is lost or given away, "his spirits should hunt / After new fancies" (58-63). Since it is the man who strays, Othello's perturbation as he defines the handkerchief is almost a betrayal of a fear of instability, which would be imaginable in the character as we have read it; too, he may obscurely be justifying, as inevitable, unhusbandlike conduct emotionally seized upon before knowledge of the loss became a live factor in his punitive scheme. After seeing him yield to a Iago who used a loverlike flirtatiousness on him, we can place him as in a sense "after new fancies"; there is a certain ironic correspondence between what he believes and what happens. He concretely sets forth the mystery: Egyptian "charmer," aged "Sibyl," "prophetic fury," "worms were hallowed," "dy'd in mummy . . . / Conserv'd of maidens' hearts" (56-57, 70-75). This poetry of the handkerchief is not entirely "private" and idiosyncratic, for its statement has a "public" equivalent in the dramatic history. "That handkerchief which I so lov'd," as Othello puts it (5.2.48), was kept by Desdemona "evermore about her / To kiss and talk to" (3.3.295-296); Iago repeatedly ("hundred times") "woo'd" Emilia to steal it (292-293)—a passion which we must recognize as long antedating any plan for using the handkerchief; Cassio says "I like the work well" and takes the trouble to ask Bianca to copy it[84] (3.4.189-191).

When Othello sums up the myth of the handkerchief, "There's magic in the web of it" (3.4.69), he guides us beyond the literal object into the symbolization of love: there is magic in the web of love and in the web of the drama itself.[85] Iago plays with gross facts, all magic out: "beast with two backs." But as soon as Brabantio finds some truth in this "slanted" journalism, he instinctively looks beyond the naturalistic: "Is there not charms / By which the property of youth and maidhood / May be abus'd?" (1.1.172-174). This is the essence of his accusation of Othello: "enchanted her!" "chains of magic," "foul charms," "arts inhibited," "spells," "witchcraft." The Duke promises relief, and Othello, picking up Brabantio's literal terms as a metaphor for defense, concludes, "This only is the witchcraft I have us'd."[86] In Brabantio's usage, witchcraft is an anesthetic; in Othello's, an awakener.

The magic in the web is manifold. The magic of the handkerchief is a seal of the spontaneous human event; it is quasi-sacramental. To Brabantio, magic is a malign working of spells, a compulsion. But at least Brabantio's sense of the magical cause makes it possible for him to understand in his way the magic of love—the harmonizing force that surmounts the barriers of "nature." On the other side is Iago with his minimizing naturalism:[87] all he admits is undifferentiated lubricity. Othello unconsciously edges toward the Iago naturalism: he reduces "charms" to "charm of personality," especially of the histrionic personality. Though his habit of mind is not reductive,[88] he here makes a slight move in a direction that becomes disastrous as he goes further. Yet here again we have a contrast, for "charm of personality" at least saves something. Even this, Iago cannot admit; it is entirely in keeping with his intellectual style to shrink Othello's "charming" story into "bragging and . . . fantastical lies" (2.1.225-226).

These, then, are the strands of magic in the dramatic web: explicitly, magic as a spell to win unwilling love; magic as the personality that stirs a willing love; magic as the talismanic preserver of love; implicitly, magic as love.[89] We instinctively

THEMATIC FORM: VERSIONS OF LOVE

look for a larger subject, for the dynamics of the personality subject to the magic of love. Iago has put this into words (again the irony of the truth-saying villain) in his sneer at Roderigo: "they say base men being in love have then a nobility in their natures more than is native to them" (2.1.217-218). This is a "magic" transformation of the personality. When we turn to see how Othello and Desdemona, who began in sentiment and romance, are transformed, we come for a necessary final look at the drama of the handkerchief. The handkerchief is stolen when Desdemona, as Emilia says, "let it drop by negligence" (3.3.311). But Desdemona, who has been trying to help Othello cure a headache, has been rebuffed, and in the direct concern of love has forgot the symbol. In rejecting her attention, Othello really rejects the magical powers of love; he *will* not be cured.[90] The handkerchief, he says, "is too little" (287). Neither the myth nor the family tradition nor the object which so stimulates the eyes and hearts of all who have to do with it can stir him, for the sense of being wronged has become self-enclosure: he will neither love nor let himself be loved. Just before Desdemona's entry he has said he'd "rather be a toad" in a dungeon "Than keep a corner in the thing I love / For others' uses" (270-273). This "all or nothing" view of love, which is really the essence of self-love, makes it impossible for him to see that he has "all," in any sense that is meaningful; and it defines an ethical nature in which there is a potential addiction to grievance (this is consistent with his pervasive need of positional assurance) and its consequence, a freezing in the posture of revenge. He closes off the possibility of a magical transformation—of discovering a new "nobility" in his "nature"—and commits himself to a mode of love action which puts the ultimate strain upon the spirit of Desdemona.

We have already spoken of Desdemona's extraordinary, unskeptical constancy, of her progress from the infatuated girl toward the devoted, enduring wife. We have to keep in mind Iago's universal vengefulness, Othello's punitive instinct,

Emilia's attributing women's misconduct to men's—the pervasive note of *lex talionis*—to appreciate Desdemona's spiritual grace (the "nobility" actualized by the tests of love). She may err in seeking a token submission and in "handling" an angry man. But even after she has been grossly mistreated, her love has not sunk into the self-love of abuse and case-making; her prayer is, "Heaven me such uses send, / Not to pick bad from bad, but by bad mend!" (4.3.107-108). She is intent on the quality of her behavior. If a villain has slandered her, she prays for him, "heaven pardon him!" (4.2.135). By putting this line between Iago's "there is no such man" and Emilia's "hell gnaw his bones," Shakespeare heightens our awareness of the love that can become charity in its rarest form of forgiveness to the deliberate evildoer. Since she can forgive, she can believe in forgiveness; hence she can intercede for Cassio. Her last words on this mission reveal the love of harmony that belongs to love: "I would do much / T'atone them, for the love I bear to Cassio" (4.1.243-244). She fails in life, but Othello and Cassio are indeed "atoned," after her death, an "atonement" which is a reminder of the great mythic act of *caritas*. The course of her actions after mid-play completes the magic theme, for in her we do see the dynamics of the personality under the magic influence of love; first she felt the static "charm" of Othello's personality and then experienced the full ripening of an outward-turning love which in this context we may call the magical transformation or the miracle of personality.[91]

In *Othello* Shakespeare dramatizes the extremes of hate and love. Without clichés or distortions he gives us devil and saint, for whom, in our more limited horizons, we no longer have an idiom but the sentimental one (hence Eliot's difficulties in dramatizing the saint). There is an almost comparable range in the very portrayal of Desdemona: she fears death and begs for life, in the manner of ordinary humanity; yet she can also achieve the miracle of more than ordinary love. Yet if Shakespeare's interpretation has the authority that comes

THEMATIC FORM: VERSIONS OF LOVE

from an inclusive awareness of human possibilities, he strengthens it with the authority of an extraordinary dramatic action. He knows the utmost extent of "nature" but also knows when to stretch it or go beyond it. There is the bald nature of the death scene: terror and animal destructive lust. Desdemona is dead. Then Emilia enters—the social reality. And then suddenly Desdemona speaks. Acting on the rationalist impulse, we reorder the scene, decide that her death was only apparent, and place the "real" death at the later point. But the fact is that we have felt Desdemona to be dead from the moment when Othello for the second time released her from his grip, and that her speaking comes as a complete shock that takes over the scene. "Still as the grave," Othello has said of her (5.2.94). We must, I think, accept the shock as intended, and must understand a bold and brilliant effort to suggest a voice coming from beyond life—the miracle which completes the pattern of magic in the web. The voice from beyond is anything but tricky theatricalism: the three speeches by Desdemona are a compact dramatic summary of the phases in the "magical transformation" (a reminder of the myth that the dying person recalls his whole life). For Desdemona becomes, rather than simply is, the saint. Her first speech—"O, falsely, falsely murder'd!" (117)—is an accusation with all the emphasis on the evildoer: the most primitive impulse. Here we can remember whatever in her actions was self-regarding—untruths, filial inconsiderateness, love of power, flight from reality, pride, tactlessness (as different critics have it). The second—"A guiltless death I die" (122)—is a self-exculpation: the impulse now freed of accusation and formalized as a legal plea, a simple factual denial of wrongdoing. Then, when Emilia asks, "O, who hath done this deed?" Desdemona speaks for the third and last time: "Nobody—I myself. Farewell. / Commend me to my kind lord. O, farewell!" (123-125). Here is the last phase: no longer a denial of wrongdoing, but the acting of goodness: the assertion not of one's own innocence or goodness but of that of the evildoer, shielding him but, more than that, forgiving him.[92] And here the verbal drama is very significant, for one of Desdemona's key words—*kind*—is in itself a summation. Once she was "Arraigning his *unkindness* with my soul," and, though she then magnanimously decided that "he's indicted falsely" (3.4.152-154), she could not banish from her mind the idea of unkindness: "his *unkindness* may defeat my life." Here, however, she got around the fact by denying its characteristic effect: "But never taint my love" (4.2.160-161). Now, with her "Commend me to my *kind* lord," she makes good her prophecy: though life has been defeated, love remains untainted for its ultimate office of denying unkindness.[93] And in *commend*, with its quest for approval, is the humility that reverses whatever pride there was. Here is the perfecting of human nature, which I have called the miracle of personality; its fitting dramatic form is an apparent miracle in the physical world, a "resurrection." Hence one's sense of a surrealistic rightness in Desdemona's return from death, as it were, to say her last words. It is an expressionistic symbol of the metaphysical quality of her love. It is the victory of spirit: the experience of *agape* in a world distraught by *eros*.

In the last scene, the certification of truth several times comes, or is felt to come, from the borders of the natural or beyond. Emilia, who repeatedly asserts Desdemona's fidelity in the face of threats and of death (135, 157, 199, 234), devotes her dying breath to the theme: "Moor, she was chaste; she lov'd thee, cruel Moor" (249). Cassio, referring metaphorically to the information in the letters found on Roderigo, or perhaps literally—it is not impossible[94]—to words actually spoken by Roderigo, reports: "and even but now he spake, / After long seeming dead—Iago hurt him, / Iago set him on" (327-329). These hints of the transnatural in the revelation of both love and hate are parts of the complex counterforce which the drama sets up against the minimal-naturalistic thinking of Iago.

Othello's tragedy is crowned by his failure to see what Desdemona's love means. Once he is disabused of his obsession,

THEMATIC FORM: VERSIONS OF LOVE

he recognizes hardly more than that she has been technically true ("Cold . . . ? / Even like thy chastity"—275-276). He has heard her say, "Nobody—I myself," and has responded only by calling her "liar," which is the first faint symptom of self-doubt or self-disgust.[95] He has also listened to her words, "Commend me to my kind lord," but there is no evidence that he has "heard" them, much less understood them. I stated, at the end of Chapter V, that to complete our estimate of Othello we would need to know how much truth there is in the best known lines of his apologia, "lov'd not wisely, but too well." Not wisely, indeed. But too well? Only if "too well" means too possessively. But the Othello who felt the magic of love that creates a union of the unlike never surrendered to the magic that transforms personality. If we can envision him as striven for, like the protagonist of the morality play, by two versions of love, we realize that he was owned for a while by that version which is a disguise of hate, that he returned to the other where he might have found salvation, but that even in the end he remained largely inaccessible to the spirit of that love. He was never wholly freed from self-love. Othello is not clear what he has done; he knows that he has lost a faithful wife, but he does not know that he has lost the woman who could forgive him and ask him to think well of her. This is his ultimate obtuseness.[96] I have said that in *Othello* we see symptoms of the domestic drama.[97] We have also intimations of the modern variant of tragedy in which the character intended as tragic (or even a whole community) never knows what has happened to him and so exists only as an unripened figure in an object lesson on the stage. The ignorant man is the one most given to self-justification. Othello is only partly ignorant, but still enough so to interlard his self-judgment with justification. "Too well" is less autobiography than a plea of "only partly guilty," but it reminds us how far he fell short of "well."

The world of magic in the web is what Iago cannot help opposing, whether love be the harmonizing force that his di-

217

visiveness cannot tolerate, or the perfecter of personality abhorrent to his cynicism.[98] To alter the terms, Desdemona represents the world of spirit which Iago must by philosophical necessity destroy. To her transcendent love he opposes a positivism of sex that takes in both Roderigo and Othello. But it is only after we have become fully aware of Desdemona as the symbolization of spirit that we can grasp all the implications of the lust-hate complex at the center of Iago's feeling for her. There is a perverse attraction toward an opposite, an attraction of which the event could not be fusion or identification but would have to be possession or spoliation. What occurs at the personal level has also a philosophic import: one value system against another, with an ironic nexus of one-sided lust, inevitably pointing not toward mutual self-fulfillment but toward conquest.[99] Hence if Iago acted overtly in the realm of sex, the indicated style would be rape and murder. (Rape is in line with the imagistic development of Iago as a trapper, and with the actional development of him as a thief. And is not the theft of the handkerchief, which he desired before he formulated a plot in which to use it, a symbolic rape?[100]) Indeed, he accomplishes both vicariously. As long as Desdemona is faithful to Othello and is alive, she is intolerable to him—a refutation of all his thought (as are, in their own ways, Emilia, whom he kills, and Bianca, whom he tries to destroy). Though he was not present at her death, he would be more likely, through the intuition of absolute enmity, than Othello, who lacked the final intuition of love, to know the spirit of her last words.

WIT AND WITCHCRAFT

Thematic Form

When Iago with unperceived scoffing reminds Roderigo that love effects an unwonted nobility in men, he states a doctrine which he "knows" is true but in which he does not "believe." Ennoblement is a real possibility; but it is to be viewed with bitterness and to be undermined. With his spontaneous antipathy to spiritual achievement, Iago must in principle deny the mysterious transformation of personality; instinctively he is the shrewd observer of all the habits that suggest infinite corruptibility as the comprehensive human truth. A believer in shrewd observation and in corruption, he holds the credo, which is not altogether unique, that man is a union of lusting, folly, and plotting.

Good sense, hard sense, common sense, no nonsense, rationality—all these terms, we may suppose, are ones which Iago might consider as defining his perspective. As he plays his love-and-honesty game, he uses words that put him on that side of the fence. First he can't tell Othello his "thoughts" because of his "manhood, honesty, or wisdom" (3.3.153-154); a little later he finds "reason" to tell them (193). Othello considers him "wise" (4.1.75). While privately he may deny his love and kid his honesty, Iago takes his brains seriously. "Thus do I ever make my fool my purse," he boasts; to spend time with Roderigo otherwise "mine own gain'd knowledge should pro-

CHAPTER 7

fane" (1.3.389-390). Othello is to be treated like an ass (1.3. 408; 2.1.318). Iago applies the term "fool" successively to Roderigo (2.3.53), Cassio (2.3.359), Desdemona (4.1.186), Emilia (4.2.148), and condescends to fools "credulous" and "gross" (3.3.404; 4.1.46). His view of himself as the clearheaded manipulator of gulls is significantly unchallenged despite the barrage of derogatory terms that eventually fall upon him.[1] He is "a smart man," apt in "deals," scornful of "suckers."[2]

It is more fun if the gull thinks he is using his own head with especial acuteness. Early in the seduction scene Iago urges Othello "that your wisdom yet" should "take no notice" of Iago's "unsure observance" (3.3.148-151); later he repeats: "Nay, but be wise" (432). The idea that he is being sharp goes to Othello's head; he resolves to be "cunning in my patience" (4.1.91), and he queries erring Desdemona, "Are you wise?" (4.1.245). After he has acted on his wisdom, Emilia tells Othello what he has become:[3] "O gull! O dolt! / As ignorant as dirt!" "O thou dull Moor," "what should such a fool / Do with so good a wife?" (5.2.163-234). How does Iago try to stop this confessional outburst? By commanding Emilia: "Be wise, and get you home" (223). Here he cannot induce that "wisdom" that serves his own end; the engineer of folly in others now by necessity collapses into senseless abuse and violence. But Othello's "O fool! fool! fool!" (323), inadequate a self-judgment as it is, acknowledges Emilia's indictment, and, inadvertently, the success of Iago's plot to make him "egregiously an ass." After all this, Othello's "lov'd not wisely" is unconsciously an understatement.

Making a fool of somebody is an aesthetic demonstration of intellectual superiority. It is implicitly partial, temporary; a comic episode after which life goes on. Let this exploit in self-aggrandizement expand with the full pressure of passion, and the attack becomes an ultimate one against sanity—putting Othello "into a jealousy so strong / That judgment cannot cure," driving him "Even to madness" (2.1.310-311, 320). It

THEMATIC FORM: WIT AND WITCHCRAFT

is the extreme revenge possible to the man of "reason," a chaos amplifying the other modes of chaos which Iago has actively sought. Twice again he speaks of Othello's madness as a likelihood or a formal objective (4.1.56, 101), and his program works well enough to elicit from Lodovico a worried inquiry about Othello (4.1.280) and from Othello himself a hinted doubt about his own sanity (5.2.111). Emilia fears lest Desdemona "run mad" (3.3.317), Othello cries out that he is "glad to see you mad" (4.1.250), and she in turn fears his "fury" (4.2.32). But "madness" recoils upon its creator: "What, are you mad?" Iago asks incredulously of truth-telling Emilia (5.2.194).

Such points in the minor theme of madness (again a brief prologue to *Lear*) set off the course of rational Iago. Insofar as he identifies rationality with his own purposes, Iago is close enough to Everyman; but he is sharply individualized—and at the same time made the representative of a recognizable human class—when the drama reveals that his purposes require the irrationalizing of life for everybody else. Of the insights that create Iago, none is deeper than the recognition that a cool rationality may itself bring about or serve the irrational. Though Brabantio thinks that Iago has "lost" his "wits" and that Roderigo comes "in madness" (1.1.92, 98), their universal technique of matching half-truths to latent fears soon has him acting as they wish, attributing "a judgment maim'd and most imperfect" (1.3.99) to anyone who takes a different view of the situation. Here Iago has simply had to make Brabantio as irrational as possible; shortly he has to curb Roderigo's own irrationality, or rather, to convert it from a less to a more serviceable form, from suicidal despair to the sexual pursuit of Desdemona. Now the first step in this conversion is the traditional argument of the "authority of . . . our wills" and of "one scale of reason to poise another of sensuality": "But we have reason to cool our raging motions, our carnal stings, our unbitted lusts" (1.3.329-332, 334-336). If in one sense this is the devil talking scripture, in another it is Iago paying

221

tribute to a faculty that he values deeply. He is the self-conscious possessor of brain-power. But reason has many functions, and the critical utility of this passage is that it points to the distinction between the ostensible and the real functions that Iago assigns to reason. In no way does he press Roderigo to apply reason to his emotional ailment, to diagnose it and to moderate and perhaps cure it; on the contrary he assures him that his cause "hath . . . reason" (373) and encourages him to found hopes of success on Desdemona's sharing in a universal unregeneracy which is evidently subject to no rational control. But more than that we see that Iago has not the slightest thought of using reason to "cool" his own "raging motions, . . . carnal stings, . . . unbitted lusts"; reason is rather the agent of his unbitted lusts and of the raging motions of his hate. It is in their behalf that he reasons with Roderigo; his reason is instrumental, serving his own unreason by playing upon Roderigo's. When he mentions the rumor about Othello and Emilia he hurries to say "I know not if't be true" (394); he'll act on "mere suspicion," so that he can act. His mind is used not to determine the truth but to convert feeling into action (and even the "will" which he has defined as the controller of the body he will now "plume up . . . / In double knavery"[4]). This is a basic Shakespearian definition of evil: the sharp mind in the service of uncriticized passion. And the final irony, as Shakespeare sees it, is that the owner of the sharp mind is eventually destroyed by the passion his mind serves.

We see the innermost mechanism of this rational instrument when the Iago-Roderigo relationship comes to its last phase. Like several of the major characters,[5] Roderigo can at times think about his own headwork: once he almost resolves to give up and return to Venice with "a little more wit" (2.3.374); he is angrily aware that he has "foolishly suffer'd" and suspects that he is "fopp'd" (4.2.182, 197). Iago retorts by praising Roderigo for both his brains, "your suspicion is not without wit and judgment," and his moral quality (214-219). The recurrent irony for Roderigo is that he cannot rely on his

THEMATIC FORM: WIT AND WITCHCRAFT

own good sense but falls back instead on Iago's version of what is good sense for him. Here comes the pay-off. When once again Iago asserts emphatically that there is a way of getting to Desdemona, Roderigo's reply is, "Well, what is it? Is it within reason and compass?" (223-224). Is it "reasonably practical"? No other question, no other issue of sanction or value. How many philosophic frills are being got rid of, and how far down to positive bedrock this is getting appears when Iago reveals the program: killing Cassio. Roderigo is still shockable. Iago soothes him, "Come, stand not amaz'd" (245-246), and offers a cure for "amazement": "I will show you such a necessity in his death that you shall think yourself bound to put it on him" (246-248). To this promise of logical demonstration Roderigo responds in the same key: "I will hear further reason for this" (251). Iago makes good his promise, "And you shall be satisfied" (252), for when Roderigo is finally lying in wait to kill Cassio, he sums up the rationale of the project: "I have no great devotion to the deed, / And yet he hath given me satisfying reasons. / 'Tis but a man gone" (5.1. 8-10). Despite his moral hesitancy, Roderigo has found "satisfying reasons" for committing murder and thinking it a way to Desdemona's bed. In this climax of his persuasion to evil, Iago's "reason" mediates between his own uncontrollable irrational drives and those of Roderigo. The rational serving one irrationality and appearing to serve another while selfishly playing upon it: this sums up, and sums up archetypally, the fundamental operating methods of the Iago way of life.

" 'Tis but a man gone" is pure Iago thought. It does away with every value or imperative or speculation that "man" or the death of man traditionally evokes and makes "a man" simply a neutral instance of a category, an object that can be acted on without moral responsibility. The philosophy " 'Tis but a man gone" (of which there are contemporary manifestations in whole political systems, in demagogic practices in our own, in some methods of business and advertising, in propaganda) is consistent with Iago's reduction of love to sexual instability, his declaration that "there is more sense" in a "bodily wound" than in "reputation," his skepticism about "honour," which he implies is unreal because unseen, and even, in a slightly different way, with his contempt for Cassio's theoretical knowledge, "Mere prattle, without practice" (1.1. 26). Theory[6] of any kind may open the door to values that transcend the immediately functional. "Iago's is a pragmatic world, and his imagery finds its authority in social usage."[7] "Let's get down to the facts," he says tacitly, that is, the tangible and the visible. (Seen from slightly different perspectives, he has affiliations with the antimetaphysical thinker, the extremist in semantics, the constitutional debunker.) We need hardly press the point that his "practical materialism"[8] is "practical" only for a very short haul.[9]

Reason as an ally of evil[10] is a subject to which Shakespeare keeps returning, as if fascinated, but with different dramatic constructions as he explores different counterforces. In *Macbeth* the rational effort to minimize the killings for ambition's sake finally runs into the force of conscience. In *Lear*, rationalized self-seeking is counterbalanced by all the fidelities implied in *pietas*.[11] And in *Othello?* Although Iago, as we saw, does not take seriously the ennobling power of love, he does not fail to let us know what he does take seriously. When, in his fake oath of loyalty to "wrong'd Othello," he vows "The execution of his wit, hands, heart" (3.3.466), Iago's words give a clue to his truth: his heart is his malice, his hands literally wound Cassio and kill Roderigo, and his wit is the genius that creates all the strategy. Wit is reality. How it enters into the dialectic of structure Iago's promises to Roderigo make clear: "If sanctimony and a frail vow betwixt an erring barbarian and a supersubtle Venetian be not too hard for my wits and all the tribe of hell, thou shalt enjoy her" (1.3.362-366). "Tribe of hell" is somewhat rhetorical; the real antagonist is "my wits"—set against the rival power of love, which he cannot tolerate. But even beyond the conscious battle there is a symbolic conflict that is at the heart of the drama. And

THEMATIC FORM: WIT AND WITCHCRAFT

for this symbolic conflict Iago, again assuaging the pain of Roderigo, inadvertently gives us a name: "Thou know'st we work by wit, and not by witchcraft; / And wit depends on dilatory time" (2.3.378-379).

Wit and witchcraft: in this antithesis[12] is the symbolic structure of *Othello*. By *witchcraft*, of course, Iago means conjuring and spells to compel desired actions and states of being. But as a whole the play dramatically develops another meaning of witchcraft which forces itself upon us: *witchcraft* is a metaphor for love. The magic in the web of the handkerchief, we saw in Chapter VI, extends into the fiber of the drama. Love is a magic bringer of harmony and may be the magic transformer of personality; its ultimate power is fittingly marked by a miraculous voice from beyond life. Such events lie outside the realm of "wit"—of the reason, cunning, and wisdom on which Iago rests—and this wit must be hostile to them. Wit must always strive to conquer witchcraft, and there is an obvious sense in which it should conquer; but there is another sense in which, though it try, it should not and cannot succeed: that is what *Othello* is about. Whatever disasters it causes, wit fails in the end: it cuts itself off in a demonic silence before death, while witchcraft—love—speaks after death.

In his recipient role in Act 5 Cassio provides another diaphanous moment in which wit and witchcraft are finely visible in their different colors. Roderigo's " 'Tis but a man gone" is a dehumanizing, an elimination of the possibility of love. Desdemona, on the other hand, has loved Cassio with "the general warranty of heaven." One precludes, the other practices, the *caritas* in which magic lies.

Between the poles of wit and witchcraft, all the major characters in the play find their orientation. Emilia looks at a good deal of life through the Iago wit, but yields to the love for Desdemona which transforms her into a sacrificial figure. Under the influence of the Iago wit, Cassio (acting through Desdemona's kindness) tries to high-pressure Othello into a charity that could only come spontaneously. Roderigo falls

225

under the witchcraft of love, but, instead of letting it take effect as it might, to bring him death or renunciation, chooses Iago's wit game and plays for what he cannot have. Emilia and Desdemona, dying, are not creatures of wit: what we have called witchcraft has led them to a transrational achievement of spirit.

We have spoken of the conflict of Desdemona and Iago, of love and hate, for Othello; of the conflict of two kinds of potentiality in the soul where both reside (the conflict, in Sewell's terms, of spirit and society, of ends and means, of integrity and expediency, of moral being and behavior). Let us restate this as the conflict of wit and witchcraft for Othello.[13] Though Othello seems to be all the naivete of Everyman, and Iago to be all his slyness, Othello gives himself more to wit than to witchcraft because he and Iago, though in different degrees, have much in common—a histrionic bent, an inadequate selfhood that crops up in self-pity[14] and an eye for slights[15] and injuries, an uncriticized instinct to soothe one's own feelings by punishing others (with an air of moral propriety), the need to possess in one's own terms or destroy, an incapacity for love that is the other side of self-love. All this is in another realm from that of witchcraft. When Othello decides to follow Iago and be "wise" and "cunning," he adopts, as we noted in Chapter III, a new code: he will "see" the facts, get the "evidence," "prove" his case, and execute "justice." This is the program of "wit." Now this is not only utterly inappropriate to the occasion on which, under Iago's tutelage, Othello elects to use it, nor is it simply one of a number of possible errors; rather he adopts an attitude or belief or style which is the direct antithesis of another mode of thought and feeling that is open to him. He essays to reason when reason is not relevant: he substitutes a disastrous wit for a saving witchcraft. Shakespeare, as one critic puts it, "forces upon the audience the question, In what strength could Othello reject Iago? The answer would seem to be, By an affirmation of faith which is beyond reason, by the act of choosing to believe in Desdemona.

THEMATIC FORM: WIT AND WITCHCRAFT

Shakespeare's point is that love is beyond reason." Or, in the formulation of C. S. Lewis, "To love involves trusting the beloved beyond the evidence, even against much evidence."[16] Othello, the prime beneficiary of witchcraft, might win all its gifts had he the faith that would open him to its action; but he is short on faith, is seduced by wit (the two actions are simply two faces of the same experience), and ruined. He knew the first miracle of love, but cut himself off from the greater miracle. His final failure is that, though he comes to recognize that he has really been witless, he is never capacious enough in spirit to know how fully he has failed or what he has thrown away. He never sees the full Desdemona witchcraft.

In the light of Desdemona's spiritual wealth we can understand Iago as a spiritual have-not. Like the have-not in the realm of things who in a materially oriented culture suffers from envy and malice, the spiritual have-not lives in characteristic vices that Shakespeare has analyzed with many-angled perception. The analogy between the material and the spiritual have-not is confirmed in Edmund's "Let me . . . have lands by wit" and in Iago's own addiction to thieving. If the analogy fails at one point—that the achievement of spiritual wealth depends on the individual and cannot essentially be helped by external accidents or blocked by external obstacles—that failure only underscores the failure of the spiritual have-not. His modes of action are exhaustively canvassed in Shakespeare's actional and verbal drama. Wit is his instrument to compensate for what he does not have. He perversely hates and lusts after what he does not have, and he undertakes to disparage it, minimize it, question its existence (debunk it), and destroy it. Rule or ruin becomes rule by ruining.[17] He must fashion the world in his own image: "And knowing what I am, I know what she shall be" (4.1.74). So it pleases him to trap those who are unlike himself—by proclaiming virtues which he does not possess (honest Iago, the universal friend), confusing the appearance of things, seeming to act in one way (as lightbringer, physician) while acting in another. Noisiness and vulgarity of style become him, though he can act the amiable, contained, and discreet adviser and consoler. His most far-reaching method is to seduce others philosophically—to woo them from assumptions in which their salvation might lie, to baser assumptions that will destroy them. Iago the individual is akin to Iago the philosopher: there is a common element in stealing purses, stealing good names, and stealing ideas needed for survival.

In sociological terms we might allegorize Iago as the criminal type, in political as the self-seeking divisive force or the patrioteer or the power seeker who will pay any price,[18] in cultural as the mass mind, in psychological as all the impulses that lead to despair of human possibility,[19] in moral as envy or hate or spiritual hardness (versions of pride), in mythical as The Enemy—the universal destroyer of ultimate values. Before all these, he is simply a human being, the apparent friend and lover of everybody. We think of these tentative formulations only because he is so variously and richly set before us as the final outcome when certain potentialities of Everyman are freed to develop fully.[20] There is no single way into this extraordinary characterization. As the spiritual have-not, Iago is universal— that is, many things at once, and of many times at once. He is our contemporary, and the special instances of his temper and style—as distinct from the Iagoism to which all men are liable—will be clear to whoever is alert to Shakespeare's abundant formulations.[21] In a limited and stereotyped form, he is the villain of the older melodrama. He is Elizabethan—as Envy or machiavel. And further back still, we see in how many parts of Dante's *Inferno* he might appear. He could be placed among the angry and the violent. But his true place is down among those who act in fraud or malice—the lowest category of sinners who had had least of spiritual substance and had relied most on wit. Here we might put him on a higher level with the panders, but again it is when we reach the lower levels that he is summoned, not once, but by group after group: the hypocrites, the thieves, the evil counselors, the sowers of dis-

THEMATIC FORM: WIT AND WITCHCRAFT

sension, and, at the very bottom of the eighth circle, the impersonators and false witnesses. Finally, in the ninth and last last circle, "damn'd beneath all depth in hell," come the treacherous. And here at last we go beyond time into our timeless myths of evil.

By an extraordinary composition of character Shakespeare has made Iago, literally or symbolically, share in all these modes of evil. And in Iago he has dramatized Dante's summary analysis: "For where the instrument of the mind is joined to evil will and potency, men can make no defence against it."[22] But he has also dramatized the hidden springs of evil action, the urgency and the immediacy and the passion of it. He contemplates, too, the evildoer's "potency" and men's defenselessness: but these he interprets tragically by making them, not absolute, but partly dependent on the flaws or desires of the victims themselves. In the *Othello* world, Iago is not a required teacher. Whoever would, could learn from Desdemona.

Appendixes

A. THE ENCHAFED FLOOD

The storm which the Venetians survive en route to Cyprus is obviously of lesser dramatic stature than the storm in *Lear*. The *Lear* storm is at the center of the play; it is vitally related to the action; it is overwhelmingly present as a physical reality; it sharply influences tone; and its symbolism is multiple. Beside this great achievement the storm in *Othello* appears to be little more than a preliminary exercise: it occurs early in the play, it is offstage, and it scarcely appears symbolic at all. Yet it disposes of the Turks and thus clears the scene for domestic broils, and it is an actional counterpart of the verbal movement that derives from the sea—for instance, the wealth of nautical imagery that Iago uses (1.1.30, 150, 153, 157-158; 1.2.17, 50), Othello's measuring the value of freedom by "the sea's worth" (1.2.28). Othello's life is a kind of sea voyage. At the start, Roderigo describes him as "an extravagant and wheeling stranger" (1.1.137), i.e., a wandering[1] foreigner; Othello would tell of literal "accidents by flood and field" (1.3.135); and at the end he declares, "Here is my journey's end, here is my butt, / And very seamark of my utmost sail" (5.2.267-268).

Early in the play our attention is turned toward the sea by the persistent references to the galleys (1.2.40ff.; 1.3.1-42). At the same time we are aware of emotional storms. Brabantio calls his grief "floodgate and o'erbearing" (1.3.56); nevertheless it comes under control.[2] Brabantio's storm is barely calmed when another comes up: Roderigo's grief, so intense that he resolves, "I will incontinently drown myself" (1.3.306). With a variety of sarcasms and cajolings Iago talks him out of it, and Shakespeare is ready to take us back to the literal sea.

If the partial calming of private storms creates an expectancy of general peace, the expectancy is furthered by the outcome of the storm itself, which is presented indirectly but rather skillfully.[3] The whole storm, in fact, is managed in the style of romance. First

231

we have the threat of enemy attack—the mode of melodrama; then the storm intervenes, the unexpected event outside of character; with romantic perfection it finishes off the enemy; but still there is the romantic excitement of the uncertain fate of "our side," played to the hilt as the Venetian boats arrive one at a time—first Cassio's, then Iago's (with Desdemona), and climactically, after as much delay as possible, Othello's.[4] This comes close to musical comedy. The point of course is the ironic contrast between the early "victory" and the later defeat: just as Othello survives the attack from without (the Turks) but succumbs to the attack from within, so he survives the storm at sea but is destroyed by the storm at home.[5] If we make the storm function as a symbol of later disaster, as some critics do, we lose a major dramatic point—that the storm is exactly the kind of trouble that Othello can and does survive. "Traitors ensteep'd to clog the guiltless keel," as Cassio phrases it (2.1.70), withheld their action—the opposite of what happens after the storm. The contrast furnishes a vivid image of human experience: the conquering of violent external threats and dangers, the defeat by internal disorders that may not even look like attacks. Musical comedy remains musical comedy by stopping at the borderline—on the shore of the happy island, after the big storm. Shakespeare, the old professional, plays that script for what it is worth and then goes on to see what happens on the island after all the dangers of wind and sea are past.

The dreadful voyage is done, and Othello rejoices in "such calms" (2.1.178)—the calm that comes *after* one storm and *before* another. The proclamation concludes, "Heaven bless the isle of Cyprus" (2.2.12)—the *isle,* at once a refuge from storms and a special target of storms, and immediately the target of Iago, who talks repeatedly of troubling the "isle" (2.3.59, 63, 133, 147).

Othello's implication that the brawlers "do that / Which heaven hath forbid the Ottomites" (171-172), by reminding us of the original storm, permits us to see the disturbance as another "foul and violent tempest" (2.1.34). When he quickly dismisses Cassio, we recall Cassio's earlier words, "The great contention of the sea and skies / Parted our fellowship" (2.1.92-93). It is just when Othello himself has been torn from all moorings ("the nature / Whom passion could not shake," as Lodovico puts it, 4.1.276-277)

APPENDIXES

that he begins, in rather orotund manner,[6] to compare himself to the elements, first in their power and relentlessness:

> All my fond love thus do I blow to heaven.
> Like to the Pontic sea,
> Whose icy current and compulsive course
> Ne'er feels retiring ebb, but keeps due on
> To the Propontic and the Hellespont;
> Even so my bloody thoughts, with violent pace,
> Shall ne'er look back, ne'er ebb, etc. (3.3.445, 453-458)

Desdemona picks up the water imagery in two statements that are ironic in different ways. She is sure he is not jealous, because "the sun where he was born / Drew all such humours from him" (3.4.30-31), and after he has first treated her harshly, declaring her hand "hot, hot, and moist" (3.4.39), she thinks only that some official business "Hath puddled his clear spirit" (3.4.143). This style is also congenial to Othello; the next time he speaks of himself, he is not the compulsive sea but a target of the elements, specifying the kind of storm he could have endured:

> Had it pleas'd heaven
> To try me with affliction, had they rain'd
> All kinds of sores and shames on my bare head,
> Steep'd me in poverty, etc. (4.2.47-50)

Then from an imaginary flood of disasters Othello turns strikingly to an actual drying up or stagnation in the sources of life:

> The fountain from the which my current runs
> Or else dries up—to be discarded thence,
> Or keep it as a cistern for foul toads
> To knot and gender in— (4.2.59-62)

Ironically, the conqueror of oceans and storms sees himself as a victim of drought, of the thirst that from the soul doth rise; from now on, the only streams are of tears and blood.[7] But at the end Othello characteristically revives the storm when he calls for punishments: "Blow me about in winds! roast me in sulphur! / Wash me in steep-down gulfs of liquid fire!" (5.2.279-280). Even after "journey's end" storms are in some way his element. They, and

233

MAGIC IN THE WEB

the kind of separation they cause, are what he can manage, or at least bear. A student of irony and symbol cannot altogether ignore the storm, though it is not a *Lear* storm.

B. THE BODY

Iago refers to his heart at 1.1.51, 62, 64; Brabantio at 1.3.193-194 ("with all my heart"); Desdemona at 1.3.251, 3.4.45; Othello at 1.3.279 ("with all my heart"), 2.1.201, 3.3.123, 3.4.38, 46, 47. There are many other uses of *heart*, both literal and figurative. Key passages in which eyes are mentioned are 1.2.28 (Iago), 3.3.166 (Iago), 189 (Othello), 198 (Iago), 3.4.61, 66 (Othello), 4.2.154 (Desdemona), 5.1.106 (Iago).

Iago will not tell Othello his secret thoughts, not even "if my heart were in your hand" (3.3.163); then he vows "wit, hands, heart / To wrong'd Othello's service" (3.3.466-467); he asks, "Give me thy hand, Roderigo" (4.2.209). He sees Cassio and Desdemona play, as he would have it, by "palm" and "fingers" (2.1.168ff., 259-260). Othello takes up a comparable palmistry: "Give me your hand. This hand is moist, my lady" (3.4.36) begins a ten-line complaint on this theme. Whether he is working on Roderigo or on Othello, Iago knows how to strike the note of sexuality by mentioning parts of the body specifically, and under his influence Othello learns to image his suspicions in the same way. For Iago, see 1.3.358; 2.1.264-265; 3.3.420-425, 439; 4.1.67. For Othello, see 3.3.341, 346; 4.1.43. Cf. the kind of image in which the physical being is not named but is implied by a word denoting function, as in Othello's "Cassio did top her" (5.2.136) and Iago's "Poor Cassio's smiles" (4.1.103).

Iago finds physical terms for his contempt for Othello, who will be "led by th' nose" (1.3.407); Cassio for his imagined sobriety, "This is my right hand, and this is my left" (2.3.118); Othello for his authority, "If I once stir / Or do but lift this arm" (2.3.207-208); Emilia for her view of men in love, "They are all but stomachs" (3.4.104), and for a woman who, in love with Lodovico, "would have walk'd barefoot to Palestine for a touch of his nether lip" (4.3.39-40); Desdemona loves Othello's "frowns" and in her sorrow hangs her "head all at one side" (4.3.20, 31-32). Othello's suffering constantly calls forth images of the body and of bodily functions. See, in addition to the passages cited earlier, 3.3.113, 388; 4.2.47-50, 55, 63, 74.

Two passages are connected by Iago's reference to Emilia's tongue. In the first, he makes a joke:

> Sir, would she give you so much of her lips
> As of her tongue she oft bestows on me,
> You would have enough.
>   *Des.*   Alas, she has no speech!
>   *Iago.* In faith, too much.
> I find it still when I have list to sleep.
> Marry, before your ladyship, I grant,
> She puts her tongue a little in her heart
> And chides with thinking.   (2.1.101-108)

In the final dialogue between Iago and Emilia, Iago's joke ironically comes true:

> *Iago.* With Cassio, mistress. Go to, charm your tongue.
> *Emil.* I will not charm my tongue; I am bound to speak.
>   (5.2.183-184)

Here she reverses the joke by putting her heart into her tongue, but, as in the joke ("before your ladyship"), it is Desdemona who provides the motive. The one time we see Emilia bestow her tongue on him, he is destroyed. There are echoes of the theme of nagging loquacity at 2.3.306-308; 3.3.19ff., 45ff.

There is a similar interaction among a number of images of curtseying and kneeling. Iago's contempt for the "duteous and knee-crooking knave" (1.1.45) finds a contrast in Cassio's enthusiastic command when Desdemona debarks, "Ye men of Cyprus, let her have your knees" (2.1.84) and in Othello's suspicion of Emilia when he calls her a "subtle whore" and adds, "And yet she'll kneel and pray; I have seen her do't" (4.2.21-23). Seconds later, Desdemona begs him to explain his "fury": "Upon my knees, what doth your speech import?" (4.2.31). Desdemona, once publicly given the Cyprians' knees, now is on her knees, but futilely. To Iago and Emilia she swears her innocence: "Here I kneel" (4.2.151)— her position the more dramatically effective because we have already seen Othello kneeling to swear revenge and Iago kneeling to swear assistance to him. Cf. the comment of John Money in "Othello's

'It is the Cause . . .': An Analysis," *Shakespeare Survey*, VI (1953), 95-96. Money remarks rightly, "Shakespearian actor and Shakespearian critic meet in the study of the words" (p. 94).

There is a very interesting repetition of *ear* in a figurative sense. Othello promises a report to the "grave ears" of Duke and Senators (1.3.124); he tells how Desdemona would "with a greedy ear / Devour up my discourse" (1.3.149-150); and Desdemona requests the Duke: "To my unfolding lend your prosperous ear" (245). To the Duke's maxims for banishing grief, Brabantio retorts ironically: "But words are words. I never yet did hear / That the bruis'd heart was pieced through the ear" (218-219). Othello, who likes listeners, on one occasion urges Iago not to make Othello's "ear / A stranger to thy thoughts" (3.3.143-144). Iago has long been preparing for this moment, resolving in one soliloquy "to abuse Othello's ear" (1.3.401) and in another, "I'll pour this pestilence into his ear" (2.3.362). Othello, who won Desdemona "by ear," is turned against her by ear.

Cf. Cassio's "she falls me thus about my neck" (4.1.139-140) with Emilia's "That men must lay their murthers on your neck" (5.2.170); Iago's "Our bodies are our gardens" (1.3.323) with Emilia's "doth abuse your bosom" (4.2.14); and the literal passages at 1.3.144, 2.1.126-127, 223, and 4.1.53, 55, 84, with the figurative ones at 3.1.52 and 3.4.184. Roderigo's term for Othello—"thick-lips" (1.1.66)—is at once a photographic image and a figure for the speaker's own feeling. Physiology is the basis of verbal comedy at 3.1.6ff.

Notes

PREFACE

The notes contain points not important enough to be included in the text; the detailed evidence for some of the points made in the text; and acknowledgment of the interpretations of other students of the play, of whom, however, I have for the most part worked independently. Though doubtless there are omissions, I have tried to include a fairly complete sampling of *Othello* criticism of the last two decades. The notes should therefore provide a selective index to the more recent commentaries, especially insofar as they deal with the aspects of the play that I discuss. To attempt to record all the earlier critical positions would needlessly add bulk, for these have already been summarized, in passages to which I refer, by other students such as Draper, Flatter, and Stoll (to read only Stoll's indefatigable replies to his critics would provide good leads to forty years of *Othello* criticism), and of course Augustus Ralli's *A History of Shakespearian Criticism* (London, 1932). In referring to other critics I try, with I hope reasonable fidelity, to note the points at which my conclusions are similar to or parallel with those of my predecessors, and to note the major areas of difference. For the most part I simply state the disagreements; occasionally I explore the issues. Though sometimes I mention other critics in the text, I have in the main confined problems of comparative criticism to the notes, for I have in mind the observation made by J. I. M. Stewart in "The Year's Contribution to Shakespearian Study," *Shakespeare Survey*, V (1952), 129: "Critical essays now frequently take the form of a progress through veritable thickets of contemporary opinion, so that the total effect is of little more than a babel of voices."

Section 1 of Chapter I, Sections 3, 4, and 5 of Chapter III, and Chapter VII appeared originally in *Sewanee Review*, *Essays in Criticism*, *PMLA*, *Virginia Quarterly Review*, and *Arizona Quarterly*, respectively.

CHAPTER 1. APPROACH

[1] One who is committed to a detailed study of parts might well wish to seize protectively on Edward A. Armstrong's observation, "There is a strange psychological bias which tempts those interested in large issues to belittle detailed work," in *Shakespeare's Imagination* (London, 1946), p. 125n. But if the study of details is at times tedious, one can but hope that the study will eventually pay off in a firmer understanding of the large issues. Cf. also G. Wilson Knight's Preface to the 4th edition of *The Wheel of Fire* (London, 1949), pp. vi-vii. Subsequent references are to this edition; "Knight" means this book unless otherwise stated. In *Flaming Minister* (Durham, N. C., 1953), G. R. Elliott makes the most detailed commentary on individual passages, moving through the five acts in

NOTES FOR PAGES 1-6

order, and consistently applying a general theory of the play. He is more complete than any other commentator in noting the interrelationship of separated passages. In this and in other matters some of our interpretations are similar. I shall try to note major points of agreement and disagreement.

[2] See the preface to the Notes, above.

[3] Cf. L. C. Knights, *Explorations* (New York, 1947), p. 31. See Section 2 of the present chapter.

[4] Cf. E. E. Stoll's phrase, "a tragedy which is also a poem, in which the parts 'mutually support and explain each other.'" This is in *Shakespeare and Other Masters* (Cambridge, Mass., 1940), p. 219. "Stoll" means this work unless otherwise stated. In *Poetry and Drama* (Cambridge, Mass., 1951), p. 43, T. S. Eliot speaks of the "perfection of verse drama, which would be a design of human action and of words, such as to present at once the two aspects of dramatic and of musical order."

[5] Professor W. H. Clemen has given numerous examples of images which link separate passages. See his *The Development of Shakespeare's Imagery* (Cambridge, Mass., 1951), pp. 83, 140, 143, 152, 163, 170. The list is not complete. Clemen also has a telling comment on the general sense of the interrelatedness of all the parts which is created by the imagery (p. 224).

[6] D. A. Traversi, *Approach to Shakespeare* (London, 1938), p. 14. Traversi's first chapter describes the problem well, it seems to me. Of *Othello* he comments: "Plot and imagery, in fact, are fused as never before" (p. 86). Cf. his "Othello," *The Wind and the Rain*, VI (1950), 268-269. On the importance of the language spoken, the "wording," there are some relevant comments by E. E. Stoll in *Poets and Playwrights* (Minneapolis, 1930), pp. 5ff., 128.

[7] On the relation of poetic language to the dramatic whole, there are some relevant observations in the opening chapter of Moody Prior's *The Language of Tragedy* (New York, 1947), pp. 1-15.

[8] Cf. Mikhail M. Morozov, "The Individualization of Shakespeare's Characters Through Imagery," *Shakespeare Survey*, II (1949), 83-106.

[9] The theory and practice of this volume are consistent, I believe, with the proposals made by R. A. Foakes in "Suggestions for a New Approach to Shakespeare's Imagery," *Shakespeare Survey*, V (1952), 81-92. Cf. the better written essay by S. L. Bethell, "Shakespeare's Imagery: The Diabolic Images in *Othello*," *Shakespeare Survey*, V (1952), 63. Cf. the chapter, "The Functions of Imagery in Drama," especially pp. 85ff., in Una Ellis-Fermor's *The Frontiers of Drama* (New York, 1946).

[10] Cf. Foakes, pp. 82, 86, 89. The importance of these elements I thought I had made clear in *This Great Stage* (Baton Rouge, 1948).

[11] In "The Life of Our Design," *Hudson Review*, II (1949-50), Alan Downer uses the term "language of props" (pp. 248ff.). I am entirely in agreement with his position that all the elements are integral parts of an indivisible whole. My terms parallel his: if Shakespeare "began by using the language of action *and* the language of poetry he soon learned to use the language of *imagery in action* which is the major characteristic of good drama" (p. 246).

[12] As Una Ellis-Fermor suggested almost two decades ago, the student of the images "in a single work of art . . . would find the work running into years."

NOTES FOR PAGES 6-12

This appears in an early and sound essay on the study of poetic language in drama, *Some Recent Research in Shakespeare's Imagery* (London, 1937), p. 6.

13 Cf., for instance, Robert F. Goheen, *The Imagery of Sophocles' Antigone: A Study of Poetic Language and Structure* (Princeton, 1951), and some of the criticism in Richmond Lattimore's Preface to his translation of Aeschylus' *Oresteia* (Chicago, 1953), pp. 15ff.

14 Hereward T. Price, *Construction in Shakespeare*, University of Michigan Contributions in Modern Philology, No. 17 (Ann Arbor, 1951), p. 11. In the ideas in this chapter I am more than once indebted to the theories set forth by Professor Price.

15 Pages 89, 180, 224. There are other observations of the same kind on pp. 223 and 224. Clemen also speaks of imagery as "a form of imaging and conceiving things" (p. 98). Cf. Price, pp. 21, 22, 28-29.

16 Page 162.

17 *The Structure of Literature* (Chicago, 1954), pp. 17, 64. Cf. also p. 27. Goodman goes on to analyze the function of the "system of images" in *Richard II* (pp. 64-66).

18 Cf. Morozov, p. 86; Bethell, "Shakespeare's Imagery," p. 69.

19 One might speak of an image pattern as an inner organism—a part of the whole that could not exist without the whole and yet an entity having parts that function with respect to each other. This would be "a verbal drama" as distinct from "verbal drama" generally. As a created thing it does not "just happen"; nor yet, I believe, is it deliberately blueprinted and executed. One may guess: a certain image or kind of image "comes up" for a speaker on a certain occasion; then it is felt consciously or perhaps semiconsciously to have some relevance to the import of the whole; and it continues to be used (with the varying degrees of consciousness presumably characteristic of the creative process) as a way of exploring character or mood or theme during the constructive process and leaving a trail by which the reader may follow the exploration in the finished work. Cf. Foakes, p. 90.

20 Cf. Price, especially pp. 24 and 35ff. George Rylands develops this idea effectively in a British Academy Shakespeare lecture, "Shakespeare's Poetic Energy," *Proceedings of the British Academy*, XXXVII (1951), 99-119. Cf. his statement that the "repetition of a word in diverse contexts throughout the play, with its correlatives and associations, often gives the clue to the poetic thought, the *dianoia*, which informs the whole" (p. 102). Cf. René Wellek and Austin Warren, *Theory of Literature* (New York, 1949), especially pp. 29-37 and 65-66.

21 Or to study the working of Shakespeare's imagination generally in accordance with the evidence of his images, as in Armstrong's *Shakespeare's Imagination*, which is concerned especially with "image clusters."

22 Eliseo Vivas, "Literature and Knowledge, *Sewanee Review*, LX (1952), 561ff. To admit intention among the objects of the mimetic process is not to embrace the "intentional fallacy." Cf. W. K. Wimsatt, *The Verbal Icon* (Lexington, Ky., 1954), pp. 3ff.

23 There is an analogous situation in criticism: the criticism of a given work of art may symbolize the critic's "perspectives and beliefs." The act of criticism may be a symbolic affirmation. This may occur very openly: everybody wants to

239

claim Shakespeare (just as Shakespeare's characters all want to be on the side of "nature" and in twentieth-century politics everybody invokes "democracy") or has to dispose of him—Christians and anti-Christians, Freudians and anti-Freudians, all with dogmatic readings. For this reason a history of Shakespeare criticism is a miniature history of ideas, and a conspectus of Shakespeare criticism at any one time gives a spectrum of current ideas. Or the affirmation may penetrate a work of ostensible detachment: the analyst of plots may find Shakespeare a repository of domestic virtues, the analyst of language may consistently find an opposition to a Christian view of life, the analyst of characters may find a nihilist who leaves us only despair. In all Shakespeare criticism there is inevitably something of the ex parte. But this does not mean a hopeless situation, an insoluble muddle of conflicting affirmations: (1) all the thought and value systems embodied in different critiques are not to be construed as equal in soundness and appropriateness; (2) a "subjective" position underlying a critique may well have the depth and breadth required for the contemplation of the literary object; (3) some critics will be graced with corrective gifts—enough literary tact and self-awareness to hold their positions with flexibility and finesse; (4) in time the generality of critical readers may be trusted to make the required discount and to distinguish the perspectives which have a large enough philosophic base from those which do not.

24 To say this is obviously not to oppose an exhausting of all literal possibilities of a text. The only trouble comes from the literalist who argues that unless the whole work is patently and primarily symbolic, it has no symbolic level. This is apparently the Chicago position.

25 In the chapter on Greek dramatists in his *History of Political Ideas*, which is to appear in 1956. I have seen this section in manuscript.

26 Norman Friedman, "Imagery: From Sensation to Symbol," *Journal of Aesthetics and Art Criticism*, XII (1953), 32. This subject is very interestingly developed, especially with reference to archetypes (pp. 32-37).

27 As William O. Raymond remarks, when asking for a critical *via media* between the romantic and historical methods: "But it does not follow that because he [Shakespeare] was an Elizabethan, he was compelled to pander to every popular taste however primitive, or every stage convention however unreasonable." This is in "Motivation and Character in *Othello*," *University of Toronto Quarterly*, XVII (1947-48), 95.

28 The fullest argument that a drama should be considered not as having a meaning partly dependent on the poetry, but as a nonsymbolic imitation of an action with a necessary generic structure and a necessary affective function to be understood in terms of theatrical experience, is developed in various parts of *Critics and Criticism*, ed. R. S. Crane (Chicago, 1952).

29 This method appears in almost pure form in Lilian Winstanley's *"Othello" as the Tragedy of Italy* (London, 1924). Miss Winstanley argues that the Othello story "is made the symbol of a *national* destiny" (p. 30); that the "peculiar greatness" of the play "is due to the fact that he incarnates the supreme type of the Spanish nation, the 'idea of Spain,' as it were, rather than any one individual" (p. 50); that "it is a study of divine retribution alike upon Philip II of Spain and upon Spain" (p. 56).

NOTES FOR PAGES 15-18

30 On the subject of this paragraph there are some sage remarks in Alfred Harbage's *As They Liked It* (New York, 1947), pp. 29ff. On the subject of the "realists" and the "historians" vs. the followers of the Coleridge tradition of viewing Shakespeare as portrayer of human nature, J. I. M. Stewart in *Character and Motive in Shakespeare* (London and New York, 1949) is excellent. See especially pp. 41-42. Fifteen years ago Benjamin T. Spencer held forth on "a monstrous and all-devouring illusion such as 'the Elizabethan mind' " and on the inconsistencies and limitations of studies rigidly oriented with respect to such a conception. "This Elizabethan Shakespeare," *Sewanee Review*, XLIX (1941), 536ff.

31 R. P. Blackmur, *The Lion and the Honeycomb* (New York, 1955), p. 197. On the need "to make Shakespeare a contemporary to see his particular relevance for our time" Knights speaks pointedly (*Explorations*, pp. 96ff.).

32 Goodman's remarks about the study of *Hamlet* are very much to the point: "So, the sentimental, the tragic, the comic: love, art, and power, and instinctual disgust and disgust in the world, and death—these constitute the magnitude of *Hamlet*. But if the attempt is made to hold them together in too simple a structure, that does not give room for the scope of the hero, then the unity is inexplicable, and the critics have recourse to explaining the failure by historical causes, revenge plots, and Renaissance psychologies" (pp. 172-173).

33 Robert M. Smith, "Current Fashions in Hamlet Criticism," *Shakespeare Association Bulletin*, XXIV (1949), 17. The limits of the historical method are expressed with great force and skill by Moody E. Prior in "Character in Relation to Action in *Othello*," *Modern Philology*, XLIV (1947), 234-237. Rufus Putney makes some sharp comments of a similar sort in "What 'Praise to Give?' Jonson vs. Stoll," *Philological Quarterly*, XXIII (1944), 307ff. For the most recent comments on this subject, and they are admirable ones, see L. C. Knights, "On Historical Scholarship and the Interpretation of Shakespeare," *Sewanee Review*, LXIII (1955), 223-240, especially 229-230, 239-240.

34 Maud Bodkin, *Archetypal Patterns in Poetry* (Oxford, 1934), pp. 333-334. The whole passage, which is especially about *Othello*, is relevant.

35 As G. Wilson Knight puts it in *The Crown of Life* (London, 1948), p. 9: "That spiritual quality which alone causes great work to endure through the centuries should be the object of our attention."

36 Arthur Sewell, *Character and Society in Shakespeare* (Oxford, 1951), p. 76. Cf. Sewell's statement in another connection that in tragedy we identify with the characters not psychologically but morally and "experience the moral community of mankind" (p. 39).

37 Donald A. Stauffer's few pages about *Othello* lay emphasis on various verbal and imagistic interconnections. This is in *Shakespeare's World of Images* (New York, 1949), pp. 170ff. Cf. Harley Granville-Barker, *Prefaces to Shakespeare* (Princeton, 1947), II, 143ff.

38 Note, also, Cassio's ignorance of the disservice he does to Desdemona when he persuades her to do him a service. Cassio takes one action which, though insignificant in itself, opens the way to his troubles: the sense of duty which leads to his personal attention to the watch at Cyprus (2.3.5-6) throws him in Iago's path and prepares for the drunkenness scene. In his repentant mood he

241

asserts, "I will rather sue to be despis'd than to deceive so good a commander" (2.3.278-279); yet Othello comes to hold him guilty of a much greater deception than being a "drunken, and . . . indiscreet . . . officer." This looks more like an irony of circumstance than an unforeseen result to which a character has himself contributed. Yet Cassio has contributed: by "suing" through Desdemona he has inadvertently given strength to Iago's insinuations.

39 Cf. Samuel Kliger, "Othello: The Man of Judgment," *Modern Philology*, XLVIII (1951), 221-224.

40 Likewise, Desdemona is confident in a just fate for a "deserving woman," i.e., "one that, in the authority of her merit, did justly put on the vouch of very malice itself" (2.1.145-148) (i.e., one whom even malicious people would vouch for). Desdemona, of course, is sparring with Iago, who promptly disposes of the virtuous woman in his final couplets. These are really a symbolic anticipation. She is "merit," he is "malice," and her fate is to win from him the expectable response, not the paradoxical response that she idealistically proposed.

41 A few lines later she is still confident: "I give thee warrant of thy place" (20). Cassio does even better than that: he gets Othello's place.

42 With his wager may be compared her guarantee of the future: if she does not "love him dearly" forever, she says, "Comfort forswear me!" (4.2.158-159). Again the presumably incompatible terms are both fulfilled: her continuing love and her loss of "comfort." A weaker form of the irony of "confidence unjustified" is that of "hope unjustified," as when Desdemona says, "The heavens forbid / But that our loves and comforts should increase / Even as our days do grow!" and Othello approves, "Amen to that, sweet powers!" (2.1.195-197). Yet this is not so simple as it may look at first, since there is a sense in which Desdemona's love (perhaps even Othello's) may be said to increase.

43 There are other examples in S. L. Bethell, *Shakespeare and the Popular Dramatic Tradition* (Durham, N. C., 1944), pp. 165-166.

44 Desdemona says of her hand, "It yet hath felt no age nor known no sorrow" (3.4.37). But she is now entering on excessive knowledge of sorrow. After Othello has ordered her to bed, she says hopefully: "He looks gentler than he did" (4.3.11). We know that this is the relative calm of the man who has fixed on a resolution—the resolution to kill Desdemona.

45 Cf. Othello's chance words after he reaches Cyprus, "If it were now to die, / 'Twere now to be most happy" (2.1.191-192), which state a truth that he does not know is true.

46 When Othello assures Desdemona that he saw Cassio with the handkerchief, she guesses at the truth: "He found it then" (5.2.66). But Othello is predetermined to believe otherwise and to act accordingly.

47 Several lines later he argues, "It is not words that shakes me thus" (4.1.42-43). He has a glimmering recognition that he is going on words alone, for a man cannot deny a possibility that he has not entertained. But despite this and the fact that he has just been noting an instance of the duplicity of words, he remains essentially impervious to that separation of words and things which is at the heart of Iago's method. For the implicit relevance of Iago to phenomena of a later age, see Richard Weaver on the dangers that follow when men begin to point out that "the word is one entity and the object it represents

NOTES FOR PAGES 19-21

is another" ("Aspects of the Southern Philosophy," *Hopkins Review*, V [Summer, 1952], 10).

48 Levin Schücking would deny the existence of such irony on the grounds that (1) if Iago speaks unfavorably about Othello, what he says has no value beyond illustrating his own character, and (2) if Iago speaks favorably of Othello, this is only a "primitive device" of characterization and proves nothing about Iago. See *Character Problems in Shakespeare's Plays* (New York, 1922), pp. 65-67. This is one way of simplifying the problem. But cf. Bethell, *Shakespeare and the Popular Dramatic Tradition*, pp. 87-88.

49 Iago's accuracy is ironic, again, when he tries to temper the vehemence of Cassio's self-condemnation: "Come, come, good wine is a good familiar creature if it be well us'd" (2.3.313-314). The man whose own passions know no limits states the virtue of moderation. Lodovico's description of Othello, "rash and most unfortunate" (5.2.283), does not have an ironic effect, since we have no reasons for not expecting such perceptive words from Lodovico. Iago's note on Cassio, "rash and very sudden in choler" (2.1.279), is psychological rather than moral, and Cassio is not a tragic hero.

50 Words which serve primarily to express Iago's own animus (contempt, cynicism, etc.) are often partly true. Cf. Bodkin, *Archetypal Patterns in Poetry*, p. 222.

51 Similarly, a character may describe another in terms that are true but do not remain true in a proper sense: the change opens the door to disaster. We cannot read Iago's view of Othello's love for Desdemona—"His soul is so enfetter'd to her love / That she may make, unmake, do what she list" (2.3.351-352)—without reflecting that the perfection of this slavery would be the salvation of Othello. But the slavery is incomplete: he escapes the bond of devotion to become the corrector.

52 An angry account of one character may be applicable to another character. Brabantio's charge against Othello actually applies rather closely to Iago and his methods with Othello: "an abuser of the world, a practiser / Of arts inhibited and out of warrant" (1.2.78-79). The repeated accusation that magic or charms have been used suggests Iago's hypnotic effect on Othello.

53 Expressed first by Iago (1.1.39ff.), approached by Emilia (4.3.89ff.), acted upon by Othello, though with some variation of style, and rejected only by Desdemona (4.3.107-108).

54 *The Language of Tragedy*, p. 6. Cf. Stoll, pp. 192ff., 205, 251.

55 Page 114. The general drift of this is right, but it fails to allow for the fact that the Duke speaks not only in prose but also in several verse styles, and for the fact that the war does, and by the management of the plot has to, divert some attention from the wedding.

56 Another variation is the sententious couplets used by the Duke in consoling Brabantio, and by Brabantio with the same rhythm in his bitter reply (1.3.202-220).

57 George H. W. Rylands, *Words and Poetry* (New York, 1928), p. 163. However, it is difficult to understand Rylands' remark that "Iago's verse soliloquies are pedestrian" (p. 160).

58 Milton Crane, *Shakespeare's Prose* (Chicago, 1951), pp. 156, 160.

NOTES FOR PAGES 21-25

59 Cf. Rylands, "Shakespeare's Poetic Energy," p. 117, and Morozov.

60 There are many such observations in Elliott, as well as in Granville-Barker, II, 14-20, *passim*, 141ff., and Traversi's "Othello."

61 Abraham B. Feldman, "Othello's Obsessions," *American Imago*, IX (1952), 150-151. See also p. 157, where Othello's wish to throw Cassio's nose to a dog is said to be "a substitute for the castration-wish."

62 Sometimes the effect is one of "bold and strange irony," as William Empson calls Othello's repetition, just before killing Desdemona, of the words used by Iago in dissuading Roderigo from drowning himself: "love thee after." This is in *The Structure of Complex Words* (Norfolk, Conn., n. d.), p. 223. "Empson" means this work unless otherwise stated.

63 Similarly, when Desdemona denies that "e'er my will did trespass 'gainst his love" (4.2.152), her choice of *will* gives her speech the effect of being a reply to Iago's insinuation to Othello: "one may smell in such a will most rank" (3.3.232; cf. 236). The various uses of *will* in the play have been noted by various critics. See, for example, John E. Hankins, *Shakespeare's Derived Imagery* (Lawrence, Kansas, 1953), pp. 94-95. As his title indicates, Hankins is mainly concerned with the possible sources of Shakespeare's imagery.

64 For instance, in Iago's last soliloquy in Act 2, the lines from "Divinity of hell" to "That shall enmesh them all" (2.3.356-368) use the contrast of black and white, the opposition of heaven and hell, the appearance theme, the contrast of the wise and foolish, the sexuality theme, and images of poisoning, the body, and trapping—all of which help regularly to animate and direct the dramatic movement. In general Iago's soliloquies recapitulate or anticipate themes, motives, and images that are structurally significant.

CHAPTER 2. IAGO: BEYOND THE GRIEVANCES

1 Kenneth Muir, "The Jealousy of Iago," *English Miscellany: A Symposium of History, Literature, and the Arts*, ed. Mario Praz, 2 (Rome, 1951), pp. 73, 74n., 82. The most complete previous discussions of the grievances are in A. C. Bradley's *Shakespearean Tragedy*, 2nd ed. (London, 1905), pp. 208-209, 212, 225; Granville-Barker, II, 102-103; Richard Flatter's *The Moor of Venice* (London, 1950), pp. 18-20, 34-38.

2 Most recently by Muir and by Frank P. Rand, "The Over Garrulous Iago," *Shakespeare Quarterly*, I (1950), 155-161, an admirably lively article. Rand takes the sensible position that jealousy does not exclude other motives. "He is in criticism, and I believe in composition, a varied if not multiple personality" (p. 161). In *Literature and Psychology* (London, 1951), F. L. Lucas suggests, without pushing it very hard, that Iago may have a "Judas-complex": "A man who loves his master and feels himself less loved than others, can be provoked to passionate resentment" (p. 76). Cf. John C. McCloskey, "The Motivation of Iago," *College English*, III (1941), 25-30; Samuel A. Tannenbaum, "The Wronged Iago," *Shakespeare Association Bulletin*, XII (1937), 57-62; M. R. Ridley, *Shakespeare's Plays: A Commentary* (New York, 1938), p. 160; Thomas D. Bowman, "A Further Study in the Characterization and Motivation of Iago," *College*

English, IV (1942-43), 460-469. In detecting a "class" feeling on Iago's part, Bowman anticipates Empson and Bethell. John W. Draper preceded all of these in defending "Honest Iago" and arguing that simply on the ground of his suspicions he had ample reason for even more vigorous action than he took. Draper cites five earlier defenders of Iago and indicates opposition to more than two dozen other critics who represent Iago "as a villain of the deepest dye." See "Honest Iago," *PMLA*, XLVI (1931), 724ff.

3 Muir has a good note on Iago as an actor (pp. 70-71). Granville-Barker has a lengthy discussion of Iago as actor and "artist" (II, 104ff.). Flatter bases his entire analysis of Iago's character on his "craze for play-acting" (pp. 8-47). This is a part-truth ingeniously built up into a whole truth; it lands Flatter in difficulties that he can get out of only by inadvertently building up Iago's greed as an equally strong motive. Cf. *Stanislavsky Produces Othello*, trans. Helen Nowak (London, 1948), p. 160.

4 On the Elizabethan attitude to self-love, see Muir, p. 74.

5 On the boorishness of his manner in this scene, see Elliott, pp. 5, 8, and elsewhere.

6 Cf. John R. Moore, "Othello, Cassio, and Iago as Soldiers," *Philological Quarterly*, XXXI (1952), 191.

7 George Lyman Kittredge, ed., *Othello* (Boston, 1941), pp. 119-120. Cf. p. x. My quotations are from this edition, though I occasionally use another reading (usually Folio in place of Kittredge's Quarto). The Kittredge text is used by permission of Ginn and Company.

8 On Iago's unimpressiveness as a soldier, see John R. Moore, "The Character of Iago," *Studies in Honor of A. H. R. Fairchild*, ed. Charles T. Prouty, University of Missouri Studies, XXI (Columbia, Mo., 1946), pp. 41-42. Henry J. Webb endeavors to rehabilitate the military merits of Iago and to dispose of Cassio as a kind of army politician in "The Military Background in *Othello*," *Philological Quarterly*, XXX (1951), 40-52, but Moore effectively disposes of his arguments in "Othello, Cassio, and Iago as Soldiers," pp. 189-194.

9 John W. Draper makes a longer defense of the appointment of Cassio in "Captain General Othello," *Anglia*, LV (1931), 296ff.

10 Though there is much difference of opinion as to the causes of Iago's hatred, the only critic to deny the reality of the hatred is Flatter (pp. 23ff.). Flatter thinks the "I hate" is only a trick to regain the confidence of Roderigo, lest his purse be lost to Iago.

11 Flatter speaks with finality on this (pp. 36-38).

12 Cf. Flatter, p. 39; Stoll, p. 237. The interpretation of Iago made in my chapter is at various points the same as Stoll's. Stoll does an excellent job of refuting critics, such as Brooke, Nicoll, and Kittredge, who find justifications for Iago or who sentimentalize him (pp. 234ff.). But Stoll, if I understand him, seems to want to treat Iago entirely as an effective stage figure made plausible by "consonance" and "identicalness" rather than as a recognizable human being and as a concentration of familiar modes of thought and feeling. In objecting to certain psychological analyses of Iago, Stoll formally would eliminate *all* "psychological" treatment of him and view him entirely in terms of his emotional impact through dramatic contrasts. Yet Stoll's practice seems to me to be better

than his theory, for his insights into Iago constantly involve the "psychological." Comments on Stoll's habit of running out other critics' "psychology" with one hand and running in his own with the other are made by Leo Kirschbaum in "The Modern Othello," *ELH,* XI (1944), 283-296. See especially pp. 287-289. Brents Stirling defines Stoll's error as "the inference that because Othello's actions are not to be integrated by any given psychological theory, psychological motivation is absent." This is in "Psychology in *Othello," Shakespeare Association Bulletin,* XIX (1944), 143.

[13] Since Coleridge's verdict of "motiveless malignity" seems to me to be just (malignity is "motiveless" when it cannot be adequately accounted for by the commonplaces of cause and effect), I should record that Coleridge puts greater trust than I do in Iago's words in 2.1. He describes Iago's "thought," once "a mere suspicion," as "now ripening—tho' perhaps Shakespeare compromised." See T. M. Raysor, ed., *Coleridge's Shakespearean Criticism* (Cambridge, Mass., 1930), I, 52.

[14] His words to Othello in another context—"it is my nature's plague / To spy into abuses" (3.3.146-147)—do tell a general truth about himself. For examples of his knowingness, see 1.1.1ff., 148ff.; 2.3.13-63, 78ff.; 4.1.95ff.; 4.2.239-241.

[15] In soliloquies he makes no other reference to her. When he expatiates on the sexuality of others, he does not mention her (1.3.340ff.; 2.1.223ff.). In talking to both Emilia and Desdemona, he is conventionally jocular or sympathetic (2.1.101ff.; 4.2.110ff.). Alone with Emilia he is easy and businesslike; there is no trace of suspicion, sharpness, or constraint (3.3.300ff.). After the second nocturnal brawl, he treats Emilia as a friendly and helpful assistant (5.1.110ff.). Nor does he accuse her at the end, as he would inevitably seem prone to do.

Those who think Iago's suspicion real call attention to Emilia's lines when she is attacking the unknown "knave" who made Othello suspicious of Desdemona: "Some such squire he was / That turn'd your wit the seamy side without / And made you to suspect me with the Moor" (4.2.145-147). But these lines strengthen the argument that Iago cannot hold the suspicion now. Emilia regards it as so ridiculous that she can equate it with Othello's suspicion of Desdemona and can even mention it in front of Desdemona; Iago tries to shut her up—"You are a fool. Go to" (148)—because he himself does not wish to appear so foolish as to have held so untenable a suspicion. Emilia's tone now indicates that she must have done a complete refutation in the past when Iago voiced his suspicion. Our whole picture of Iago suggests that he did not even have a real suspicion of Emilia then, but found the suspicion useful in some maneuver of the time.

[16] Schücking notes this *"excess of motives,"* but in his literalist zeal to deprive such matters of characterological status attributes it to a *"mistake"* by Shakespeare (p. 213). He gives a convenient summary of critical opinions on the validity of Iago's grievances (pp. 206ff.). He thinks the grievances are real but the real source of Iago's conduct is his "evil disposition" (p. 211).

[17] One should allow for the possibility of a sexual *double entendre* in the joke. If the secondary meaning is present, it represents, not an implication of illicit conduct, but Iago's characteristic awareness of the physical circumstances of sexuality.

NOTES FOR PAGES 34-37

[18] Sewell identifies Iago with earlier Shakespeare characters who "establish a *rapport* with the audience not unlike that established by the comedian in the music-hall" (p. 81).

[19] Taking off from a statement by John Jay Chapman (*A Glance Toward Shakespeare* [Boston, 1922]), Stoll deals convincingly with this aspect of Iago (pp. 247ff., 265-268, 277).

[20] In Christian terms, he took over the divine function: "Vengeance is mine." Cf. the statement of this in Lily Bess Campbell, *Shakespeare's Tragic Heroes: Slaves of Passion* (Cambridge, Eng., 1930), p. 172.

[21] In *Shakespeare* (London, 1951), George I. Duthie suggests "psychological inconsistency" (pp. 18, 38) because Iago alleges sexual jealousy but does not act like a jealous man. But such allegations may be consistent with other aspects of personality.

[22] See *Variorum*, p. 124; Arden ed., p. 90. Schücking denies that Iago has a conscience (p. 210). Empson has the interesting idea that motive-hunting is an aspect of Iago's "honesty": he is "quite open to his own motives or preferences and interested to find out what they are" (p. 223).

[23] In commenting on the falsity of the grievances, Stauffer contends that Iago is "an outcast from society" who "glories in" his state (pp. 174-175). This is questionable.

[24] This is a different problem from that of giving him a reality which he is not accorded in popular melodrama, where his defeat is preassured. Iago's reality is made convincing and immediate by the success of his machinations against people "like ourselves."

[25] Page 83. Cf. Flatter: "The Iago family is large, its members are many" (p. viii). Cf. Bowman: Iago has "the energy to actuate natural impulses" ("A Further Study," p. 469). The dramatic situation, as I see it, is such that Harbage's phrase concerning the evil in the play, "comfortably localized" (*As They Liked It*, p. 55), is a little too comfortable.

[26] Stoll quotes John Palmer's statement, in *Studies in the Contemporary Theatre* (London, 1927), that Iago's evil is "evil for its own sake" (p. 238). Cf. Harbage: "Vice is something absolute, rooted irremovably in some individuals and lodged temporarily in others; it is not a mere natural effect of a natural cause" (*As They Liked It*, p. 137). Cf. Stauffer: "Iago is a vision of evil" (p. 174).

[27] This comes very close to Stewart, *Character and Motive in Shakespeare,* pp. 108-110, with an exception to be noted later. Cf. Elliott, pp. 116, 126, 135, 137-138; F. R. Leavis, "Diabolic Intellect and the Noble Hero: A Note on *Othello,*" *Scrutiny*, VI (1937), 264. In Granville-Barker's terms, "the evil is externalized in Iago" (II, 100).

[28] *Archetypal Patterns in Poetry*, p. 245. It is put very similarly by Thomas F. Connolly in "Shakespeare and the Double Man," *Shakespeare Quarterly*, I (1950), 31: "He is that side of man which is hidden from the light of day, but which cannot be denied." There is a psychoanalytic version of this in Feldman, pp. 156-157.

[29] *The Works of Herman Melville*, ed. Raymond W. Weaver (London, 1924), XIII, 43.

[30] The references are to chapters 10, 11, and 15 in the edition cited; they

NOTES FOR PAGES 37-39

occur respectively on pp. 45, 46, 51, and 62. The passage on Claggart which applies most remarkably to Iago—as well as to Edmund, Goneril, and Regan—is in the sixth and fifth paragraphs from the end of Chapter 10 in the Weaver edition (p. 46).

31 Especially at 3.3.177ff., 183ff., 192; 3.4.26ff.; 4.1.102; 5.2.345. For a summary of various opinions on whether Othello is "jealous," see Muir, pp. 65-68. It would be wrong to deny Othello's "jealousy" in order to establish his "nobility," for his nobility is dubious; but it is important to determine the status of his jealousy. Stoll replies effectively to French critics who argue either that Othello was always somewhat jealous or else that he was not jealous at all (pp. 223 and earlier). There is a complete survey of opinions on Othello's jealousy in Stoll's *Othello*, University of Minnesota Studies in Language and Literature, No. 2 (Minneapolis, 1915), pp. 9-11, 15-16. Cumberland Clark gives a very elementary account of Othello's jealousy in *Shakespeare and Psychology* (London, 1936), pp. 27-30. Flatter argues that what moved Othello was "not jealousy, but conviction," which "should not be confused with jealousy" (pp. 127-135). A. H. R. Fairchild argues that what underlies Othello's jealousy is honor and that the whole play is to be read in this light. What we see in his domestic actions is a "misapplied honor" taken over from his military attitudes. This is in *Shakespeare and the Tragic Theme*, University of Missouri Studies, XXIX (Columbia, Mo., 1944), 28ff.

32 There are minor echoes at various points—e.g., Bianca's jealousy in the matter of the handkerchief (3.4.185; 4.1.153ff.). Cassio has just enough private jealousy of position to insist, when he is drunk, "The lieutenant is to be saved before the ancient" (2.3.114). In the subsequent disciplinary episode Othello displays, I am convinced, jealousy of his own position (see Chapter V).

33 Cf. Iago's scorn for "bookish theorics" with latter-day sneers at "theorists," "intellectuals," "brain trusters," etc.

34 Edith Sitwell puts it: "he must be first in everything." See *The Poet's Notebook* (Boston, 1950), p. 107.

35 With overtones that we call "modern," Shakespeare presents Brabantio's jealousy as at once the jealousy of position and the anguish of the deceived lover (cf. 1.1.162, 166; 1.3.194-195).

36 See 2.1.309-311; 3.3.165-167, 175-176.

37 Cf. John Draper, "he well knew the torments that he planned to inflict," "The Jealousy of Iago," *Neophilologus*, XXV (1939), 57, and Empson, p. 246.

38 Cf. J. V. Cunningham, *Woe or Wonder: The Emotional Effect of Elizabethan Tragedy* (Denver, 1951), p. 51. Cf. Harbage: "The enemy in . . . *Othello* [is] envious malice" (*As They Liked It*, p. 146). Lily Bess Campbell's statement is much to the point: "But Iago is, as we might expect, not merely jealous. With him jealousy is but one phase of envy, and in his heart is perfect hatred. In him passion has already worked its destruction. . . . Envy . . . is vile and servile, and is moreover secretive: . . . It is then on a theme of hate that the play opens. It is a hate of inveterate anger. It is a hate that is bound up with envy" (p. 153). What is interesting here is the way in which a close textual study and a close historical study support each other. There are differences, of course: Miss Campbell evidently accepts the validity of Iago's grievances. Bradley uses a

NOTES FOR PAGES 39-41

much too narrow conception of envy when he argues that Iago is not envious because he shows no real competitive spirit (pp. 220-221). Bradley could hardly say anything better than that Iago "has a spite against goodness in men" (p. 221), but his assignment of intellectual reasons for this seems to me to be weak. Elliott uses the term "envious arrogance" (p. 79). Granville-Barker calls Iago "bitterly envious, pettily spiteful, morbidly vain" (II, 99). In *Shakespeare's Use of Learning* (San Marino, Calif., 1953), Virgil Whitaker states, "Iago's character is founded upon pride or self-love, the very source of all sin" (p. 281). Flatter calls Iago an "inside cripple" (p. 8). Cf. Paul V. Kreider, *Repetition in Shakespeare's Plays* (Princeton, 1941), p. 69: "The vengeful spirit of a disgruntled egotist." About half of Kreider's book is devoted to a generic account of Shakespeare's villains. In *An Interpretation of Shakespeare* (New York, 1948) Hardin Craig identifies in Iago "the creed of the ego" but adds surprisingly, "he has little positive ill will. He has spite only against anything that might weaken his self-esteem. His want of passion is horrible" (p. 196). Cf. Wolfgang Weilgart, *Shakespeare: Psychognostic* (Tokyo, 1952), p. 196: "Iago's deeds flow out of the hateful blackness of his soul, his demon of negation."

[39] Cf. Elliott, p. 61; Stanislavsky, p. 19.

[40] Cf. Elliott, p. 208. That the jealousy is prior to the specific "abuses" and "faults" on which Iago's case rests not only depends on inference from the overall style of the character but is directly established in a remark of Iago's to Roderigo: "I have told thee often, and I retell thee again and again, I hate the Moor" (1.3.372-373). There is no reason to question "told thee oft"; and Iago had time for his oft-told tale only if he began telling it *long before* the recent failure of promotion. Roderigo has already said to him, "Thou told'st me thou didst hold him in thy hate" (1.1.7)—*before* Iago told him the army story.

[41] Apropos of *Othello*, Cunningham takes a tack that comes in appropriately here: he chides the modern "optimistic assumption that men are not likely to go wrong unless there is sufficient cause" (p. 120).

[42] Robert Speaight says the play cannot be understood without "une conception métaphysique du mal" and speaks of the "oppositions profondément métaphysiques" of Othello and Iago. This is in "Réflexions sur 'Othello,' " *Mercure de France*, No. 1079 (July, 1953), pp. 478, 489.

[43] "Mass mind" is a metaphor for a complex of attitudes about which I shall say more later. The attitudes are restricted to no social or economic level. In explaining Iago, Empson gives some weight to "lower class" resentments (pp. 233-235). If this is sound history, what is critically important is the way in which Shakespeare has generalized the limited historical fact. To work in terms of the "lower class" theory is still to be concerned with genetics, which sometimes do not take us all the way. In "mass mind" I am using, I believe, the same kind of metaphor which Sewell uses when he describes the basic structure of *Othello* in terms of "secular society" versus "a single human soul" (pp. 91ff.). Though I value his treatment, the difficulty I find is that if Iago is really a representative of "all society whatsoever" (p. 94), then society could hardly exist at all. Iago seems rather a precipitate of the evils that exist in solution along with appropriate virtues in society, and this fact I try to express in "mass mind." Now Sewell says something like this a little later in a statement in which, it seems to

249

NOTES FOR PAGE 41

me, he virtually surrenders his metaphor: "Society, we may suppose, is not absolutely represented in Iago. Valour and devoted love are values which society must respect, if it would continue itself" (p. 97). In *The Lion and the Fox* (New York and London, [1927]), Wyndham Lewis works out a similar interpretation, describing Othello as a "Colossus," for whose nobility, simplicity, and purity his admiration is almost hysterical, and applying to Iago such terms as these: "commonplace worldly person," "man in the street," "man of the world," "*small* destroyer," "ideal *little man*," "Everyman, the Judas of the world, the representative of the crowds around the crucifix," "man about town," "commonplace and maniacal," "small and shoddy" (pp. 188-194).

44 The approach sketched here has been worked out in almost these terms by Paul N. Siegel in "The Damnation of Othello," *PMLA*, LXVIII (1953), 1068-1078. He has made a very full collection of all the passages in the play that contribute to this reading. He argues that Othello undergoes a "fall," like Adam, and that, like Faustus, he makes a pact with the devil and is damned. Bradley compares Iago to Mephistopheles (p. 208). Cf. Bodkin, *Archetypal Patterns in Poetry*, pp. 224ff. On Iago as devil, see Sitwell, pp. 103ff., especially pp. 108 and 111. But Elliott finds Desdemona guilty of failure in Christian virtues. Sewell also uses the metaphor of the Fall of Man and finds at the end of the play "no hint of regeneration or redemption" (pp. 94-95, 97). The Faust-Mephistopheles comparison is also made by Connolly, p. 33. Cf. Joseph Kerman, "Verdi's *Otello*, or Shakespeare Explained," *Hudson Review*, VI (1952), 274. In *Shakespeare Studies* (New York, 1927) E. E. Stoll puts it this way: "Iago is the great devil of the seventeenth century, as Goethe's Mephistopheles is of the nineteenth" (p. 383). Making Iago a devil has for Stoll the advantage of exorcizing that other devil, Psychology. Cf. Henri Fluchère, *Shakespeare* (Cahiers du Sud, 1948), p. 301. In *In the East My Pleasure Lies: An Esoteric Interpretation of Some Plays of Shakespeare* (London, 1950), pp. 11-22, Beryl Pogson argues that Iago, who appears as Diabolos or the Slanderer, is the "Divine Tempter," trying to awaken Othello "to his spiritual possibilities"; Desdemona is the "Redeemer"; Othello, in killing himself, "suffers the Mystical Death as a Prelude to Re-Birth."

45 This is the Folio reading. Editors differ widely here. The Folio reading is important for interpretations based on the Christian myth. Cf. Richmond Noble, *Shakespeare's Biblical Knowledge* (London, 1935), p. 273.

46 To look at the play in this way would call attention to a distinction between the "outside" evil and the "inside" evil. In the mythic readings which I have sketched, the principal detail—the enemy attacking the garden—suggests an attack from "outside." I have argued, however, that Iago works from within the community. The point may be clearer if we consider that, in a Christian world, an attack from "outside" would necessarily be an attack from a different mythic order (rather than an attack from an inimical force accounted for in the Christian myth). Now the play does contain a threat of just such an attack—that from the Turks. That such a menace is present in men's imaginations appears a number of times in the imagery. If "such actions may have passage free," Brabantio warns (referring to Othello's supposed drugging of Desdemona), "Bondslaves and pagans shall our statesmen be" (1.2.99), a mode of thought

250

NOTES FOR PAGE 41

echoed in Cassio's eventual judgment of Iago, "Most heathenish and most gross!" (5.2.313). After the V-day quarrel at Cyprus, Othello demands, "Are we turn'd Turks, and to ourselves do that / Which heaven hath forbid the Ottomites?" (2.3.170-171). And in his final despair he claims the mitigating fact that he killed an offensive Turk (5.2.351ff.). But the irony of it is that the attack from without fails and that from within succeeds. As individual or as mythic figure, Iago is comprehended within the Christian order.

[47] All the characters call upon "God" and "heaven" in a conventional expletive sense: Othello at 2.3.204, 3.3.106, 162, 4.1.19, 36, 163, 5.2.62; Desdemona at 4.2.81; Brabantio at 1.3.189; Cassio at 2.3.66, 77, 101, 290, 5.1.50; Roderigo at 1.1.34; Montano at 2.3.164; Emilia at 3.3.298, 5.2.218; Iago at 1.1.4, 33, 59, 86, 108, 2.3.162, 261, 384, 4.1.61, 5.1.90, 5.2.219. At one point Iago swears "By Janus" (1.2.33), a choice of oath which, whatever its literal applicability in the context (Kittredge, p. 132), has symbolic value also. "A large portion of the Biblical allusions proceed from the mouth of Iago" (Noble, p. 216).

Exclamation frequently shades into invocation, prayer, and oath: Othello at 1.3.122, 267, 2.1.197, 3.3.460; Montano at 2.1.34; the Herald at 2.2.12; Emilia at 3.4.155, 4.2.136, 141, 5.2.221, 232, 250; All, 5.2.186; Cassio at 2.1.44, 77,–85, 2.3.115; Desdemona at 1.3.163, 2.1.195, 3.4.77, 81, 126, 163, 4.2.135, 4.3.107. Twice Iago speaks as if in prayer, ironically, at 3.3.175, 373.

Christian sacraments, beliefs, ideals, and cosmology are drawn upon repeatedly for the interpretation of conduct and as a source of images: Othello at 1.3.141, 2.1.190-191, 2.3.171, 172, 5.2.2; Montano at 2.3.203; Iago at 2.3.349-350, 3.3.202; Cassio at 3.4.184; Emilia at 4.3.79; Gratiano at 5.2.208.

Cassio invokes divine aid for the voyagers to Cyprus (2.1.44, 73, 77, 85), drunkenly discusses the fate of souls (2.3.105-115), castigates himself for being drunk (2.3.260-312). His repeated use of *devil* to describe drunkenness and its accompanying vices reminds us that the drunkenness was engineered by Iago, who is repeatedly called devil elsewhere.

Roderigo and Iago argue whether Desdemona is of "blessed condition" (2.1.255-259; cf. 2.3.325). Desdemona's regular indications of Christian faith increase in number and intensity when she is under Othello's attack (4.2.38, 81, 82, 86, 88, 129; cf. 5.2.60, 83).

Othello tends to deck out his thoughts with allusions to God and heavens (3.3.278, 355-356, 371-373), often of a flamboyant or spectacular sort (3.3.445-447). In his sense of divine activity in his affairs he acts almost literally on the theory that the hairs of his head are numbered. "Had it pleas'd heaven / To try me with affliction" (4.2.47-48); "If heaven would make me such another world" (5.2.144). The patience which he cannot achieve he apostrophizes "Ay, there look grim as hell!" (4.2.64). In fact, when he wants to express the idea of something going wrong, he is likely to think of hell. In "Perdition catch my soul / But I do love thee!" (3.3.90-91) he is of course using a conventional order of exclamation. But when he tells Desdemona that to lose the handkerchief or give it away "were such perdition / As nothing else could match" (3.4.67-68), his use of *perdition* contains some interesting wordplay: *perdition* as "loss" and as "destruction" or "damnation." Thus, like "Chaos is come again," the statement is unconsciously prophetic. Othello thinks of the divine as taking his side

251

NOTES FOR PAGES 41-42

(4.1.6-8; 4.2.39, 77). His decisions about Desdemona, and his accusations of her, are full of "devil" and "damnation" (3.4.42; 4.1.44, 191; 4.2.35-37, 90-92), and eventually he claims these for himself in the same magniloquent terms in which he has allotted them to Desdemona (5.2.274ff.). In Othello's expectation of punishment in hell lies another ironic tie with the early scenes in the play, when Brabantio accused Othello of "arts inhibited" and "practices of cunning hell" (1.2.79; 1.3.102), and Iago called him "devil" (1.1.91; 2.1.229).

Iago is perfectly willing to call on the devil or to be the devil or his cousin (1.3.365, 409-410; 2.3.356; 3.4.136; 4.1.71; cf. 1.1.155; 1.2.9), although once he swears "by the faith of man" (1.1.10). Is the diabolistic villain here invoking (1) man's faith in God? (2) the individual man's faith in himself? (3) man's faith in man generally—a humanistic credo? Each of these possible readings has its own ironic value. See also the section, "Essay on Man," in Chapter IV.

48 Whitaker, p. 275. "Three definite relationships of reason, will, and appetite are presented in the play" (p. 278).

49 There has been a great deal of study of the play in these terms. See the article by Paul Siegel referred to in n. 44. In "Shakespeare and the Tragedy of Our Time," *Theology Today*, VIII (1952), 518-534, Roy Battenhouse definitely treats Iago as a Satan-figure and Othello as a Judas-figure. But Clifford Leech insists that the play presents a view of the world "that cannot be reconciled with Christianity." See *Shakespeare's Tragedies* (New York, 1950), pp. 103-105. This is in a chapter in which Leech successfully, though modestly, undertakes to supply the defect so strangely insisted on by T. S. Eliot—an adequate answer to Rymer. The most complete Christian reading that I know of is in Elliott's *Flaming Minister*. As he interprets the play, the main characters progress from a wicked pride to a Christian love and humility. See p. 202. He is especially good in tracing the theme of "divinity of hell" (pp. 106, 139, 140, 188, etc.). Sewell's *Character and Society in Shakespeare* is less a "Christian" in this sense than it is a "religious" reading of the play. Whitaker's *Shakespeare's Use of Learning* squares the play with theological doctrine. One of the pioneer studies of the Christian materials is Kenneth O. Myrick's "The Theme of Damnation in Shakespearean Tragedy," *Studies in Philology*, XXXVIII (1941), 221-245.

50 There would be more of a situation for the student of form if, given the conditions in *Othello*, the drama turned out to be other than Christian, or if, given an opposite probability, as in say the Roman plays or *Lear*, there were grounds for arguing that the drama is essentially Christian. What is important, however, is less the reversal of expectation than the sense of discovery, which may be served in various ways—for instance, in the recognition of the latently beneath the patently Christian, as in Roy Battenhouse's "Hamlet's Apostrophe on Man: Clue to the Tragedy," *PMLA*, LXVI (1951), 1073-1113; "*Measure for Measure* and the Christian Doctrine of Atonement," *PMLA*, LXI (1946), 1029-1059.

51 Milton's presentation of Satan, as described by Arnold Stein in *Answerable Style* (Minneapolis, 1953), is at various points very similar to Shakespeare's presentation of Iago. "Seeing is believing," the theory implicit in Satan's argument to Abdiel (p. 29), is what Iago gets Othello to accept as a basis for judging Desdemona. The Son's analysis of the rebels, "me they have despis'd, / Yet

envied" (p. 30), might, with due changes, be said of Iago by Othello. Stein's paraphrase of Satan, "The mind must be preserved unhurt . . . so that it can search out material means to gain a material superiority" (p. 31), in part describes the Iago program. Likewise this comment: "He is . . . referring inward to self for moral sanction" (p. 36). And this: "the inner hardness provides unrelenting drive to the opportunism that shrewdly seeks the point of maximum penetration" (p. 49). Finally, and most remarkably, some of Milton's imagery is identical with Shakespeare's: "Finally Satan enters, like a wolf, or a thief" (p. 60). Some of these aspects of Shakespeare's treatment of Iago I shall look at more fully in later chapters. Incidentally, Bradley calls it "almost absurd" to compare Iago and Milton's Satan (p. 207).

52 For a list of critics who have treated Iago as a Satanic character, see Stoll, p. 233. This is essentially Stoll's own position; he frequently uses phrases such as "infernal angel" (p. 258). I am in sympathy with any critical metaphor that will keep the scope of Iago wide enough. But we get into difficulty if we accept Chapman's statement that Iago is a "demon" but "not a human being at all" (Stoll, p. 247).

53 Empson carries on a running attack on the idea that Iago "is Evil," but one may doubt whether much is gained by the substitute theory that "he is a critique on an unconscious pun" (p. 230). Or let us put it in this form: Empson's theory does not so much dispose of the theory that Iago "is Evil" as it explicates another way in which "Evil" functions—which is the critical problem in *Othello*. Empson is being a little disingenuous in saying that Evil "has no unity" (p. 231); neither Evil nor Hypocrisy nor Sturdy Independence (which is where Empson locates the Iago soul) has unity until the drama absorbs it into its own unity. The better the dramatization that Evil gets, the more it may have the appearance, or even the reality, of multiplicity; when the dramatization gets very good, as it does in Iago, we may have to seek some virtue beyond unity.

54 The best statement of this is in Bethell's "Shakespeare's Imagery." He argues that the play can be interpreted on three levels—the personal (Cinthio's story), the social (the "new man" who suggested to Shakespeare the "atheist-machiavel with his principle of pure self-interest"), and the metaphysical ("the agelong warfare of Good and Evil")—and that these "coalesce into something like unity" under the diabolic imagery, a symbolization of the disruption of order felt at all three levels (pp. 71ff.). This underlying theme is also developed by other types of imagery, as I shall show. Cf. Price: "Shakespeare constructs in such a way that his persons are public and private at the same time" (p. 40). Foakes' remark that "poetic imagery" may serve "to display a particular situation as a symbol or type of a universal condition" (p. 90) is also relevant.

55 Bethell, *Shakespeare and the Popular Dramatic Tradition*, p. 26. Bethell elaborates the point in a statement that is particularly applicable to Iago (p. 141). I cannot understand the *either-or* logic that sometimes governs discussions of Iago's character. Two good critics come at this in different ways: Bradley is unwilling to let Iago be "Evil for Evil's sake" lest this make him a symbol and keep him from being a character (p. 209); Stewart believes that Iago is "unreal" as a character and therefore has to be read as a symbol (*Character and Motive in Shakespeare*, p. 110). Our principle must be *both-and*;

NOTES FOR PAGES 43-48

to make Iago simply one thing or another will restrict and reduce the actual figure of the play.

56 Cf. Bethell's remark that in dealing with Cleopatra he is concerned with "the concrete poetic expression of a complex interpretation of experience" *(Shakespeare and the Popular Dramatic Tradition,* p. 163).

57 Cf. the quotation from Rand in n. 2 above. The multiplicity of Iago as a character is the obverse of a coin of which the reverse is the multiplicity of the sources from which he is derived. The best treatment of this is in Stoll, pp. 231ff., 276. Cf. Theodore Spencer, *Shakespeare and the Nature of Man,* 2nd ed. (New York, 1949), pp. 131-132; Granville-Barker, II, 111. Numerous commentators identify Iago as a machiavel. Mario Praz rebukes Wyndham Lewis for finding Machiavelli "everywhere," asserts that Seneca was "at the back of every Tudor mind" more than Machiavelli, and claims that Shakespeare's Iago is much less Machiavellian than Cinthio's. See "Machiavelli and the Elizabethans," *Proceedings of the British Academy,* XIV (1928), 71, 76-77; "Shakespeare's Italy," *Shakespeare Survey,* VII (1954), 103.

58 Bodkin, *Archetypal Patterns in Poetry,* p. 223. There is another illuminating comment on p. 333.

59 Iago is indeed a test of the prevalent views of human nature. Whatever the problems of the nineteenth century in facing Iago, our own are partly due, perhaps, to a predisposition to look at manifestations of evil only genetically and therapeutically. And yet it may be suggested that in one way the twentieth century is unusually well equipped to recognize and appreciate Iago: our part of the stage of history is frequently walked by individuals whose existence—and appeal, and partial authority, and partial insight—testifies again to the Shakespearian perceptiveness (cf. Putney, p. 318). How can Iago seem unconvincing?

60 Cf. Traversi, "Othello," p. 259; Fairchild, pp. 37-43.

61 Elliott is constantly trying to make Iago little more than a nasty nincompoop. Leavis more mildly tries to cut Iago down to size (pp. 277ff.). This is a by-product of his desire to cut Bradley down to size. The terms which Granville-Barker applies to Iago also have the effect of emphasizing his pettiness, which is by no means his dominant characteristic (II, 99-101). Somewhat the same line is taken by Moore in "The Character of Iago," pp. 44-45. Duthie makes a good statement of the balance of the two characters (pp. 164-165).

CHAPTER 3. THE IAGO WORLD: STYLES IN DECEPTION

1 True, Othello has known Iago longer than he has known Desdemona. Doubtless that contributes to his misjudgment of them. But it is not a sufficient cause.

2 Pages 218ff. The analysis of the "honesty" passages is much more fully worked out than in the present essay. Empson claims that the puns on *honest* which he finds "at least allow Iago a reasonable basis for his legerdemain" (p. 242).

3 When Brabantio tells Roderigo, "In honest plainness thou hast heard me say / My daughter is not for thee" (1.1.97-98), he provides one of the rare instances in which "honest plainness" is just that. In suggesting that it would be an "honest action" to report to Othello Cassio's inability to drink (2.3.146),

254

NOTES FOR PAGES 48-53

Montano makes possible Iago's denial, "Not I" (147)—a rare failure to capitalize on "honest," as if for once he were not carefully thinking out his "line." There is a minor jocular echo of the honesty theme at 3.1.22-23.

4 3.3.97, 98, 105, 107, 115, 116, 131, 132, 136, 143, 144, 154, 162.

5 As Paul A. Jorgensen says in "Honesty in *Othello*," *Studies in Philology*, XLVII (1950), 557-567, the irony is not merely that of "a villain posing as an honest man" but of "a knave posing as Honesty, a hunter of knaves" (p. 566). It is interesting that, in attempting to describe Iago's "honesty game" as representatively human, I reach conclusions like those of Jorgensen, who is viewing the "honesty game" in the light of a prevalent Elizabethan situation.

6 Although Stoll in general defends Othello against charges of stupidity, he acknowledges that the "loyalty" which Iago exhibits in this scene is suspect (p. 254). Empson regards Iago as pretty clumsy here (p. 234).

7 Iago does not quite adopt the style of the petty larcenist in Saul Bellow's novel who, noting some apparent diffidence in a possible recruit to the profession, inquires, "What's the matter, are you honest or something?"—as if honesty were an eccentricity or a disorder or a handicap in coming to terms with actuality: a mode of thought, even if wholly ironic, presumably unlikely before modern biological and economic thought. Roderigo begins to slip toward honesty when he despairs of his end (4.2.174ff.) and Iago's method is to restore his faith in the pragmatic validity of the line of action until now followed by him without profit. Here Iago is modern enough, for he implicitly accuses Roderigo of "failure of nerve."

8 Cf. "shows of service" (1.1.52) and "show out a flag and sign of love" (1.1.157).

9 The atmosphere of stratagem envelops even the activities of the Turkish navy. At first the Turks feint at Rhodes—a "pageant / To keep us in false gaze" (1.3.18-19)—but then bear with "frank appearance" toward Cyprus (38). This detail is considered an organic part of the play by Harold C. Goddard in *The Meaning of Shakespeare* (Chicago, 1951), p. 467.

10 Theodore Spencer makes this issue the dramatic center of the play (pp. 130, 135). Cf. Bethell: "I do not think that the ramifications of deceitful appearance in *Othello* have ever received comment" ("Shakespeare's Imagery," p. 72). My development of this theme differs considerably from Bethell's. Cf. Kreider, pp. 134-135; Weilgart, pp. 204-205.

11 Even the latecomer Lodovico seems infected by the world Iago has created in the image of his idea (5.1.43).

12 Cf. Stoll: "the villain derives a perilous pleasure out of skating on thin ice and almost giving himself away" (p. 248).

13 Sister Miriam Joseph remarks that "Whenever Shakespeare wishes to represent the acme of disorder and confusion, he introduces logical confusion, that is, a mutually destructive merging of incompatibles." See *Shakespeare's Use of the Arts of Language* (New York, 1947), p. 132. In "Dramatic Illusion in *Othello*," *Shakespeare Quarterly*, I (1950), 146-152, Hoover H. Jordan notes that Othello does not reason well about appearances, but attributes this to "unyielding devotion to duty and honor" (p. 148).

14 Cf. Flatter, pp. 87-88.

NOTES FOR PAGES 53-56

15 She can dissemble only as a matter of self-control; during Iago's jokes before Othello has reached Cyprus she explains, "I am not merry; but I do beguile / The thing I am by seeming otherwise" (2.1.123-124).

16 Cf. Ruth L. Anderson's statement in *Elizabethan Psychology and Shakespeare's Plays*, University of Iowa Humanistic Studies, III (Iowa City, 1927), p. 90: "Shakespeare's characters believe so implicitly in a correspondence between outward seeming and the inward state of the soul, indeed, that a revelation of gross disparity is baffling." Cf. pp. 119, 144.

17 Elliott singularly reads *shows* as if it were *is* and thus concludes that Othello is now aware of "all his own sin" (p. 226).

18 Cf. 4.1.16: "Her honour is an essence that's not seen." For an extended comment on the implications of the clothing imagery, see E. E. Kellett, *Suggestions* (Cambridge, Eng., 1923), pp. 75-77. See also Kittredge, p. 142.

19 William Maginn suggests (*Variorum*, p. 17) that "I am not what I am" is a "profane allusion" to the terms in which God reveals himself to Moses, "I am that I am." The proposal is worth keeping in mind, since the diabolical in Iago is more than once suggested in the play. See the section on The Christian Myth in Chapter II and the concluding part of Section 5 in the present chapter.

20 Literally when he adjures Brabantio, "Zounds, sir, y' are robb'd! For shame, put on your gown!" (1.1.86) and in a different sense when he promises to "bind" Cassio's wound "with my shirt" (5.1.73). (Cf. Desdemona at 3.3.76-77.) Referring to himself: "plume up my will / In double knavery" (1.3.399-400). Referring to others: "Abuse him to the Moor in the rank garb / (For I fear Cassio with my night cap too)" (2.1.315-316); "Wear your eye thus" (to Othello; 3.3.198); "Wear thy good rapier bare" (to Roderigo; 5.1.2).

Cf. Cassio: "So shall I clothe me in a forc'd content" (3.4.120). Cf. Elizabeth Holmes, *Aspects of Elizabethan Imagery* (Oxford, 1929), p. 53.

Iago notes derangement as the effect of love, describing Roderigo as a man "Whom love hath turn'd almost the wrong side out" (2.3.54), a figure echoed by Emilia when she reminds Iago of the rascal "that turn'd your wit the seamy side without" (4.2.146). Iago even sings a song about clothes (2.3.92ff.).

> To vouch this is no proof
> Without more certain and more overt test
> Than these thin habits and poor likelihoods
> Of modern seeming do prefer against him.   (1.3.106-109)

Desdemona: To my unfolding lend your prosperous ear.   (1.3.245)

> This honest creature doubtless
> Sees and knows more, much more, than he unfolds.   (3.3.242-243)

Emilia:
> O heaven, that such companions thou'dst unfold,
> And put in every honest hand a whip
> To lash the rascals naked through the world.   (4.2.141-143)

Iago: the Moor / May unfold me to him.   (5.1.20-21)

The final unfolding, ironically, comes from "the pocket of the slain Roderigo" (5.2.309), Iago's dupe. For other dramatic uses of clothes, note the comparable passages at 1.1.10 and 1.2.22-23.

22 Cf. Othello's inquiry: "What's the matter / That you unlace your reputation

NOTES FOR PAGES 56-59

thus" (2.3.193-194). Then Cassio is stripped of his reputation and his job.

23 The clothing imagery, indeed, links the three scenes in Act 2. Scene 1 begins with Iago's intimating that Cassio and Desdemona have been "naked in bed"; Scene 2 begins with Othello's check-up on Desdemona, including his question about "her fan, her gloves, her mask," and continues with the "brothel scene"; Scene 3 begins with Othello's ordering Desedmona to bed and continues with her undressing for bed. The irony of Othello's inquiry about Desdemona's "disguise" is that she really needs a little more of the mask for self-protection.

24 Her note that "a lady in Venice would have walk'd barefoot to Palestine" for love of Lodovico (4.3.39-40) and her intimation that she could be unfaithful to her husband "for all the whole world" if not "for measures of lawn, nor for gowns, petticoats, nor caps" (74-77).

25 Shakespeare's habit is to tie his recurrent images to literal facts of the drama—setting, weather, properties, characteristics of the dramatis personae— and thus to interweave all his literary means. We have seen, indeed, the functional interweaving of metaphors of dress ("lin'd their coats," "rank garb"), literal images ("lash the rascals naked through the world"), and stage facts referred to (Desdemona's mask and gloves, Roderigo's pockets) or actually present (Iago's shirt as bandage, Desdemona's undressing for bed). These means work with the most conspicuous dramatic fact in *Othello*—the "disguise" of Iago, that is, the concealment of intention and motive that remains punctureproof until the final scene. And then there is the handkerchief, not "clothes," really, but not altogether ornament either. Yet it is functionally allied to the pattern of dress and appearance: when Desdemona has the handkerchief, her appearance is in a sense "right"; her "ensemble" is complete; she is protected. When she is robbed of the handkerchief, her safety is gone; she is symbolically naked and defenseless.

26 Othello, he says, should have given the lieutenancy to him, "of whom his eyes had seen the proof" (1.1.28). In *The Counter-Renaissance* (New York, 1950), p. 657, Hiram Haydn comments on this passage: "Iago also belongs, then, to the hand-in-the-wound (*C'est moi qui l'ai vu*) school; he is a devotee of the 'science of the particular.'" In *Othello*, of course, there are many words of seeing which have only mechanical, as opposed to thematic, functions and which are not dealt with in this section.

27 Since he is so successful, Iago subtly flatters himself in defining himself as an improviser: "Knavery's plain face is never seen till us'd" (2.1.321). From Brabantio he gets a dual response that is dramatically valuable—on the one hand, a rushing to visual evidence and reliance upon it (cf. 1.1.141ff., 164, 167; 1.3.62-63, 98), and on the other hand, a distrust of the seen: "Fathers, from hence trust not your daughters' minds / By what you see them act" (1.1.171-172).

28 At the beginning of this scene Iago imputes a protective vision to Cassio: why should he "steal away so guilty-like, / Seeing you coming" (3.3.39-40)?

29 "Discern'st thou aught in that?" and "Show me thy thought" (102, 116).

30 ". . . it is my nature's plague / To spy into abuses" (146-147), of which Empson oddly says that Iago "believes this and thinks it creditable" (p. 223); "take no notice" of my "scattering and unsure observance" (150-151); "beware . . . the green-ey'd monster" (166).

257

NOTES FOR PAGES 59-62

31 In part by a general assertion about the Venetians, who "do let heaven see the pranks / They dare not show their husbands" (202-203). Iago's words imply that he knows what may be seen from a celestial point of view.

32 Cassio has a similar confidence in his seeing. When Othello tells him to "look . . . to the guard tonight," he replies, "with my personal eye / Will I look to 't" (2.3.1-6). Then he gets "blind drunk."

33 Elliott argues that these words lodge poisonously in Othello's subconscious because he does not "inwardly confute" them (p. 39). Cf. Granville-Barker, II, 36. The longest of the many discussions of the repetition of *deceive* is by Flatter, pp. 72-88; he argues that Brabantio is in the play only to say these words and thus contribute to the effectiveness of the deception. There is almost a "deception theme." Just as Othello is "deceived" by Desdemona, so Lodovico says of Othello, "I am sorry that I am deceiv'd in him" (4.1.293). And Cassio insists, "I will rather sue to be despis'd than to deceive so good a commander" (2.3.278-279). Cf. Stauffer, p. 171.

34 There is a psychological note on this transfer in Lucas, pp. 72-73, 75.

35 Othello's growing intention of keeping an eye on Desdemona is in effect commented on when he complains of "a pain upon my forehead" and she replies, "Faith, that's with watching" (3.3.284-285). His *double entendre* is intentional, hers is not. *Watching* may have a primary meaning of "waking," but the meaning "To be on the look out, to keep a person or thing in sight" was also possible at the time (see OED, "*watch*, v., I. Intransitive, 4 and 6," and also "*watching*. vbl. sb."). His "pain" and his "watching" are connected in other ways than Desdemona supposes.

Iago fakes one more gesture of restraint—"scan this thing no further" (245)—but then goes ahead with the visual program: "You shall by that perceive," "Note if your lady strain," "Much will be seen in that" (249-252). Othello commands, "If more thou dost perceive, let me know more. / Set on thy wife to observe" (239-240); surmises, "This honest creature doubtless / Sees" more than he tells (242-243); regrets seeing what he thinks he is seeing: "I saw't not [Desdemona's transgression], . . . it harm'd not me" (339).

36 "I'll see before I doubt; when I doubt, prove" (190).

37 Winifred M. T. Nowottny, "Justice and Love in *Othello*," *University of Toronto Quarterly*, XXI (1952), 332, 335. This article is excellent. My analysis differs in that to me the opposing forces seem not to be love and justice but love and the whole world of rational demonstration, of which justice is but one part. Cf. another formulation by Miss Nowottny: "the tragic conjunction set up when the nature and processes of love become involved with the utterly different nature and processes of judgment" (p. 333).

38 Cf. Cunningham on Othello's intellectual perplexity (pp. 119ff.). Cunningham, however, is referring to Othello's "proof" of Desdemona's guilt by syllogistic means. He is interested in establishing the plausibility of the action at this point, and so he enumerates all the factors in the situation that contribute to the apparent adequacy of the proof.

39 Cf. Weilgart on Iago: "intellect without love" (p. 53).

40 Elliott says she is disastrously self-deceptive (p. 153).

41 Not only *might* Othello have saved himself and his wife by being able to

NOTES FOR PAGES 62-63

"see Desdemona's visage in her mind," but there is dramatic reason why he *should* have done so: he not only heard her words "saw Othello's visage in his mind" but spoke words which must have had for him some reminder of hers— "For she had eyes, and chose me" (3.3.189).

42 Iago: Would you, the supervisor, grossly gape on?
              Behold her topp'd?   (3.3.395-396; cf. 397-402)
                      Yet we see nothing done.   (3.3.432)
                      did I today
           See Cassio wipe his beard with.   (3.3.438-439)
Othello: Now do I see 'tis true.   (3.3.444)
                      Fetch't, let me see't!   (3.4.85)

43 After saying, "What / If I had said I had seen him do you wrong?" (4.1.23-24), Iago sets up his play within the play, directing Othello, "mark the fleers," "mark his gesture," "Did you perceive . . . ?" "And did you see . . . ?" (4.1.83, 88, 181, 183). Cf. 4.1.250.

44 His cross-examining of Emilia (4.2.1-9) hardly represents what Bradley calls "an ineradicable instinct of justice" (p. 197). He questions Desdemona at 4.2.25ff. There is a strong visual element throughout Othello's lines here. He has a visual image of himself as cuckold—"A fixed figure for the time of scorn / To point his slow unmoving finger at!" (54-55); he comments on Desdemona's fairness (68-71); and he imagines that "the moon winks"—i.e., shuts her eyes in shame (Kittredge)—because of what it has seen (77). This last line is a reminder of Iago's comment that Venetians "let heaven see" their pranks (3.3.202).

45 "By heaven, I saw my handkerchief in's hand!" "I saw the handkerchief" (5.2.62, 66). Desdemona has already said, "you are fatal then / When your eyes roll so" (5.2.37-38). Rolling eyes, it may be assumed, were a fairly conventional symbol of an emotional state (cf. Arden ed. of *Othello*, p. 233). But an emotional state may grossly distort powers of observation, as we have seen happen in *Othello*.

46 He says to them, "Nay, stare not, masters" (5.2.188), as if they were not seeing aright. Cf. Stoll, *Poets and Playwrights*, pp. 78-79.

47 Sister Miriam Joseph comments on the handkerchief as "circumstantial evidence" (p. 97).

48 This is not the only time that Shakespeare is interested in the tragic hero's impulse to dismiss literally a person who has the key to the hero's well-being. Cf. Lear to Kent: "Out of my sight!" (1.1.159).

49 When Iago has got Cassio drunk and told Montano that drink "rocks Cassio's cradle" nightly, Montano says that Othello should know about this: "Perhaps he sees it not, or his good nature / Prizes the virtue that appears in Cassio / And looks not on his evils" (2.3.138-140). Though his conjecture is necessarily inaccurate in this case, Montano's words give a good general picture of Othello: to "see it not" and to "look on" only part of what "appears" mark his tragic course.

His phrase "subdu'd eyes" (5.2.348), which Kittredge defines as yielding to emotion (p. 231), is symbolically true, for it expresses his turning from visual detection to grief, where his eyes do not err except by falling short. Likewise "unused to the melting mood" (349) has more than its literal meaning. Once

NOTES FOR PAGES 63-74

he sneered at Desdemona's "crocodile tears" (4.1.255-257), and when she feared that Cassio was dead, he was outraged: "Weep'st thou for him to my face?" (5.2.77). The "melting mood," which earlier he misread, he now experiences.

50 Elsewhere Othello called it "precious eye" (3.4.66), and our attention is focused on it by the contrasting praises of Iago and Cassio (2.3.21-25; cf. 2.1.227-229). Unlike Othello, she is aware of how others see a situation: she would not stay in Venice "To put my father in impatient thoughts / By being in his eye" (1.3.243-244). Note the echo of this in Gratiano's words after her death, "This sight would make him [Brabantio] do a desperate turn" (5.2.207).

51 Some of the points which are brought together systematically in this chapter are scattered through the textual commentary of Elliott's *Flaming Minister*. See, for instance, pp. 133n., 137, 139, 172, 193, 211, 213n. Some of these points are also made by Caroline Spurgeon in *Shakespeare's Imagery* (Cambridge, Eng., 1952), pp. 64, 159. One of the fullest treatments of the light-and-darkness theme is that of Goddard (pp. 459ff., 474).

52 Cf. Bradley, p. 191.

53 The contrast is noticed by Clemen, p. 131. Knight elaborates upon it (pp. 114-115). Cf. lines 133, 135, 137, 148-149, 157, 164.

54 Cf. Knight, pp. 111-112.

55 All of Act 1 takes place at night—Iago's first move against Othello, the Turkish crisis. More than half of Act 2 deals with the drunken brawl during the nocturnal revels at Cyprus. In Act 3 Iago tells the lie about the night he slept with Cassio and overheard his dream about Desdemona. Act 4 is full of anticipations of the coming night—plans for revenge, Desdemona's preparing for bed. The actions on this night occupy all of Act 5.

56 See 1.3.278, 279; 2.1.272; 2.2.10-11; 2.3.1-11, 45, 196, 201, 216; 3.3.57-61; 4.1.191, 216-219; 4.2.104, 218-219, 243, 249; 4.3.15-16, 30-31, 107; 5.2.25.

57 There is a fuller discussion of the love-death linkage in Chapter VI.

58 On the archetypal relation between darkness and hell, and light and paradise, see Friedman, p. 37.

59 The couplet is paralleled by Iago's lines that close the next to last scene in the play: "This is the night / That either makes me or fordoes me quite" (5.1.128-129). For a somewhat different interpretation of the light-and-darkness passages, see Hankins, pp. 47-48, 72-74.

60 The terminology of wealth appears in literal ways, of course. See 1.3.29-30; 2.1.83; 3.1.25-26. There are other metaphorical uses at 1.3.215-260, and 4.1.185-186.

61 For instance, Othello's bitter dismissal of Desdemona after the brothel episode reverses his style of addressing her after their safe arrival in Cyprus. His earlier words: "Come, my dear love. / The purchase made, the fruits are to ensue; / The profit's yet to come 'tween me and you" (2.3.8-10). In the later scene the "profit" has by implication taken place, and Othello sardonically completes the "purchase"—"There's money for your pains" (4.2.93).

On some occasions, also, the economic figures minister to the theme of "private property in human affections" which Kenneth Burke uses in interpreting *Othello* in "Othello: An Essay to Illustrate a Method," *Hudson Review*, IV (1951), 165-203, esp. pp. 166ff.

NOTES FOR PAGES 74-79

62 Cf. Burke: "Property fears theft because it is theft" (p. 167).

63 Clemen, p. 223.

64 He sneers at Cassio as "debitor and creditor, this counter-caster" (1.1.31). Ostensibly warning Othello against jealousy, he discourses with philosophic mien: "Poor and content is rich, and rich enough; / But riches fineless is as poor as winter / To him that ever fears he shall be poor" (3.3.172-174).

65 Stauffer remarks that "to Iago the material world is the real world, and money buys anything" (p. 169).

66 Even Burke, who usually squeezes every possible meaning out of whatever character or scene he discusses, does not go as far as possible with Roderigo (p. 180).

67 Roderigo's experience varies the theme of loss, his misery in the disappointment of a very tenuous hope illuminating the vast anguish of a man who, like Othello, undergoes the deprivation of a joy not merely aspired to but apparently possessed for life. Likewise Roderigo is at once a victim and a self-deceiver. Shakespeare often uses such "analogous" action, as Francis Fergusson calls it in *The Idea of a Theatre* (Princeton, 1949), pp. 104ff. See also n. 68 below.

68 Iago faces two analogous but dissimilar problems: making Othello disbelieve in a love that is actually his, and making Roderigo believe in a love that can never be his. Iago is ingenious enough to adopt utterly opposite personal facades for his different victims: in prying Othello loose from the truth, he appears high-minded, "honest," saddened by the frailty of women; in attaching Roderigo to an expectation that can· never become a truth, he enunciates a cynical disbelief in the fidelity of women. This is the sleight of hand of a formidable entrepreneur. Burke lists other ways in which Iago's skill in deceit is established before he takes on Othello (p. 173). Clemen has a good comment on Iago's use of different speech styles for different victims (p. 122).

69 The historical background of the relationship between Iago and Roderigo is discussed by John W. Draper in "This Poor Trash of Venice," *Journal of English and Germanic Philology*, XXX (1931), 508-515.

70 In his acting edition of 1876 Wilhelm Oechelhauser stressed the "plebeian" character of Iago (*Variorum*, p. 442).

71 Sewell, p. 93.

72 Iago also calls Bianca "this trash" (5.1.85). Although his immediate concern is to implicate her in the Cassio-Roderigo brawl, Iago's term indicates his actual evaluation of her. He cannot or will not understand her love for Cassio.

73 Cf. Elliott, pp. 44, 79.

74 Yet the thief-to-be has, with his cry of thief, made an astonishing impression that is not wholly removed by the technicality of a court decision. The note of theft curiously recurs in the last of the four homiletic couplets on patience which the Duke rather heavily delivers to Brabantio: "The robb'd that smiles steals something from the thief; / He robs himself that spends a bootless grief" (1.3.208-209). Though a distinction in values is made by means of an image of theft, as in Iago's purse-trash speech later, we note that the Duke's management of the image in effect reconverts Brabantio into "the robb'd" and Othello into "the thief." The Duke perhaps has secret sympathies.

261

Burke relates the images of theft to the property motif (p. 167).

[75] William Hazlitt discussed this aspect of Iago in *Characters of Shakespeare's Plays* (London, 1817). The relevant passage is quoted by Muir, pp. 68-69. Stoll also makes this point. Granville-Barker says Iago "plays high and recklessly" (II, 71).

[76] Again there is a Chaucer echo: "To yeve and lene him of his owene good / And have a thank, and yet a gowne and hood."

[77] "Shakespeare and the Tragedy of Our Time," p. 531.

[78] Empson says of Iago here, "Of course, I assume his feelings are very sincere" (p. 248). Cf. Harbage's chapter on "The Unreliable Spokesman" in *As They Liked It*, pp. 105ff. Also cf. Stauffer's remarks on Iago's "double-talk" (p. 176).

[79] Cf. his words to Cassio drunk, "You will be sham'd for ever" (2.3.163).

[80] Stoll has some excellent passages on this subject. See pp. 256, 258, 273, 275.

[81] Sitwell, in noting Iago's willingness to forfeit his own life, describes him in a phrase quoted from Baudelaire: "la vraie grandeur des pariahs" (p. 113).

[82] In doing so, she must face the passion of both Iago and Othello—the faithful servant whose subordination of self in a moral crisis counterbalances the evil selfishness and thus gives hope for the survival of human quality. The archetype of the devoted follower has undergone a singular transformation in our day. In a nominally nonhierarchic society it cannot be literally meaningful, so that in popular literature it is reduced to a sentimental stereotype. The persistence of the stereotype suggests a psychic sneak back into a social order which it is not permissible to admire publicly.

[83] Cf. Burke's explanation of Emilia's role as "protecting" the "tragic engrossment" by presenting the "low" while the audience, "by the rules of the game," wishes to be identified with the "high" (p. 185). This is very shrewd. But I suggest that even without rules of the game the audience wants to take the "high," *provided* that its terms are acceptable—i.e., not pompous, peremptory, or as here, so youthful as to make Desdemona's partisan identify himself with more ingenuousness than he finds comfortable. Emilia gives him an alternative style to tie to, thus preventing resistance to Desdemona's values as well as to her manner. Thomas D. Bowman argues that Emilia is "rather sensibly though gently rebuking her girlish charge for exaggerated trust in her own sex" and correcting "an innocence too strongly grounded in ignorance to be completely becoming." See "In Defense of Emilia," *Shakespeare Association Bulletin*, XXII (1947), 101.

[84] Cf. Flatter, p. 54.

[85] Kittredge calls Emilia's argument "unassailable" (p. 217). But Kittredge strangely reads the argument thus: that a misbehaving husband "cannot blame" a wife for misbehaving similarly! Emilia isn't saying this; rather she falls into the now commonplace justification by cause.

[86] Stanislavsky's fanciful and yet often useful reconstruction of events and relationships before the opening of the play includes this: "Iago slept in his tent. He was Othello's servant, even his doctor. Better than others he knew how to dress a wound" (p. 17).

[87] Cf. 3.3.276.

NOTES FOR PAGES 89-100

88 No wonder that, when Emilia charges him with murder and Iago with subornation of murder, he "Falls on the bed" (5.2.198).

89 He describes an illness of a kind when he pictures the Englishman as so "potent in potting" that "he gives your Hollander a vomit ere the next pottle can be fill'd" (2.3.79, 85-86).

90 Brabantio partly shares Iago's view. Cf. 1.3.62-63. But there is an implied refutation of Iago in Desdemona's use of his very word *abhor*. She does not "abhor" Othello. Rather, "I cannot say 'whore.' / It doth abhor me now I speak the word" (4.2.161-162). We are more likely to observe the immediate pun than the long-distance wordplay.

91 Besides situations which are literally "medical" (2.3.253, 259-260; 5.1.30), the medical metaphor appears also at 1.1.35; 1.3.202-203; 2.1.50-51.

92 Cf. Clemen, p. 128.

93 Hardin Craig observes that in this speech of Iago's Shakespeare anticipates the psychology of the "fixed idea unhinging the reason," which would permit us to view Iago as a psychiatrist in reverse. See *The Enchanted Glass* (New York, 1936), p. 128.

94 Cf. Bradley, pp. 436-437; Granville-Barker, II, 56.

95 Iago instinctively tries to "make it hot" for his enemies. Note an image that at first seems casually illustrative: when he is directing Roderigo to raise a commotion with a "dire yell," he uses this comparison, "As when . . . the fire / Is spied in populous cities" (1.1.75-77). Fire and destruction come naturally to his mind.

96 Carlyle-Wicksteed translation. Hankins comments on the serpent-devil connection (p. 51).

CHAPTER 4. THE IAGO WORLD: STYLES IN REVELATION

1 Clemen stresses Othello's tendency to *"sense* all abstract matters as palpable, tastable, audible and visible things" (p. 124). Iago uses sensory material as much; the difference is that for him the sensory is reality. Cf. Morozov: "His images are generally concrete and substantial" (p. 88).

2 Cassio, 3.3.15; Brabantio, 1.1.99, 1.3.57; Othello, 1.3.149-150, 3.3.183-184. Iago is quick to use occasions of eating and drinking to further his plots—the victory revel (2.3), Bianca's supper invitation to Cassio (4.1.165ff.; 4.2.239ff.; 5.1.117ff.). For sharp contrasts in the conduct and style of Desdemona, see 3.3.24, 57, 58, 78.

3 Cf. 2.1.111, 161, 303; 3.3.166-167. Emilia's kinship with him is shown in her use of his metaphorical style: "They are all but stomachs, and we all but food, etc." (3.4.104ff.).

4 As for Othello: 1.3.354-356; 3.3.327. Iago has contributed to Brabantio's bitterness; cf. 1.1.104, 163; 1.3.68, 216. Othello's style is slightly reminiscent of Iago's when he uses taste metaphors in speaking of Desdemona at 1.3.263 and 3.3.345-347.

5 Othello regularly thinks of Desdemona as "sweet" (2.1.207; 3.3.55, 56; 4.1.189, 193; 4.2.68; 5.2.15-20); this is the background for his saying that

263

"Heaven stops the nose" at her deeds (4.2.77). Cf. Emilia, "Villany, villany, villany! / . . . I smell't!" (5.2.190-191). Cassio makes a similar shift of terms for Bianca (3.4.171; 4.1.150-151). Cf. Spurgeon, pp. 80, 161-162.

[6] Iago also uses images of birth at 2.1.128-129 and 2.3.382-383. Note Emilia's definition of jealousy at 3.4.162 and Othello's use of birth images in ferocious attacks on Desdemona at 4.1.256-257 and 4.2.61-62, 66-67.

[7] Knight states only that "we have the spirit of negation set against the spirit of creation" (p. 119). But the paradox is also present. Weilgart refers to "the tragedy of creation, procreation, without love" (p. 85). Brabantio says he is glad he has "no other child" (1.3.196), and Othello wishes Desdemona had never been born (4.2.69).

[8] I am not concerned here with the problem of rationalizing the time scheme of the play, on which there has been much discussion, nor with the problem of "double time," nor with such matters of time as appear at 2.3.385; 3.3.169; 3.4.172-176.

[9] The first part of *Othello* is dominated by a sense of urgency; see 1.1.88; 1.2.37-38, 41-42; 1.3.46, 277-278, 299, 301. The problem is to distinguish between the urgency produced by a situation which leaves men with no choice, and that which is produced by unapprehended or uncontrolled elements in the personality or by outer influences which play upon these.

[10] Cf. 2.3.335-336; 3.1.33ff.; 3.3.14ff.; 3.4.114.

[11] She swears that her love is enduring (4.2.157ff.). She is understandably urgent in begging Othello to prolong her life (5.2.52, 80-83).

[12] Compare Emilia's "may his pernicious soul / Rot half a grain a day" (5.2.155-156), which is not a wish to protract the torturer's ecstasy, but a temporal adjustment of the punishment to the crime.

[13] Cf. Cassio's "I am maim'd for ever" (5.1.27), in which *for ever* is an immediate product of fear and pain. Just once Othello's absolutizing of time is right: when he sentences Iago, "If thou dost slander her and torture me, / Never pray more" (3.3.368-369). Cf. his vindicatory exaggeration (5.2.212).

[14] There is a somewhat similar case when, replying to Othello's unsure statement that he thinks Desdemona is honest, Iago wishes, "Long live she so! and long live you to think so!" (3.3.226). Othello is suspicious; to the suggestion of his being a dupe the *long* adds the note of protraction which, as we have seen from other passages, Othello is peculiarly unable to bear.

[15] Clemen observes this (p. 128). Cf. Hankins, pp. 49-50.

[16] Granville-Barker, II, 112.

[17] On "Plague him with flies" (1.1.71), see Sitwell, who regards this as a piece of diabolical symbolism (p. 116). In the "ram-ewe," "Barbary horse," and "beast with two backs" passages (1.1.88-89, 111-117), we see Iago's great liveliness of figurative language. When Clemen speaks of the "static" quality and the "prosaic brevity" of Iago's imagery he is, I think, too much bent on making a contrast between Iago's style and Othello's (p. 123). Cf. Stoll on Iago: "in speech what a poet!" (*Poets and Playwrights*, p. 124).

[18] The point was first made by Spurgeon, pp. 335-336, later by Morozov, pp. 87ff. For instances, see 1.3.341-342, 391; 2.1.111, 171, 318; 2.3.52-53, 274-277. In

NOTES FOR PAGES 105-108

saying that she does not wish to be a "moth of peace" (1.3.257), Desdemona uses the image *moth* to denote triviality, as if it were a failure of humanness. When Emilia plans to "play the swan, / And die in music" (5.2.247-248), her image suggests, not the nonhuman, but a creature uniquely endowed with a human gift.

19 Cf. Cassio's terms of self-condemnation after he has got drunk: 2.3.280ff.

20 Elliott seems to me to misinterpret this scene badly (pp. 94-99).

21 Cf. Elliott's comment that Iago's "desire has always been to murder souls, not bodies" (p. 206). Sewell describes the Iago world as one "from which spirit has been drained" (p. 93).

22 Kittredge says that *blown* is "literally, 'flyblown'" (p. 187). If this is valid—there are other interpretations—then the jealousy into which Othello is falling is doubly characterized as non- or anti-human.

23 Clemen notes this, pp. 125 and 132, but gives it less emphasis than the contrast of Iago's and Othello's image styles. For examples of Othello's animal imagery, see 3.3.270-273; 4.1.63, 146-147; 4.2.61-62, 65-66. Cf. Emilia's speech at 5.2.198; Cassio's contrastingly mild language at 4.1.131, 150; Iago's reply to Othello at 4.1.64-65. Note how Iago's reference to "goats" and "monkeys" at 3.3.403-404 is echoed in Othello's "Goats and monkeys!" at 4.1.274. Cf. Stoll, *Poets and Playwrights*, p. 111.

24 *Man's* is First Quarto; *my* is Second and Third Quarto; *mine* in the Folios. Editors have various preferences.

25 Empson, p. 230.

26 Cf. Armstrong, p. 76.

27 *Nature*, of course, may simply mean character, faculties, kind, or class; see 3.3.199; 3.4.144; 4.1.39, 276; 5.2.11. *Soul* is often used casually in mild oaths or exclamations, or as a loose equivalent of *man, life, mind,* or *conscience:* 1.1.107, 152; 1.3.196, 267. There are references to jealous souls at 3.3.175; 3.4.159. Cf. also 1.3.114; 2.3.174; 3.3.374, 416; 4.2.13, 52.

28 The word is not used frequently enough for it to have a major structural role. It is used in the old sense by Brabantio at 1.3.62, 96, 101, by Othello at 3.3.227, and by Desdemona at 5.2.42. There is another mild anticipation of *Lear* in Othello's use of images from disordered nature—"huge eclipse," "error of the moon" (5.2.99-101, 109-111; cf. the echo of Iago at 2.3.182). But these marks of "chaos" fall very short of the cosmic symbolization of ruptured order in *Lear;* these isolated expressions are less passionate than sententious, less discovered than recollected, for Othello has a lesser range of thought and feeling than Lear and his entourage, and as yet he is caught uncertainly between his official and cultivated theory that he has executed justice and his private and resisted intimations that he has done something else. Cf. B. Ifor Evans, *The Language of Shakespeare's Plays* (London, 1952), p. 133. The note of "nature erring from itself" is present in another way: lightly in Othello's travel-poster account of monsters he has seen (1.3.143ff.), seriously in the recurrence of the words *monster* and *monstrous* (cf. Stauffer, pp. 170, 177): 1.3.410; 2.3.217; 3.3.107, 166, 427; 3.4.163; 4.1.63; 5.2.190.

If the major function of such terms as *monstrous* is to define and castigate, yet in some way they are resistant and protective, fending off a dehumanization that seems unbelievable. The narrow margin between human and animal is in most danger when the enemy of the margin can with sardonic histrionism ape the style of the human being who dreads encroachment by the nonhuman. A case in point is Iago's defensive mock despair when Othello briefly challenges him: "O monstrous world!" (3.3.377). While Iago by crying "monster" actually aids the progress of his own "monstrous birth," he exemplifies classically the pose of injured innocence adopted by the patrioteer-troublemaker threatened with identification.

[29] Iago also calls Cassio "loose of soul" because he talks in his sleep (3.3.416), and urges Roderigo, "let thy soul be instructed" (2.1.223) when he analyzes the love of Desdemona and Othello as transitory lust. Thus the soul is a psychological mechanism and apprehends love as lust. Desdemona conceives her union with Othello as a "consecration" of her "soul and fortunes" (1.3.255); when she tries to estimate her love for Othello, she puts it thus: "I wonder in my soul / What you could ask me that I should deny" (3.3.68-69); she reproves herself for "Arraigning his unkindness with my soul" (3.4.152); that she did not give the handkerchief to Cassio she swears "by my life and soul" (5.2.49). These are more than convenient hyperboles; her love is, as the drama unfolds it, a great devotion of spirit. There is, then, a certain irony in Othello's theological decorum, "I would not kill thy unprepared spirit. / . . . I would not kill thy soul" (5.2.31-32), and in his calling her "sweet soul" when he is blind to the sweet soul and is about to execute her for unspiritual conduct. After the storm Othello greets Desdemona, "O my soul's joy!" and adds that he "fears" that "My soul hath her content so absolute / That not another comfort like to this / Succeeds in unknown fate" (2.1.186, 193-195). In part the accuracy of his fear reflects, though he does not know it, a narrower view of the soul as the sensorium of an incomplete love: he shades away from the obligation implied in Desdemona's phrases. When he is about to kill Desdemona, he reassures himself: "It is the cause, it is the cause, my soul" (5.2.1). *My* sense of things cannot be wrong. Early in the play he says, of the expected meeting with furious Brabantio, "My parts, my title, and my perfect soul / Shall manifest me rightly" (1.2.31-32). Presumably he means only that in terms of his conduct with Desdemona, he is morally ready for the encounter; yet the term he uses is unqualified, and the effect is at least one of a somewhat uninquiring confidence. Othello is of a lesser spiritual range than Desdemona, and a few lines such as these exhibit in another way the readiness of the victim. Cf. 3.3.90-91; 5.2.302. Battenhouse argues that the "center of Othello's actual faith" is "his own soul, in which his own virtues are treasured as eternal law" ("Shakespeare and the Tragedy of Our Time," p. 529).

[30] I.e., "by the Christian faith" or "by the faith of men" (the "three great ones" who "off-capp'd").

[31] Cf. 3.3.153; 4.2.134.

[32] Cunningham argues that "soul" means "rational soul" (p. 118). Thus Iago doubles his instrument of control: it is "rational" as well as "manly" to follow his line. Goneril and Regan use the same tactic in trying to control Lear.

NOTES FOR PAGES 120-126

51 Elliott, who constantly attributes closemouthedness to pride (in both Cassio and Othello), singularly misses the meaning of Iago's final speech (pp. 229-230). Granville-Barker uses an appropriate phrase: "satanic conceit" (II, 94).

52 Cf. Othello's earlier lines addressed to Iago: "If thou dost slander her and torture me, / Never pray more; abandon all remorse" (3.3.368-369).

53 On Iago's virtues, see Bradley, p. 234.

54 Knight traces the theme of developing chaos (pp. 116ff.). Cf. Bradley, pp. 178, 196; Stauffer, p. 173; Theodore Spencer, p. 129.

55 5.1.27, 37, 45, 48, 64, 72, 79, 84, 86; cf. 101, 112, 114.

56 5.2.31, 32, 33, 35, 41, 42, 51, 52, 56, 65, 78, 80.

57 5.2.106, 112, 113, 114, 115, 117, 122, 126, 130.

58 Note also the language of painful irritation, 2.1.98; 4.3.58, 93-95; 5.1.11; the talk of hanging and drowning, 1.1.34; 1.3.366-368; the metaphors of injury, 1.3.99, 173-174, 219. The continuing note of injury early in the play is predictive. In contrast, the effect of injury and suffering is sterilized by being attached to a romanticized past in Othello's account of "disastrous chances," etc., 1.3.134-157.

59 He injures Othello "symbolically" by declaring him "defective" in such matters as "loveliness in favour, . . . beauties" (2.1.232-234).

60 1.1.49, 71, 87, 149, 155.

61 Cf. 2.3.221-222. It is as if Iago were wounding himself as a guarantee of his fidelity to fact—just as earlier, in guarantee of his fidelity to his chief, he appeared barely able to restrain himself from wounding Roderigo: "I hold it very stuff o' th' conscience / To do no contriv'd murther" and "Nine or ten times / I had thought t'have yerk'd him here under the ribs" (1.2.2-5). Injury is an instrument of policy; compare his invention of a "raging tooth" as the cause of the wakefulness which led him to hear Cassio's alleged dream (3.3.414ff.). Shakespeare is interested in the pseudo injury as a characterizing device; it is practiced both by Falstaff and by Edmund in *King Lear*. The verbal self-injury is really a hyperbole of the sort analyzed in Laurence Sterne's *Sentimental Journey*, when the Paris wigmaker vouches for the excellence of his work by suggesting that the customer can safely dip the wig "into the ocean" ("The Wig: Paris"). Sterne comments "that the grandeur is *more* in the *word;* and *less* in the *thing.*" Cf., in a culture with a monetary orientation, the stylized regret: "I'd rather lose a million dollars than have this happen."

62 Cf. Knight, pp. 116-117.

63 3.3.284, 335, 368, 388-390.

64 3.3.449-450, 431, 477; 4.1.38, 146-147, 180, 188, 211.

65 Cf. 4.2.13, 133, 136, 142-144.

66 The distinction between the artwork that imposes order on the segment of life and that which proposes to move on the current of life may have a validity that extends beyond the present context. In the former, one can see affiliations with the "classical," and possibilities of artificiality and formalism; in the latter, the "romantic," with possibilities in one direction of mimetic form and in another of naturalistic formlessness.

67 Cf. Traversi: "The prevailing tenour of the play is still destructive; so much so, I think, that it is lacking in proper moral balance and does not give complete satisfaction as a work of art" ("Othello," p. 268).

33 A joke by the Clown glances at the theme (3.4.21-22).

34 "Knave," of course, may be used neutrally. As a denigratory term it app[ears] at 1.3.400 and 2.1.242-252. There are other examples of the Iago vocabular[y] 2.1.262-265, 312, 321; 2.3.53, 61. Drunken Cassio talks like him at 2.3.150-[;] cf. Othello at 2.3.172, 196, 210, 256.

35 With animal images and terms like "villain," "minx," "bawd," etc. 3.3.359, 475; 4.2.20, 21, 72, 73, 81, 86, 89.

36 See 4.1.25-29, 46, 95, 97, 129, 187; 5.1.11, 56-69, 78, 85. As in Act [5] victims fall into abuse and cry "villain" repeatedly (5.1.23, 41, 54).

37 Stoll has some sharp descriptions of Iago's vulgarity (pp. 251-252).

38 By Emilia: 4.2.15, 130-132, 139-140; 5.2.151, 155-156, 172-174, 190-19[1]; others: 5.2.235, 239, 242, 285, 296, 313, 316, 318, 368.

39 Cf. Sitwell, p. 94.

40 At 1.3.138; 3.3.442.

41 Folio reading. The Quartos have a single "cursed." It is possib[le] Othello refers to himself. H. H. Furness, following Edwin Booth, s[ays] reference is to Iago (*Variorum*, p. 323).

42 The literal and metaphorical meanings of *slave* are paralleled by th[e] and metaphorical meanings of *poor white* as used in southeastern Unite[d] In educated usage, the word is largely a metaphor for qualities of m[ind or] spirit—qualities very much the same as those suggested by *slave* in [;] in the main, the understanding of the human being at his lowest possi[ble] of desire and fulfillment.

43 For a different treatment of the music, and for its relation to the s[ee] G. Wilson Knight, *The Shakespearian Tempest*, 3rd ed. (London, 1953) 183.

44 Armstrong notes that the swan is the only "singing bird" in *Othel[lo*].

45 See 1.1.101, 141-142, 181; 1.2.57, 62ff., 94; 1.3.59ff.

46 The tools later express their chagrin appropriately. Cassio lamen[ts his] noisiness (2.3.279ff.). Roderigo regrets that he has only been noisy a[nd] nothing out of it: "I do follow here in the chase, not like a hound [ ] but one that fills up the cry" (2.3.369-370).

47 In the midst of one outburst, however, Othello uses a cosmic s[ound] symbol of the enormity of what he thinks Desdemona has done (4.2[ ). He] ends the brothel scene by shouting for Emilia (90), whom earl[ier he] ordered, "Cough or cry hem if anybody come" (29). It is one [of the] scenes terminated by sounds from within rather than from without.

There is a long series of official calls, signals, and announcement[s of] action: 1.2.44; 1.3.12; 2.1.1ff.; 2.2.1ff.; 4.1.226ff.; 4.2.169. Extraordinar[y as] these outbreaks of sound combine to create the effect of a constan[tly] and discordant atmosphere.

48 Cf. Spurgeon, p. 79.

49 This statement is very close to Knight, p. 119. Knight, howe[ver,] heavy weight of symbolism on the music.

50 Stoll apparently sees greatness and dignity in the character [at] the end (pp. 271-272, 274, 276).

NOTES FOR PAGES 126-131

68 Granville-Barker, as far as I know, is the only critic to comment specifically on the effect of Iago's remaining alive (II, 114).

69 Bethell notes that Desdemona is "the only important personage in the play" to use no diabolic imagery, and he comments that this "has considerable significance for character: 'O, the more angel she'" ("Shakespeare's Imagery," p. 69).

70 See 2.3.184; 5.1.63, 94. His opening word is "'Sblood" (1.1.4)—the oath, ironically, of an anti-redeemer. *Blood* may have stylistically neutral meanings such as "family," "nature," etc. Cf. 1.1.170; 1.3.104, 123.

71 Compare these speeches of the wounded:

Montano: Zounds, I bleed still. I am hurt to the death.	(2.3.164)
Roderigo: Nobody come? Then shall I bleed to death.	(5.1.45)
Iago:　　I bleed, sir, but not kill'd.	(5.2.288)

Iago's "moral victory" over an inept attacker, whatever else it is, is also the triumph of one who has caused others to bleed until they feared death, or died. Iago has been efficient.

72 Traversi believes that the blood imagery is the principal imagistic means of marking Iago's perversion of Othello ("Othello," pp. 251-268).

73 Iago at 1.1.16, 38, 59; Roderigo at 1.1.140; Brabantio at 1.2.72.

74 Othello's concern with justice appears in a concern with justness; see 1.3.124; 3.3.385; 5.1.31.

75 She admits she was "Arraigning his unkindness with my soul" and adds, "But now I find I had suborn'd the witness, / And he's indicted falsely" (3.4.151-154). Compare her prayer for her traducer, "heaven pardon him!" with Emilia's immediately following, "A halter pardon him!" (4.2.135-136).

76 See 1.1.147-148; 1.2.14-16, 95; 1.3.69-70.

77 On Othello's lines as an example of the "defendant's speech," see Milton B. Kennedy, *The Oration in Shakespeare* (Chapel Hill, N. C., 1942), pp. 33, 81, 108, 113, 137.

78 Stoll remarks that Othello "shows scarcely a judicial spirit" (p. 201), but seems to me not to give this observation sufficient weight in his general estimate of Othello's character. Bradley notes the "ominous words" that Othello speaks during this scene (p. 190), but drops the subject: his virtual idealization of Othello leaves him no way of dealing with such facts. However, as recent a critic as Evans believes that in this scene Othello speaks "the language of a general in action; bold, effective, with no word wasted, straight statements of an assured mind" (p. 128). Elliott notes everything that is wrong with Othello's conduct in this scene but fails to see the roots in Othello's personality, because, as elsewhere, he is so intent on working out his allegory of love and pride (pp. 87-92, 108-110).

79 "Suit" and "suitor" at 3.3.42, 80; 3.4.87, 166; "deny" at 3.3.69, 76, 83; "advocation" at 3.4.123.

80 Stanislavsky's notes for the production of the scene include such terms as "The examining magistrate," "The Oath," "The Verdict" (pp. 188-190).

81 The quest for the air of legality has been given subtle assistance by Iago's use of a metaphor that serves to confer an official propriety upon even "vile and

269

NOTES FOR PAGES 131-137

false" thoughts: "Who has a breast so pure / But some uncleanly apprehensions / Keep leets and law days, and in session sit / With meditations lawful?" (3.3.138-141). Malice of mind is like a periodic session of court.

[82] There has been much discussion of Othello's failure to talk candidly to Desdemona about Iago's charges. Stirling attributes this to "morbid and malignant secretiveness" ("Psychology in *Othello*," p. 139). But the conduct seems fairly expectable or "normal"; this is put in different ways by Samuel A. Tannenbaum, "The Jealousy of Othello," *Shakespeare Association Bulletin*, X (1935), 246, and Putney, p. 314. Whatever the psychological genesis, the action itself has a certain moral quality. Elliott calls it "pride." I am here looking at it as a part of the extensive judicial metaphor in the play. My discussion of the judicial metaphor is in some details similar to that of Brents Stirling in his book *Unity in Shakespearian Tragedy: The Interplay of Theme and Character* (New York, 1956). However, our perspectives and emphases differ.

CHAPTER 5. OTHELLO: ACTION AND LANGUAGE

[1] Stoll, p. 263, as well as in every work since *Othello* (1915), in which he first formulated it. He changes the terms slightly in "Slander in Drama," *Shakespeare Quarterly*, IV (1953), 433-450. (His *Othello* contains a good summary of critical opinions on the characters of Iago and Othello from the seventeenth century to 1915.) Stoll keeps insisting that in drama we must find effect, not reality; theater, not life; stage, not home. But when a convention like "the calumniator credited" has been dead for a long time and the play said to rely on it is very much alive, the critic's responsibility is to try to find out with what transconventional life the poet has inspired the actions where the ancient convention is said to be the controlling factor. Speaight says it is "étonnant" how Shakespeare, while obeying all the rules of the theater, "savait illustrer, spontanément, les immuables lois de l'univers" (p. 489). Stoll's position, by the way, is really a vast elaboration of that of G. B. Shaw, *Collected Works* (New York, 1931), XXIII, 154-158, 332.

[2] Here the main line of descent is from Bradley through Granville-Barker (II, 112ff.) and Knight. Here also may be included H. B. Charlton, *Shakespearian Tragedy* (Cambridge, Eng., 1948), pp. 113-140. Sitwell attributes to Othello "the greatness and simplicity . . . of Nature before it was altered by civilization" (p. 94). Sewell, who is clear about Othello's decline, nevertheless seems to me to overrate Othello's initial status as a man of the world of spirit, a result, apparently of his overvaluing the significance of Othello's cosmic imagery (pp. 32, 78, 95). Willard Farnham lists Othello among the heroes "at heart incorruptible" and in contrast with the later Shakespeare hero who "has faulty substance reaching to the very center of his character." This is in *Shakespeare's Tragic Frontier* (Berkeley and Los Angeles, 1950), pp. 5, 8. If Othello is, as I believe, seriously flawed, he would have to be reinterpreted as an anticipation of such later heroes as Macbeth, Antony, and Coriolanus.

[3] Here the line of descent is from Eliot and Leavis and, in the application of Jungian psychology, from Bodkin. Leavis makes a vigorous attack on

NOTES FOR PAGES 137-140

Bradley's idealization of Othello. Leavis' pioneer article—in *Scrutiny*, VI (1937), 259-283—has been inadequately noticed.

4 Kirschbaum, pp. 283ff. Kirschbaum derives partly from Bodkin. He lists Allardyce Nicoll, Theodore Spencer, and Mark Van Doren as among those who attribute Othello's disaster to his own flaws, and J. D. Wilson, Kittredge, and E. K. Chambers as continuers of the "noble Othello" tradition. In *Shakespeare: A Survey* (London, 1925), Chambers calls Othello "a gracious and doomed creature, a child in spirit, walking on the abyss" (p. 225).

5 Elliott, who seems to me to be too rigorous and inflexible in applying the dogma of pride to all the characters; nevertheless, he has a good analysis of Othello's shortcomings. Other analyses of Othello by Battenhouse, Siegel, and Traversi, I refer to elsewhere.

6 Such as that of Stewart in *Character and Motive in Shakespeare*, pp. 105, 106, 109. Stewart reaffirms "nobility" as the main impression given by Othello.

7 I hope my reading represents what Bodkin calls "attending with all the resources of our minds to the words and structure of the drama" (*Archetypal Patterns in Poetry*, p. 333), and takes due account of what Prior calls the "technique of cumulative revelation and of interrelationship between action and character" ("Character in Relation to Action in *Othello*," pp. 226, 234, 237).

8 Cunningham, disagreeing with Stoll's argument about convention, argues that Iago's conversion of Othello is made plausible by Othello's syllogistic operation at 3.3.384ff. (pp. 118ff.). Stirling argues for "Othello's personal initiative and persistence in reaching the conclusion of Desdemona's guilt" ("Psychology in *Othello*," p. 136). In "Othello's Crucial Moment," *Shakespeare Association Bulletin*, XXIV (1949), 181-192, John Wilcox argues that Iago gave Othello the first hints about Desdemona's infidelity offstage. For a recent example of the traditional argument that Iago's technique of deception is irresistible, see Flatter, pp. 136ff. For other arguments that are explicitly or implicitly anti-Stoll, see Putney, pp. 307-319; Prior, "Character in Relation to Action in *Othello*," pp. 226-233; Raymond, pp. 84-94; Duthie, pp. 13ff. Cf. Speaight, pp. 482-485.

9 He conjectures that Desdemona may be "gone" because "I am black"; yet he virtually equates this with two other possible causes—his social deficiencies and his age (3.3.263-266). (All three doubts are "positional.") In "Do you triumph, Roman?" (4.1.121) there may be some trans-Mediterranean feeling. Again, "Are we turn'd Turks . . . ?" (2.3.170) may reflect a vague sense of insecurity in his own Christianity, which Battenhouse interprets as largely a veneer.

10 E.g., 3.3.202-203, 207, 229-237.

11 Stoll notes that this idea, started by Schlegel, still crops up occasionally (p. 194). Cf. *Poets and Playwrights*, p. 133. Bradley makes a lively attack on particularist views of Othello (pp. 187, 210). On the other side of the fence is Campbell, pp. 157, 161ff.

12 Cf. John Money on Othello's "inarticulacy" and its relation to "this inarticulacy, or impotence, of the man" ("Othello's 'It is the Cause . . .': An Analysis," *Shakespeare Survey*, VI (1953), 99-100).

13 Traversi, "Othello," p. 253.

NOTES FOR PAGES 140-151

[14] Fairchild uses the term *romantic* to describe Othello's attitude to his experiences. Fairchild's little-known study has a good analysis of Othello as he appears in Act 1 (pp. 35-36).

[15] Leavis, p. 265. Cf. p. 270. Traversi analyzes Othello similarly in "Othello," pp. 252-253.

[16] Stanislavsky, p. 109.

[17] For example, Bodkin and Kirschbaum; see "The Modern Othello," pp. 289ff. Leavis speaks of Othello's "ideal conception" of himself and of the "romantic idealizing love . . . dubiously grounded in reality" (pp. 264, 267, 271). Cf. Traversi: "he dramatizes as 'nobility' his own innate incapacity to cope with life" ("Othello," p. 249). On Othello's personality generally, see Theodore Spencer, p. 124; Leavis, pp. 261, 264. The full scope of the characterization is lost if we interpret Othello simply as a military man confronted by non-military problems. Rather he is a representative kind of human being, the kind, we may speculate, that tends toward the military life.

[18] 3.3.97-99, 105-107, 115-116, 125-126, 131-136, 143-144, 153-154, 162-164.

[19] Leavis, p. 268; Elliott, pp. 120, 189.

[20] Cf. Granville-Barker, II, 38; Leech, pp. 84-85.

[21] Cf. Traversi: "The problem of *Othello* is the problem of consciousness, of the relationship of instinctive life to critical detachment" ("Othello," p. 264).

[22] There is a nice play of modal auxiliaries in this passage. Othello says, "Would I were satisfied!" (390). Iago: "You would be satisfied?" (393). Othello: "Would? Nay, I will" (393). Iago, wrily: "And may" (394).

[23] Stirling, "Psychology in *Othello*," p. 137. Stirling here refers to "certainty" with regard to Desdemona, but the phrase serves for a general description of Othello's difficulty.

[24] Fairchild, pp. 33-34.

[25] Charlton says correctly that "living has been for him a continuity of passionate experience and not a series of intellectual states" (p. 121). But next thing Charlton has converted "passionate experience" into "soul": "His mind is unequal to his soul" (p. 123).

[26] Pages 286-287. Cf. Elliott, pp. 117, 121, 134, 135, 206. But Elliott locates Othello's disposition to believe Iago not in his personality generally but in a secret inclination to doubt Desdemona along with other women. Cf. Leavis, p. 267.

[27] Empson says Iago "feels he is now in danger" (p. 226). This is doubtful. Rather, the master "stunt man" feels the excitement of a close call. Still more questionable is Empson's statement that Iago is unwilling "to be the Fool he thinks he is taken for."

[28] The game becomes a habit with Iago. When Lodovico, amazed at Othello's striking Desdemona, makes inquiries of Iago, Iago replies, "It is not honesty in me to speak / What I have seen and known" (4.1.288-289)—the archetypal technique of the ambiguous statement that encourages inferences which are half-right and hence more difficult to deal with than if they were all wrong.

[29] *Archetypal Patterns in Poetry*, p. 223. This is qualified on p. 333. Cf. Connolly's comparable point that Iago "is in fact what is now called the subconscious" (p. 31).

NOTES FOR PAGE 151

30 Empson is good on this passage (pp. 228-229). Cf. Kittredge, p. 227.

31 He sneers at her "well-painted passion" (4.1.268) but he does not seriously challenge the "passion" that has "my best judgment collied" (2.3.206), nor the "shadowing passion" (4.1.39); he is sure that Iago's signs of unwillingness to tell his thoughts come "from the heart / That passion cannot rule" (3.3.123-124) —i.e., the heart that cannot control its (honest) passion. Iago, always feinting, encourages Othello's passion by seeming to inveigh against it (3.3.391; 4.1.78); Lodovico's astonishment shows how far this passion has gone (4.1.276-277); and Desdemona is horrified by it.

32 *Othello* briefly anticipates the patience theme to be developed in *Lear*. In the opening scenes Roderigo, Othello, and the Duke successively ask "patience" of Brabantio (1.1.104; 1.3.89, 207), and though Brabantio replies ironically (1.3.215), he so conducts himself that, as in the matter of justice, the achievement of Act 1 is the measure for a later failure: at least to the extent that Brabantio has been "patient" enough to discover the facts and be governed by them as best he may. Cf. 1.3.243.

Iago is a connoisseur of the impatience of others, spurring it or checking it at need. (There is only one reference, a trivial one, to his own patience. See 2.1.98.) After the fight he suggests that Cassio had suffered "some strange indignity, / Which patience could not pass" (2.3.245-246)—thus subtly planting in Othello's mind the idea of grievance too large for patience. The game is to create the impatience and then control it toward an end: leadership, of a sort. When Iago gets to the stage of urging restraint, his victims are seriously in the toils. See 2.3.376 and 5.1.87. As always, Iago works by corrupting a virtue. And he is aided by Desdemona's bad judgment in her new wifely role; she promises to work on Othello and "talk him out of patience" (3.3.23). (Cf. her advice to Cassio at 3.4.129.) Then Iago urges Othello, "Patience, I say. Your mind perhaps may change" (3.3.452)—simulating the purity of the detached consultant as he uses *patience* to stir impatience. Later he repeats: "Confine yourself but in a patient list" and "Marry, patience!" (4.1.76, 88). At this point Othello, who has in the main been too deeply immersed in his passion to have much self-awareness, comes out with what is in effect a sardonic witticism about himself. He is humorless, and the heavy irony he falls into is right for him: "Dost thou hear, Iago? / I will be found most cunning in my patience; / But (dost thou hear?) most bloody" (90-92); i.e.: "That's *my* kind of patience." Here he knows what to expect of himself—and accepts the expected, which is his tragedy. His final contribution to the patience theme—this is in the "brothel scene" with Desdemona— is an imaging of the plagues under which, Joblike, he would have been capable of patience (4.2.47-56). This is a very fine picture of the being in torment who imagines that any other kind of torment would be more bearable than his own. For Othello it has the value of enabling him to see himself as a more than ordinarily patient man; the very construction of the speech to this point strengthens the "ideal image" of himself, for he seems to set the widest limits of patience and then with a second wind goes on to describe a still harsher test for which he could summon up a still further reserve of endurance. But there are absolute limits to Jobism, he implies. Having found himself capable of bearing almost unspeakable afflictions—the old soldier, rhetorically recalling a past in which he did succeed—he is now justified in finding his present situation beyond the bounds of all patience (57-64). A farewell to patience, he implies, is not to be construed as an act of savagery by one who can know or do no better; it is an extremity to which the good man is compelled, as if by a "strange indignity / Which patience could not pass." The idea of inevitability is a powerful source of assurance.

33 On one occasion he might fall into pity: when he says to Iago, "But yet the pity of it, Iago! O Iago, the pity of it, Iago!" (4.1.206-207). Othello's use of *pity* might stir some memory, some resensing, of his own words just before leaving Venice: "She swore . . . / 'Twas pitiful, 'twas wondrous pitiful" and "She lov'd me for the dangers I had pass'd, / And I lov'd her that she did pity them" (1.3.160-161, 167-168). But he has already resolved to be governed by his hard side: "No, my heart is turn'd to stone" (4.1.192-193).

34 Kirschbaum, p. 292. Cf. Craig: "taking on himself the justice of God, the acme of tragic madness in both ancient and modern drama" (*An Interpretation of Shakespeare*, p. 204).

35 Cf. Stoll, pp. 205-206. Elliott's analysis of this part of Act 5 seems to me to be excellent (pp. 213ff.), despite his somewhat schoolmasterish rebuking of Desdemona (pp. 217-218). Money analyzes the passage acutely and sensitively (pp. 94-105). The rarity of a recent critic who takes Othello at his own words is provided by Flatter, who believes Othello's case is that "of mankind . . . of honesty, of truth, of faith—of belief in the goodness of creation" (p. 156). Othello sees "through his personal grievance" and recognizes "beyond it, the wrong done to mankind" (pp. 157-158). His "real and unique greatness" is the "indestructibility of his love" (p. 158). Cf. n. 38.

36 Nowottny, p. 340. Nowottny's analysis of this scene is one of the best I know. One of her most interesting contentions is that all four of the Elizabethan meanings of *cause* are implied in Othello's use of the word, so that by it he unites all of his feelings for one action. But the feelings split apart before he acts.

37 Sister Miriam Joseph refers to Othello's "own rating, as a sort of private priest sacrificing to justice what he most loves" (p. 264).

38 In the scene in which he reads Desdemona's palm and prescribes "A sequester from liberty, etc." (3.4.40-43). Othello's acting as confessor to Desdemona ironically reverses—another of those echoes from passage to passage that are so continuously fascinating in Shakespeare—Desdemona's enthusiastic promise constantly to plead for Cassio with Othello: "His bed shall seem a school, his board a shrift" (3.3.24).

39 Flatter praises Othello for his Christian solicitude here, not noting that when Desdemona asks time "to say one prayer" (83), Othello answers only with an unceremonious "it is too late" and kills her. Flatter praises Othello as a "practicing Christian" but says that of course we grant him the usual tragic hero's right, "to take the law into his own hands" (pp. 151, 156). Somewhere, Christian doctrine gets lost.

40 Cf. Charlton, p. 120.

41 Cf. Nowottny's remark that the killing is "symbolic" in that it "stands for all the warring emotions pent up in Othello" (p. 341).

NOTES FOR PAGES 156-166

42 See conclusion to Chapter IV.

43 *Variorum*, p. 300.

44 Cf. Granville-Barker, II, 88.

45 He uses the word only after her death, and then not directly as an epithet for her: "She's like a liar gone to burning hell!" (5.2.129).

46 In "The World of Homer," *Review of Politics*, XV (1953), 491ff., Eric Voegelin discusses the wrath of Achilles in terms that may profitably be applied to Iago, not only as a murderer but as a plotter generally. "The wrath of Achilles . . . is something outside human order. It is a gap in the order that binds men together, and through the gap pours an uncontrollable darkness from beyond" (p. 494). "The conduct of Achilles . . . is a sinister failing of the heart that places the hero outside the order of Gods and men" (p. 498). ". . . this outbreak is sensed by the others as something more than a fitting reaction to the situation; its roots seem to reach deeper into a disorderly disposition of Achilles" (p. 500).

47 Cf. Leavis, p. 274.

48 Cf. Nowottny: "the man who accepts justice as the supreme value in life will, if he be wholly consistent, at last execute himself" (p. 340).

49 Kirschbaum calls these lines "uncontrolled screaming" (p. 288), Granville-Barker, "the howling of the damned" (II, 121). Cf. Money, p. 100.

50 My reading is in complete disagreement with that of Elliott, who sees Othello in the final scene going through a spiritual apotheosis, purged of pride, coming into right love, achieving perfect justice, etc. (pp. 224-240). It is a little surprising that Elliott, who has been so meticulous in detecting pride in Desdemona, should so tolerantly say of Othello, "Humanly he wishes to justify himself" (p. 235). He seems not to know the criticisms of Eliot, Leavis, Kirschbaum, Traversi, etc.

51 Knight says that "Othello's fault is simplicity alone" (p. 118).

52 Sewell puts this very effectively: "The settlement he is making now is with society, not with the universe" (p. 96).

53 1.2.83-84. Cf. E. K. Chambers, *Shakespeare Gleanings* (Oxford, 1944), p. 47.

54 It is pleasant to find how close this comes to Leavis' description of this effect as a "superb *coup de théâtre*" (p. 276). He speculates most interestingly as to why so many critics have been taken in. My analysis of Othello's lines in the latter part of 5.2 parallels his, except that he lays more emphasis on the "tragic and grand" element that coexists with the sentimental and the histrionic. Fluchère calls Othello "un peu comédien" and insists repeatedly on the self-conscious theatricalism of the suicide (pp. 161, 284-285, 326). In *Themes and Conventions of Elizabethan Tragedy* (Cambridge, Eng., 1935), pp. 134-135, M. C. Bradbrook identifies Othello's speech with the convention of self-dramatization and adds that the convention must be "judged by its possibilities and its results."

55 The only other student of the play to comment on this is, as far as I know, Granville-Barker, II, 149. He is one of the few critics who regard Othello at the end as simply lost.

56 T. S. Eliot's brief comment on this passage, written more than twenty years ago, is one of the more telling paragraphs in *Othello* criticism. Note especially

275

the sentence: "He takes in the spectator, but the human motive is primarily to take in himself." The paragraph is in the essay "Shakespeare and the Stoicism of Seneca," *Selected Essays 1917-1932* (New York, 1932), p. 111. Traversi elaborates effectively (*Approach*, p. 85), as does Money, pp. 104-105. For a dissent see Stoll, *Poets and Playwrights*, p. 59n., 70. Knight reads this final speech literally (p. 118). However, Knight's sense of the text seems to me, in his interpretation of Othello, to be resisting his formal theory. Though he officially views Othello as an ideal of valor, he is aware of his sentimentality and flamboyance (p. 117); but he brushes off such matters because he lacks a theory to account for them. He has a comparable difficulty in dealing with Othello's change of style. Knight not only sees Othello's decline into vulgarity and grossness, which everybody sees, but he also notes his rhetoric and bombast at 5.2.260ff. (p. 102); however, all these changes become for him merely a symbol of Iago's influence, without having any roots in Othello's character and personality. It is all right to speak of Iago's "corroding" Othello, as several critics do; but the problem is, What is there in the first place that makes Othello corrode so easily? The whole text of the play gives us, in my opinion, an emphatic answer to that question. Leech speaks of the "fortitude that makes even Othello end in dignity" (p. 119), but criticizes adversely Elliott's optimistic interpretation (*Shakespeare Quarterly*, V [1954], 89). E. M. W. Tillyard believes that the final Othello is a man "of more capacious mind" than the initial Othello, that the conclusion of the play hints at a "rebirth," pointing to the late plays. See *Shakespeare's Last Plays* (London, 1951), pp. 17, 18, 21. Kirschbaum is right in saying that critics tend to see Othello "as he sees himself" (p. 294). See his list of critics who think Othello is nobler at the end of the play (p. 288n.). Among those who think he is damned are Bethell ("Shakespeare's Imagery," pp. 78-79), Siegel, Battenhouse.

[57] Knight calls the play "eminently a domestic tragedy" (p. 108), but he uses the term in a quite different sense. Cf. Granville-Barker, II, 47. Bethell talks regularly of the "domestic" element in *Othello* but objects to letting this element obscure the "profoundly theological structure" ("Shakespeare's Imagery," p. 66).

[58] Cf. Traversi: "The great speeches in which he attains tragic stature by expressing his 'nobility' are, at the same time, merciless exposures of weakness" ("Othello," p. 267).

CHAPTER 6. THEMATIC FORM: VERSIONS OF LOVE

[1] Nowottny, p. 334.

[2] Cf. Traversi, *Approach*, p. 80; Elliott, pp. 8ff., 45-48, 61-73, *passim*. Various critics identify love and hate as the conflicting forces. The most complete discussion of the love theme is Elliott's, with which I shall indicate only major points of agreement and disagreement. One of Elliott's most interesting ideas is that Iago's hatred of Desdemona is intensified because he cannot evoke any self-love in her.

[3] II, 9. Cf. Flatter, pp. 208-209; Weilgart, pp. 53, 85.

[4] The contents of this paragraph will suggest in the main the extent of my agreement and disagreement with Knight's version of the conflict: "The play turns on this theme: the cynical intellect pitted against a lovable humanity

transfigured by qualities of heroism and grace" (p. 112). Knight's analysis of Iago and my own are generally consistent. But Knight, in idealizing Othello, seems to me to make the play verge on melodrama.

5 Charlton, pp. 128, 130.

6 Cf. Battenhouse, "Shakespeare and the Tragedy of Our Time," p. 528. My analysis of Othello's defects as a lover is close to that of Elliott, pp. 19-40, *passim*. These defects, which are noted by most recent critics, are given a psychoanalytical interpretation by Feldman, pp. 148ff. In Feldman's view, Othello is homosexually attracted to Cassio but disguises this from himself by the "makeshift passion" for Desdemona. The ostensible jealousy of Desdemona is really a jealousy of Cassio. Othello is really "effeminate" (p. 159); fearful of his lack of manliness, he seeks manly glory in the military profession (p. 162). This view throws out all the evidence of conscious behavior in favor of inferences about the unconscious, and appears to create as many difficulties as it solves. See the theory of Wangh in n. 71. In view of the increasing awareness of Othello's shortcomings as a lover, it is surprising to find G. Bonnard arguing that Othello's flaw is that he loves Desdemona so much that he loses common sense and does not persuade her to stay in Venice as he should. This is in "Are Othello and Desdemona Innocent or Guilty?" *English Studies*, XXX (1949), 181ff.

7 Elliott, pp. 29ff., 126.

8 Leavis, p. 265. Note his further comments on the limitations of Othello's love, pp. 268-270. Cf. Money: "His love for Desdemona is subtly presented from the start as inadequate" (p. 102).

9 Cf. Kirschbaum, pp. 291-292. My treatment is partly akin to Traversi's in "Othello," pp. 253ff., except that he argues for the constant presence of sensual passion. It appears only later, I think—the product of converted egoism and the enormously stimulating images used by Iago. If Othello concealed sexual feeling, 2.3.8ff. are hard to explain.

10 In *The Secret Self* (New York, 1952), Theodore Reik comments on the mixture of the masculine and the feminine in Desdemona in the love-making period (pp. 60-62).

11 Flatter, p. 74. One may sympathize with Flatter's objection to critics' calling Desdemona "saint" without having to go to his extreme of referring to her "cool and calculated indifference" and the "height of her *hubris*" (pp. 75, 81). In Stanislavsky's production plan, she "very tenderly addresses her father" (p. 65).

12 The evidence will hardly sustain the theory of sexual precocity in Desdemona that is toyed with by Flatter and by Speaight, p. 482.

13 Battenhouse argues that Desdemona, in her awareness of sex, "has a more Christian notion of marriage" than Othello, who disparages the flesh ("Shakespeare and the Tragedy of Our Time," p. 529).

14 Kirschbaum, calling it "almost inhuman" (p. 290n.), makes an acute analysis of this part of the play. So does Elliott, though he seems to read into Desdemona's character a much more elaborate awareness of the situation than the lines justify. He imputes to her a knowledge that Othello's love is limited and suggests that she wants to go along to war "to win his full love" (pp. 28ff, 34ff.). Sewell says surprisingly that "Othello's thought and feeling at the beginning of the play are free from the pressures of temporal things" (p. 94).

15 Traversi is very good on this subject. He notes the "coldness" of Othello's style, "with a fire beneath that makes it all the more capable of corruption" (*Approach*, p. 81).

16 Elliott's constant harping on Othello's pride seems to me to suffer somewhat from his failure to connect it with other elements in his personality. In a stronger character than Othello, pride would take a quite different form.

17 The most astonishing comment in twentieth-century criticism of *Othello* concerns this passage. In "Husbands in Shakespeare," *Shakespeare Association Bulletin*, XX (1945), Sibyl C. Holbrook says that these lines show the "essentially light vain nature of the woman," who, she says, "has an empty little mind" (p. 175).

18 Cf. Kirschbaum, pp. 290-291 and nn. On Othello's use of first-person pronouns, see Elliott, pp. 62-65, and Fairchild, pp. 35-36.

19 See 3.3.6-7, 10, 48, 71, 80-82.

20 He tells Montano he loves Cassio (2.3.148), and Othello refers publicly to Iago's love for Cassio (246-247). For implied love-making to Brabantio, see 1.1.110; to Roderigo, 1.3.342, 371; to Othello, 1.2.7. He asks Othello, "Are you fast married?" and says Brabantio "will divorce you" (1.2.11, 14). But Brabantio accepts the marriage and Iago does the divorcing. Iago betrays his own motive by attributing it to Brabantio.

21 Since his "love" and his "honesty" are Iago's major strategic means of seduction, one wonders whether the meaning of *honesty* does not strengthen the meaning of *love* in more than the obvious way (i.e., the love of an honorable man). Since there is so much talk of Desdemona's "honesty" and since Iago's protestations occur mainly in a context in which fidelity is the sole subject, might not Iago's "honesty" also implicitly become Iago's "chastity," so that he would thus become Othello's "true love"? This reversal of the usual play of meanings in the word is a familiar enough poetic event.

22 Iago prepares for this by an earlier remark, "Cassio's my worthy friend" (3.3.223).

23 Sitwell makes a sharp observation on this passage (p. 104). Cf. Elliott, p. 143; Granville-Barker, II, 46; Feldman, p. 156.

24 Cf. 3.4.171, 196. Cf. Cassio's "leave me for this time" (3.4.191) and Othello's "leave me but a little to myself" (3.3.85). For Desdemona's emphasis on the love of Cassio and Othello, see n. 19. Emilia assures Cassio of Othello's continuing love (3.1.50), but Cassio is still worried lest the "general will forget my love and service" (3.3.18; cf. 3.4.112, 118). Cassio's own affection survives everything, as his "Dear General" makes clear (5.2.299).

25 This perhaps adds a little something to our knowledge of Shakespeare's imaginative resourcefulness in characterization, since it reverses the usual situation as described by Alfred Harbage, "A striking feature of Shakespeare's work is that women who have shifted lovers assimilate the traits of common prostitutes," in *Shakespeare and the Rival Traditions* (New York, 1952), p. 197. Cf. Elliott, p. 212.

26 Cf. Bowman, "In Defense of Emilia," pp. 99-104.

27 Cf. Bradley, pp. 239-241.

28 Literal use of military terms: 2.3.126-127, 381, 386. References to himself at

war: 1.2.1; 2.3.186-187; 3.4.134-137. Cf. 3.3.467. Military-naval metaphors: 1.1.153, 157; 1.2.17.

[29] Drunk and sober, Cassio is concerned for his spiritual well-being (2.3.106ff., 263ff.).

[30] When Cassio tells Bianca that he does not want Othello to "see me woman'd" (3.4.195), his self-protectiveness is ironic: had Othello known about Bianca from the start, the story of Cassio's affair with Desdemona might have seemed less plausible. Granted, of course, that Cassio could have carried on doubly. But it is only after Othello is already convinced that Iago tells him that Cassio gave Desdemona's handkerchief to "his whore" (4.1.187).

[31] 1.2.37ff.; 1.3.232ff., 279, 299-301; 2.3.257-258; 3.2.1ff.; 3.3.58-59.

[32] ". . . she wish'd / That heaven had made her such a man" (1.3.162-163). Editors split widely on whether *her* is dative or accusative. The line holds both meanings in solution.

[33] Perhaps beyond that they allude to the use of *guerrière* in the sense of "mistress." See the notes in the *Variorum* and in the Arden edition.

[34] On the relationship among these passages, see also the notes on 2.1.184 in the Kittredge and Arden editions.

[35] These comparisons are made by Iago (3.4.134-137) and Lodovico (4.1.276-279).

[36] Cf. Granville-Barker, II, 119.

[37] Draper, "The Jealousy of Iago," p. 50. See also Draper's "This Poor Trash of Venice," especially p. 512.

[38] The difference between my interpretation and Knight's is epitomized in the fact that Knight refers to the "farewell" speech as "this noble eulogy of war" (p. 107). Knight consistently thinks of Othello as the noble warrior, as a "symbol" of "purpose, courage, and valour."

[39] Traversi, "Othello," p. 267. Morozov states that at the end the "lofty theme" again dominates Othello's imagery (p. 87). Morozov tends to take the imagery at face value. Bethell disposes of the critics who "still talk of the poetic imagination of Othello" ("Shakespeare's Imagery," p. 64).

[40] In the fact, for instance, that *pugno* and *f--k* are cognate. See Helge Kökeritz, *Shakespeare's Pronunciation* (New Haven, Conn., 1953), p. 74n. We might recall, also, the enormous erotism of army language generally, notably in the intrusion of metaphors of erotic origin into all the nonerotic phases of existence.

[41] E.g., erotogenic flagellation and killing; necrophilia. For the spread of the sadistic impulse in erotic language, see Eric Partridge, *Shakespeare's Bawdy* (New York, 1948), p. 118.

[42] For an extremely interesting theoretical discussion of the love-death nexus, see M. C. D'Arcy, *The Mind and Heart of Love* (New York, 1947), pp. 28ff. Cf. Armstrong, pp. 93-99; the passage contains several illuminating comments on *Othello*.

[43] Some of the conclusions drawn in this section are hinted at by Money, pp. 101-104.

[44] Brabantio describes the pattern for the events of two nights when he tells what "Hath rais'd me from my bed" (1.3.54).

279

45 Desdemona's "Tonight, my lord?" (1.3.279) is echoed later in Bianca's request to Cassio, "And say if I shall see you soon at night" (3.4.198).

46 Othello's comment to Desdemona, "'Tis the soldiers' life / To have their balmy slumbers wak'd with strife" (2.3.257-258), is a kind of "sentence," suitable for the public ear. But in the context we have been examining, the words go beyond the decorous generality: "strife" (i.e., war) interferes here with love—the love that had its origin in war (the tales and bearing of a warrior).

47 Ernest Brennecke, "Nay, That's Not Next!" *Shakespeare Quarterly,* IV (1953), 35-38. Cf. Othello's "betray more men" (5.2.6).

48 Cf. Leavis: "that characteristic voluptuousness of Othello's which, since it is unassociated with any real interest in Desdemona as a person, slips so readily into possessive jealousy" (pp. 272-273). In attacking Bradley's interpretation of this speech, Leavis analyzes it shrewdly. Nowottny speaks of his "need to possess her again—for murder is now the only act of possession open to him" (p. 341). But if he could practice the "faith" of love, he could again "possess" her in a more inclusive sense.

49 William Empson, *Seven Types of Ambiguity,* 2nd ed., rev. (London, 1949), p. 186.

50 This stage direction, placed at line 198, is only in the First Quarto. Kittredge accepts it, but Flatter has a strong argument against it (p. 186).

51 The conveyance of this meaning might be aided by the word *kiss,* which could also mean intercourse. See Partridge, p. 137.

52 Spoken when he takes the poison (5.3.120). Juliet then comes to, stabs herself, and falls on Romeo's body. Her words to the dagger are also ambiguous, "This is thy sheath; there rust, and let me die" (170). But the play goes on for another 130 lines, so that the passages lack the emphasis which Othello's final words receive from their position, twelve lines from the end.

53 "I will be / A bridegroom in my death, and run into't / As to a lover's bed" (4.14.99-101). Here there is no missing the pun on *death.* Cf. also 4.15.38-39; 5.2.298-299.

54 The only commentators whom I have seen come near this point are Granville-Barker, II, 83-84, and Flatter, pp. 168-169.

55 Flatter, p. 44. But Flatter circumscribes the possibilities in this when he imputes to Iago "the mentality of a crazy actor" (p. 46) rather than a resemblance to Jekyll and Hyde.

56 Wyndham Lewis, p. 197. Lewis is more aware than some critics of this complication in Iago's character.

57 We must allow for still other possibilities in these tantalizing lines. (1) In using such a phrase as "worthy and chaste dames," Iago is taking on, as he does elsewhere, protective coloring, i.e., convincing the audience that he can share its general working principle of sexual fidelity. Though it may be betrayed, fidelity, and not infidelity, is still primary. (2) The horror of Iago is increased if one can view him as a person who understands fidelity and perhaps would like to believe in it, and in a sense does, and yet takes deliberately to another practical philosophy. (3) The phrase is to be understood as in quotation marks, and the tone is cynical. See the Arden ed., p. 182, for the view that Iago is finding deep

satisfaction in the ruin of the innocent. Similarly, cherishing his philosophy is a means of annihilating what is held by other people to be a reality.

58 Knight remarks that what Iago says to Roderigo about sex is "probably" his "sincere belief" and that he proceeds from theory to action based on the theory stated (pp. 112, 113).

59 This passage is analyzed in Cunningham, pp. 25-27. In refuting Hardin Craig's interpretation of the passage, Cunningham points out that Iago speaks "plain and hoary orthodoxy" and to a good end at the moment, if not ultimately.

60 Cf. Bethell: "It may also be indicative of Shakespeare's intention for Iago that Edmund in *Lear*, his literary scion, professes to worship Nature as his goddess" ("Shakespeare's Imagery," p. 70). The naturalism held by both is fully discussed by Traversi, "Othello," pp. 256-257.

61 Sewell, p. 30. Sewell is analyzing Iago's imagery, but the statement fits here in a more general sense.

62 Eric Voegelin, "The Origins of Scientism," *Social Research*, XV (1948), 489ff.

63 Cf. Kittredge's comment on Iago's argument, p. 189.

64 Cf. Traversi's phrase: "Othello's passion turning to corruption in contact with the canker of Iago's cynicism" (*Approach*, p. 84).

65 Othello's errors are not the same as Lear's but enough like them so that they may be seen as an anticipation of Lear's. Lear also suddenly loses faith in all he knows, and he wants, in effect, to "prove" love, but by measuring it, whether in words or property.

66 He expends only two general ideas on Othello (4.1.16-17, 67-68), an implicit one on Cassio (118ff.), one on his effort to incriminate Bianca (5.1.116).

67 This has been described in different ways. See Evans, pp. 125-130. Evans notes other symptoms of decline in the language of Othello. Kirschbaum's theory is that before, Othello held a false view of Desdemona and himself (pp. 288ff.).

68 To Iago: 3.3.359, 475; 4.1.188-189. Cf. 4.2.20-21. To Desdemona: 4.1.250-251; 4.2.72-81, 84-90; 5.1.34; 5.2.77, 79, 131, 136.

69 Various critics make this point: Stauffer, p. 183; Granville-Barker, II, 110; Weilgart, p. 86.

70 Bradley, believing that the use of this phrase is inconsistent with Iago's general ideas, argues that the phrase shows the presence of a conscience in Iago (p. 235n.). But atheists constantly use blasphemous oaths.

71 This interpretation is made in Muir's "The Jealousy of Iago" (pp. 73ff.), one of the strong essays on the play. His interpretation and mine differ in that Muir believes that Iago is also motivated by a resentful suspicion that he has been cuckolded, a suspicion traceable to pathological jealousy. As I see it, this narrows Iago down too much, does not take enough account of his general enviousness of spirit. Yet it is precisely such a general enviousness that is indicated by various parts of Muir's own essay: his reference to Iago's "dog-in-the-manger attitude" (p. 78), his discussion of the wide range of feelings and attitudes covered by the Elizabethan concept of jealousy (pp. 79-81), his acute remark on Iago's "feelings of inferiority" (p. 81), which I think goes to the

heart of the matter. Bradley thinks Iago "unassailable by the temptations of . . . sensuality" and insists that of the love of Desdemona mentioned in the second soliloquy "there is not the faintest trace . . . in word or deed either before or after" (pp. 218, 225). Theodore Spencer follows in this tradition (pp. 132-133), as do Elliott (p. 74), and Granville-Barker (II, 108). But Moore describes Iago as a "sensual fellow" ("The Character of Iago," p. 44). Cf. Stoll, "Slander in Drama," p. 439. In "Othello: The Tragedy of Iago," *Psychoanalytic Quarterly*, XIX (1950), Martin Wangh argues that Iago "is jealous of Desdemona and hates her" because he "loves Othello" (p. 203). Because he is also attracted to Cassio, he suspects an affair between Cassio and Desdemona (p. 208). He identifies Desdemona with Emilia, so that his killing of Emilia has a double meaning (p. 211). Wangh refers to other psychoanalytic interpretations.

[72] Cf. Muir: "In Iago the 'false within' is projected as the false without" (p. 83).

[73] Cf. Traversi on the intensity of Iago's sexuality (*Approach*, pp. 82-83).

[74] Stoll makes many observations on Iago that lead him close to such a conclusion. See pp. 200, 237, 238, 270. But he apparently approves Lytton Strachey's theory that Shakespeare improved on Cinthio by omitting Iago's passion for Desdemona (*Characters and Commentaries* [New York, 1935], pp. 295-296), since this gave Iago the larger dimension of motivelessness. However much we may think that *motiveless* is the right word for Iago, we should not carelessly cast out elements in his character lest they turn out to provide "motives." Iago would act as he acted whether or not Desdemona excited him sexually. The point is that lust is one of the ways in which abstract evil is humanized and concretized in him. (On Stoll: n.b. his later opinion, in "Slander in Drama," p. 439.)

[75] Haydn calls him "the impotent . . . and sexually frustrated man who is envious of healthy men and women" (p. 658). Haydn treats Iago in general as a figure of "Counter-Renaissance naturalism." Cf. Speaight on Iago's "sexualité profondément désaxée" (p. 492) and Traversi's phrase, "perverted sensuality" ("Othello," p. 252).

[76] This appears also in his assurance to Roderigo, "If thou canst cuckold him, thou dost thyself a pleasure, me a sport" (1.3.376-377). Any discomfiture for Desdemona's chosen bedfellow would be a gain.

[77] See 3.3.421-426.

[78] August Goll uses the phrase "an erotic instinct of cruelty" in "Criminal Types in Shakespeare," *Journal of Criminal Law and Criminology*, XXX (1939), 43. In some details Goll's discussion parallels my section, "I Do Love Her Too." In his exemplification of the "intimate connexion between cruelty and desire" Iago anticipates an aspect of the romantic sensibility discussed by Mario Praz in *The Romantic Agony*, tr. Angus Davidson (Oxford, 1933), p. 28 and *passim*. See especially Chapter I, Section 2; Chapter II, Sections 10 and 11; Chapter V, Section 23. Empson several times talks of the "Puritanism" which for Iago is a part of his honesty line, if not something more (p. 226). The role of puritan, one suspects, is a special histrionic pleasure for a man of lively carnal imagination.

[79] As Bonnard argues, "Are Othello and Desdemona Innocent or Guilty?" pp. 176ff. Perhaps a Renaissance audience felt Desdemona to be imperfectly filial (though the Duke's refraining from rebuke makes this questionable) in Act 1, but to argue that this is what makes Desdemona's suffering bearable is to invoke

NOTES FOR PAGES 209-213

a calculus of guilt and suffering which is simply not established in the dramatic progression.

[80] Leech, p. 76; Allardyce Nicoll, *Shakespeare: An Introduction* (New York, 1952), p. 144.

[81] Nicoll, pp. 144-145.

[82] On willfulness, see Flatter, p. 103. In his comments on Acts 3 and 4 Elliott convicts Desdemona of severe errors of pride and self-deception (pp. 111ff.), giving a moral color to what seem at most errors of judgment. For instance, her effort to take a charitable view of Othello, even after he has acted badly, Elliott interprets as deliberate cherishing of a false view of Othello (pp. 157ff., 183ff., and elsewhere). He says that her charity for Othello "is far more kind than just and right—unlike the wise charity of the 'good Father' (23) to whom she prays" (p. 204). It is a high standard to apply, even to the "divine Desdemona." This should be contrasted with Granville-Barker's analysis, II, 48-50. In *Shakespeare's Tragedies* (London, 1951), G. B. Harrison says Desdemona "soon turns from adoration to a zest for conquest" and calls her "a determined young woman, . . . eager to get her own way" (pp. 137, 143). But shortly, without analyzing the change, he describes her as "this terrified child" (p. 151).

[83] Fernand Baldensperger writes: "But Othello is a decided Christian and at the same time an inborn fetichist: a 'divided duty' would be his lot, if an exacting talisman was not the dominant affair, and here it is a pity to see many commentators apt to believe that the 'handkerchief' was the same bit of linen it is for our laundress, while it is an amulet without equal: when Th. Rymer . . . ironically christened *Othello The Tragedy of the Handkerchief,* he did not suspect how right he was after all, but *mutatis mutandis*" (personal letter dated Paris, September 14, 1953).

[84] Thus initiating a side drama of jealousy that has some parallels to the main plot: the handkerchief itself seems evidence of infidelity, Bianca flings it back at Cassio (to "give't away"!) in the same scene (4.1.159-161) in which under Iago's influence he decides to break with her, and then her devotion appears to mature (and her explicit self-regard to diminish).

[85] Cf. Knight on "the significance of the magic handkerchief *as both a symbol of domestic sanctity and the play's one link with the supernatural*" (p. 109n.).

[86] 1.2.63-65, 73, 79; 1.3.61, 64, 66, 91-92, 156, 169.

[87] But compare his use of a metaphor from magic when Emilia is about to tell the whole truth in the last scene: "Go to, charm your tongue"; she replies, "I will not charm my tongue" (5.2.183-184).

[88] He needs the idea of magical powers to describe the "charm" of Desdemona: "O, she will sing the savageness out of a bear!" (4.1.200-201). He must think of himself as a judge resisting charms: "Forth of my heart those charms, thine eyes, are blotted" (5.1.35).

[89] Cf. Charlton, p. 127.

[90] On Desdemona's forgetting about the dropped handkerchief, see Goddard, p. 472. On this scene generally, cf. J. M. Murry, *Shakespeare* (New York, 1936). According to Murry, Othello's rejection of the handkerchief exemplifies the saying that "we kill the thing we love" (p. 264); since it did not serve Othello, it becomes simply a "thing," and Desdemona *"must . . . forget clean about it"*

(p. 263). Murry defines Iago as "the element of death that is in love" (p. 266) and as "the awareness of the potentiality of death in love" (p. 267).

91 "Miracle" means banishment of self-love, not the "conversion" or radical redirection of energies described in Maud Bodkin's *The Quest for Salvation in an Ancient and a Modern Play* (London, 1941). Knight calls Desdemona "a symbol of man's ideal, the supreme value of love" (p. 109). Cf. Stauffer, p. 181.

92 My interpretation is close to Elliott's here except that at this point Elliott insists that she knows how much she has been "to blame for Othello's jealousy" (p. 223).

93 *Kind*, of course, means "natural" as well as "considerate," "gentle," etc. The word is more than a casual clue to Desdemona's personality. She describes the split between Othello and Cassio as "An unkind breach" (4.1.237). Bradley has a good comment on Desdemona's final words (p. 206 and n.). Flatter's enthusiastic discussion is perceptive (pp. 107-121).

94 After Cassio has been wounded and Roderigo stabbed, Cassio and Roderigo are carried off together (5.1.104). There is no stage direction indicating the death of Roderigo after his last words at 5.1.62. Indeed "after long seeming dead" would be more applicable if he had actually spoken than if he spoke only through letters, since he has been dead only an hour or so. On the two voices from beyond life, cf. Goddard, p. 491.

95 This is the one point at which Othello's real character begins to break through to Bradley (pp. 438-439), who ducks back in shock at what he has almost let himself see.

96 Granville-Barker is very good on the end of Othello (II, 112-114). There is no textual warrant for Flatter's conclusion that at the end Othello knows he has been forgiven (p. 170) or for his conclusion that Othello "regains his faith in himself, his human dignity, his belief in woman's goodness" (p. 166), has "an almost blissful feeling of relief " (p. 167), and "overwhelmed with joy, welcomes back the wife whom he had feared lost" (p. 168).

97 For a statement of some of the distinctions between *Othello* and the domestic drama as exemplified in *A Woman Killed with Kindness*, see Prior, *The Language of Tragedy*, p. 96. One wonders whether the repetition of *kind* and *kindness* in *Othello* might not have been felt as an allusion to Heywood's play.

98 Cf. Goll, pp. 39-40. Iago's "egoism" hates "altruism."

99 On Shakespeare's manifold treatment of lust there is an apposite passage in Stauffer, pp. 167-168.

100 Just before her death Emilia reports that he "often with a solemn earnestness / ... / ... begg'd of me to steal it" (5.2.227-229). Her comment on "earnestness"—"More than indeed belong'd to such a trifle"—indicates her unawareness of a symbolic import.

CHAPTER 7. THEMATIC FORM: WIT AND WITCHCRAFT

1 The only suggestion of an intellectual shortcoming in Iago is made by Emilia, who refers to a past occasion when a gossip "turn'd your wit the seamy side without" (4.2.146).

² Many critics raise the question how much real depth of mind he has. Elliott insists repeatedly on Iago's essential stupidity (pp. 76, 166, 228-229, and elsewhere). Elliott makes a considerable contribution to the large collection of denunciatory rhetoric lavished upon Iago, who seems likely to make frenetic moralists of us all. It seems more important to identify the Iagoism always present under different forms. Goddard calls Iago "the most terrific indictment of pure intellect" in all literature (p. 462).

³ Cf. Whitaker, pp. 285-286.

⁴ 1.3.399-400. Only a few lines after he has twice used "wills" in the sense of "moral authority," he goes on to speak of "wills" in the sense of "sexual desires" (324ff., 352-353). The second meaning may well undermine—by underlying—the first; it is possible that Iago is consciously disintegrating his own sermon by making another meaning available to those who can detect it. And any talk of his own "will" may be an oblique reference to his sexual feeling for Desdemona.

⁵ Cassio at 2.3.34-35, 291-292, 309, 4.1.123; Desdemona at 4.3.23 (cf. Othello, 4.1.200). When Othello feels that "in wholesome wisdom" he cannot immediately reinstate Cassio (3.1.49), *wisdom* connotes "administrative expediency"—a meaning somewhere between "knowledge of truth" and Iago's "personal expediency." Desdemona's insistence that Cassio "errs in ignorance and not in cunning" (3.3.49) contrasts him with what we know Iago to be and with the Othello who resolves to be "cunning"; and her argument that Cassio's fault is "in our common reason" minor (3.3.64) involves the idea of "common sense." There is a contrast between Othello's doctrine that "ignorance is bliss" (3.3.339ff.) and Iago's theory of "No, let me know" (4.1.73). Here again is the irony of Iago's putting into words sound doctrine which he does not "believe" in, i.e., does not act on, witness his preference of his own feelings to the truth of the case (Othello and Emilia) as the ground of action.

⁶ Iago always has implied "theories," of course, as do all "practical" thinkers. What he must oppose is the formal admission of the theoretical.

⁷ Sewell, p. 32.

⁸ Bethell's phrase, "Shakespeare's Imagery," p. 69.

⁹ Cf. Elliott, p. 44. Elliott stresses this point repeatedly.

¹⁰ In Elizabethan psychological terms the evil results from "reason" which is "perverted" (Anderson, p. 149). Cf. Whitaker, pp. 281-282; cf. Goddard, p. 464.

¹¹ Cf. F. C. Kolbe, *Shakespeare's Way* (London, 1930), pp. 131-132.

¹² The same dualism is implied by Iago at 3.3.211.

¹³ This formulation is analogous to that of Stewart in *Character and Motive in Shakespeare*, pp. 108-109, but there is some difference in terms. Stewart's treatment of the Iago-Othello tension as a kind of debate of the Body and Soul is extremely illuminating, but it seems to me to have two defects which are interlocked: it exalts Othello's role because it ignores Desdemona's role. But Stewart approaches the problem only from the point of view of the plausibility of the seduction scene. Likewise, in my opinion, Sewell errs by identifying the ideal alternative with Othello, who can go either way, rather than with Desdemona, who can go only one way. Thus he is able to say surprisingly that "Othello himself has that superiority of spiritual being over Desdemona which Adam had over Eve" (pp. 94-95). My formulation is closer to Stauffer's: "Desdemona

and Iago represent relatively fixed and unchanging forces that war for Othello's soul. The hero partakes of both their natures" (p. 186). Cf. Goddard, pp. 456, 474, 492. Goddard identifies Desdemona with "spirit" and Iago with "war."

[14] On Othello's self-pity, see Elliott, pp. 115, 123.

[15] Empson remarks that both "are versions of the Independent Man" (p. 243). Empson lays much stress on Iago's sensitiveness to slights, apparently with the feeling that as a member of a class he was a victim.

[16] C. S. Lewis, "On Obstinacy in Belief," *Sewanee Review*, LXIII (1955), 535. The preceding quotation is from Nowottny, p. 334.

[17] As Tillyard puts it: "The desire to destroy is a very simple derivative from the power-instinct, the instinct which in its evil form goes by the name of the first of the deadly sins, Pride. It was by that sin that the angels fell, and at the end of *Othello* Iago is explicitly equated with the Devil. Shakespeare embodied all his horror of this type of original sin in Iago" (p. 44). Cf. Granville-Barker's "a braggart decrying in others the qualities he himself lacks" (II, 99). Speaight remarks that Iago is not a cynic because of personal bitterness but belongs to those who are "naturellement cyniques, par besoin de détruire chez eux et chez autrui toute verité, toute bonté, toute vertu" (p. 492).

[18] We might summarize Iago as a political type by saying that his tactics are "based on exhibitionism, identification with the lowest common denominator of the electorate, an easy way with the truth, appeal to prejudice, and intemperate abuse." Actually, this is a book reviewer's summary of the generic traits of the American demagogue discovered by a student of American demagoguery (*New Yorker*, December 18, 1954, p. 134).

[19] Goll remarks that the "innermost crime is the destruction of confidence" (p. 49).

[20] Stanislavsky describes Iago as having "much temperament and the capacity of all human vices" (p. 160).

[21] Battenhouse finds parallels between Iago and Communists and between Othello and liberal humanists ("Shakespeare and the Tragedy of Our Time," pp. 525ff.). Muir summarizes well: "He is the Italianate, Machiavellian villain, raised to the highest pitch of intensity. He is the malcontent. He is what Blake called

> The idiot questioner, who is always questioning
> But never capable of answering, who sits with a sly grin
> Silent plotting when to question, like a thief in a cave,
> Who publishes doubt and calls it knowledge, whose science is Despair,
> Whose pretence to knowledge is envy, whose whole science is
> To destroy the wisdom of ages to gratify ravenous envy.

He is the Intellect divorced from the Imagination. He is the corrosive acid which eats away love and trust" (p. 83). Cf. Stoll: "In life itself there is an affinity between cynicism and swindling, jesting and licentiousness" (p. 273). There is a very lively description of Iago's counterpart in a modern army in Moore's "The Character of Iago," p. 46.

[22] *Inferno*, Canto XXI, verse 19. Carlyle-Wicksteed translation, Modern Library Edition, p. 168.

APPENDIX A. THE ENCHAFED FLOOD

1 Cf. Iago's "erring barbarian" (1.3.363-364).

2 The public and the private troubles are brought together skillfully when Brabantio sneeringly makes application of the Duke's principle of consolation for the loss of his daughter: "So let the Turk of Cyprus us beguile: / We lose it not, so long as we can smile" (1.3.210-211).

3 By the feelings of Cyprians describing the storm and waiting to see its effects (2.1.1-73).

4 Cf. Granville-Barker, II, 15-16.

5 Cf. Knight: "The storm of sea or bruit of cannonade are powerless to hurt them: yet there is another storm brewing in the venomed mind of Iago. Instead of merging with and accompanying tragedy the storm is here contrasted with the following events: as usual in *Othello*, contrast and separation take the place of fusion and unity" (p. 111). He gives the storm somewhat more dramatic weight than I do. Cf. Elliott, pp. 54, 57, 67. Goddard reads the poststorm reunion of Desdemona and Othello as presaging a "transcendental reunion" after their separation by an emotional storm (pp. 485ff.).

6 Since many critics habitually regard all such lines of Othello's as "noble poetry," it is a relief to find Elliott saying that the Pontic sea lines are "too adjectival to be noble." But in the next sentence he talks about their "highly wrought grandeur" (p. 139).

7 4.2.103-104, 124; 4.3.47, 58-59; 5.2.20-21, 348-350. Cf. also, "The fresh streams ran by her and murmur'd her moans" (4.3.45).

Index

The page numbers for the more important passages are in italics.

Abuse, language of, *110-13*, 136
"Actional drama," 6, 11, 17, 24, 25, 42, 44, 45, 73, 78, 82, 99, 124, 185, 188, 227, 231, 238
Adultery problem, *30-34*, 84-85, 246
Aeschylus, *Oresteia*, 12, 239
Affective analysis in criticism, 9-10, 240
Allegory, avoidance of, 115, 170, 193; danger of, 81; relation of *Othello* to, 37, 96, 208
Analogy in structure, 99, 120, 156, 180, 261
Anderson, Ruth L., *Elizabethan Psychology and Shakespeare's Plays*, 256, 285
Animal imagery, 8, 94-95, 97, *105-108*, 112, 135, 199, 264-65
Antony and Cleopatra, 8, 147, 169, 193, 270
Appearance and reality, theme of, *50-58*, 60, 63, 64, 67, 87, 91, 99, 113, 135, 150, 155, 194, 227, 244, 255-56, 257
Archetype, 11-12, 42, 61, 240, 260, 262. *See* Iago, as archetype
Arden edition of *Othello*, 247, 259, 279, 280
Aristophanes, 188
Aristotle, *Poetics*, 7
Armstrong, Edward A., *Shakespeare's Imagination*, 237, 239, 265, 267, 279
Army life, language of, 2, 7, *182-87*. *See* War, as theme

Baldensperger, Fernand, 283
Battenhouse, Roy, "Hamlet's Apostrophe on Man," 252; "*Measure for Measure* and the Christian Doctrine of Atonement," 252; "Shakespeare and the Tragedy of Our Time," 80-81, 252, 262, 266, 271, 276, 277, 286
Baudelaire, Charles, 262
Bellow, Saul, 255

Bethell, S. L., *Shakespeare and the Popular Dramatic Tradition*, 242, 243, 253, 254; "Shakespeare's Imagery: The Diabolic Images in *Othello*," 238, 239, 245, 253, 255, 269, 276, 279, 281, 285
Bianca, 3, 179-81, 200, 218, 280, 283
Birth, images of, 100, 264
Black-and-white imagery. *See* Light and darkness
Blackmur, R. P., *The Lion and the Honeycomb*, 15, 241
Blake, William, 286
Blindness and sight. *See* "Seeing is believing"
Bodkin, Maud, *Archetypal Patterns in Poetry*, 16, 36, 150-51, 241, 243, 247, 250, 254, 270, 271, 272; *The Quest for Salvation in an Ancient and a Modern Play*, 284
Bonnard, G., "Are Othello and Desdemona Innocent or Guilty?" 277, 282-83
Booth, Edwin, 267
Bowman, Thomas D., "A Further Study in the Characterization and Motivation of Iago," 244-45, 247; "In Defense of Emilia," 262, 278
Brabantio:
acted on by Iago, 39, 70-71, 78, 221, 257; charges against Othello, 90, 129-30, 212; ironic statement of truth by, 19
Bradbrook, M. C., *Themes and Conventions of Elizabethan Tragedy,* 277
Bradley, A. C., *Shakespearean Tragedy*, 137, 244, 248-49, 250, 253, 254, 259, 260, 263, 268, 269, 270, 271, 278, 280, 281, 282, 284
Brennecke, Ernest, "Nay, That's Not Next!" 280
Bridal night, theme of, 56-58, 69-73, 174, *188-93*

289

INDEX

Brooke, Tucker, 245
Burke, Kenneth, 12; "*Othello:* An Essay to Illustrate a Method," 260, 261, 262
Burning, imagery of, 94, 97

Campbell, Lily Bess, *Shakespeare's Tragic Heroes: Slaves of Passion*, 247, 248, 271
Cassio:
and handkerchief, 211; as lesser Othello, 180, 279; as lover, 179-80, 183, 279; as lover of Emilia, 33; attitude to Othello, 113, 169, 179-80, 183, 278; drunkenness, 2, 27-28, 79, 102, 107, 110, 115, 123, 162, 241, 265; irony of survival, 18, 242; lieutenancy problem, *25-30*, 245; on reputation, 80, 105; suit for reinstatement, 102, 162, 179-80, 225, 241-42
Chambers, E. K., 271; *Shakespeare: A Survey*, 271; *Shakespeare Gleanings*, 275
Chaos, as theme, 122, 127, 134-35, 160, 170, 175-76, 198-99, 265, 268. See Iago, as producer of chaos
Chapman, John Jay, *A Glance Toward Shakespeare*, 247, 252
Charlton, H. B., *Shakespearian Tragedy*, 270, 272, 274, 277, 283
Chaucer, Geoffrey, 81, 262
Chekhov, Anton, 10
Chicago critics, 240
Christian theme, *41-43*, 84, 214, 216, *250-53*, 256, 276
Cinthio, Giovanni Giraldi, 42, 139, 253
Circumstantial drama, 6
Clark, Cumberland, *Shakespeare and Psychology*, 248
Clemen, W. H., *The Development of Shakespeare's Imagery*, 7, 8, 9, 238, 239, 260, 261, 263, 264, 265
Clothing, imagery of, 7, *55-58*, 64, 120, *256-57*
Clown, 114
Coleridge, Samuel Taylor, 25, 75, 96, 241; *Coleridge's Shakespearean Criticism*, ed. T. M. Raysor, 246; "motiveless malignity," 40, 78, 246
Connolly, Thomas F., "Shakespeare and the Double Man," 247, 250, 272

Conrad, Joseph, 36
Contrast, dramatic use of, 61, 83-84
Conventions, Shakespeare's treatment of, 91, 126, 137, 270, 271, 275
Coriolanus, 270
Costume, 6, 257
Craig, Hardin, *The Enchanted Glass*, 263; *An Interpretation of Shakespeare*, 249, 274, 281
Crane, Milton, *Shakespeare's Prose,* 243
Crane, R. S., *Critics and Criticism*, 240
Critics, of *Othello*, 237, 245; of Shakespeare generally, 240. *See also individual names*, Anderson, Armstrong, etc.
Cunningham, J. V., *Woe or Wonder: the Emotional Effect of Elizabethan Tragedy*, 248, 249, 258, 266, 271, 281

Dante Alighieri, *Inferno*, 77, 97-98, 228-29, 263, 286; *Purgatorio*, 106
D'Arcy, M. C., *The Mind and Heart of Love*, 279
Death, language of. *See* Injury, Pain and torture, War
Demonic in Iago. *See* Iago, as Satan
Desdemona:
and handkerchief, 88, 210-11, *213*, 283-84; as Christian figure, 41, 277; as defendant, *131-34;* as element in Othello, 226, 286; as helper of Cassio, 102, 131, 175-76, 214; as lover, *169-76, 183-84, 189-93,* 200, *208-18,* 226, 277, 279, 283-84; as opposite of Iago, 58, 63, 177, 206, 214, 217, *224-26,* 269, 285-86; as physician, 87-88; as sacrificial figure, 41, 250; as saint, *214-18*, 277; attitude to Iago, 92, 147, 174; attitude to Othello, 110, 129, 173-75, *208-16;* contrasted with Emilia, 68, 72, 84, 107, 209; contribution to tragedy, 210; death scene, 71-73, *152-57*, 191-92, *215-16;* delicacy, 199, 208; "economics," 83-85; irony of her promise, 18, 19, 242; naivete, 209, 210; on conduct of wives, 2; on jealousy, 39-40; on visual evidence, 61-62, 173, 259; self-regarding elements, 215-16, 258, 278, 282-83; her song, 115, 190; undressing for bed, 57, 190
Design, 20, 25. *See* Structure

INDEX

Diabolism. *See* Iago, as Satan
Disease and medicine, language of, 2, 5, 46, *86-95*, 263
Domestic drama, 166, 217, 276, 284
Downer, Alan, "The Life of Our Design," 240
Draper, John, 237; "Captain General Othello," 245; "Honest Iago," 245; "The Jealousy of Iago," 248, 279; "This Poor Trash of Venice," 261, 279
Duthie, George I., *Shakespeare*, 247, 254, 271

Economics, language of, 4, *73-85*, 260-61
Eliot, George, 141
Eliot, T. S., 214, 252, 270, 275; *Poetry and Drama*, 238; "Shakespeare and the Stoicism of Seneca," 275-76
"Elizabethan mind," 240, 241
Elliott, G. R., *Flaming Minister*, 146, 237-38, 244, 245, 247, 249, 250, 252, 253, 255, 257, 260, 261, 265, 268, 269, 270, 271, 272, 274, 275, 276, 277, 278, 282, 283, 284, 285, 286, 287
Ellis-Fermor, Una, *The Frontiers of Drama*, 238; *Some Recent Research in Shakespeare's Imagery*, 238-39
Emilia:
attitude to Iago, 26, 85, 110, 118-19, 178, *181-82*, 262; attitude to Othello, 124, 161, 262; "economics," 84, 262; Iago's attitude to, 32-33; on sexual jealousy, 39-40; relations with Cassio, 26, 33; relations with Desdemona, 68, 84, 95, 115, *181-82*, 199-200, 216, 225; resemblance to Iago, 85, 181, 199, 214, 263; self-recognition, 111, 182; theft of handkerchief, 2, 83, 88, *181-82;* theory of love, *199-200*
Empson, William, *Seven Types of Ambiguity*, 192, 280; *The Structure of Complex Words*, 46-47, 49, 244, 245, 247, 248, 249, 253, 254, 255, 262, 265, 272, 273, 282, 286
Envy, as theme. *See* Jealousy
Euripides, 10, 11
Evans, B. Ifor, *The Language of Shakespeare's Plays*, 265, 269, 281
Evidence. *See* "Seeing is believing," Handkerchief

Evil, dramatization of, 4, 5, 16, 35-37, 50, 63, 64, 65, 67, 69-70, 77-78, 81, 82, 87, 89-90, 91, 94, 99-100, 105, 107, 115, 121, 123, 126, 135, 154, 176, 208, 222-24, 229, 249, 282; Shakespeare's definition of, 222-24, 229

Fairchild, A. H. R., *Shakespeare and the Tragic Theme*, 248, 272, 278
Falstaff, 14, 268
Farce, materials of, 190
Farnham, Willard, *Shakespeare's Tragic Frontier*, 270
Faulkner, William, 206
Feldman, Abraham B., "Othello's Obsessions," 244, 247, 277, 278
Fergusson, Francis, 106; *The Idea of a Theatre*, 261
Fielding, Henry, 45
Figures of speech, as connective devices, 21-22
Flatter, Richard, 237; *The Moor of Venice*, 244, 245, 247, 248, 249, 255, 258, 262, 271, 274, 276, 277, 280, 283, 284
Fluchère, Henri, *Shakespeare*, 250, 275
Foakes, R. A., "Suggestions for a New Approach to Shakespeare's Imagery," 238, 239, 253
Form, 1, 17, 160, 168, 200. *See* Spatial form, Structure
Friedman, Norman, "Imagery: From Sensation to Symbol," 13, 240, 260
Furness, H. H., 267

Generic analysis, 10, 15, 240
Genesis, 96, 97
Goddard, Harold C., *The Meaning of Shakespeare*, 255, 260, 283, 284, 285, 286, 287
Goethe, Johann W. von, *Faust*, 250
Goheen, Robert F., *The Imagery of Sophocles' Antigone*, 239
Goll, August, "Criminal Types in Shakespeare," 282, 284, 286
Goodman, Paul, *The Structure of Literature*, 8, 15, 21, 239, 241, 243
Granville-Barker, Harley, *Prefaces to Shakespeare*, 170, 241, 244, 245, 247, 249, 254, 258, 262, 263, 264, 268, 269, 270, 272, 275, 276, 278, 279, 280, 281, 282, 283, 284, 286, 287

291

INDEX

Greek drama, 7

Hamlet, 72, 92, 147, 241
Handkerchief, 62, 83, 87-88, 124, 132, 155-56, 161, 181-82, 192, *211-14*, 257, 259, 283-84
Hankins, John E., *Shakespeare's Derived Imagery*, 244, 260, 263, 264
Harbage, Alfred, *As They Liked It*, 241, 247, 248, 262; *Shakespeare and the Rival Traditions*, 278
Harrison, G. B., *Shakespeare's Tragedies*, 283
Haydn, Hiram, *The Counter-Renaissance*, 257, 282
Hazlitt, William, *Characters of Shakespeare's Plays*, 262
Heywood, Thomas, *A Woman Killed with Kindness*, 284
Historical study of drama, 14-16, 240, 241, 248, 255
Holbrook, Sibyl C., "Husbands in Shakespeare," 278
Holmes, Elizabeth, *Aspects of Elizabethan Imagery*, 256
Honesty theme, 2, *147-52*, 155, 254-55. See Iago, as "Honest Iago"
Hunting and trapping, language of, 4, *104-105*, 244

Iago:
as antihuman, *95-98, 104-13*, 114, 120, 122, 134-35, 180, 199-200; as archetype, 12, 63, 78, 92, 97, 108, 109, 115, 118, 121, 125, 223, 286; as comedian and joker, 34, 48, 68, 71, 150; as criminal, 120-21, *157-60*, 162, 181, 228; as debunker, 82, 108, 195, 207, 212, 224, 227; as deceiver, *45-98*, 99, 111, *131-34*, 155, 176, 220, 227-28, 258, 261; as destroyer of love, 115, 170-71, 177, 179-80, 182-83, 194, 199-200, 207-208, 217-18, 224-26, 286; as director of Othello's seeing, *58-64*, 73, 226, 258; as disturber of the peace, 114, 117, 121, 123-24, 130, 170; as "economist," *73-83*, 218, 261; as element in Othello, 36, 118, 125, 128, 226, 247, 272, 286; as Everyman, 35-36, 39, 42, 43, 44, 126, 127, 221, 226, 228, 247; as "Evil," 16, *35-37*, 40-41, 43, 44, 45, 46, 50, 72, 73, 87, 90, 116, 121, 129, 228-29, 247, 249, 253, 254, 267; as false friend, 11, 43, 44, 50-51, 96; as gambler, 52, 79, 80, 81, 83, 255, 262, 272; as "Honest Iago," *46-50*, 99, *147-52*, 155, 247, 254-55, 272, 282; as hunter and trapper, *104-105*, 107, 150, 158, 198, 218, 227; as informer, 63, 134; as jealous man, *39-41*, 44, 96, 104, 113, 203-204, 206-208, 213, 228, 244, 245, 248-49, 281; as Judas, 244, 250;

as lightbearer, *64-72*, 87, 91, 113, 189, 196, 227; as "lover," *176-79, 200-208*, 226, 278; as machiavel, 11, 44, 91, 228, 254; as "man of blood," 127-28, 269; as man of reason, *219-28*, 276, 284-85; as "mass mind," 41, 85, 111-13, 205, 228, 249-50; as melodrama villain, 35-36, 44, 91, 96, 228; as opposite of Desdemona, 58, 63, 127, 149, 177, 206, 214, 217, 218, 224-26, 285-86; as perceptive man and truth-teller, 19, 81, 82, 194-95, 213, 219, 243, 282-83, 285; as philosopher, 44, 51-52, 55-56, 67-68, 82, 108, 112-13, *193-200*, 212, 219, *221-24*, 281; as philosophical corrupter, 52-53, 61, 67-68, 196-98, 228, 242, 273; as physician, 5, 86-87, *89-98*, 99, 113, 122, 155, 227, 262-63; as poisoner, 5, *91-98*, 105; as producer of chaos, 71, 90, 93, 99-100, 112-13, 119, 122, 123, 170, 176, 198, 221, 275; as prosecuting attorney, *131-34*; as psychologist, 105, 106, 108-13, 263; as Satan, *41-43*, 44, 78, 81, 82, 93, *94-98*, 99, 104, 105, 107, 114, 120, 126, 214, 225, 228, 229, 238, 250, 252-53, 256, 264, 286; as thief, *77-83*, 87, 91, 92, 99, 113, 196, 227, 228, 255, 261-62; as "timer," *101-104*; as Tristram, 206;

attitude to Bianca, 89, 180-81, 261; attitude to (and actions against) Cassio, 33-34, 37, 38, 40, 47, 78, 79, 86, 89, 176, 178, 203-204, 206-207; attitude to Desdemona, 38, 47, 56-57, 64, 89, 93-94, 195, *200-208*, 218, 276, 281-82, 284, 285; attitude to Emilia, 32-33, 39, 157-60, 220, 246; attitude to Roderigo, 50, 71, *75-78*, 89, 109, 176, 178, 195, 213, 221-23, 231, 255, 261; his conscience, 35, 247, 281; griev-

292

INDEX

Iago (continued):
ances, *25-37*, 39, 75, 94, 201, 244, 245, 246; grievances as a dramaturgic device, *34-37*, 96; hatred of Othello, 29-30, 31, 37, 78, 113, 169-70, *176-79*, 193, 206, 226, 245; histrionism, 26, 47, 51, 72, 80, 125, 140, 226, 245, 247, 266, 280, 282; imagistic style, 21, *100-27*, 158, 181-82, 218, 224, 243, 263, 264, 267; lieutenancy problem, *25-30*, 245; love of noise, *113-20*, 121, 227; multiplicity, 43-44, 99-100, 176, 194, 200, *228-29*, 244, 253, 254, 280, 286; on reputation, 2, 31, 73-74, 79-82, 196, 224; on the unseen, 62, 196, 224; position in *Inferno*, 97-98, 228-29; pride, 106, 120-21, 228, 249, 252, 268, 286; readiness in his victims, 44, 45, 74, 75, 101, 103, 129, 137, 176, 196, 229; recognized by others, 111-13, 267; relation to Melville's Claggart, 37, 43, 113, 116, 247-48; self-knowledge, 92, 227; self-love, 170, 249; strategy against Othello, *92-95*, 109, 127-28, 131, 137, 144-45, *147-52*, 172, 196, 273; suspicion of adultery, *30-34*, 38, 95-96, 201, 246, 281; theft of handkerchief, 4, 83, 211, 218; theories of sex, 2, 3, 32-33, 89, 105, 106, 108, 109, 170, 180, *193-200*, 211, 219, 223-24, 280-82; use of animal imagery, 8, *105-108*, 195; vulgarity, 76, 77, 82, 116, 118, 120, 158, 199, 220, 228, 250, 261, 267
Image pattern, 239, 257
Imagery, recurrent, 7-9, 23-24, 59, 238, 239, 241, 257, in characterization, 8, 238, 239, in structure of meaning, 9, 10, 238, 239; secondary meanings, 22, 72-73, 138, 269; Shakespeare's use of, 7, 21, 238, 239, 244, 257. *See* Animal, Birth, Burning, Clothing, Nature, Pain and torture, Physiological, Sound effects, Taste and smell, *and the entries under* Language *and* Theme
Imitation (mimesis), 10-11; objects of, 11, 126, 239, 268
Injury, in language and action, 119, *122-27*, 136, *152-68*, 268
Intentional Fallacy, 239
Invidia. *See* Jealousy

Irony, modes of, *17-21*, 83, 242, 243: occurrence of, 42, 46, 48, 59, 62, 68, 73, 81, 106, 118, 120, 125, 150, 166, 176, 177, 181, 189-90, 193, 211, 213, 222, 232, 234, 242, 243, 244, 251, 257, 285. *See* Othello, irony; Iago, as perceptive man and truth-teller

Jealousy, as theme, *38-41*, 96, 104, 113, 203-204, 206-208, 248, 249, 283
Johnson, Samuel, 157, 176
Jordan, Hoover H., "Dramatic Illusion in *Othello*," 255
Jorgensen, Paul A., "Honesty in *Othello*," 255
Justice theme, 93-94, 119, 121-22, 126, *128-36*, *142-44*, *152-68*, 184, 207, 226, 258-59, 269-70, 274-76

Kellett, E. E., *Suggestions*, 256
Kennedy, Milton B., *The Oration in Shakespeare*, 269
Kerman, Joseph, "Verdi's *Otello*, or Shakespeare Explained," 250
King Lear, 11, 51, 60, 80, 107, 108, 109, 121, 132, 147, 159, 185, 188, 195, 196, 210, 221, 224, 227, 231, 234, 252, 259, 265, 266, 268, 273, 281
Kirschbaum, Leo, "The Modern Othello," 149, 246, 271, 272, 274, 275, 276, 277, 278, 281
Kittredge, George Lyman, 245, 271; ed. *Othello*, 245, 251, 256, 259, 262, 265, 273, 280, 281
Kliger, Samuel, "Othello: the Man of Judgment," 242
Knight, G. Wilson, *The Crown of Life*, 241; *The Shakespearian Tempest*, 267; *The Wheel of Fire*, 237, 260, 264, 267, 268, 270, 275, 276, 276-77, 279, 281, 283, 287
Knights, L. C., *Explorations*, 238, 241; "On Historical Scholarship and the Interpretation of Shakespeare," 241
Kökeritz, Helge, *Shakespeare's Pronunciation*, 279
Kolbe, F. C., *Shakespeare's Way*, 285
Kreider, Paul V., *Repetition in Shakespeare's Plays*, 249, 255

Language. *See* Abuse, Army life, Disease and medicine, Economics, Hunt-

293

INDEX

ing and trapping, Injury, Light and dark, Storm, Theft, Value. *See also* the entries under Image pattern, Imagery, Theme

Lattimore, Richmond, tr., Aeschylus' *Oresteia,* 239

Leavis, F. R., "Diabolic Intellect and the Noble Hero: A Note on *Othello,*" 146, 247, 254, 270-71, 272, 275, 277, 280

Leech, Clifford, *Shakespeare's Tragedies,* 252, 272, 276, 283

Lewis, C. S., "On Obstinacy in Belief," 227, 286

Lewis, Wyndham, *The Lion and the Fox,* 250, 280

Light and dark, in language and stage effects, 2, 46, *64-73,* 78, 86, 87, 91, 99, 115, 122, 135, 152, 189, 244, 260

Literalist criticism, 12, 240, 246

Literary history. *See* Historical study of drama, Theatrical conditions

Literature, *Othello* as, 13-14

Lodovico, closing speech of, 24, 95

Love, as theme, 3, 4, 6, 29, 37, 60-61, 87-88, 100, 105-106, 115, 120, 135, 146, 168, *169-218, 225-29, 276-84;* Shakespeare's doctrine of, 185

Love-and-death, as theme, 57, 70, *187-93,* 279-80, 284

Love-and-hate, as theme, 70, 164, 169-70, 176-79, 188, 191, 207-208, 214, 217, 218, 276, 282

Love-and-war, as theme, 182-87, 188, 279, 280

Lucas, F. L., *Literature and Psychology,* 244, 258

Macbeth, 109, 147, 159, 224, 270

McCloskey, John C., "The Motivation of Iago," 244

Madness theme, 220-21, 285. *See* Rationalism; Iago, as man of reason

"Magic in the web," 3, 6, 16, 17, 20, 23, 44, 173, *208-18,* 283-84

Maginn, William, 256

Manliness, theme of, *108-13,* 135, 277

Marlowe, Christopher, *Dr. Faustus,* 40

Meaning, as object of criticism, 3, 4, 5, 6, 10, 13, 15, 16, 40, 159; structure of, 6, 9, 42

Medicine. *See* Disease and medicine

Melodrama, conditions of, 160, 185, 232; problem of, 35-36

Melville, Herman, *Billy Budd,* 37, 43, 113, 116, 247-48

Merchant of Venice, 139

Miller, Arthur, 10

Milton, John, 42

Miriam Joseph, Sister, *Shakespeare's Use of the Arts of Language,* 255, 259, 274

Money, John, "Othello's 'It is the Cause . . .': An Analysis," 235-36, 271, 274, 275, 276, 277, 279

Montano, attitude to Cassio, 28

Moore, John R., "The Character of Iago," 245, 254, 282, 286; "Othello, Cassio, and Iago as Soldiers," 245

Morality play, relation of *Othello* to, 36, 37

Morozov, Mikhail M., "The Individualization of Shakespeare's Characters through Imagery," 238, 239, 263, 264, 279

Muir, Kenneth, "The Jealousy of Iago," 25, 36, 244, 245, 247, 248, 262, 281-82, 282, 286

Murry, J. M., *Shakespeare,* 283-84

Music, *114-16,* 120, 267

Myrick, Kenneth O., "The Theme of Damnation in Shakespearean Tragedy," 252

Myth, problem of, *41-43;* mythic elements in *Othello,* 41-43, 44, 61, 96, 169-70, 183-84, 196, 198, 199, 200, 208, 211-12, 213, 214, 215, 228, 229, 251

Nature, imagery of, 9, 265-66; in *King Lear,* 11

Nautical imagery. *See* Storm

Nicoll, Allardyce, 245, 271; *Shakespeare: An Introduction,* 283

Night, dramatic use of, 2, *68-73,* 78, 260

Noble, Richmond, *Shakespeare's Biblical Knowledge,* 250

Noise, *113-21,* 122, 267

Nowottny, Winifred M. T., "Justice and Love in *Othello,*" 169, 227, 258, 274, 275, 276, 280, 286

Oechelhauser, William, 261

294

INDEX

Othello:
as adulterer, *30-34;* as Christian, 41, 274, 283; as Everyman, 36, 139, 142, 145, 166-67, 226; as executive, 145, 148, 163, 171-72, 174, 269; as "idealist," 80, 137, 138, 270-71, 272; as jealous man, 38, 39, 248, 265, 280; as Judas, 41, 252; as judge, *128-36, 142-44,* 148, *152-68,* 207, 226, 259, 269-70, 274-76; as lover, 85, *139-42,* 145, 146, 150-51, 152-57, 168, *169-76,* 178, 187, *189-93,* 198, *211-18,* 226-27, 274, 275, 277, 280; as man of reason, 220, 226-27, 272; as military man, 141, 142, 146, 149, 164, 171-72, *182-87,* 272, 279, 280; as Moor, 138-39, 146-47, 156, 172, 271; as noisemaker, 118, 136; as object of conflict, *226-29,* 285-86; as philosopher, *52-54,* 60-61, 131, 133, 135, 145-46, 152-53, 193, 196-98, 212, 272; as physician, 88, 135; as priest, 88, *154-56,* 159-60, 274; as romantic, 140, 141, 145, 171, *183-86,* 193, 199, 272; as sick man, 86-87, 88-89, 93; as tragic hero, 85, 142, 146, 152, 159, 161, *166-68, 185-87,* 216-18, 259, 270, 276;
  abusive language, 110, 111, 135-36, 158, 164, *198-200,* 276, 281; attitude to Cassio, 27, 144, 145, 148, 278; black Othello and fair Desdemona, 64ff.; brothel scene, 3, 189-90, 198, 273; conception of honor, 164, 248; deception of, by Iago, 2, 52-53, *144-52,* 177-79, 196-98; distance from Desdemona, 57-58, 72, 171, 174; "economics," 85, 261; egotism, 102, 138, 140, 146, 167, 172, 174, 175, 178, 180, 186, 213, 217, 266, 278; farewell to arms, 2, *118, 184-86;* general analysis of, *135-36, 137-68,* 250, *270-76;* histrionism, 140-41, 144, 145, 146, 161, 164, 165-66, 171, 187, 212, 226, 275; immaturity, 140, 141, 142, 145, 147, 148, 167, 187; impatience, 102-103, 135, 149, 150-51, 165, 264, 273; irony of action by, 18, 83, 142, 147; irony of words by, 19, 20, 151, 154, 164, 211; manner with Iago, 26; multiplicity, 138, 155, 156, 163, 166-68; murder of Desdemona, 72-73, 94, 119, 123-24, 135, *152-57,* 159-60, 190-92, *215-16;* need of "positional assurance," 138-39, 141, 142, 143, 144, 145, *147-52,* 153-54, 160, 164-65, 168, 172, 175, 176, 199, 213, 274; nobility, 137, 144, 156, 167, 171, 271, 276, 278, 279; obtuseness, 50, 60, 217; passion, 130-36, 142, 146-47, 150, 152, 156, 161, 166, 173, 247, 273, 281; pride, 137, 138, 142, 174, 252, 268, 269, 270, 271, 275; puritanism, 138, 142, 146; readiness as victim, 45, 92, 103, 129, 137, 144-45, 176, 266, 276; revelry in Cyprus, 142, 143, 144, 148, 184; rhetoric, *137-38,* 144, 158, 159, 172, 174, 273, 276, 287; "seeing is believing," *58-64,* 131, 226, 257-59; self-deception, 138, 141, 142, 144, 145, 152, 153, 155-56, 159, 162, 164, 172-73; self-recognition, 73, 85, 107, 111, 143, 145, 161, *163-67,* 187, *217-18,* 220, 227, 273, 276, 284; sexuality, 138, 172-73, 175, 277, 280; stoicism, 138, 141, 144, 164, 172; use of animal imagery, 8, 106, 135, 199; view of honesty, 46ff., *147-52;* violence, 125-27, 128, 136, *152-57,* 164, 167, 172, 198-200, 232; virtues, 137-38, 141, 149, 167, 172, 174, 276, 277, 279; vulgarity, 118, 199, 276

Pain and torture, imagery of, 9, 86, *122-27,* 268
Palmer, John, *Studies in the Contemporary Theatre,* 247
Paradox, 66, 70, 118, 122-23, 160, 185, 187-88, 264
Partridge, Eric, *Shakespeare's Bawdy,* 14, 279, 280
Parts, nature of, 2, 3, 12, *see* Plot, Poetry; relation of, *1-7,* 12, *17-24,* 25, 59, 71, 74, 88, 99, 104-105, *129-36, 157-60,* 163, 186, 237-38, *241-44,* 257, 274, 279; separation of, 20-21
Patience theme, 273-74. *See* Othello, impatience
Physiological imagery, 122, *234-36,* 244, 263-64
Plot, as a basic part, 2ff., 5, 15, 238
Poem, *Othello* as, *3-6,* 10, 14, 184, 238
"Poetic drama," 6
Poetic method, 59, 278
Poetic structure. *See* Verbal drama
Poetry (poetic language), 239, 244; as

295

INDEX

a basic part, 2ff., 5, 238; as dramatic, 5, 238, 254; as source of symbolism, 12, 13; effect of, *3-7*, 9, 21
Pogson, Beryl, *In the East My Pleasure Lies*, 250
Poison theme, 5, 46, *90-98*, 244. See Disease and medicine
Praz, Mario, "Machiavelli and the Elizabethans," 254; *The Romantic Agony*, 282; "Shakespeare's Italy," 254
Price, Hereward T., *Construction in Shakespeare*, 7, 239, 253
Prior, Moody, "Character in Relation to Action in *Othello*," 241, 271; *The Language of Tragedy*, 21, 238, 243, 284
Prometheus, 73
Proof, Othello's quest of. See "Seeing is believing"
Properties, 6, 238, 257
Prose, effect of, 21, 243; limitations of, 3, 4-5; Shakespeare's development of, 21; use of, 196, 243
Psychoanalytic criticism, 22, 43, 244, 247, 270, 272, 278, 282
Pun, in dramatic form, 193, 253
Purse. See Economics, language of
Putney, Rufus, "What 'Praise to Give?' Jonson vs. Stoll," 241, 269, 271

Ralli, Augustus, *A History of Shakespearian Criticism*, 237
Rand, Frank P., "The Over Garrulous Iago," 244, 254
Rationalism in Shakespearian tragedy, 61, 92, 106, 107, 132, 135, 158, 173, *221-24*, 258. See Madness theme; Iago, as a man of reason
Raymond, William O., "Motivation and Character in *Othello*," 240, 271
Recurrency, verbal, 7, 22-24. See Imagery, Language, Theme
Reik, Theodore, *The Secret Self*, 277
Repetition, dramatic, 157. See Recurrency
Reputation theme, 31, *79-82*
Revenge, 159-60
Rhythm, 23; as element in structure, 110, 161; as separative device, 21, 243, 244; of tragedy, 111

Ridley, M. R., *Shakespeare's Plays: A Commentary*, 244
Ritual, 29, 30, 32, 155, 160, 162
Roderigo:
as lover, 179, 225-26; as man of reason, 222-23, 225, 226; as tragic character, 76-77, 111, 162; deceived by Iago, 2; importance of his role, *75-78*, 216, 261, 284; prosaic style, 21; relations with Iago, 50, 75-78; relation to Othello, 75
Roman plays, 252
Romeo and Juliet, 169, 193
Rylands, George, "Shakespeare's Poetic Energy," 239, 244; *Words and Poetry*, 243
Rymer, Thomas, 211, 283

Schücking, Levin, *Character Problems in Shakespeare's Plays*, 243, 246, 247
"Seeing is believing," as theme, *58-64*, 131, 135, 150, 226, *257-59*
Seen and unseen. See "Seeing is believing"
Serpent images. See Iago, as Satan
Setting, 6, 68ff., 257
Sewell, Arthur, *Character and Society in Shakespeare*, 16, 226, 241, 247, 249-50, 252, 261, 265, 270, 275, 277, 281, 285
Shaw, G. B., 17, 270
Siegel, Paul, "The Damnation of Othello," 250, 252, 271, 276
Sight theme. See "Seeing is believing"
Sitwell, Edith, *The Poet's Notebook*, 248, 250, 262, 264, 267, 270, 278
Slavishness, theme of, *111-13*, 243, 267
Smith, Robert M., "Current Fashions in Hamlet Criticism," 16, 241
Sophocles, *Antigone*, 239; *Oedipus Rex*, 11, 62, 159, 160; *Trachiniae*, 11
Soul, meanings of, 266
Sound effects, *113-20*
Spatial form, 170-71
Speaight, Robert, "Réflexions sur 'Othello,'" 249, 270, 271, 277, 282, 286
Spencer, Benjamin T., "This Elizabethan Shakespeare," 241
Spencer, Theodore, 272; *Shakespeare and the Nature of Man*, 254, 255, 268, 272, 282

296

INDEX

Spurgeon, Caroline, *Shakespeare's Imagery*, 260, 264, 267
Stage effects, 65, 66, 70-72, 88, 215. *See* Light and dark, Sound effects, Storm
Stanislavsky Produces Othello, tr. Helen Nowak, 245, 249, 262, 269, 272, 277, 286
Stauffer, Donald A., *Shakespeare's World of Images*, 241, 247, 258, 261, 262, 265, 268, 281, 284, 285-86
Stein, Arnold, *Answerable Style*, 252-53
Sterne, Laurence, *Sentimental Journey*, 268
Stewart, J. I. M., *Character and Motive in Shakespeare*, 241, 247, 253, 271, 285; "The Year's Contribution to Shakespearian Study," 237
Stirling, Brents, "Psychology in *Othello*," 246, 270, 271, 272; *Unity in Shakespearian Tragedy: The Interplay of Theme and Character*, 270
Stoll, E. E., 238; *Othello*, 248, 270; *Poets and Playwrights*, 238, 259, 264, 265, 271, 276; *Shakespeare and Other Masters*, 238, 243, 245-46, 247, 248, 250, 252, 254, 255, 262, 267, 269, 270, 271, 274, 282, 286; "Slander in Drama," 270, 282
Storm, in language and action, 101, 114, 115, 122, 143-44, *231-34*, 287
Strachey, Lytton, *Characters and Commentaries*, 282
Structure, *1-6*, 10, 42, 97, 156, 157, 163, 211, *224-29*, 244, 276; Shakespearian, 61. *See* Parts, nature of *and* relation of
Style, as index of character, 21, 84, 100, 125, 127, 138, 150, 158, 159-60, 199, 202, 264, 265, 269, 276, 279; in Iago's strategy, 196-97
Symbolic action, 12, 166, 239-40, 273
Symbolism, as a quality of literature generally, 11-13, 14, 15, 240-41; in *Othello*, 43, 45, 65, 67, 69, 70, 72-73, 74, 86, 87, 88, 101, 104, 113, 117, 120, 160, 185, 189, 190, 193, 198, *211-18*, *225-29*, 231, 234, 242, 257

Tannenbaum, Samuel A., "The Jealousy of Othello," 270
Taste and smell, imagery of, 100, 263-64

Theatrical conditions, in criticism of drama, 13-14, 15
Theft, in language and action, 74, 78, 79, 81-82, 85, 87, 88, 91, 97, 99, 113, 227, 228, 261-62
Theme. *See* Appearance and reality, Bridal night, Chaos, Christian, Honesty, Jealousy, Justice, Love, Love-and-death, Love-and-hate, Love-and-war, Madness, Manliness, Patience, Poison, Reputation, "Seeing is believing," Slavishness, War, *and the entries under* Imagery *and* Language
Tillyard, E. M. W., *Shakespeare's Last Plays*, 276, 286
Time problem, *101-104*, 135, 264
Tone, 113, 190, 268
Tragedy, nature of, 73, 111, 120, 126, 160, 182, 185, 217; structure of, 35, 83, 111, 161, 193
Tragic hero, defined by Iago, 19; Othello as, 85, 142, 146, 152, 161, 185, 259; Shakespearian, 60-61, 76, 132, 152, 153
Tragic method, Shakespearian, 60-61, 83
Trapping. *See* Hunting and trapping, language of
Traversi, D. A., *Approach to Shakespeare*, 4, 238, 276, 278, 281, 282; "Othello," 238, 244, 254, 268, 269, 271, 272, 275, 276, 277, 279, 281, 282

Value terms, 74ff., 79, 80-82, 83-85
Van Doren, Mark, 271
Variorum edition of *Othello*, 247, 256, 261, 267, 275, 279
Verbal drama, *5-7*, 17, 24, 25, 42, 44, 45, 55, 82, 83, 99, 124, 185, 188, 205, 227, 231, 238, 239, 271, 274; relation to meaning, 9, 11, 67, 74, 78, 91-93, 94, 97, 239
Verse, verse style. *See* Poetry
Villains, Shakespearian, 61, 91, 107, 116
Violence. *See* Injury, Pain and torture, War
Visual evidence. *See* "Seeing is believing"
Vivas, Eliseo, "Literature and Knowledge," 11, 239
Voegelin, Eric, 196; *History of Political Ideas*, 12, 240; "The Origins of

297

INDEX

Scientism," 281; "The World of Homer," 275

Wagner, Richard, 188
Wangh, Martin, "Othello: The Tragedy of Iago," 277, 282
War, as theme, *121-27*, 243, 286; language of, *182-87*, *278-79*. See Love-and-war, theme of
Water imagery. See Storm
Weaver, Raymond W., ed., *The Works of Herman Melville*, 247-48
Weaver, Richard, "Aspects of the Southern Philosophy," 242-43
Webb, Henry J., "The Military Background in *Othello*," 245
Weilgart, Wolfgang, *Shakespeare: Psychognostic*, 249, 255, 258, 264, 276, 281
Wellek, René, and Warren, Austin, *Theory of Literature*, 239
Whitaker, Virgil, *Shakespeare's Use of Learning*, 249, 252, 285
Wilcox, John, "Othello's Crucial Moment," 271
Williams, Tennessee, 10
Wilson, J. Dover, 271
Wimsatt, W. K., *The Verbal Icon*, 239
Winstanley, Lilian, "*Othello*" *As the Tragedy of Italy*, 240
"Wit and witchcraft," 1, 3, 16, *219-29*
Worldliness, the world. See Economics, language of